D0252806

Continuing the Reformation

Continuing the Reformation

Re-Visioning Baptism in the Episcopal Church

Ruth A. Meyers

 CHURCH

Church Publishing Incorporated, New York

Library of Congress Cataloging-in-Publication Data

Meyers, Ruth A., 1957–
    Continuing the Reformation: re-visioning baptism in the Episcopal
Church / by Ruth A. Meyers

    p.   cm.
    Includes bibliographical references and index.
    ISBN 0-89869-195-8
    1. Baptism—Episcopal Church. 2. Baptism—Anglican Communion.
3. Baptism (Liturgy) 4. Episcopal Church—Liturgy. 5. Anglican
Communion—Liturgy.
I. Title.
BX5949.B2M49 1997   97-38357
264' . 03081—dc21   CIP

Church Publishing Incorporated
445 Fifth Avenue
New York NY 10016

5 4 3 2 1

Table of Contents

Abbreviations

ATR	*Anglican Theological Review*
BCP	The Book of Common Prayer
BOS	*The Book of Occasional Services*
DC VI	Drafting Committee VI (Drafting Committee on Christian Initiation)
PBS	*Prayer Book Studies*
SLC	Standing Liturgical Commission

Acknowledgments

This book began as part of my doctoral work at the University of Notre Dame. I am indebted to Dr. Paul Bradshaw, director of my dissertation, who has helped me clarify my thinking about liturgical renewal and provided significant encouragement and guidance as the dissertation gradually took shape.

The research for the dissertation was facilitated by a number of people and organizations. A grant from the Zahm Research Travel Fund enabled me to travel to the Archives of the Episcopal Church in Austin, Texas, and to New York and Massachusetts to interview Bonnell Spencer, Chair of the Drafting Committee on Christian Initiation, and Daniel Stevick, a member of the drafting committee. A Visiting Fellowship from the Episcopal Theological Seminary of the Southwest in Austin provided the opportunity for me to make a second visit to the archives to complete my research. The staff of the Archives of the Episcopal Church offered their support and assistance during my research there. The staff at the United Library at Seabury-Western Theological Seminary, particularly Newland Smith, librarian at Seabury-Western, assisted me in obtaining materials needed for research. Bonnell Spencer, Daniel Stevick and Leonel Mitchell all consented to be interviewed about the revision process and offered much helpful insight. Spencer and Mitchell also shared their personal files from their work with the drafting committee. The Sedgwick family, Tim, Martha, Sarah and Ellen, graciously provided housing and hospitality for me during numerous research trips to Seabury-Western.

It has been nearly five years since I completed work on the dissertation. Subsequent opportunities to write and to speak have helped me develop my thought. Some material from my essay "Liturgy and Society: Cultural Influences on Contemporary Liturgical Revision," published in *Liturgy in Dialogue*, edited by Paul Bradshaw and Bryan Spinks (London: SPCK, 1993), appears in chapter 2 of this book. At various points in the book, I have also drawn upon my work in "Christian Rites of Adolescence," published in *Life Cycles in Jewish and Christian Worship*, edited by Paul Bradshaw and Lawrence Hoffman (University of Notre Dame Press, 1996). More recently, an

x

invitation to speak at a Diocese of Chicago liturgy day on "The Power and Promise of Baptism" provided the opportunity to give further consideration to the meaning of baptism for the Church in our post-Christian era, and an opportunity to address clergy and musicians in the Diocese of Pennsylvania on "Anglican Worship in the Next Millennium" likewise encouraged me to consider the influence of contemporary social and cultural changes on our worship. I am grateful to those diocesan liturgical commissions for their kind invitations.

A number of people have supported and encouraged me in the process of preparing this book for publication. Byron Stuhlman read the dissertation manuscript and offered many helpful suggestions which have strengthened my work. Clay Morris and John McCausland also read the manuscript at different stages and encouraged me to pursue my editing for publication. The Sisters of St. Helena in Vails Gate, New York, offered several days of hospitality, providing a quiet and prayerful place in the final stages of editing.

Finally, my family has suffered through my inattention as I poured my energy into writing and editing. Yet my husband Daniel has been a constant source of support, and it is to him that this book is dedicated.

Ruth A. Meyers
Good Friday 1997

Foreword

For those of us who were fortunate enough to be a part of it, the re-shaping, re-forming, and re-visioning of Christian initiation was the most exciting theological enterprise of the last half of the twentieth century. The Book of Common Prayer 1979 bears witness to an ecumenical consensus already attained concerning the eucharist, but discussion of baptism had barely begun. I had read Dix's *The Theology of Confirmation in Relation to Baptism* prior to writing my doctoral dissertation on *Baptismal Anointing*, and that had led me to read Lampe, Mason, Thornton, and the reports of the English Convocations; but these were not widely read in the United States. My research led me to publish "The Shape of the Baptismal Liturgy" in *Anglican Theological Review*.

At that point I was asked to become a consultant to the Standing Liturgical Commission to work with Bonnell Spencer on the revision of the baptismal rite. When the drafting committee was fully constituted, we began work on what was to become *Prayer Book Studies* 18. By and large we encountered not opposition but mystification from those to whom we presented our work. Most people had never thought about any of the questions which the study raised, and those who had were supporters of Gregory Dix's view.

We saw *PBS* 18 as a platform from which to raise these issues and hoped that many of them would eventually be accepted. The committee wished to present a proposal to the Standing Liturgical Commission which embodied our theology of baptism without compromise. There would be plenty of time for compromise before it could be finally adopted and find a place in the Prayer Book.

PBS 26, our revised proposal, attracted both supporters and critics on all sides. One priest, I remember, accused me personally of blasphemy for having had a part in it. It was a theologically exciting time, and the Episcopal Church has still not resolved all of the questions which *PBS* 26 raised.

Ruth Meyers has given us a theological and historical study of the entire process, through the scholarly eyes of one who was not personally involved;

and she has done it while she was still able to interview many of the participants and to read our notes. Bonnell Spencer has died since she interviewed him. And Bill Spilman, Terry Holmes, and Margaret Mead had already died. Most of the rest of us are retired. Dr. Meyers's work is both timely and important if the vision of Christian initiation which came into shape in these years is to have its place in the life of the Church, as I believe it should.

It is a particular joy to me to introduce this work by a former student and now my successor at Seabury-Western, since it deals so well with the area to which I have devoted the better part of my working life.

Leonel L. Mitchell
Professor Emeritus of Liturgics
Seabury-Western Theological Seminary
September 1997

Introduction

Being a cradle Episcopalian, I was baptized at the tender age of one month. Thus my earliest memory of baptism (the picture of me as an infant in my long white christening robe doesn't count) is the baptism of my cousin Darryl. I was six or eight years old, and one Sunday afternoon my parents gathered my two brothers, my sister and me, and off we went to Grandma's church. This was not the parish Darryl and my aunt and uncle attended, but the church where my mother and my aunt had been raised. My most vivid memory of that afternoon remains the large, dark, nearly empty church. In addition to my grandparents, several of my aunts and uncles and cousins were there, but aside from the rector, perhaps an Altar Guild member, and, of course, my grandparents, no member of that parish was at the baptism. The ceremony in the church was a vivid contrast with the warmth and intimacy of my grandparents' house where the family gathered to celebrate after the baptism.

I had a very different experience two years ago when my son Jerry was baptized. The baptism was scheduled for a Sunday morning when the bishop visited our home parish. Jerry's godparents included not only a close family member but also members of the parish, linked to our family by our common baptism in Christ, not by blood relation. The church was full—grandparents and other family members had traveled from out of town to be with us, but most of the people in the pews were members of the parish. At the time of the baptism, everyone processed out of their pews and gathered around the font, where we poured as much water on Jerry as we could—it was one of those ninety-degree humid summer days, and he giggled with delight as the cool water washed over him. Then the bishop anointed him, smearing the fragrant chrism over his face and signing him with the cross. Jerry had his first communion that day. After the service, we gathered downstairs for a festive reception hosted by the parish. Gifts were presented publicly—a Bible from his parish sponsors, a prayer book from my husband and me. Jerry was indeed welcomed into the household of God, a household visibly present in the many hugs and acts of love shown to him and to us that morning.

During the past half century, a revolution has been quietly taking place in the Episcopal Church, a revolution in the way we celebrate baptism and a revolution in the way we understand baptism. The traditional Anglican pattern of initiation into the Church, which began with baptism, usually in infancy, and was completed by confirmation and first communion during adolescence, has been replaced by a rite of baptism defined by the 1979 prayer book as "full initiation by water and the Holy Spirit into Christ's Body the Church." In many places infants are admitted to communion at their baptism. The new rite of "Confirmation with forms for Reception and for the Reaffirmation of Baptismal Vows" can be understood as a repeatable rite of affirmation of faith, not an initiatory rite. Baptism is more and more seen as central to the life of the Church, the sacrament which forms and empowers the body of Christ.

The radical changes in the Episcopal Church's practice and theology of baptism are part of a much broader liturgical movement which has profoundly reshaped worship in the Episcopal Church and other Christian churches during the twentieth century. This liturgical movement took place against the backdrop of massive social and cultural upheaval. We are moving out of the era of Christendom, an age when the ethos of Christianity pervaded society and our world was presumed to be Christian. Our time is often described as "post-Christendom," or "post-Christian," a time in which broader societal supports for Christian life are rapidly crumbling and the Church is increasingly understood as a distinctive community whose values are not identical with those of the society and the state. This profound transition in the relation between Church and society is challenging the Church to rediscover its identity as the body of Christ.

In *Anglicanism and the Christian Church*, the English theologian Paul Avis traces interpretations of Anglican identity from the Reformation to the present day. He concludes by advocating a "baptismal ecclesiology," an understanding of the Church founded neither upon an erastian paradigm in which Church and society are intertwined in a single Christian commonwealth, nor upon an apostolic paradigm in which bishops as successors of the apostles are the primary symbol of the Church. A baptismal ecclesiology understands the Church to be rooted in baptism, the sacrament of incorporation into the Church and the foundation of our unity within Anglicanism and with other Christians. Avis argues that a baptismal paradigm has been part of Anglicanism, in some official formularies and in the writings of some Anglican theologians, since the Reformation. Nevertheless, he urges the Anglican

Communion to embrace more fully this baptismal paradigm as the way forward in ecumenical dialogues.

I believe that the twentieth-century revolution in baptismal practice and theology in the Episcopal Church is bringing about a baptismal ecclesiology, an understanding of the Church as a community formed by baptism and empowered by baptism and the eucharist to carry out the reconciling ministry of Christ in the world. This baptismal ecclesiology is significant not only in contemporary ecumenical dialogue but also as a basis for the identity of the Church in a post-Christendom world. Increasingly, baptism is no longer viewed as a mark of citizenship in the world, but rather signifies entry into a distinctive community that has experienced the power of the risen Christ and so chooses to live as Christ's people in the world.

This book traces the emergence of a baptismal ecclesiology in the Episcopal Church, a revolutionary change brought about not only by the official process of prayer book revision leading to the 1979 prayer book, but also by changes in the life of the Church which have enabled the acceptance of a radically different initiatory pattern. But the reformation continues as communities continue to implement the rites of the 1979 prayer book and grasp the power of baptism to shape Christian life.

A note about inclusive language: Many of the materials cited here, dating from earlier decades of this century, use masculine nouns and pronouns where the reference is clearly to humanity. A shift to widespread use of inclusive language is just one aspect of the many changes experienced during this century. Throughout the book, I have cited historical documents and published texts without modification, rather than judge that material by the standards of a later generation.

Chapter 1

The Traditional Anglican Pattern: Baptism, Confirmation, Admission to Communion

I am what is sometimes known as a "cradle Episcopalian." The child of active Episcopalians, I was baptized at the rather tender age of one month, confirmed when I was in the ninth grade after a full school year of confirmation classes, and admitted to communion at the time of my confirmation. My experience reflects the traditional Anglican pattern of Christian initiation, a pattern established by the first Anglican prayer books at the time of the Reformation in the sixteenth century and essentially unchanged until the 1979 Book of Common Prayer. But this pattern was the product of the rather complex evolution of baptism and confirmation in the life of the Church, an evolution that has been widely studied and discussed during the twentieth century. To understand the radical changes introduced in the 1979 Book of Common Prayer, it is necessary to begin with a brief survey of this history.[1]

The New Testament and the Early Church: A Single Initiatory Rite

Numerous references and allusions to baptism can be found in the New Testament, but nowhere is there a full description or text of a baptismal rite. The book of Acts includes several reports of baptisms as part of its story of the missionary spread of the Gospel, beginning with the baptism of three thousand converts in response to Peter's Pentecost sermon following the descent of the Spirit on the disciples (Acts 2). From these descriptions and from other New Testament references to baptism, we can conclude that baptism followed conversion and was administered with water in the name of Jesus or in the name of the Father, Son and Holy Spirit.

While in several places the New Testament associates the gift of the Holy Spirit with baptism, there is no evidence for the regular administration of a rite

1

bestowing the Spirit separate from baptism. Acts 8:14-17 tells of the journey of Peter and John to Samaria in order to lay hands on converts who had been baptized but had not received the Spirit, and Acts 19:1-6 relates Paul's encounter at Ephesus with disciples who had been baptized into John's baptism but did not know of the Holy Spirit. In each of these tales, the Holy Spirit is bestowed through laying on of hands by the apostles. But in Acts 10:44-48, the Spirit descends upon a group of Gentiles while Peter is preaching to them, and in response the converts are baptized. Elsewhere in Acts, baptisms are reported without any mention of the bestowal of the Spirit. The primary intent of each of these stories is not to provide an accurate description of the sacramental practice of the nascent church, but to bear witness to the missionary spread of the church, empowered by the Holy Spirit.

What can be learned from these reports of baptism and other New Testament references to baptism is that converts were initiated into Christian life by baptism with water in the name of Jesus or in the triune name. Baptism was interpreted as incorporation into the Christian community, cleansing from sin, rebirth, participation in Christ's death and resurrection, entrance into the reign of God, sealing with the Spirit, being clothed with Christ. Some of these metaphors suggest ritual actions, for example, anointing or putting on new garments. However, there is no conclusive evidence that such actions were customarily part of the baptismal rite during the first century.

As the Church grew and ritual practices developed, the multifaceted dimensions of baptism gradually came to be expressed symbolically through various interpretive gestures and actions, including anointing and the laying on of hands. The normative candidate was an adult, although from at least as early as the end of the second century, the children of believers, including infants, were incorporated into the Christian community by the same rite. Baptism culminated in the celebration of the eucharist, at which the newly baptized, including infants, were present and received communion for the first time. The bishop customarily presided at the initiatory rite, and by the fourth century, baptism was usually administered at the Easter vigil. No additional rite, for adults or for children, was considered necessary to complete Christian initiation.

The Middle Ages: Adaptation and Division of the Rite

The official recognition of the Church after the peace of Constantine (313) had a number of consequences for the Church's initiatory practice. Throughout the fourth century, large numbers of adults were initiated through an elaborate process that included several months or years of preparation (the "catechumenate"), culminating in the celebration of the initiatory rites at the Easter vigil. But as the empire came to be predominantly Christian, there remained few adult converts to be baptized, and the normative candidates were infants. The catechumenate was shortened and adjustments made to the preliminary rites. Baptism continued to be administered at the vigils of Easter and Pentecost, with exceptions permitted for those in danger of death. However, in the later Middle Ages, owing to concern about infants dying suddenly, without warning, baptism came to be allowed to infants at any time. By the fourteenth century, several synods required that baptism be administered within eight days of birth.

In the early Middle Ages, outside of Rome and central Italy, where dioceses were large and travel difficult, bishops could not be present at most celebrations of baptism. Instead, a priest administered the entire rite, including a single postbaptismal anointing and the concluding eucharist, and this was viewed as full Christian initiation. This continues to be the initiatory pattern of Eastern Orthodox churches today. But in Rome and the dioceses of central Italy, in addition to a postbaptismal anointing on the head by a priest, the bishop administered a second anointing on the forehead. In cases where a bishop was unable to be present for the rite, this final anointing could be readily supplied within a short period of time, effectively preserving a role for the bishop in Christian initiation.

When in the eighth century the rites of Rome were imposed by the emperor Charlemagne throughout the West, the Roman initiatory rite with its second postbaptismal anointing administered by a bishop gradually became the standard rite of western Christianity. However, due to the difficulty of travel and the negligence of bishops and parents, the rite did not function nearly as well outside of Rome. Often several years lapsed between baptism and the bishop's anointing, a rite which came to be called "confirmation." Local ecclesiastical councils began to adopt legislation setting maximum ages by which children should be confirmed and providing penalties for parents who did not comply. Eventually these maximum age limits came to be seen as minimum ages for confirmation.

As confirmation emerged as a separate rite administered several years after baptism, a theological rationale developed. Confirmation came to be understood as a strengthening of the Spirit, equipping the person for the spiritual battles of this world. Thomas Aquinas offered a biological analogy: baptism is to human birth as confirmation is to growth.

While confirmation gradually came to be administered several years after baptism, up until the twelfth century infants continued to be communicated at the time of their baptism, and the reception of communion was considered necessary to their salvation. However, in the ninth century a doctrine of sacramental realism began to emerge, emphasizing that in the eucharist the bread and wine actually become the body and blood of Jesus. Eventually doubts arose as to the propriety of communicating infants, lest they desecrate the sacrament by spitting up the host. Infants began to be communicated with wine only, and by the thirteenth century, as the same sacramental realism resulted in the withdrawal of laity from receiving the chalice, infants ceased to be communicated at all. Legislation then restricted communion to those who had reached the age of discretion. In England, a Council of Lambeth, held under Archbishop John Peckham in 1281, decreed that no one should be admitted to communion until confirmed. The intent, however, was not to discourage communion, but rather to encourage parents to bring their children for confirmation.

The Reformation:
Confirmation as a Profession of Faith

The reformers of the sixteenth century inherited a process of initiation that included infant baptism and, usually at the age of discretion (age seven or ten), an anointing by the bishop called "confirmation," followed by admission to communion. To this the reformers added their concern to provide members of the Church with a firmer foundation in the essentials of the faith.

Martin Luther and John Calvin denounced the medieval practice of confirmation as an idle and superstitious ceremony but saw great value in catechesis prior to admission to communion. While Luther and Calvin did not themselves introduce rites to replace confirmation, churches in the Lutheran and Reformed traditions gradually began to produce rites for adolescents to profess their faith and be admitted to communion.

In the Church of England, a rite of confirmation similar to the medieval rite was retained, but with imposition of hands by the bishop instead of anointing. However, in the prayer book the confirmation rite was prefaced by "a catechism for children," and children were required to learn the responses to this catechism as well as the Creed, the Lord's Prayer and the Ten Commandments prior to their confirmation. Moreover, the "confirmation rubric" requiring confirmation before admission to communion was retained, making admission to communion as well as confirmation contingent upon catechesis.

An explicit profession of faith was added to the Anglican confirmation rite in 1662.

The more radical reformers abolished infant baptism altogether and introduced instead a practice of believers' baptism. This eliminated a separate rite of confirmation or profession of faith for those baptized in infancy. Yet in the following centuries, as churches in these traditions became more firmly established, rites of infant "dedication" became increasingly common. Furthermore, although conversion was requisite for baptism, the appropriate experience tended to occur at about the expected age. In short, although churches in believers' baptist traditions interpreted baptism quite differently from those in the Anglican, Lutheran and Reformed traditions, the initiatory patterns came to be quite similar. A rite in infancy was followed by catechesis throughout childhood, leading to a public ritual that included a profession of faith and granted admission to full communicant membership.

In the Roman Catholic tradition, the initiatory pattern was much the same. The Council of Trent in the sixteenth century issued several decrees that institutionalized the late medieval separation of baptism, confirmation and admission to communion. Up until that time, though rare in practice, it was possible for infants to be confirmed and admitted to communion. Well known examples include Prince Arthur and Princess Elizabeth in England. But the Council of Trent, while affirming the necessity of confirmation, directed that confirmation be postponed to the age of seven, if not age twelve, and likewise declared that children under the age of reason were under no obligation to receive the eucharist.

By the early twentieth century, in some places in the Roman Catholic Church, the customary age for first reception of communion had risen to age ten or twelve, or even fourteen or older. The decree *Quam singulari*, issued in 1910 by the Sacred Congregation of the Sacraments under Pope Pius X, affirmed that the age for first communion was the age of reason, understood to be age seven and further defined as the age at which a child could discern eucharistic bread from ordinary bread. While the decree did not discuss confirmation, it had the effect of reversing the sequence of sacraments: first reception of communion began to precede confirmation in many congregations of the Roman Catholic Church.[2] Eventually this practice encouraged Episcopalians to reconsider their pattern of Christian initiation, but in the early twentieth century, the inherited Reformation pattern remained firmly in place.

This Reformation pattern, evident in most American churches at the beginning of the twentieth century, reflected the era of Christendom, in which the entire society is presumed to be Christian, or at least to be based upon Christian values. Baptism (or, in believers' baptist traditions, a rite of infant dedication) was administered as a matter of course and was primarily a rite of passage marking physical birth, a social occasion significant in the lives of the immediate family and friends of the child. There was an assumption that Christian formation and nurture would occur through daily living as well as regular participation in Sunday School, because the values of Church, family and society were closely intertwined. At an appropriate age, usually at some point in adolescence, children made a public profession of faith (baptism, for believers' baptists), a rite marking growth and acceptance of "adult" responsibilities. Following this rite, young people were considered full communicant members of the Church. Glimpses of this process in the Episcopal Church can be found in pastoral manuals which helped clergy interpret the prayer book rubrics.

Baptism as a Private Rite

The 1892 Book of Common Prayer provided three versions of the rite of baptism: "The Ministration of Public Baptism of Infants, to be used in the church," "The Ministration of Private Baptism of Children, in houses," and "The Ministration of Baptism to such as are of Riper Years, and able to answer for themselves." While the baptismal rites in the sixteenth-century prayer books of the Church of England had assumed infant candidates, in the seventeenth century a rite for adults became necessary because of the neglect of the sacraments during the period of the Commonwealth, the growth of the Anabaptist movement (which practiced believers' baptism), and the desire to convert and baptize native people and slaves in the developing British colonies. Hence the 1662 English prayer book introduced a rite for adult baptism, modeled on that for the baptism of infants, and the American Episcopalian books of 1789 and 1892 followed suit. Nonetheless, in the early twentieth century, infant baptism continued to be the norm and adult baptism the exception.

In the 1892 Book of Common Prayer, the opening rubric of the service of public baptism of infants directed that "Baptism should not be administered but upon Sundays and other Holy-Days, or Prayer-Days."[3] The English rite further specified that baptism was to be administered

> when the most number of people come together; as well as for that the Congregation there present may testify the receiving of them that be newly baptized in the number of Christ's Church; as also because in the Baptism of Infants every

man present may be put in remembrance of his own profession made to God in his Baptism.[4]

This rationale for the administration of baptism on Sundays and holy days had been omitted from the first (1789) American prayer book, perhaps because most baptisms were being performed privately. Certainly by the early twentieth century, most baptisms were administered privately, in the presence of family and close friends but apart from the regularly scheduled worship of most parishes. Moreover, although the prayer book also directed that baptism be administered after the last lesson at Morning or Evening Prayer,[5] this rubric was widely ignored. Authors of pastoral manuals made some attempts to stress the significance of public baptism, but their writings suggest that the prevailing custom was private, not public baptism.

In a text for use in his pastoral theology classes, William DeWitt, Dean of Western Theological Seminary in Chicago, acknowledged the significance of a public rite of baptism but allowed numerous exceptions to public baptism at the main Sunday service. In large parishes where it was likely that baptisms would occur nearly every Sunday, it was appropriate to limit to one or two Sundays each month the times at which children might be brought to be baptized. Alternatively, "a special congregation can usually be secured, by a little effort, for a Sunday afternoon baptismal service."[6] Moreover, while the rubrics prefacing the rite of private baptism stipulated that children should not be baptized at home without "great cause and necessity,"[7] DeWitt opined that a mother's "pious reason that she wants no delay in making [the child] a member of Christ and the child of God" was sufficient cause. Although a child privately baptized should be brought to the church to be received by the congregation, DeWitt acknowledged that "it is usually difficult to get parents" to do so.[8]

Such a gap between theory and practice is also evident in an Anglo-Catholic manual written by Charles Burnett, Curate of St. Ignatius' Church, New York City. For Burnett, "public baptism" meant the rite of Public Baptism of Infants, held in the church, with or without a congregation beyond the immediate family:

> It is certainly most agreeable to the character of the baptismal service and to ancient custom that many Christian people should be present and take some part in the service when holy Baptism is publicly administered. Therefore the parish Priest will do well, generally, to try to secure such an attendance at Public Baptisms. But as a matter of fact *it is not often possible to do this*...
>
> Moreover, it may often happen that the parish Priest, out of consideration for the feelings of poor people...will do well to appoint, for the Baptism, an

hour when the congregation will be limited to the persons of the baptismal party.

> And finally, custom, of long continuance and almost universal among us, *allows us to baptize publicly in church at any hour which may be most convenient for all who are immediately concerned. This customary action on the part of many or most of our Bishops and the great body of our parochial and missionary clergy makes the rubric in question not obligatory.*[9]

While Burnett allowed numerous exceptions to the rubrical directive for public baptism, William Paret, Bishop of Maryland from 1885 to 1911, encouraged his clergy to adhere rigorously to the rubrics. Only under conditions of great necessity should exceptions be made. Even in his missionary practice, when it was often necessary for him to hold baptisms at homes far from the church, Paret would gather a congregation of neighbors and hold a full service of Morning or Evening Prayer with baptism after the second lesson. Paret was particularly insistent because he recognized that his own practice was atypical:

> Holy Baptism is thrust aside... They needlessly break the rubrics. They take it away from the prominence the Church demands for it and its place in the public service, and fear to weary their people by putting it after the second lesson. They have it before Service, or after Service, or they hand it over to the Sunday School, or to the Children's Service... How often do you suppose the average layman or lay-woman sees the administration of Baptism? And when they do see it, how often are they impressed by reverent solemnity?[10]

Preparation for Baptism

Not only was baptism administered privately as a separate office, little or no preparation was expected. For the baptism of infants, the pertinent rubrics, essentially unchanged since the 1549 Book of Common Prayer, directed that parents or sponsors notify the minister prior to the beginning of Morning Prayer and that the parents and godparents along with the child be ready at the font as the priest directed. The fact that the rubrics required only very short notice in itself precluded any significant preparation.

DeWitt suggested that the minister search out children for baptism and provide "a printed blank for the instruction of parents, and to serve as a memorandum."[11] Such instruction was minimal, as indicated by this statement on the recommended application form:

> Sponsors should read the service for the PUBLIC BAPTISM OF INFANTS before coming to church, that they may understand their duties and make proper

responses. If they have no PRAYER BOOKS, the clergy will furnish them upon application.

This "instruction" offered no interpretation of the meaning of the baptismal service or the nature of Christian life, nor did DeWitt recommend any other instruction by the priest.[12] It appears that for DeWitt the meaning of the prayer book service was self-evident.

Although DeWitt stressed the serious nature of baptism, he was realistic, perhaps even despairing, with regard to the attitude of many parents: "Parents frequently regard Holy Baptism as a sentimental or superstitious ceremony of no more importance than is indicated by their willingness 'to have baby sprinkled.'" To remedy this, DeWitt emphasized the importance of sponsors who understood their responsibilities, even if it meant having fewer than three sponsors (the number stipulated by the prayer book) or having a sponsor who was a stranger to the family:

> It will be necessary in such cases to impress upon the parents that the Church means every word contained in the baptismal office; and that it is your duty to see to it that sponsors can be relied upon to do their duty by infants whom the Church commits to their spiritual care.[13]

Careful selection and preparation of sponsors was also recommended by Burnett, who stated that it was the duty of the priest to ascertain "that persons competent to act as sponsors are chosen and that such persons are sufficiently instructed in regard to the ceremonies of holy Baptism, and about the obligations of sponsorship."[14] But like DeWitt, Burnett provided few specific suggestions for the preparation of parents and sponsors. Paret made no recommendations regarding their instruction, although he emphasized the obligations of sponsors: "let me beg you to do all in your power to make the sponsors' act and office a deep reality."[15]

In contrast to the rubrical provision for parents to present children for baptism with little notice, the service for the baptism of adults called for "timely notice" to be given to the minister, who was to examine the candidates as to whether they were sufficiently instructed in the principles of Christian religion, and to exhort them to prepare by prayers and fasting.[16] Paret commented:

> I have reason to know that very often in such cases hardly any care at all is taken. A person of decent, respectable reputation says to the minister, "I wish to be baptized." And the minister takes that profession of a wish as assurance of the person's fitness, and asking no further questions, says, "Come on Wednesday next, after the second lesson."

Furthermore, Paret complained, there was a dearth of instructional manuals for use by adults prior to their baptism, although numerous manuals were available for prayer and instruction prior to confirmation and for preparation for communion.[17] This lack of preparatory materials may reflect laxity in the instruction of adults, as Paret implied, but it might also indicate that adult baptism was rare in practice.

Certainly the predominant practice in the early twentieth century was for infants to be baptized with virtually no preparation of their parents and godparents. Baptism was a social event, an occasion for celebrating the birth of the child and a religious rite affirming the child's place in Church and society. It was assumed that the child would be raised in a social context in which Christianity was normative and Christian teachings were widely accepted. What was needed for those beginning their Christian life was to be raised as a citizen of this Christian nation. Hence, little special preparation was necessary for those primarily responsible for the Christian upbringing of the child, that is, the parents and godparents, although it was appropriate to underscore their responsibilities.

The Office of Confirmation

While minimal ritual attention was given to baptism, by the early twentieth century confirmation was of great significance in most parishes and dioceses. During the colonial period, the absence of bishops had precluded confirmation unless an individual traveled to England, a difficult journey seldom if ever undertaken for this sole purpose. Even after the Episcopal Church was constituted following the American Revolution, bishops customarily retained their parochial responsibilities and seldom made parish visitations. It was only in the early nineteenth century that bishops began to carry out with great zeal their responsibility of presiding over confirmation services. Bishops such as John Henry Hobart, Bishop of New York from 1811 to 1830, and Alexander Viets Griswold, Bishop of the Eastern Diocese (comprising all the New England states that did not have resident bishops) from 1811 to 1843, viewed their episcopal visitations as integral to the missionary work of the Church and traveled widely in their dioceses to administer confirmation.

Bishops in the early twentieth century continued to view confirmation as an important aspect of their ministry. The practice of David Greer, Bishop of New York from 1908 to 1919, was described in this manner: "ordinarily he would have a confirmation in the evening, and on Sundays he would visit two or three other parishes for confirmation."[18] Charles Lewis Slattery, bishop in Massachusetts from 1922 to 1930, approached his work of confirmation with great eagerness:

Episcopal visitations began at once [following his consecration as bishop], and in this part of his work Bishop Slattery from the beginning and throughout his episcopate took greatest pleasure... [H]e valued most in his work as bishop the opportunity which confirmation brought to him in the relationship with the young at the most sacred moment of their lives.[19]

The same devotion was described by Anson Rogers Graves, Missionary Bishop in Nebraska from 1890 to 1910. His autobiography related his travels throughout Western Nebraska, with continuing emphasis on visitations and confirmations. On one trip, "in the three days we drove eighty miles, held two services with baptism and confirmation and secured seventy game birds with our guns,"[20] a typical description of Graves' journeys. On another occasion, after holding services in an outlying town, he returned to the home where he was staying with a family, and there:

The man requested us to baptize him, which we did. Then for an hour or more we instructed him, his wife and daughter in the fundamental principles of the Christian religion. Then the three were confirmed and received the holy communion. As the place was off our usual beat, there was no certainty of our being there again, hence we crowded these functions together, working until after midnight.[21]

Graves' work in a missionary district necessitated some compromises in the administration of sacraments. Yet in this setting, as in the more settled diocese of New York, the administration of confirmation was a high priority for the bishop.

In contrast to baptism, which was to be administered in the context of Morning or Evening Prayer (a rubric which, as we have seen, was frequently ignored), the prayer book made no provision for confirmation to be joined to any other office. Arthur C. A. Hall, Bishop of Vermont from 1894 to 1929, explained: "The office [of confirmation] is complete in itself, and may often conveniently be used as a separate service, with accompanying hymns and an address."[22] In some places Morning or Evening Prayer no doubt preceded the office of confirmation. However, it was in particular the presence of the bishop, who customarily gave an "address," that gave the occasion great ritual significance. Pastoral necessity might at times necessitate a private confirmation, but the office was usually celebrated publicly with family and friends of the confirmands as well as members of the local congregation in attendance.

Preparation for Confirmation

The description of Bishop Graves' baptism and subsequent catechesis and confirmation of a family reflects the customary practice of giving instruction in the Christian faith in preparation for confirmation rather than prior to baptism. In this missionary situation, it would have been possible to catechize the family and then baptize and confirm them in a single ritual event. But it appears that the sequence of events, compressed into a single evening because of the exigencies of the mission field, was determined by the prevailing pattern in which catechesis and confirmation followed baptism.

The 1892 prayer book maintained the pattern of previous Anglican prayer books, in which confirmation was preceded by the catechism and children were expected to know the responses to this catechism in addition to the Creed, the Lord's Prayer, and the Ten Commandments prior to being confirmed. But although these parameters were established, the actual content and means of instruction varied. Preparation was usually conducted by the clergy and emphasized religious instruction and intellectual achievement. For many clergy, confirmation preparation was an opportunity to instill in candidates a wide range of information covering such areas as church history, the prayer book, and worship.

Many clergy relied on commercially prepared confirmation manuals in addition to or instead of the catechism. In his manual for priests, DeWitt described the wide assortment of materials available:

> There are a great many manuals for Confirmation Classes. Some are distinctly partisan; some too brief, and some too long. Some pay little attention to the meaning of the Catechism, and some do not give it all as it stands. Not a few are so worded as to overtax the intellectual ability of children. Some have no form for self-examination, and some are not preparatory to the Holy Communion. My own experience in this matter led me to publish a manual, which I venture to suggest.[23]

But it was not only the manuals for confirmation instruction which sometimes were of dubious quality. DeWitt had disparaging words for preparation which was merely "mechanical":

> The mechanical grinding of the ecclesiastical mill which is set agoing "for Confirmation" once a year, some six weeks before the Bishop comes; just taking in whatever is offered and saturating all that is offered with fixed proportions of Apostolic Succession, fully explained sacramental mysteries, damnation of schism, ridicule of Rome, pet ritual precepts...; the grinding of the mill that never stirred a heart to love-engendered penitence...; the grinding of the mill that has to grind each year to keep the enrollment of communi-

cants up to where it has been for a decade...; this grinding of the mill is not attuned to the melody, "God so loved the world."

DeWitt recommended a course of instruction of at least twelve weeks wherever possible, that is, if the bishop would give sufficient notice. His proposed course was intended to convey the basics of the faith, to invite individuals to open their hearts to God, and to inculcate a habit of self-examination.[24] While DeWitt urged both intellectual preparation and spiritual conversion, his rather cynical description of "the ecclesiastical mill" implied that thorough preparation for confirmation was all too often lacking.

Like DeWitt, Paret stressed the importance of careful preparation for confirmation. He recommended that clergy teach about confirmation in sermons throughout the year, as well as preach a series of sermons on confirmation prior to the bishop's visitation. In addition to these sermons, confirmation classes were to provide specific teaching as the prayer book directed. Paret urged that clergy adhere to the standards set forth by the prayer book but not add further criteria. These supplementary requirements, which Paret himself had observed, included learning the *Te Deum* or Nicene Creed, understanding "the points of history, order, and worship in which the Church differs from other Christian bodies," and studying questions additional to those found in the catechism.[25]

The Age for Confirmation

DeWitt's criticism included a denunciation of "the grinding of the Confirmation mill which turns out 'the largest class' [and] 'includes three lawyers, one physician, and the mayor.'"[26] Although this implied confirmation of adults, adolescents were more commonly the candidates. The prayer book expected that children would be brought to confirmation when they had reached the age of discretion, usually considered to be early adolescence. Paret told the clergy that although there would be older people not yet confirmed, "in the places where the Church has long been doing its work, the children must be the staple of the [confirmation] class."[27]

A 1918 article by Lester Bradner, a member of the General Board of Religious Education of the Episcopal Church, suggested that the average age of confirmation had been dropping, from age sixteen, customary during the nineteenth century, to age fourteen and even as young as ages ten or eleven. According to Bradner, the age considered most appropriate depended upon the understanding of what was being accomplished in confirmation:

> Those who would emphasize the necessity of cooperation on the part of the individual, and especially his fitness to understand the moral and doctrinal positions to which he is giving personal assent and allegiance, and his capacity to assume the responsibility which must rest upon a self-directed membership in the Church, will naturally choose a later age. Those who emphasize more exclusively the divine blessing conferred upon the individual by virtue of the sacrament or rite will naturally seek whatever benefit there is in this at the earliest possible moment.[28]

Bradner recommended, on the basis of psychological understandings of adolescence, that confirmation occur in early adolescence, at age twelve or thirteen. Confirmation at this age would coincide with the beginning of a child's physical, emotional, and social transition to adulthood, and introduce the child "to a Guide with whom he is to undertake the great adventure of faith."[29] Yet Bradner also pointed out that variations in the development of individual adolescents called for flexibility and careful judgment in the age chosen for confirmation, and he acknowledged that some would desire confirmation at an even earlier age, to permit admission to communion, and others would opt for a much later age, at which fuller intellectual comprehension was possible.[30]

As we will see, the appropriate age for an adolescent rite of commitment has been widely debated throughout much of this century, not only in the Episcopal Church but also in most Christian denominations. The disagreement reflects, at least in part, the emergence of a more extended developmental period of adolescence, a phenomenon which has its origins in the complexities of modern industrial society. With childhood devoted to education and psycho-social development rather than apprenticeship for adult labor, there is no single clear transition point from childhood to adulthood, but rather a series of events marking stages of growth and the gradual assumption of adult responsibilities. This extended developmental period of adolescence offers no readily agreed upon point at which a rite of public profession of faith is most appropriate. Bradner's 1918 work marks an early recognition of the range of possibilities and the contours of the debate.

Prayer Book Revision

The American prayer book had been revised in 1892 to provide flexibility and enrichment in the liturgy. Owing to a stipulation that no alterations be made touching upon either statements or standards of doctrine, the revision was rather minor. This revision, however, did not fully satisfy the desire for prayer book revision in the Episcopal Church. In 1913, scarcely twenty years after the last revision, a memorial resolution from the Diocese of California to the

General Convention initiated another round of revision, leading to the 1928 Book of Common Prayer. Once again the revision commission was charged to make no decision affecting the faith and doctrine of the Church, but this time the stipulation was interpreted to mean the limits of Anglican orthodoxy, an interpretation permitting much greater latitude.

The primary change in the baptismal offices was the consolidation of the three separate offices for baptism. The rubrics in the 1789 and 1892 prayer books had given directions for combining the offices of infant and adult baptism, for receiving a person privately baptized, and for conditional baptism. But these rubrics were confusing and complicated. Most clergy resorted to a supplemental (and unofficial) prayer book for directions when they found it necessary to combine the different offices, while the members of the congregation were left to muddle through as best they could. The revisers sought to eliminate this confusion by providing one office with instructions for various circumstances.

In structure and content, the 1928 baptismal rite was much like the 1892 rites of infant and adult baptism. The latter rites were quite similar to each other, necessitating only minor adjustments when they were combined into a single rite. Provisions for private baptism and the reception of persons so baptized were included as rubrics at the conclusion of the 1928 baptismal rite, using a structure akin to the 1892 rite of private baptism.

Perhaps the most significant theological change introduced in the 1928 baptismal rite was the elimination of several references to original sin and God's wrath. This principle for revision was in keeping with the rejection of the Augustinian doctrine of original sin by theologians of the late nineteenth century. In a paper given at a Church Congress in 1919, Charles Slattery, chair of the revision commission, argued that such a revision was appropriate and desirable because of this shift in theological opinion:

> There is also apparent readiness on the part of the whole Church, in all its parties or schools of thought, to repudiate the once current belief in original sin, as that doctrine was technically and exactly defined, wherever that doctrine is or appears to be embedded in the Book of Common Prayer, as in connection, for instance, with the Church's thought of Baptism.[31]

But Slattery was mistaken in his claim that the entire Church was ready to eliminate the doctrine of original sin. Several Evangelical groups objected to omissions from the proposed baptismal office, including "all men are conceived and born in sin"; "none can enter into the Kingdom of God, except he be regenerate and born anew of water and of the Holy Ghost"; "being delivered from thy wrath"; "crucify the old man, and utterly abolish the whole body of sin."[32]

Despite the Evangelicals' objections, most of the phrases were not restored, and similar changes were made in the Catechism. In an introduction to the 1928 prayer book, Slattery provided a rationale for the elimination of each phrase from the baptismal rite. "Conceived and born in sin" had been troublesome for many parents, to whom it implied sinfulness in the act of conception. "Being delivered from thy wrath" was not in keeping with more modern theology which emphasized God's love rather than God's wrath. As for "crucify the old man," Slattery commented that the phrase "aroused the mirth of the unregenerate as applying to the child's father."[33] Only the phrase "...be regenerate and born anew..." was retained in the revision finally adopted. While Slattery's remarks skirted the issue of original sin, it should be noted that the 1928 revisions were intended to remove reference to a particular doctrine of sin as it had been developed by Augustine in the early fifth century and by later medieval theologians, particularly phrases that were commonly misconstrued. The 1928 revisions did not excise altogether a scriptural understanding of sin and redemption, and indeed retained the renunciation of the devil, the world and the flesh.

In addition to excising phrases referring to original sin, the revisers eliminated in entirety the "Flood Prayer," a prayer for the candidates that related baptism not only to the deliverance of Noah and his family from the flood, but also to the Israelites' passage through the Red Sea and to Jesus' baptism in the Jordan. Without this prayer, the 1928 baptismal rite contained no references to the Hebrew scriptures or to the baptism of Jesus. An article about the proposed revision said of the flood prayer:

> [T]he prayer is about the worst in the Prayer Book. It was never known in the Church until Luther translated it from some obscure Latin source. It offends in many ways, especially in making Baptism, first of all the deliverance from God's wrath and the Church of God merely an Ark of Safety.[34]

Slattery commented that the prayer created difficulty in applying the figure of Noah to baptism.[35]

The gospels appointed, which continued to be the only scriptural readings in the rite, included the 1892 readings for infant baptism—Mark 10:13-16—and adult baptism—John 3:1-8—along with a new alternative, Matthew 28:18-20. The possibility of using any of these readings at the baptism of either an infant or an adult could be employed creatively, as Slattery suggested:

[I]f the Minister wishes to impress on unbaptized adults the importance of Baptism, he may read the passage about Nicodemus [John 3] at a child's Baptism. Or, if he wishes to impress upon adults the necessity of humility, he will read at their baptism the Lesson about little children [Mark 10].[36]

While there were numerous changes, mostly minor, in the baptismal rite, little was changed in the office of confirmation. The Preface, an introductory address by the bishop which had been made optional in 1892, was dropped because it had "laid emphasis on Confirmation as the renewing of Baptismal vows."[37] Yet the renewal of baptismal vows remained in the question addressed to the candidate by the bishop, "Do ye here...renew the solemn promise and vow that ye made, or that was made in your name, at your Baptism...?" The renewal of baptism was further emphasized by the addition of the question, "Do ye promise to follow Jesus Christ as your Lord and Savior?", which paralleled a question addressed to adult baptismal candidates.[38]

The overall impact of the 1928 prayer book on the understanding and practice of baptism and confirmation was slight. The celebration of baptism was simplified in cases where the combination of offices had been necessary. Some archaic language was modified to give greater clarity. References to original sin and God's wrath were diminished, with new emphasis placed upon God's mercy and love. The requirement of instruction prior to confirmation and the reception of communion remained, and confirmation continued to include prayer for the gift of the Holy Spirit as well as the ratifying of baptismal promises.

However, the revisers were aware that further revision of the prayer book was likely, even inevitable, since liturgy is by its nature constantly evolving. After 1928, the Revision Commission was reconstituted as a Liturgical Commission:

> to which Commission may be referred, for preservation and study, all matters relating to the Book of Common Prayer, with the idea of developing and conserving for some possible future use, the liturgical experience and scholarship of the Church.[39]

The new commission provided an official mechanism by which proposed revisions could be examined and brought before the Church for approval or rejection, and was an acknowledgment by the Episcopal Church of the ongoing nature of liturgical change. However, the revolutionary changes in baptism and confirmation that would be incorporated into the next (1979) prayer book were not solely the work of this commission. To the contrary, as we shall see in the following chapters, numerous changes in the theology and practice of

Christian initiation were gradually accepted due to many factors both within and beyond the Episcopal Church.

NOTES

1. The survey that follows is of necessity brief and without annotation. Fuller discussion may be found in:

Gerard Austin, *Anointing with the Spirit: The Rite of Confirmation: The Use of Oil and Chrism* (New York: Pueblo, 1985), pp. 3-37;

Aidan Kavanagh, *The Shape of Baptism: The Rite of Christian Initiation* (New York: Pueblo, 1978), pp. 3-78;

Made, Not Born: New Perspectives on Christian Initiation and the Catechumenate (Notre Dame: University of Notre Dame Press, 1976);

Daniel B. Stevick, *Baptismal Moments; Baptismal Meanings* (New York: Church Hymnal Corporation, 1987), pp. 5-26;

Byron David Stuhlman, *Occasions of Grace* (New York: Church Hymnal Corporation, 1995), pp. 18-71.

2. Paul Turner, *Confirmation: The Baby in Solomon's Court* (New York: Paulist Press, 1993), pp. 86-7, 147-9. Although in some countries confirmation was administered before the age of reason and even in infancy, and confirmation could always be administered to infants and young children in danger of death, these were viewed as exceptions to the prevailing norm in the Roman Catholic Church.

3. BCP 1892, p. 244.

4. Paul V. Marshall, *Prayer Book Parallels: The Public Services of the Church Arranged for Comparative Study*, Anglican Liturgy in America, Vol. 1 (New York: Church Hymnal Corporation, 1989), p. 232.

5. BCP 1892, p. 244.

6. William C. DeWitt, *Decently and in Order: Pastoral Suggestions in Matters Official and Personal* (Milwaukee: The Young Churchman Co., 1914), pp. 105-6.

7. BCP 1892, p. 251.

8. DeWitt, pp. 114-15.

9. Charles P. A. Burnett, *A Ritual and Ceremonial Commentary on the Occasional Offices of Holy Baptism, Matrimony, Penance, Communion of the Sick, and Extreme Unction* (New York: Longmans, Green, and Co., 1907), p. 35 (emphasis added).

10. William Paret, *The Pastoral Use of the Prayer Book: The Substance of Plain Talks Given to His Students and Younger Clergy* (Baltimore: Maryland Diocesan Library, 1904), pp. 148-52.

11. DeWitt, p. 106.

12. Ibid., p. 312.

13. Ibid., p. 106.

14. Burnett, p. 48.

15. Paret, pp. 154-5.

16. BCP 1892, p. 257.

17. Paret, pp. 167-70.

18. Charles Lewis Slattery, *David Hammell Greer: Eighth Bishop of New York* (New York: Longmans, Green, and Co., 1921), p. 256.

19. Howard Chandler Robbins, *Charles Lewis Slattery* (New York and London: Harper & Brothers, 1931), p. 231.

20. Anson Rogers Graves, *The Farmer Boy Who Became a Bishop* (Akron, OH: The New Werner Company, 1911), p. 127.

21. Ibid., p. 138.

22. Arthur C. A. Hall, *Notes on the Use of the Prayer Book* (New York: E. & J. B. Young, 1896), p. 51.

23. DeWitt, pp. 304-5, n. 20.

24. Ibid., pp. 119-23.

25. Paret, p. 198.

26. DeWitt, pp. 119-20.

27. Paret, p. 188.

28. Lester Bradner, "The Educational Aspect of Confirmation," *Anglican Theological Review* 1 (1918): 135.

29. Ibid., p. 142.

30. Ibid., pp. 143-6.

31. Charles Lewis Slattery, "Essentials of Prayer Book Revision," in *The Church and Its American Opportunity: Papers by Various Writers Read at the Church Congress in 1919* (New York: Macmillan, 1919), p. 106.

32. Lucius Waterman, *Prayer Book Papers*, Series II, No. 2, The Protestant Episcopal Church, *The Duty of Parties toward Proposals for Prayer Book Revision* and *Proposed Supplanting of Our Baptismal Offices* (New York: The Prayer Book Papers Joint Committee, n.d.), pp. 16-26.

33. Charles Lewis Slattery, *The New Prayer Book: An Introduction* (New York: Edwin S. Gorham, n.d.), pp. 19-20.

34. Charles M. Addison, "The Baptismal Office: A Liturgical Blunder," *The Churchman*, Feb. 9, 1924, p. 16.

35. Slattery, *The New Prayer Book*, p. 19.

36. Ibid.

37. Ibid., p. 24.

38. BCP 1928, pp. 278, 296-7.

39. *Journal of the General Convention*, 1928, p. 352.

Chapter 2

The Emergence of
A Eucharistic Ecclesiology

The revolutionary changes in the Episcopal Church's initiatory theology and practice must be viewed within the larger framework of liturgical change during the middle decades of the twentieth century. In these years, a "liturgical movement" swept through not only the Episcopal Church but also other churches of the Anglican Communion, the Roman Catholic Church and several mainline Protestant churches. It was a time of enormous liturgical ferment, with extensive experimentation in virtually every aspect of the liturgy, including ritual action, congregational participation, hymnody, architecture, and the visual arts. New liturgical books appeared in many different worshiping traditions, and in several of these traditions there were successive revisions issued over the course of two or three decades.

The driving force of the liturgical movement was the belief of its leaders that the renewal of the liturgy would lead to the renewal of the Church. Drawing upon a Pauline theology of the Church as the mystical body of Christ, adherents of the liturgical movement called for active participation of all the faithful in worship and emphasized the relationship between liturgy and the life and mission of the Church. Celebration of the eucharist was central to this vision: gathered around the altar as a community of believers, the people of God are united to one another and to Christians of all times and places in a common action which forms and transforms them to be the body of Christ. As this *eucharistic ecclesiology* gradually took root in the Episcopal Church, Sunday worship in Episcopal churches began to change and the stage was set for the substantial revisions in the 1979 Book of Common Prayer.

Societal and Cultural Change during the Twentieth Century

The causes of this twentieth-century liturgical reform cannot be located entirely within the churches. Certainly developments in biblical and historical scholarship and the discovery of ancient texts unknown to earlier generations offered new insights into the evolution of liturgical forms and practices over the centuries. The increasing ecumenical cooperation of this century fostered exchange of the riches of diverse traditions and allowed the fruits of the liturgical movement to be shared across denominational lines. But churches exist in the wider framework of culture and society, and their worship is always situated in a particular historical context. German Martinez maintains that the interplay between "religious-theological ideas and socio-cultural phenomena" has been the basis for the evolution of worship throughout Christian history: "The style of worship and its understanding by people has been in fact structured at every stage by that complex system of interdependent theological and cultural ideas that permeate and are permeated by the predominant Christian vision of the day."[1] Thus to understand the widespread and substantial liturgical changes of the twentieth century, we must look beyond the churches to their historical and cultural context.

It is apparent to even a casual observer that the twentieth century has been a time of monumental change and global crises. Two world wars and an intervening economic depression were followed by the dawn of the nuclear age and the threat of global annihilation. Scientific and technological change has proceeded at an ever-increasing pace, as Arthur M. Schlesinger, Jr., points out:

> A boy who saw the Wright brothers fly for a few seconds at Kitty Hawk in 1903 could have watched Apollo 11 land on the moon in 1969. The first rockets were launched in the 1920s; today astronauts roam outer space. The first electronic computer was built in 1946; today the world rushes from the mechanical into the electronic age. The double helix was first unveiled in 1953; today, biotechnology threatens to remake mankind.[2]

The twentieth century has seen the rise of mass communication, the development of ever more rapid transportation, and the growth of an entertainment industry as movies, radio and television have come to the fore. All of these changes have affected the way we live and the way we perceive ourselves and our world. Our horizons have been expanded, and at the same time the world has "shrunk" as the nightly news brings worldwide events into our living rooms and modern transportation permits global travel with an ease never before known.

The United States has been affected by these changes and has experienced its own crises which have dramatically altered the shape of society. The demand for labor in the defense industry during World War II increased the participation of women in the work force and encouraged the migration of blacks from the rural South to urban industrial centers in the North, Midwest and West. The decade following World War II was a time of relative prosperity and expansion of cities and suburbs, although even this postwar period of recovery was disturbed by the emerging cold war and the Korean War; by the anti-Communism associated with Senator Joseph McCarthy; and by racial tensions, evident in the 1954 Supreme Court decision striking down separate but equal schools, the forced integration of schools in Little Rock, Arkansas, and the Montgomery, Alabama, bus boycott. Yet this upheaval was mild in comparison to the 1960s. One study catalogued the changes of this decade:

> the election of the first Roman Catholic as President of the United States and his tragic death in 1963; the continuation and escalation of the cold war, including both the Berlin Wall and the Bay of Pigs; rapid technological advances...; the full flowering of the civil rights movement—sit-ins, freedom rides, white citizens' councils, bombings, racial murders, the March on Washington, and the passage of the 1964 Civil Rights Act; the urban riots of the late 1960s and the assassinations of Martin Luther King, Jr., Malcolm X, and Robert Kennedy; antiwar protests over Viet Nam; the rise of student protests against both the military-industrial complex and the universities; the beginnings of the women's liberation movement; and, finally, the rise of the counterculture, including the search for alternative life styles, drug use, communes, and a variety of new religious movements.[3]

In short, the 1960s were a time of massive social and cultural disturbance.

Church life in the United States followed a pattern similar to the broader socio-cultural changes. The 1950s saw renewed vigor in church life, with rapid growth in church membership and a rise in the construction of new church buildings. The cataclysmic events of the 1960s were accompanied by widespread questioning of institutional church structures, essential theological principles and traditional understandings of morality. Church membership and attendance and the importance people attached to traditional religion declined markedly, but there was also increasing church involvement in social justice issues, including civil rights and antiwar protests. The massive upheaval of the 1960s yielded to disillusionment and despair in the early 1970s. Energetic social activism was replaced by concern for personal fulfillment. Participation in mainstream Protestant and Roman Catholic churches continued to decline, although George Gallup found that levels of religious belief continued to be extremely high. By the end of the 1970s the decline appeared to have halted and the 1980s were a time of relative stability.[4] But the relationship of Church and culture had undergone a fundamental change.

A 1968 sociological study of American religious commitment led its authors to draw this conclusion:

> the religious beliefs which have been the bedrocks of Christian faith for nearly two millennia are on their way out; this may very well be the dawn of a post-Christian era.... The new reformation in religious thought reflects the fact that a demythologized modernism is overwhelming the traditional, Christ-centered, mystical faith.[5]

The authors of this study pointed out that challenges to traditional Christian tenets had been discussed by theologians at least since the time of Kierkegaard, but in the 1960s this criticism of the tradition was being popularized by theologians, for example, Bishop J. A. T. Robinson in *Honest to God* and Harvey Cox in *The Secular City*.

The changing relationship between Church and culture during the 1960s was described not only as a shift to a post-Christian era but also as "secularization." In a secular world, the supernatural or transcendent was viewed with skepticism, and hence traditional beliefs and practices seemed irrelevant to the contemporary world where science and technology were accorded more and more importance. A secular world-view had been emerging since the Enlightenment or even since the Renaissance, but it came to full flower in the years after World War II. International competition and accelerating achievements in science and technology led to greater emphasis on education in these areas, and the federal government played an important role in providing financial resources for higher education. Mass communication permitted widespread dissemination of theological challenges to traditional Christian beliefs, including talk of the "death of God."[6]

Although secularization was a primary concern of theological discourse during the 1960s, Martin Marty observed that the very opposite of the secular was also present in the contemporary culture: a new religiosity, evident in the growing popularity of such phenomena as astrology, mysticism, the occult, yoga and Zen. Marty commented, "Their coexistence [i.e., secular and religious perspectives] points to the protean and evanescent aspects of a culture which is uncertain about authority and direction." In this culture, both the significance of tradition and the reality of the supernatural receded into the background, while immanence and the immediacy of the spiritual experience were stressed. What had become important was the "here and now."[7]

In this climate, where "relevance" was a primary value, liturgical experimentation flourished. Social and cultural upheaval was accompanied by a rejection of much of the tradition or at least radical questioning of its significance for contemporary people. Almost nothing was too extreme to be attempted in worship. Yet change was also resisted in some quarters, and many of the more extreme forms of liturgical experimentation did not endure.

In an assessment of the social and cultural dynamics that influence religious change, Robert Wuthnow posited a number of interrelated factors that play a role in facilitating the emergence of new ideas. Environmental factors include the size, access to material resources and social location of a potential audience for change; the availability of a medium by which new ideas can be communicated to this audience; and the symbolic or mental capacities with which the audience can process the new ideas. The institutional context for change refers to the availability of material and cultural resources and the particular organizational constraints as well as relationships between institutions. Wuthnow also identified what he called "action sequences," suggesting that ideas are produced in response to specific crises or triggering events and that particular persons or groups work to bring about specific changes.[8] He did not address in depth the question of liturgical change, but his identification of sets of variables offers some guidance in exploring factors influencing contemporary liturgical experimentation and revision.

A primary audience for liturgical innovation was found on college campuses during the 1960s, a decade of enormous expansion in higher education. This widespread liturgical experimentation may reflect not only the liberalization associated with education, but also the availability of an audience open to new forms of worship. Campuses provided a location where significant numbers of students were gathered and thus offered a critical mass of people able to consider new liturgical ideas. Furthermore, according to one study, the college students of the 1960s, born in the years following World War II, were far more open to innovation than students of the previous decade. In contrast to students of the 1950s, who tended to conform to the norms and expectations of others and maintain a high commitment to family life and a low interest in political activity, students during the 1960s emphasized individual freedom and autonomy rather than conformity to social norms, experimentation with new forms of marriage and family life-styles, and political activism to bring about social change.[9]

A different survey of religious belief during the 1960s found a substantial difference between those over fifty and those under fifty, with the older generation more likely to hold traditional beliefs and also more likely to attend church each week and to contribute financially to the church. These attitudinal differences were attributed to the cultural shift marked by World War II:

"World War II seems to mark a watershed between the older America of small town and rural living (or stable urban neighborhood), and the contemporary America of highly mobile, urban life and the development of a mass culture."[10]

While this latter survey, published in 1968, acknowledged some liturgical experimentation, its authors argued that significant institutional change had not occurred. This lack of change they attributed to institutional inertia and more specifically to the fact that supporters of a more traditional theological perspective remained in most congregations and were more active than more liberal laity. Clergy tended to be liberal, but they met resistance to change within their congregations. Robert Wuthnow has noted a similar gap between, on the one hand, less educated and more conservative laity, and, on the other hand, clergy and more educated laity who supported liberal social causes.[11]

These studies do not provide empirical evidence of attitudes towards liturgical change. However, if we accept the premise that theologically liberal laity and clergy were more open to new religious ideas, then it is plausible that liturgical experimentation was accepted primarily by younger and more highly educated laity and by many clergy. It is likely that clergy provided much of the leadership for innovations which were introduced, and that the audience most receptive to these new ideas was found on college and university campuses and among other laity with at least some college education.

In addition to the environmental factors that create an audience receptive to change, Wuthnow identified the institutional context for change and "action sequences" as factors that facilitate the emergence of new religious ideas. The institutional context is particularly significant in the process of official liturgical revision and so will be taken up in Chapter 6. Action sequences, that is, persons or groups working to bring about change, are evident in the people and processes of the liturgical movement, and it is to this movement that we now turn.

Origins of the Liturgical Movement

The first stirrings of the liturgical movement may be found in the 1830s. As in the twentieth century, the nineteenth-century liturgical revival was prompted by societal and cultural factors, including romanticism, reaction to the rationalism of the eighteenth-century Enlightenment, and the industrial revolution. Leaders in the Roman Catholic and several Protestant churches in Europe and the United States sought the recovery of the Church's authentic liturgical tradition as they understood it. In their eyes, the Middle Ages represented the ideal, a time when Church and society were integrated as a cohesive whole. By restoring medieval patterns, the Church might best respond to the needs presented by an emerging industrial society.[12]

In Anglican churches, including the Church of England and the Episcopal Church, changes in ritual practice were largely an outgrowth of the Oxford Movement, which emphasized the sacraments as an important means of grace. While the Oxford Movement was initially concerned more with doctrine than liturgical practice, this early emphasis gradually gave way to a ritualism that idealized medieval Gothic architecture and ornamentation. For models of this liturgical practice, Anglican clergy turned to medieval and nineteenth-century Roman Catholic ceremonial. As a result, Episcopal churches began to adopt such practices as the use of altar crosses and candles, processions with processional crosses and torches, the use of colored stoles, and vested choirs and acolytes, ornamentation and ceremonial which are widely accepted in the Episcopal Church of the late twentieth century but which aroused enormous controversy when they were introduced in the nineteenth century. While this was typically accompanied by an individualistic piety, the ritualist controversy served to break the rigid uniformity which had characterized Anglican worship for two centuries and alter what one twentieth-century observer described as the "arid, overly intellectualized and formalized use of the Prayer Book."[13]

The ritualists also succeeded in encouraging more frequent celebration of communion, leading to the nearly universal practice in the Episcopal Church of an early celebration of communion every Sunday morning. This was accomplished through an appeal to personal devotion rather than on the basis of a corporate understanding of the eucharist. The principal Sunday service in these Anglo-Catholic services was customarily solemn high mass with few members of the congregation receiving communion. The eucharist remained at the periphery of congregational life, significant as an act of individual devotion but not as a celebration by the body of Christ. The assessment of Louis Bouyer, a twentieth-century Roman Catholic liturgical scholar, is telling:

> what the Anglo-Catholics of a hundred years ago were able to borrow from the Catholics of the time were precisely those features which now appear to Catholics to be among the weakest points in their recent liturgical practice. For example, a preference for low Mass (as private as possible) rather than a public celebration; the high Mass itself carried out so as to do without Communion or any participation at all by the faithful; and, above all, an enthusiasm for Benediction of the Blessed Sacrament which tended to make it, rather than the Mass itself, the focus of congregational worship.[14]

As Bouyer's comments suggest, a new phase of the liturgical movement began in the Roman Catholic Church during the twentieth century. It focused on three primary concerns: a theology of the Church as the mystical body of Christ; the importance of the active participation of all the faithful in worship; and the vital relationship between liturgy and social justice. These teachings were spread by informal contacts among liturgical leaders; during Liturgical Weeks and other such gatherings, first for clergy and later for laity as well; and by publications both scholarly and popular, including new periodicals. Several Benedictine monasteries were centers of liturgical renewal, including the Abbey of Maria Laach in Germany and St. John's Abbey in Collegeville, Minnesota.

The teachings of the Roman Catholic liturgical leaders inspired the Anglican Arthur Gabriel Hebert, a member of the Society of the Sacred Mission whose work is widely recognized as a significant influence in popularizing the liturgical movement in the Church of England. Hebert's 1935 book *Liturgy and Society* articulated a theological rationale for liturgical renewal.[15] It was followed two years later by *The Parish Communion*, a collection of essays edited by Hebert and intended to provide practical guidance in the implementation of the parish communion, defined as "the celebration of the Holy Eucharist, with the communion of the people, in a parish church, as the chief service of the day, or better, as the assembly of the Christian community for the worship of God."[16]

Both the Roman Catholic liturgical movement in Europe and the liturgical renewal in the Church of England had some influence on liturgical renewal in the Episcopal Church. However, the liturgical movement in the Episcopal Church developed its own shape with its own leadership.

William Palmer Ladd

The first prominent leader of the modern liturgical movement in the Episcopal Church was William Palmer Ladd, dean of Berkeley Divinity School in New Haven, Connecticut, from 1918 until his death in 1941. In 1937 Ladd began a biweekly column, "Prayer Book Interleaves," in *The Witness*, at that time a weekly Episcopal Church periodical. His columns provided historical, theological, and practical insights on a broad range of topics related to liturgy. Ladd intended to write an extensive series of columns, but for reasons of health ceased writing after three years. His columns were published posthumously as a collection under the same title.[17]

Ladd was familiar with the liturgical movement in both the Roman Catholic Church and the Church of England. While he looked favorably on the primary goals of those movements, Ladd had a far more negative appraisal of the Oxford Movement, whose legacy he described as "an evil heritage."[18] In Ladd's opinion, Anglo-Catholics had abandoned Anglican tradition and distorted Anglican eucharistic theology and practice:

> They made eucharistic worship individual rather than corporate. They brought back to ghastly life all the medieval and Reformation metaphysical wrangles over the manner of the presence. They took as their standard first the Sarum use, then the degenerate, legalistic ritual and ceremonial of the Church of Rome, and tried to force the Prayer Book into that procrustean bed.[19]

Ladd was concerned that the "liturgical movement should take the right direction in this country at the present time." He sought the adaptation of "our inherited forms of worship to the modern situation," in order that the Church might "meet the needs of a generation it has done so much to mislead and to alienate."[20] In the face of "commercialism and humanism in America, fascism, communism, nationalism, and totalitarianism in Europe," Ladd desired the restoration of unity in God and in Christ, celebrated in Word and Sacrament.[21]

For Ladd, the renewal of the eucharist was of primary importance, the ideal being that "every parish should unite around the Lord's table on every Lord's day."[22] To achieve this ideal, Ladd urged that parishes adopt a monthly parish communion service, building upon the eighteenth-century practice of a late communion service on the first Sunday of the month. More was intended than simply holding a communion service. The parish communion would be "in the fullest measure congregational," with hymns and service music selected to encourage congregational singing.[23] To counter the "wretched medieval idea" that the eucharist is the "monopoly of the priest," wardens and vestrymen (few if any women served on vestries at the time) should assist by reading lessons, presenting the oblations and perhaps also administering the chalice.[24] The celebration might include "important announcements and interesting parish news" as well as special prayers and thanksgivings for both parochial and community concerns. "The newly-confirmed should make their first communion at this service, and it is the proper time for adult baptisms." The sacrament could be brought to those kept away by illness.[25] The bread used should be not individual wafers but rather "always in one piece (the 'one loaf' of St. Paul)."[26] These practical suggestions were intended to emphasize "the corporate character of eucharistic worship" and so to deepen understanding and appreciation of the eucharist.[27]

Ladd believed that the renewal of the eucharist had social and political implications:

> No eucharistically minded Christian can possibly say his whole duty is to save his soul and other people's souls. He must be concerned about the body, about hunger and poverty, about unsanitary tenements, ugly cities, and every social injustice.[28]

This concern for human welfare was integrally linked with eucharistic offering. The bread and wine offered at the altar represented both God's creation and the products of human labor. Furthermore, self-offering and sacrifice were part of the eucharistic action, although, according to Ladd, Episcopalians had not yet grasped the connections between this self-offering and Christian life in social service and mission.[29]

The concerns of contemporary life were also important subjects for the intercessory prayers of the eucharist. The prayer "for the whole state of Christ's Church" was antiquated and failed to address contemporary needs.[30] Times had changed, and intercessions ought to pray for the needs of the parish and the community, to recognize contemporary evils such as unemployment, to be concerned with missions and social justice, parish and family life, Christian education, international relations. These matters of current concern could be included as the rubrics allowed, that is, in addition to the fixed prayer for the Church.[31]

Ladd influenced the Episcopal Church not only through his writing but also through his leadership of Berkeley Divinity School. For Ladd, theological education began at the altar. Visitors to the school were expected to attend morning chapel services so they might become part of the community.[32] Furthermore, at the "very heart of the theological curriculum" was "liturgiology," an essential subject of study for parsons and seminarians alike. The neglect of this all-important subject accounted for low standards of Anglican worship as well as low attendance at Sunday worship.[33]

Study of liturgiology would also be of benefit in efforts toward Christian unity. "If we do not know our own mind, how shall we guide our Presbyterian, Methodist, and Roman Catholic brethren?"[34] One step in this education was the formation of a "Liturgical League," organized in the mid-1930s "to promote the study of the various Christian liturgies and to stimulate a love of worship." Growing out of conferences designed by students at Berkeley to popularize the eucharist among young people, the Liturgical League attracted young people from all denominations for study and prayer to further Christian understanding and seek Christian unity. Study outlines used at these conferences were included in *Prayer Book Interleaves*.[35]

Prayer Book Interleaves is Ladd's legacy to the Episcopal Church. In this little book, reissued in 1957 to introduce a younger generation to his ideas, Ladd showed himself to be grounded in the best of contemporary scholarship yet also possessing a keen pastoral sense. Evident on every page is his passion for liturgy as a living entity and his fervent concern that liturgy be constantly adapted so that it might be relevant to the issues of human society. His work was an important catalyst in the twentieth-century shift toward a eucharistic ecclesiology.

Other Liturgical Pioneers

While Ladd is widely regarded as the forebear of the liturgical movement in the Episcopal Church, other liturgical leaders contemporaneous with Ladd played a role in educating Episcopalians about liturgy and its renewal. These first pioneers were followed by succeeding generations of scholars and pastoral leaders who helped spread the vision of the liturgical movement and so gradually change the understanding and practice of worship in the Episcopal Church.

One means of education and enrichment was music. *The Hymnal 1940* was adopted by the Episcopal Church as a companion to the 1928 prayer book. A primary intent of this hymnal was to provide both hymns and service music that would be suitable for congregational singing. It included texts both ancient and modern, with music representing England and continental Europe as well as American and Canadian composers.

A primary architect of *The Hymnal 1940* was Winfred Douglas, who "almost single-handedly reshaped the practice and taste of the Church in liturgical music."[36] Douglas' 1937 book *Church Music in History and Practice* was intended to introduce clergy, seminarians and organists to the underlying principles of music and its relation to liturgy. For Douglas, these principles could be seen most clearly in the Gregorian chant of the seventh century. From this repertoire, Douglas identified standards that applied to contemporary church music: music was sung to the praise and glory of God; music, "the voice of the whole Church," was an integral part of each service, not merely a decorative addition; every member of the body joined in the active praise of the whole body; music was subordinate to liturgical text, and so no changes might be made solely for musical reasons.[37]

Douglas believed that church music at its best expressed the organic life of the body of Christ. While some music was appropriately sung by the choir, at the heart of the eucharist was a dialogue between celebrant and congregation, a dialogue which included the *sursum corda* and Lord's Prayer as well as lesser dialogues involved in the prayers and reading of scripture. Thus the congregation was essential to the celebration of eucharist.[38] Douglas urged that "each member of the mystical body of Christ...actively participate...with heart and mind and voice."[39]

In the same year that Douglas' text on church music appeared, Edward Lambe Parsons and Bayard Hale Jones published *The American Prayer Book*, which was widely used and became a standard seminary text for a generation. Parsons, Bishop of California from 1924 to 1940, had been one of the principal architects of the 1928 prayer book. Jones, whose interest in liturgical studies was complemented by his facility in ancient and modern languages, taught liturgics at the Church Divinity School of the Pacific and later at St. Luke's School of Theology in Sewanee, Tennessee.

In the preface, Parsons explained that the revision of 1928 had been influenced by a new understanding of ancient sources while at the same time introducing thoroughly modern elements. No book then available satisfactorily addressed these dimensions in a way that was widely accessible. This new book thus sought to place the 1928 prayer book in light of the most recent liturgical scholarship. The authors hoped not only to treat their subject objectively, in a manner acceptable to a broad spectrum of the Episcopal Church, but also to contribute to the goal of Christian unity, which should be anchored in worship.[40]

The American Prayer Book dealt in a straightforward manner with the literary history of The Book of Common Prayer and then with the sources and rationale of each of the prayer book offices in turn. While Parsons and Jones had access to the most recent liturgical studies, they lamented that much work remained to be done in the field of comparative liturgics:

> Hitherto, the study has fallen in the lines of the ancient conflict between Eastern and Western standards of doctrine, discipline, and worship. What has been needed is a complete account of the origin and evolution of Christian worship, in order to find its essential meaning in its ultimate sources, and to make it possible to assay the value of competing forms symbolizing historic "positions" by assigning them a place in a comprehensive scheme of historic evolution which shall account for them.[41]

This need identified by Parsons and Jones was largely met by the 1945 publication of *The Shape of the Liturgy* by Gregory Dix, an Anglican monk from Nashdom Abbey in England.[42] One scholar made this assessment soon after the book appeared:

It would be difficult to exaggerate the excellence and usefulness of his study. It brings together in a comprehensive as well as analytical treatment the results of modern critical scholarship in the history of Christian worship from the Last Supper through the Reformation. It clarifies the problems which need further investigation and interpretation.[43]

Although scholars have challenged the authenticity of some of Dix's sources as well as aspects of his reconstruction and interpretation of his sources, *The Shape of the Liturgy* proved to be of enormous influence, not only in the Anglican Communion but across denominations. Perhaps its most enduring legacy is Dix's identification of a fourfold "shape" of the liturgy, that is, that the eucharist over the ages has consisted of taking bread and wine, blessing the bread and wine, breaking the bread, and sharing the bread and wine. Dix helped contemporary Christians understand that the eucharist is fundamentally an action done by a community, not a rite said by a priest while the people listened or watched.[44]

In addition to his writing, Dix's influence was felt in his speaking tours of the United States in 1947 and 1950 to 1951. These tours included not only lectures but also "reenactments" of the eucharist as it might have been celebrated according to ancient rites. Dix thus helped popularize the insights of his study.[45]

The development of liturgical scholarship continued to be an important dimension of the liturgical movement. "Original and creative American [Episcopalian] scholars such as B. S. Easton, Frank Gavin, Felix L. Cirlot, R. K. Yerkes, and Edward R. Hardy investigated ancient and Eastern sources."[46] While not active in the liturgical movement, these scholars were important in the development of the discipline of historical liturgical study.

But in this ecumenical century, scholarship was not narrowly partisan, and its influence stretched across denominational lines:

Protestants listen today [1958] to what Roman Catholic interpreters, such as Romano Guardini, Joseph Jungmann, and Louis Bouyer, have to say about the liturgy, not merely because these men are prepared to admit that all is not well with the liturgical life of the great Latin Church, but chiefly because they speak to the central themes of our common Christian faith. On the other side, Roman Catholics respect the liturgical opinions of such scholars as the Lutheran Hans Lietzmann, the Anglican Gregory Dix, or the Reformed Oscar Cullmann, because these men seek to be honest with history, without special favor to their own ecclesiastical commitment, and because they build their liturgical reconstructions not narrowly, on the slender materials of the New Testament alone, but on the broader foundations of the whole patristic age of the great Fathers of the Universal Church.[47]

Guardini, one of the early thinkers of the liturgical movement, wrote *The Spirit of the Liturgy* and *Liturgical Education* while a student. Both books offered a vision of the liturgy which profoundly affected the liturgical movement in the United States. Jungmann's monumental study *The Mass of the Roman Rite*, first published in English in 1951,[48] was a detailed scholarly study of the development of the Roman mass and its component parts. More accessible was Jungmann's *The Early Liturgy to the Time of Gregory the Great*, published in 1959,[49] which offered a picture of patristic liturgy, focusing on the eucharist and initiatory rites. Bouyer's *Liturgical Piety*[50] made available to an English-speaking audience the work of Odo Casel, a monk of Maria Laach. Casel is responsible for mystery-theology, the teaching that liturgy is rooted in the paschal mystery of Jesus' passion, death and resurrection. Casel's teaching proved to be a major influence on contemporary sacramental theology, and Bouyer, building upon Casel's insights, explored the embodiment of the Christian mystery in the liturgies of the Church. In *Mass and Lord's Supper*, Lietzmann argued that the eucharist could be traced to two distinct types of liturgy in the early Church.[51] Cullmann, a New Testament scholar, contributed several studies of worship in the New Testament and the early Church.[52]

While these and many other scholars contributed to liturgical renewal through their careful historical study and their theological acumen, in the Episcopal Church seminary faculty played a vital role in encouraging the spread of the liturgical movement. Foremost in this regard was Massey Hamilton Shepherd, Jr., who taught early and medieval church history at Episcopal Theological School in Cambridge, Massachusetts, from 1940 until 1951 and then accepted a chair in liturgics at Church Divinity School of the Pacific in Berkeley, California, where he taught until his retirement in the 1980s.[53]

Shepherd had visited Berkeley Divinity School in 1938 and then spent six months studying and lecturing at the school in 1941, shortly before William Palmer Ladd's death. As both mentor and friend to Shepherd, Ladd was a significant influence on Shepherd. Shepherd followed Ladd in writing a column, "The Living Liturgy," which appeared in *The Witness* from 1944 through 1948 and from which selections were published in a book of the same title.[54] He continued to write numerous articles on liturgy in *The Witness* and other popular periodicals throughout the 1950s and 1960s. A central figure in the process of liturgical renewal leading to the 1979 prayer book, Shepherd influenced the Episcopal Church through his writing, his teaching and his membership on the Standing Liturgical Commission, as well as his many ecumenical contacts. Shepherd's commentary on the 1928 prayer book[55] became a valuable resource that helped an entire generation of church leaders understand the background and content of the rites in that prayer book as well as the limitations of the book.

Another significant leader was H. Boone Porter, who taught liturgics at Nashotah House in Wisconsin and then at General Theological Seminary in New York City. His book *The Day of Light*[56] helped underscore the relation between Sunday and forms of Christian worship, especially the eucharist. But he was also influential in the supervision of doctoral studies for a new generation of liturgical scholars, including Marion Hatchett, who later taught at the School of Theology in Sewanee, Tennessee; Thomas Talley, who went to Nashotah House and then succeeded Porter at General; and Leonel Mitchell, who taught at the University of Notre Dame and then joined the faculty of Seabury-Western Theological Seminary in Evanston, Illinois. The work of these scholars was complemented by others, including Charles Price at Virginia Seminary; Louis Weil, who succeeded Talley at Nashotah House and many years later followed Shepherd at CDSP; and Daniel Stevick at Philadelphia Divinity School and then, after its merger with Episcopal Theological School, part of the faculty at Episcopal Divinity School in Cambridge, Massachusetts.

This later generation of scholars, now retired or nearing retirement, began their teaching at a time when the liturgical movement was in full flower. As the emphasis of the liturgical movement shifted from the implementation of the 1928 prayer book to a radical revision of that book, these scholars played important roles in interpreting to the Church the rites that were evolving. Before that revision got underway, however, the teachings of the liturgical movement gradually took root and were spread throughout the Episcopal Church.

Associated Parishes

During the 1940s the liturgical movement grew slowly. Articles on the subject of liturgy appeared in popular periodicals, especially *The Witness*, and a few conferences were reported. The English Anglican A. G. Hebert spent the fall term of 1948-49 as a visiting lecturer at Berkeley Divinity School and had a number of speaking and preaching engagements around the country. In 1949 the four-hundredth anniversary of the first English Book of Common Prayer was celebrated with the publication of books about the prayer book, articles in various periodicals, and a commemoration at the 1949 General Convention.[57] The widespread recognition of this anniversary suggests growing popular interest in liturgy and the BCP.

Liturgical reform was encouraged by the Anglican Society, founded in the United States in 1934. The goals of the Society were to promote and preserve the Catholic faith in strict accordance with BCP principles and to uphold "English" liturgical ceremonial, that is, the Sarum usage popularized in England during the early twentieth century by Percy Dearmer in *The Parson's Handbook.* Although the Society remained small, its early meetings were reported in Episcopal Church periodicals, and in 1944 the Society began publication of its own quarterly journal, *The Anglican.* The latter became a forum for articles relating to liturgical renewal.

Far more influence came to be wielded by a different organization, Associated Parishes (later called The Associated Parishes for Liturgy and Mission). The group was founded by twelve clergy, including Massey Shepherd, who gathered in November 1946 at the College of Preachers in Washington, D.C., "to share their 'despair over Sunday morning' and to see if something could be done to educate the church for better liturgy."[58] Its members wanted to bring the insights of the liturgical movement to parishes in the Episcopal Church. To begin this task, they would work in their own parishes to implement the goals of the liturgical movement, namely that parish life would be centered in the celebration of the eucharist and that this life would be integrally linked with mission beyond the Church. This was to be accomplished within the bounds of the existing liturgy of the Episcopal Church; members of Associated Parishes committed themselves to the use of authorized liturgical materials, that is, the 1928 Book of Common Prayer, *The Hymnal 1940* and materials authorized by the Ordinary (i.e., the diocesan bishop). At their semiannual meetings, members of Associated Parishes shared their hopes and frustrations and debated how best to advance the liturgical movement in the Episcopal Church.[59]

As the organization developed, Associated Parishes eventually became more widely known. In 1950 its first publication appeared: a pamphlet entitled *What I Promise as a Sponsor in Baptism.* As the title suggests, it was an instruction for sponsors, describing their duties "in light of the theology of baptism and confirmation and the facts of spiritual growth."[60] This was followed by several pamphlets which set forth the theology and practice of the services of the 1928 prayer book, including eucharist, baptism and confirmation.[61]

In the pamphlet on the eucharist the vision of the liturgical movement is evident. Throughout the pamphlet, the centrality of the eucharist, the active participation of the entire community in the celebration of eucharist, and the vital connection between liturgy and life were stressed. The introduction asserted, "Every part of our parish life must be related to this fellowship at the Altar where we are all members one of another."[62] The "Choral Parish Eucharist with Sermon" was described as "the principal act of worship of the Church every week."[63] The link between liturgy and life was found in the offertory and in the sharing of communion. The commentary noted that "today, in many parishes, representatives of the congregation bring these offerings reverently in procession to the celebrant"; in the presentation of the bread and wine "every thought and word and deed, every aspiration and accomplishment, all that goes to make up the whole of ourselves is presented to God in sacrifice."[64] The commentary on "the Communion" concluded with an exhortation to the communicants who had been united with God and one another: "Into every area of human activity, political, economic, social and cultural, we must extend the Holy Fellowship of the Altar."[65]

While the goals of the liturgical movement were evident, so too was the commitment of Associated Parishes to the 1928 prayer book. The structure of the 1928 rite was closely followed. Although asserting that "the Church's worship is centered in the Bible and the Eucharist,"[66] the pamphlet included the proclamation of the Word under the heading "The Preparation" (the portion of the rite elsewhere entitled "Ante-Communion"). Shepherd had stressed (in his commentary on the 1928 prayer book) that the two parts of the service, Ante-Communion and Communion, "are coordinate and complementary expressions of the Christian Faith, in Word and Sacrament,"[67] but the Associated Parishes pamphlet does not give the same emphasis to the ministry of the Word. Rather, the "Eucharist proper" was subdivided into three sections, Offertory, Consecration and Communion, rather than Dix's fourfold take, bless, break and give. The Offertory corresponded approximately to "take" but included, in addition to the offering of alms, bread and wine, the offering of prayer (the Prayer for the Whole State of Christ's Church) and penitence (Confession and Absolution), which in the 1928 prayer book followed the collection of alms and preparation of the table. It is likely that the Dixian "blessing" of bread and wine was entitled "The Consecration" because the 1928 prayer book used the title "Prayer of Consecration."[68] The breaking of bread did not appear as a distinct action; the 1928 rubrics directed that the bread be broken during the recitation of the words of institution in the Prayer of Consecration and not as a separate action just prior to communion. Nevertheless, the commentary stated, "the bread is broken either during the Consecration or after the Prayer of Humble Access."[69] The limitations of the 1928 prayer book were evident even as Associated Parishes interpreted that eucharistic rite as consistently as possible with the ideals of the liturgical movement.

A review of Associated Parishes records indicates that this pamphlet on the eucharist was widely distributed. After exhausting a first printing of 10,000, a second printing sold 17,300 copies. Associated Parishes also granted several requests for use of the brochure by overseas clergy.[70] Doubtless the pamphlet helped teach many Episcopalians about the vision of the liturgical movement. Those who read the pamphlet, and many others in parishes influenced by its teaching, would be encouraged to see themselves as active participants in the liturgy, offering themselves as a sacrifice to God and joined to one another in a community called to ministry in the Church and in the world.

In addition to its publications, several conferences were sponsored or cosponsored by Associated Parishes, beginning in 1958 with a conference at Grace Church in Madison, Wisconsin. This first conference, attended by about 130 people, focused on the objectives of the liturgical movement and its implications for clergy and laity. The proceedings of the conference were later published in a volume edited by Massey Shepherd.[71] The next year a second conference was held, this one in San Antonio, Texas, with over 700 people in attendance, two-thirds of whom were lay, representing 35 dioceses in 24 states and Mexico. The theme of this conference was the eucharist and liturgical renewal, and the addresses were once again published.[72] Three years later a conference in Wichita, Kansas, drew over 950 persons from 46 states. This conference sought to relate the liturgical movement to the mission of the church.[73] After these national conferences, Associated Parishes directed its efforts toward regional conferences, and several were held around the country from 1965 until 1970.[74]

Through its conferences and publications, Associated Parishes was instrumental in bringing the vision of the liturgical movement to the parishes and people of the Episcopal Church. Their emphasis on the eucharist as the corporate action of the people of God, an action integrally linked to every aspect of life, was an important factor in the emergence of a eucharistic ecclesiology.

Initiatives in Religious Education

Changes in the understanding and practice of worship resulted not only from the spread of the liturgical movement but also through the religious education movement which flourished in the years following World War II. In response to concerns about the lack of a national curriculum and a large drop in church school attendance between 1933 and 1943, a reorganized Department of Christian Education began in 1947 to develop a national program of Christian education for all ages. A 1952 statement explained the purpose of the new program:

> to provide ways in which children, youth, and adults can respond to the Gospel through progressive, conscious, and meaningful participation in the Drama of Human Redemption as comprehended in the Book of Common Prayer.

The program emphasized relationship as experienced in "the redemptive fellowship." The BCP was not simply a book for worship but a focal point for Christian life:

> [T]he Prayer Book way of life provides us with the axis around which our life revolves. Specifically this means that the living Gospel is our primary value, and man's great need for the faith experience of living in relationship to this Gospel is our principal concern. The natural relationships of life, particularly within the blood family and the fellowship of the parish church, are the channels in which a response to the Gospel may be found.
>
> Without minimizing the importance of man's personal relationship to God, the Department accepts as basic the relationship which man must have to his Redeemer through the fellowship of the Church. The Church has the unique and specific task of responding to the action of God the Holy Ghost as He strengthens us through the fellowship of God's people.

To accomplish these goals, the Department of Christian Education decided that their curriculum would emphasize the total educational process rather than more traditional didactic materials.[75]

The goals were communicated through leadership training programs held for laity and clergy around the country. Beginning in 1954, training was also done through Parish Life Conferences, weekend retreats for leaders gathered from different parishes of a diocese. In 1953 the Department of Christian Education began publication of *Christian Education Findings*. This periodical reported on leadership training events and parish life conferences sponsored by the Department and addressed other matters pertinent to religious education.[76]

An important figure was Reuel Howe, a member of the faculty at Virginia Theological Seminary, who gave numerous lectures as part of the leadership training programs. Howe eventually published the substance of his talks in a book entitled *Man's Need and God's Action*.[77] The book went through many printings and was widely discussed in the Episcopal Church. Howe emphasized the importance of reconciliation and of the ministry of the Church as a reconciling community. Christians are brought into the redemptive fellowship of the Church through baptism and renewed in that fellowship through com-

munion: "in Holy Communion we may participate in the reunion of the separated and the reconciliation of the alienated." Such reconciliation through
participation in communion had implications for Christian living; Christian
witness and service were to be directed not back to the Church but from the
Church to the community. "The test is not in what I do for my church but what
I do as a member of the Church in the political, social, economic, educational,
recreational life of the world."[78] Howe's approach was thus consistent with the
liturgical movement's emphasis on the connection between liturgy and
mission.

Publication of the new curriculum, *The Seabury Series*, began in 1955.
Parishes were expected to meet four conditions before introducing the
curriculum:

1) An ever-widening group of individuals with the congregation "genuinely
   concerned about the redemptive task of the parish"...

2) An emphasis on family worship...

3) A weekly class for parents and godparents...

4) Religious and educational preparation of teachers.

Although the series was controversial and used in only one-third of the parishes around the country,[79] the family service began to take root. Articles in
national church periodicals provided practical suggestions for how best to
organize these services.

The idea of the family service was for the entire family to worship together
on Sunday morning as an integral component of parish education. The goals of
the liturgical movement were evident to some extent. An article assessing the
effect of *The Seabury Series* noted:

> Many parishes have accepted the family service, "the parish Communion," as
> the heart of parish life.
>
> Many churchpeople have attended parish life conferences and come
> home resolved to play their proper role in the life of the redeemed commu-
> nity.[80]

However, the primary intent of family services was not to restore weekly parish communions but to emphasize the centrality of worship in parish life,
whether the Sunday service was Morning Prayer or Holy Communion. Additionally, there was debate as to whether BCP rites should be abbreviated to
accommodate the presence of children.

Thus the religious education movement helped to further the liturgical
movement insofar as it emphasized the centrality of worship in the life of a

congregation. However, it remained for the liturgical movement to bring about the restoration of the eucharist as the central act of Christian worship.

A Eucharistic Ecclesiology

The religious education movement and the liturgical movement gradually introduced new liturgical practices and helped shape a new approach to liturgy in the Episcopal Church. The large attendance at the Associated Parishes conferences is indicative of growing interest in the liturgical movement during the 1950s. Other conferences, national and diocesan, also addressed the goals of the liturgical movement. *Parish Worship on Community Occasions*, a 1950 pamphlet sponsored by the National Council of the Episcopal Church, presented the ideals of the liturgical movement along with practical suggestions for parish worship. These were accompanied by liturgical experimentation of various kinds, including services which claimed to imitate Christian practice from the earliest centuries of the Church, celebration of the eucharist with the priest facing the people, the congregation standing during the prayers and the *sursum corda*, the use of baked bread rather than wafers, and the introduction of jazz and other contemporary musical settings for the eucharist. Articles appeared regularly in popular periodicals, explaining the purposes of the liturgical movement and its significance in parish life.

During the 1950s and 1960s, more and more parishes introduced a number of practices that would emphasize the active participation of the people. The offertory procession was given particular significance. People were taught that their money, bread and wine were tokens of their whole selves, symbols of their stewardship over God's gifts of creation, and representative of the entire economic and social order in which they lived. Congregations were encouraged to join in saying the Prayer of Humble Access and the postcommunion prayer, a practice which Ladd had described as "a novel idea but perhaps a good one in that it makes the service more congregational."[81]

Lay liturgical leadership was gradually permitted. Since 1871 the canons of the Episcopal Church had provided for licensed lay readers to lead worship, i.e., Morning Prayer, in congregations where the services of an ordained minister were not available, but it was only in 1952 that the canons were amended to permit a licensed lay reader to read the Epistle at Holy Communion. There is some evidence that during the 1960s lay persons also began to lead the prayer for the Church, although this was never specifically authorized by the canons. Some latitude was introduced with a 1961 canon which permitted lay persons not licensed as lay readers to assist a presbyter on special occasions in the conduct of public worship. Attempts to allow lay readers to administer the chalice were introduced and defeated at nearly every General Convention beginning in 1931 until an amendment to the canons was finally adopted in 1967. Women, who had been explicitly excluded from the office of lay reader in 1904, were in 1961 allowed to be licensed as lay readers in situations where no ordained clergyman or male lay reader was available, and then an amendment adopted by the Special Convention of 1969 permitted women to be licensed as lay readers on the same basis as men.[82] These canonical changes reflect a growing understanding that the eucharist is not a solo performance by a priest on behalf of a largely passive laity but rather an action involving the whole congregation. The provision for lay administration of the chalice doubtless is also a response to need created by an increasing frequency of celebration of the eucharist and growing numbers of communicants regularly receiving communion.

Architectural changes also pointed to a new understanding of the eucharist as a celebration of the community. The Associated Parishes pamphlet on the eucharist includes a full-page sketch of a priest elevating a chalice and host while facing an altar over which a large Christus Rex shines brightly; surrounding the priest are people kneeling, many with their faces shielded from the bright manifestation. This sketch is evocative of the neo-Gothic architectural style that became popular during the nineteenth century: with the altar against the wall, the attention of the people is drawn through the priest to the transcendent beyond. But in this same pamphlet another full-page sketch shows a priest, arm uplifted in a gesture of blessing, standing behind a freestanding altar, facing a congregation and looking out into the world beyond. Two other smaller sketches show a priest behind a freestanding altar, facing a congregation for the celebration of communion; the third sketch on this page suggests Jesus with his disciples gathered around a table at the Last Supper.[83] Clearly Associated Parishes was introducing a different manner of celebrating eucharist, albeit subtly, without direct comment. That this shift was no small matter is evident in a pamphlet published by Seabury Press to explain to priests in detail, complete with diagrams and pictures, how to celebrate the eucharist while facing the people.[84]

During the late 1950s, the question of whether Morning Prayer or Holy Communion should be the central act of Sunday worship began to be actively debated. More frequent communion had been urged by the sixteenth-century reformers, some eighteenth-century evangelicals, including John and Charles Wesley, and the nineteenth-century Oxford Movement, but none of these movements had succeeded in establishing a weekly communion as the principal Sunday service in a majority of parishes in the Episcopal Church. The writings of William Palmer Ladd, Massey Shepherd and Associated Parishes all stressed that the eucharist was the principal act of the Church's worship every Sunday. But that change occurred slowly. Ladd called for a true parish communion once a month, which he saw as the most realistic way for the average parish to begin to reform its practice. The family services as introduced by the religious education movement emphasized the importance of the entire family worshiping together every Sunday but saw Morning Prayer and Holy Communion as equivalent alternatives. As weekly celebration of the eucharist was more widely discussed, proponents of Morning Prayer expressed concern that the weekly celebration of the eucharist would diminish the significance of the eucharist and argued that alternation of Morning Prayer and Holy Communion permitted a desirable variety in the worship life of congregations. Despite this opposition, during the 1960s an increasing number of parishes shifted to weekly celebration of the eucharist as the principal Sunday service.

As these "new" practices gradually became normative in the Episcopal Church, a eucharistic ecclesiology began to emerge. The celebration of the eucharist with the active participation of all the people was more and more central to the life and mission of the Church. The eucharist came to be understood not just as an act of individual devotional piety but also as a primary corporate expression of faith. In an age of rapid social and cultural change, when the foundations of Christendom were crumbling, the corporate act of eucharist became a primary means by which the Church's identity was established.

This renewed understanding and practice of the eucharist was an important factor both in determining the need for a radically revised prayer book and in shaping the rites of that new book. But the renewal of the eucharist and the liturgical movement which helped bring it about also played a significant role in the changing understandings and practices of baptism and confirmation.

NOTES

1. "Cult and Culture: The Structure of the Evolution of Worship," *Worship* 64 (1990): 408.

2. *The New York Times Magazine*, July 25, 1986, p. 20, cited by John Booty, *The Episcopal Church in Crisis* (Cambridge, MA: Cowley Publications, 1988), pp. 12-13.

3. Jackson W. Carroll, "Continuity and Change: The Shape of Religious Life in the United States, 1950 to the Present," in Jackson W. Carroll, Douglas W. Johnson, and Martin E. Marty, *Religion in America: 1950 to the Present* (San Francisco: Harper & Row, 1979), p. 6.

4. Ibid., pp. 6-37; Sydney E. Ahlstrom, *A Religious History of the American People* (New Haven, CT: Yale University Press, 1972), pp. 1079-96; George Gallup and Jim Castelli, *The People's Religion: American Faith in the 90's* (New York: Macmillan, 1989), pp. 8-17.

5. Rodney Stark and Charles Y. Glock, *American Piety: The Nature of Religious Commitment* (Berkeley/Los Angeles: University of California Press, 1968), p. 205.

6. See Joseph L. Allen, "Continuity and Change: The Church and the Contemporary Social Revolution," *Interpretation* 22 (1968): 464-9; Booty, *The Episcopal Church in Crisis*, pp. 18-19; Leigh Jordahl, "Secularity: The Crisis of Belief and the Reality of Christian Worship," *Dialog* 9 (1970): 16-18; Robert Wuthnow, *The Restructuring of American Religion: Society and Faith Since World War II* (Princeton, NJ: Princeton University Press, 1988), pp. 314-17.

7. "The Context of Liturgy: Here and Now, There and Then," *Worship* 43 (1969): 468.

8. *Rediscovering the Sacred: Perspectives on Religion in Contemporary Society* (Grand Rapids, MI: Eerdmans, 1992), pp. 105-8, 122-6.

9. Carroll, "Continuity and Change," in *Religion in America*, p. 39.

10. Stark and Glock, *American Piety*, p. 207, n. 2.

11. Ibid., pp. 211-12; Wuthnow, *The Restructuring of American Religion*, pp. 160-4.

12. Michael Moriarty, "William Palmer Ladd and the Origins of the Episcopal Liturgical Movement," *Church History* (1995): 439. For a fuller discussion, see, among others, R. W. Franklin, "The Nineteenth Century Liturgical Movement," *Worship* 53 (1979): 12-39; Ernest Koenker, *The Liturgical Renaissance in the Roman Catholic Church* (St. Louis: Concordia, 1966); Massey Hamilton Shepherd, "The History of the Liturgical Renewal," in Shepherd (ed.), *The Liturgical Renewal of the Church* (New York: Oxford University Press, 1960), pp. 21-52.

13. Shepherd, "History of the Liturgical Renewal," in *The Liturgical Renewal of the Church*, p. 47. For further discussion of the Oxford Movement and ritualism, see, among others, Massey H. Shepherd, *The Reform of Liturgical Worship: Perspectives and Prospects* (New York: Oxford University Press, 1961), pp. 11-33; Byron Stuhlman, *Eucharistic Celebration 1789-1979* (New York: Church Hymnal Corporation, 1988), pp. 75-95; James F. White, *The Cambridge Movement: The Ecclesiologists and the Gothic Revival* (Cambridge: Cambridge University Press, 1962).

14. Louis Bouyer, *Liturgical Piety* (Notre Dame, IN: University of Notre Dame Press, 1955), p. 48.

15. A. G. Hebert, *Liturgy and Society: The Function of the Church in the Modern World* (London: Faber and Faber, 1935).

16. A. G. Hebert, "The Parish Communion in Its Spiritual Aspect," in Hebert (ed.), *The Parish Communion* (London: SPCK, 1937), p. 3. While Hebert is credited with popularizing the teachings of the liturgical movement, Donald Gray, *Earth and Altar: The Evolution of the Parish Communion in the Church of England to 1945*,

Alcuin Club Collections 68 (Norwich: Canterbury Press, 1986), maintains that the origins of the parish communion predate Hebert and are independent of the Roman Catholic Church. Gray identifies the beginnings in the nineteenth century in the teachings of what he terms "sacramental socialists," Christian socialists who taught that the Church as God's instrument in the world gathers to celebrate the eucharist not only for personal salvation but for the sake of the world.

17. William Palmer Ladd, *Prayer Book Interleaves: Some Reflections on How the Book of Common Prayer Might Be Made More Influential in Our English-speaking World* (New York: Oxford University Press, 1942).

18. Ibid., p. 166.

19. Ibid., pp. 20-21.

20. Ibid., p. 167.

21. Ibid., pp. 113-14.

22. Ibid., p. 53.

23. Ibid., p. 56.

24. Ibid., p. 82.

25. Ibid., pp. 55-6.

26. Ibid., p. 70.

27. Ibid., pp. 56-7.

28. Ibid., p. 51.

29. Ibid., pp. 7-8, 51-3.

30. The 1928 prayer "for the whole state of Christ's Church" appears in revised form as the prayer "for the whole state of Christ's Church *and the world*" in the 1979 BCP, pp. 328-30.

31. Ladd, *Prayer Book Interleaves*, pp. 64-6, 110, 156-7.

32. Massey H. Shepherd, *The Living Liturgy* (New York: Oxford University Press, 1946), p. 124.

33. Ladd, *Prayer Book Interleaves*, p. 133.

34. Ibid., p. 114.

35. Ibid., pp. 118-22.

36. Shepherd, "History of the Liturgical Renewal," in Shepherd (ed.), *The Liturgical Renewal of the Church*, p. 48.

37. Winfred Douglas, *Church Music in History and Practice: Studies in the Praise of God* (New York: Charles Scribner's Sons, 1937), pp. 27-8.

38. Ibid., pp. 39-44.

39. Ibid., p. 272.

40. Edward Lambe Parsons and Bayard Hale Jones, *The American Prayer Book: Its Origins and Principles* (New York: Charles Scribner's Sons, 1937), pp. vii-ix.

41. Ibid., pp. 57-8.

42. London: Dacre Press, 1945; new edition with additional notes by Paul V. Marshall, New York: Seabury Press, 1982.

43. Massey H. Shepherd, *The Liturgical Movement and the Prayer Book* (Evanston, IL: Seabury-Western Theological Seminary, 1946), p. 13.

44. For more recent assessments of Dix's contributions in *The Shape of the Liturgy*, see Paul F. Bradshaw, *The Search for the Origins of Christian Worship: Sources and Methods for the Study of Early Liturgy* (New York: Oxford University Press, 1992), pp. 137-43; Bryan D. Spinks, "Mis-Shapen: Gregory Dix and the Four-Action Shape of the Liturgy," *Lutheran Quarterly* 4 (1990): 161-77; Kenneth Stevenson, *Gregory Dix—Twenty-Five Years on* (Bramcote, Nottingham: Grove Books, 1977), pp. 23-39.

45. Michael Moriarty, "The Associated Parishes for Liturgy and Mission, 1946-1991; The Liturgical Movement in the Episcopal Church" (Ph.D. Dissertation, University of Notre Dame, 1993), pp. 64-6.

46. H. Boone Porter, "Toward an Unofficial History of Episcopal Worship," in Malcolm C. Burson (ed.), *Worship Points the Way: A Celebration of the Life and Work of Massey Hamilton Shepherd, Jr.* (New York: Seabury Press, 1981), p. 110.

47. Shepherd, "History of the Liturgical Renewal," in Shepherd (ed.), *The Liturgical Renewal of the Church*, pp. 29-30.

48. New York: Benziger Brothers; the English translation of Volume II was published in 1955.

49. Notre Dame, IN: University of Notre Dame Press.

50. Notre Dame, IN: University of Notre Dame Press, 1955.

51. Leiden: E. J. Brill, 1979.

52. *Baptism in the New Testament* (London: SCM Press, 1950); *Christ and Time* (London: SCM, 1951); *Early Christian Worship* (London: SCM, 1953); "The Meaning of the Lord's Supper in Primitive Christianity," in O. Cullman and F. J. Leenhardt, *Essays on the Lord's Supper* (London: Lutterworth, 1958).

53. Burson (ed.), *Worship Points the Way*, includes several articles relating to Shepherd's work and the liturgical movement.

54. Massey Hamilton Shepherd, *The Living Liturgy* (New York: Oxford University Press, 1946). For Ladd's influence on Shepherd, see *The Living Liturgy*, pp. 124-6; Holmes, "Education for Liturgy," in Burson (ed.), *Worship Points the Way*, p. 121.

55. *The Oxford American Prayer Book Commentary* (New York: Oxford University Press, 1950).

56. Greenwich, CT: Seabury Press, 1960; republished, Washington, DC: The Pastoral Press, 1987.

57. Verney Johnstone, *The Story of the Prayer Book* (New York: Morehouse-Gorham, 1949); John Suter and George Cleaveland, *The American Book of Common Prayer: Its Origin and Development* (New York: Oxford University Press, 1949).

58. Holmes, "Education for Liturgy," in Burson (ed.), *Worship Points the Way*, pp. 122-3.

59. Michael Moriarty, *The Liturgical Revolution* (New York: Church Hymnal Corporation, 1996), pp. 44-54. (*The Liturgical Revolution* is the published version of

Moriarty's dissertation, "The Associated Parishes"; the dissertation will be cited only where a reference does not appear in the published text.) In his study, based upon original documents, Moriarty offers several significant correctives to the account given by Holmes, "Education for Liturgy," pp. 122-3.

60. Book review, *The Living Church*, Oct. 8, 1950, p. 19. This review notwithstanding, Associated Parishes has no record of the publication of this pamphlet, and Moriarty uncovered no evidence of it in his study of the Associated Parishes.

61. *The Parish Eucharist*, 1950; *Christian Initiation: Part I—Holy Baptism*, 1953; *Christian Initiation: Part II—Confirmation*, 1954.

62. *The Parish Eucharist*, p. 4.

63. Ibid., p. 16.

64. Ibid., pp. 10-11.

65. Ibid., p. 20.

66. Ibid., p. 1.

67. *Oxford American Prayer Book Commentary*, p. 65.

68. BCP 1928, p. 80.

69. Associated Parishes, *The Parish Eucharist*, p. 18.

70. Moriarty, *The Liturgical Revolution*, pp. 66, 234 n. 22.

71. *The Liturgical Renewal of the Church*.

72. Massey Shepherd (ed.), *The Eucharist and Liturgical Renewal* (New York: Oxford, 1960).

73. Frank Stephen Cellier (ed.), *Liturgy is Mission* (New York: Seabury, 1964).

74. Moriarty, *The Liturgical Revolution*, pp. 133-4.

75. "The Philosophy and Procedures of the Department of Christian Education," pp. 1-3, cited by Dorothy L. Braun, "A Historical Study of the Origin and Development of the Seabury Series of the Protestant Episcopal Church" (Ph.D. dissertation, New York University, 1960), pp. 201-2.

76. David E. Sumner, *The Episcopal Church's History: 1945-1985* (Wilton, CT: Morehouse-Barlow, 1987), pp. 74-82.

77. New York: Seabury, 1953.

78. Ibid., p. 150.

79. Sumner, *The Episcopal Church's History*, pp. 79-81.

80. Peter Day, "Beachhead Established: Revolution in the Sunday School Begins to Penetrate the Parishes," *The Living Church*, June 17, 1956, p. 5.

81. *Prayer Book Interleaves*, p. 148.

82. Edwin Augustine White and Jackson Dykman, *Annotated Constitution and Canons for the Government of the Protestant Episcopal Church in the United States of America otherwise known as The Episcopal Church*, revised and updated by the Standing Commission on Constitution and Canons of the General Convention (New York: Office of the General Convention, 1985), Vol. II, pp. 928-47. A 1989 Supplement to the 1981 edition takes account of subsequent amendments which distinguish Lay Readers, Lectors and Lay Eucharistic Ministers and allow the latter to administer

bread as well as wine. For further discussion of women as lay readers, see Pamela Darling, *New Wine: The Story of Women Transforming Leadership and Power in the Episcopal Church* (Cambridge, MA: Cowley Publications, 1994), pp. 102-4.

83. Associated Parishes, *The Parish Eucharist*, pp. 13, 17, 21.

84. Massey Shepherd et al. (eds.), *Before the Holy Table: A Guide to the Celebration of the Holy Eucharist, Facing the People, According to The Book of Common Prayer* (Greenwich, CT: Seabury, 1956).

Chapter 3

The Renewal of Baptism

Leaders of the liturgical movement gave much of their attention to the renewal of the eucharist, the principal act of public worship. Far less consideration was given to baptism. For example, Ladd's *Prayer Book Interleaves* includes only four articles under the heading "Baptism," while eleven articles appear under "The Holy Eucharist" and frequent references to the eucharist are found in many of the articles in other sections of the book. None of the articles discuss confirmation. In *The Living Liturgy*, Shepherd devoted just two essays to baptism and one to confirmation in contrast to sixteen on the eucharist.

Yet baptism was not neglected altogether. As a eucharistic ecclesiology began to emerge, with new attention given to the active participation of the community which was the body of Christ gathered in a particular time and place, calls were issued for reform of baptismal practice. The obstacles were significant. Baptism was important primarily as a rite of passage marking physical birth. While it was often a significant event for the family of the infant to be baptized, baptism was on the periphery of congregational life. Most Episcopalians were quite content with this approach, especially since the baptismal rite in the 1928 prayer book made no provision for congregational participation and so the rite simply added length to a service of Morning or Evening Prayer. Reforms urged by leaders of the liturgical movement were intended to restore to baptism its significance as a rite of incorporation into the body of Christ and so to bring baptism into a more central place in the life of the Church.

A Call for Public Baptism

Baptism in the early twentieth-century Church was most frequently a private or semiprivate rite, having little or no apparent connection to the ongoing life of the worshiping community. Efforts to change this practice can be found beginning in the late 1930s.

In *The American Prayer Book*, Parsons and Jones provided an extended description of the baptismal liturgy in the recently discovered and translated document *Apostolic Tradition*, attributed to Hippolytus of Rome and thus indicative of practice in the early third century. According to this document, baptism in the early Church was a public sacrament celebrated annually at the Easter vigil. Those baptized were usually adults who had spent months or even years in preparation for the solemn occasion.[1] After surveying the development of the baptismal rite, especially in Anglican prayer books, Parsons and Jones commented with regard to the 1928 rite:

> Baptism is a corporate act of the Church, not the expression of the whim of individuals. Children should be brought to the church, to be received by the congregation, instead of being subjected to the too common abuse of submerging a sacred rite in a social function.
>
> It is likewise advisable...that Baptism, when practicable, be solemnly performed at a principal service on a Sunday.

Parsons and Jones acknowledged that baptism could be administered at other days and times but urged that "mere convenience" not be the determining factor. Rather, the sacrament should be administered in the presence of a congregation.[2]

In a 1938 column entitled "Easter and Baptism," William Palmer Ladd described the elaborate ceremonies of baptismal preparation and baptism in ancient Rome, emphasizing the public celebration of baptism at the Easter vigil. He acknowledged that baptism lost its "ancient prestige" during the Middle Ages and had not been restored either by the reformers of the sixteenth century or by the Anglo-Catholics of the nineteenth century. Deploring the current state of baptismal practice, Ladd urged a return to at least occasional public celebrations of baptism:

> We baptize adults in private, thus denying that baptism has any social implication, and in total disregard of our Lord's admonition about confessing him before men. We baptize infants semiprivately, and sometimes as a Sunday school feature...
>
> If we believe in the importance of the Church as a society, why not make as much as possible of the ceremony of initiation into that society? We cannot build baptisteries or revive the Easter vigil, but we might occasionally allow our congregations to witness the admission of new members to their fellowship, and we can dignify the baptismal service with the ceremonial aid of processions, lights, and music.[3]

While Ladd set forth succinctly the historical precedent, his call for a return to public baptism was a call to recognize the importance of baptism in the life of the contemporary worshiping community. Historical continuity was of value, but for Ladd the real value in the "early church" model of public baptism was its expression of the significance of baptism for the Church as a living body. Thus he did not call for wholesale reform which would be primarily an imitation of early church forms. Rather, his recommendations were limited: occasional public baptism and heightened ceremonial. Perhaps Ladd recognized that liturgical practices change slowly and that more limited changes were more likely to be implemented in the average parish.

Ladd's column engendered at least one response, from A. Q. Bailey, rector of the Episcopal Church in Collingswood, New Jersey. In a letter to *The Witness*, Bailey stated that his practice for thirty-seven years as a parish priest had been to have baptism as part of the regular service of the church, "either in the rubrical place after the Second Lesson or at the beginning of the Communion Service after the procession." The only exceptions he made were for private baptisms in sickness and baptism at the Sunday school service. Bailey claimed that he had never "lost a baptism" as a result of this stance, nor did he encounter much opposition.[4]

While the norm in Bailey's parish may have been public baptism, he seems to have been an exception in the Church at large. Nor did Ladd's column lead to an immediate and widespread change in baptismal practice. A 1944 article by Thomas E. Jessett, rector of Trinity Church in Everett, Washington, lamented that baptism was all too frequently treated as a purely social matter. He called for adherence to the rubric directing that baptism take place after the second lesson at Morning or Evening Prayer. Jessett himself had instituted this practice in every parish where he had been a rector. Although it was generally viewed as an innovation, he reported that "it has always been an innovation that has brought unanimous approval."[5]

The Living Church also encouraged a return to public baptism. A 1942 editorial expressed this concern:

> the prevailing custom throughout the Church is to administer Holy Baptism at odd hours when the serenity of a dignified congregation will not be disturbed by the vocal offerings of an overdressed infant.

The editorial made a plea similar to that of Ladd's a few years earlier. In addition to the historical argument, it called for public baptism on the basis of prayer book rubrics: the 1892 BCP had entitled the office, "The Ministration of the *Public* Baptism of Infants," and the first rubric in the Church of England BCP called for baptism on Sundays or other Holy Days "when the most number of people come together," to witness to the newly baptized being received into Christ's Church and to be put in mind of their own baptism. Baptism should not be understood as "a personal privilege conferred by a priest upon a family group," but rather as "an act of the Church... possessed of an inherently public character."[6]

Responses to this editorial indicate that it had some influence in fostering a practice of public baptism. The June 20, 1943, edition reported that at least two parishes in the Diocese of Massachusetts, St. John's Church in Roxbury and Christ Church in Quincy, were experimenting with public baptism at their 11:00 a.m. Sunday services.[7] Several months later, Francis Lightbourn, a parish priest from Glassboro, New Jersey, wrote to say that he had baptized his infant daughter at a Sunday service in his parish. While he supported the editorial call for public baptism, he was not ready to make it the policy for his parish: "for my own child I could have the kind of service I wanted. It remains to be seen whether any others ask for that kind [i.e., public baptism at the Sunday service]."[8] Five years later, *The Living Church* reported that Lightbourn, now at a parish in another state, had done a public baptism at the request of one of the godparents, who "had witnessed such a service elsewhere and liked the idea."[9]

The need for the restoration of public baptism was stressed at a 1945 conference of the Episcopal Evangelical Fellowship. Frederick Grant of Union Seminary addressed the gathering on "The Theology of Baptism," and Reuel Howe spoke on "Personal and Social Implications of Baptism." Grant and Howe emphasized the corporate nature of baptism and urged that baptism be administered as part of regular Sunday worship. Howe's lecture reached an even wider audience when it was published as an article in *Anglican Theological Review*.[10]

The shift to a practice of public baptism occurred gradually. A 1945 article in *The Living Church* stated that "many of us clergy are insisting on the public baptism of infants," not only in adherence to the intent of the rubrics but also because of the importance of baptism for the corporate life of the Church.[11] Yet in 1950 a priest lamented that baptism "has of late become a little, private get-together, with small amount of knowledge displayed about the true meaning of the rite, and from which the public in general has been excluded."[12]

For a change in practice to take root, the call for public baptism needed to be sounded at many times in different ways. In 1945 Howe urged that public baptism was necessary to convey the full meaning of baptism as entrance into the redemptive fellowship. A few years later, Lane Barton, Bishop of Eastern Oregon, suggested that baptism might be administered publicly on special days in the liturgical year, such as Easter Eve and Whitsunday (Pentecost), to emphasize the centrality of baptism.[13] In 1952, Angus Dun, Bishop of Washington, D.C., issued a pastoral letter suggesting that public baptism become the customary practice of parishes:

> Holy Baptism is not a private act of a human family. It is an act of the family of God...
>
> Therefore the rubrics, or little directives, of our Prayer Book clearly intend that Baptism should normally be administered in the church and in the presence of a congregation of Christ's flock. Thus it is made clear that the Church is present and welcomes the new member for whose growth in the new life every member shares responsibility. And in this way every man present is reminded of his own profession made to God in his Baptism.

Dun's letter concluded, "For the ordering and strengthening of our common life I bid you think on these things."[14] His statements thus appear more as episcopal counsel rather than firm directive.

The practice of public baptism became increasingly common during the 1950s. Baptism came to be administered publicly as part of family services. The Associated Parishes pamphlet about baptism urged the importance of public baptism:

> Baptism is a public service of the Church. Hence it should take place when as many members of the Church as possible can be present. Thus the people of God may both witness the initiation of new members, and receive them into their fellowship.

According to the pamphlet, the congregation was also important as a witness to the universal Church in all times and places. The presence of a congregation was underscored by a sketch entitled "baptism today" that depicted a full congregation looking on as a priest baptizes an infant.[15]

Yet the call for public baptism continued to be sounded for many years, suggesting that private or semiprivate baptism was still occurring with some frequency. Nevertheless, alongside this usage the practice of public baptism gradually developed and eventually replaced the private rite. This was not seen as merely an imitation of the practice of the early Church nor as formal adherence to older prayer book rubrics. These provided historical precedent, but the primary rationale for the return to public baptism was the renewed emphasis upon the corporate nature of the Church, fostered by the liturgical and religious education movements, and the consequent understanding of the importance of baptism in the life of the Church.

The Role of Parents and Godparents

In addition to the call for public baptism, there was renewed emphasis upon the role of godparents at baptism. As greater attention was given to the importance of godparents in Christian nurture, the term "sponsor" was increasingly used.

The role of the sponsors in ensuring a child's Christian nurture and upbringing was frequently discussed in the Episcopal Church press during the 1940s and 1950s. Howe described the responsibilities of sponsors in this manner:

> The sponsor or godparent should be a baptized practicing Christian who has a special interest in the child and is willing through the years to assist the parents and others in his care and instruction. He will seek to bring to the child's experiences a relationship of trust, love and understanding that will awaken in the child the response of love, trust, and integrity.

Sponsors were responsible not only for their own godchildren but also "for all the children of the household of faith." Thus they should expect to teach Sunday school or in other ways contribute to the welfare of children. However, sponsors did not bear their responsibility alone, but shared this burden with the whole body of Christ by reminding everyone of their duties toward children. Sponsors were thus representative of the entire community.[16]

The Associated Parishes pamphlet on baptism also pointed out the responsibilities of sponsors, who could be parents or godparents. Essentially, sponsors were responsible for the Christian nurture of their godchildren. "When Christian nurture is properly done, a baptized infant should grow to Christian maturity never knowing the time when he was not a Christian."[17]

Careful election of sponsors had been encouraged in pastoral manuals of the late nineteenth and early twentieth centuries. However, these manuals had provided few guidelines for the instruction of parents and sponsors. As public baptism was increasingly advocated, more attention was given to this preparation. Barton encouraged careful preparation of the parents.[18] Dun, in his pastoral letter, asked that parents and "sponsors or godparents" be "loyal and practicing members of the Church," and that they be instructed about the meaning of baptism and their responsibilities.[19] The Associated Parishes pamphlet stated that sponsors for infants were instructed in their duties and responsibilities but did not specify further the content of this instruction.[20] There is little to indicate how extensive any instruction of sponsors would have been, although the expectation of some instruction is certainly a step toward a more rigorous baptismal discipline.

A wider acceptance of the need for instruction of parents and godparents is evident in the 1949 General Convention's adoption of an amendment to the canon enumerating the duties of the clergy. Introduced by a deputy from North Carolina, the new canon directed that before baptizing infants or children, the ministers were

> to prepare the sponsors by instructing both the parents and the Godparents concerning the significance of Holy Baptism, the responsibilities of parents and Godparents for the Christian training of the baptized child, and how these obligations may properly be discharged.

As the proposal moved through the General Convention legislative process, the Committee on the State of the Church, noting that instruction was already required for adult baptism, confirmation, and marriage, "strongly" recommended adoption of the canon. The Committee on Canons then opined that the proposed amendment would "bring to parents and sponsors in many instances a realization of the meaning and purpose of Holy Baptism, of which they would otherwise be ignorant or heedless." Though the adoption of the amendment does not mean that all clergy immediately introduced new processes of instruction, the convention's action does reflect growing commitment to the necessity of instruction of sponsors of infants.[21]

The Baptismal Font

Ladd had pointed out that baptisteries were prominent in ancient church buildings but had become a negligible feature in contemporary churches: "Those ancient baptisteries... demonstrate the honor in which baptism was held by the first Christians, and the separation they believed baptism made between themselves and the pagan world. But in our churches the font is often a negligible feature."[22] In keeping with his moderate approach to liturgical change, Ladd did not recommend building baptisteries. Yet as increasing emphasis was given to public baptism, some attention was also given to the location and type of the baptismal font.

During the 1950s there were a few reports of baptismal tanks and baptism by immersion in Episcopal churches. However, most of the changes recommended were more modest. Shepherd commented:

> [A] vigorous protest is in order against the practice of some architects of providing a mere cubbyhole or tiny recessed chapel for the erection of the font, where so few people may conveniently witness the baptisms or take an active part in the service. And the font ought to be larger than a bird-bath.[23]

Howe expressed similar sentiment. He pointed out that when public baptism once again became customary, "it will be necessary for the fonts to be pulled out of the closets and corners where they have been hidden, dusted off, and put in a conspicuous and symbolically appropriate place."[24]

The growing appreciation of the importance of baptismal symbolism is evident in a comparison of two editions of *A Prayer Book Manual*, issued by the Boston Clergy Group of the Episcopal Evangelical Fellowship. The 1943 edition made no mention of the place of the font in the church building. A new edition issued during the 1960s pointed out that in many churches the font was not in an appropriate place for public baptism. It suggested that a basin could be placed on a table in the chancel since "the important thing is that everyone present be given an opportunity to participate fully in the service." The 1943 edition had directed the priest to "sprinkle" water on the person's head, while the later edition instructed the priest to "pour" water on the baptizand's head. The latter verb implies a somewhat more effusive use of water, although immersion was not strongly recommended. Both editions of the manual acknowledged that the prayer book rubric permitted "dipping," but the only advice was, "If you want to try it, practice it at home on your own child first, to be sure you can hold him without slipping."[25] The more explicit directions for sprinkling or pouring suggest that this was the method more likely to be used.

The Revival of the Easter Vigil

In the 1928 prayer book, no provision was made for Holy Week and Easter services beyond the daily propers. The only reference to baptism was found on Easter Eve in the Epistle, 1 Peter 3:17-22 (the flood as an Old Testament prefiguring or "type" of baptism), and the collect:

> Grant, O Lord, that as we are baptized into the death of thy blessed Son, our Saviour Jesus Christ, so by continual mortifying our corrupt affections we may be buried with him; and that through the grave, and gate of death, we may pass to our joyful resurrection; for his merits, who died, and was buried, and rose again for us, the same thy Son Jesus Christ our Lord.[26]

Although the Collect and the Epistle referred to baptism, the focus of the celebration was the commemoration of Jesus' burial and descent into hell, not baptism.[27]

An Easter vigil first appeared in the Episcopal Church as part of the Anglican missal, an unofficial liturgical resource closely patterned upon the Roman Catholic missal. Such missals reflect the desire of Anglo-Catholics to reproduce the ceremonies and in some instances the texts of the Roman mass, including the Holy Saturday liturgy from the Roman missal. This was a full Easter vigil, but in the Roman Catholic Church it had come to be celebrated on the morning of Holy Saturday in addition to an Easter mass on Easter Sunday morning.

The editors' foreword to the first edition of the American missal, published in 1931, stated that the increasing restoration of the ancient ceremonies of Holy Week made it desirable to have those ceremonies in a book appropriate for liturgical use. The rubrics for the vigil on "Easter Even" instructed that the service begin at a "suitable hour (preferably at night)." The liturgy included the administration of baptism in accordance with the 1928 BCP but did not call for congregational participation, either by being sprinkled with the newly blessed water or by renewing baptismal vows.[28] It is difficult to know the extent to which this Easter vigil liturgy was the actual practice of any parish in the Episcopal Church. At most, it would have been implemented in some Anglo-Catholic parishes.

Ladd believed that the Easter vigil could not be restored and suggested instead that the use of the paschal candle be revived as a significant link with the early Church.[29] The use of the paschal candle on Easter Eve was proposed as early as 1929, in an article by Howard B. St. George, professor of liturgics at Nashotah House.[30] Fifteen years later, an article describing Holy Week services using resources available in the Bible, prayer book and hymnal included the blessing of the new fire and the blessing of the paschal candle on Easter Eve but stopped short of calling for a full vigil service. The author pointed out, "The modern custom of anticipating, holding the ceremony in the morning, spoils the intended effect of beginning in comparative darkness and ending in light."[31] This comment suggests that few parishes were celebrating a nighttime Easter vigil.

Yet the relation between baptism and Easter was beginning to be recognized. Massey Shepherd commented in 1945 that "many of the parish clergy are returning to the ancient custom of appointing stated times for Baptism, particularly Easter Even."[32]

While the earliest efforts were directed at restoring one aspect of the ceremonial, by the late 1940s there were attempts to restore the full vigil. A manual of Holy Week services, published during Lent 1946 under the auspices of the Episcopal Church Society of Saint John the Evangelist, included a liturgy for Easter Eve, described as "the great service of the Easter Vigil."[33] A discussion of variations of this service stated: "In some places the ancient custom of offering this service in the nighttime has been restored.... In some places portions of the liturgy are used as a late afternoon or early evening devotion." Suggestions were made for appropriate portions of the service to be used at different times.[34] This indicates that there was some experimentation as this "new" service, with quite elaborate ceremonial and extensive prayer and scripture, was introduced.

The vigil liturgy in *An American Holy Week Manual* followed the outline of the Roman Catholic Holy Saturday vigil, including the blessing of the new fire, the blessing of the paschal candle, the *Exsultet*, the "Prophecies" (twelve Old Testament lessons, each with a concluding collect), a blessing of the font, baptisms (when there were candidates to be baptized), the Litany of the Saints and the first mass of Easter. The prophecies were explicitly baptismal. A rubric prior to each reading provided a baptismal interpretation of the lesson, for example, this introduction to the first prophecy (Genesis 1:1-2:2):

> Our forefathers saw in these ancient lessons types of Baptism and of our redemption, wrought by the life, death, and resurrection of our Lord. In this first Prophecy, the Spirit of God moving over the waters is a type of the Spirit moving over the waters of Baptism today. Light out of darkness is a symbol of Christ's resurrection from the tomb, and of our resurrection from the waters of Baptism. In Baptism we regain our share in the divine nature of him who became partaker of our humanity that he might restore that which mankind lost in the Fall.[35]

The blessing of the font included the sprinkling of the congregation with the newly blessed water, in accord with Roman Catholic practice. This insured that the worshipers would be reminded of their baptism whether or not there were candidates for baptism. The collect for the first mass of Easter, also taken from the Roman missal, emphasized baptism in the petition that God would "preserve in the new children of thy family the spirit of adoption which thou hast given them."[36] Any congregation which implemented this vigil, or a significant portion thereof, would be reminded throughout of the paschal dimensions of baptism.

The efforts of one parish to implement an Easter vigil on Holy Saturday night were described in a 1953 article in *The Living Church*. Wilfred F. Penny, rector of St. Ignatius' Church in New York City, explained that the parish had decided in 1950 to celebrate the vigil at night since "we found difficulty in accommodating our souls, minds, bodies, and emotions to the assumption that Saturday morning is the 'night verily blessed.'" According to him, the service was well-attended from its inception, the primary difficulty being that there were at first no candidates for baptism. But in 1952 there was one adult baptism, and in 1953 he was expecting to baptize three infants at the service. The renewal of baptismal promises, a "new section," was also included "as an effective means of making the faithful enter more consciously into the spiritual content of the Easter mystery." The introduction to this renewal as quoted by Penny is markedly similar to the comparable text from the Roman Catholic vigil as restored in 1951, and thus the renewal of baptismal vows appears to have been introduced in imitation of the Roman Catholic practice.[37]

At least one parish, St. Andrew's in Harriman, Tennessee, followed Penny's recommendation and celebrated Easter with a vigil service. The rector, Frank McClain, stated in a letter to the editor, "the service, with certain modifications, has proved one of the most wonderful things in the life of this small parish in the hill country of Tennessee."[38]

The growing interest in celebrating the Easter vigil is evident in the various liturgical texts which were published during the 1950s. In 1951, Pius XII had authorized the celebration of the vigil in the Roman Catholic Church on Holy Saturday night as a one-year experiment. This permission was then renewed for three years and finally made general law in 1955. An English version of the Ordo authorized in 1952 was published in London by the Church Literature Association for use in Anglican churches.[39] This English version was little more than a translation of the Latin, with few adaptations. Massey Shepherd lamented in a review:

> It is certainly a pity that the entire baptismal office of the Ordo is not made more nearly conformable to the Prayer Book—inasmuch as many of our parishes do have the administration of Holy Baptism on Easter Even. Also, the Collect, Epistle, Gospel of the Mass, and Litany should be those of the Prayer Book.[40]

Shepherd's remarks indicate an increasing tendency to administer baptism on Easter Eve. Whether or not this was linked with a full vigil service, it suggests that there was a growing awareness of the connection between baptism and Easter. This may reflect in part a desire to return to the worship patterns of the early Church. But when baptism was administered in the context of some or all of the Easter vigil, the Easter liturgy would bring into prominence the death and resurrection motif of baptism.

To provide texts for the celebration of the Easter vigil in the Episcopal Church, Associated Parishes produced *Holy Week Offices*, edited by Massey Shepherd and published in 1958. The book drew primarily upon the Bible, prayer book and hymnal as sources, in conformity to the requirements of Article X of the Episcopal Church Constitution and a prayer book rubric permitting the use of special forms of worship at the discretion of the Ordinary (i.e., the diocesan bishop).[41] Following the lighting of the paschal candle and the *Exsultet*, the service offered the option of continuing with Evening Prayer or with the vigil, both of which were to be followed by baptism and then either the Ante-Communion or Holy Eucharist (the latter to be celebrated if the vigil and baptisms were concluded at midnight). If the bishop was present, confirmation could also be celebrated.[42]

In response to pressure for official texts for Holy Week services, including Easter Eve, the 1960 edition of *The Book of Offices* included a rite comprising the lighting of the paschal candle and the *Exsultet* followed by Evening Prayer.[43] Attempts had been made to include the entire rite for Easter Eve from *Holy Week Offices*, but the publisher granted permission only for use of the Blessing of the Paschal Candle. The more limited rite in *The Book of Offices* did not prevent the use of the full rite from *Holy Week Offices*, but the latter book did not have the same official status as the former, which had the approval of General Convention.

The revival of the Easter vigil in its various forms provided a sense of the paschal dimensions of baptism. One author reflected on his experience of the vigil at St. Mary the Virgin in New York City in 1948:

> It was a turning point in my life, for here, however corruptly, I perceived the panoply of the faith; the church dark, the reading of the prophecies, and the lighting of the new fire, the blessing of the Font with its very sloshy drama...and then the bursting from the tomb with lights coming on, rattles and bells, and Ernest White going berserk on the great organ. It may have been on Saturday, with a smallish congregation, but I had seen the Lord arise and connected it with my baptism and had been deeply moved intellectually and viscerally.[44]

The connection of baptism with the mystery of Jesus' death and resurrection, emphasized in the celebration of the Easter vigil, gradually became more central in the life of the Church as the vigil was more widely celebrated. In this way, the revival of the vigil contributed to changing understandings of baptism.

Other Baptismal Days

Prior to the 1979 prayer book, the connections made between baptism and the liturgical year centered for the most part on Easter, particularly the vigil. But there was also some awareness of the significance of Pentecost and of Jesus' baptism for the contemporary Church's practice of baptism.

In 1935, the Presiding Bishop of the Episcopal Church and the Commission on the Forward Movement issued "An Act of Affirmation" for use on Whitsunday (Pentecost). The rite called people to rededicate their lives to the service of God and to reaffirm the vows of their baptism. It was essentially a modification of the 1928 BCP confirmation rite. The two questions asked by the bishop at confirmation were to be recited in declarative form by the congregation, the priest said the prayer for the sevenfold gifts of the Spirit, and the congregation then joined in saying a modified form of the confirmation formula ("defend, O Lord, this thy child..."). The rite was published in *The Southern Churchman* in 1935.[45] An editorial the following year claimed that, due to the efforts of the Forward Movement in 1935, "Whitsunday found an unusual number of communicants rededicating themselves as disciples of the Living Lord and asking that the Holy Spirit descend upon us today."[46] Despite this claim, no other Episcopal Church periodical took note of the Act of Affirmation, and there was no mention of it in *The Southern Churchman* after 1936.

Later articles called attention to Pentecost as a baptismal day. Bishop Barton had recommended a Pentecost celebration of baptism in order to emphasize the centrality of baptism.[47] A decade later, an article in *Christian Education Findings* described the origins of the feast of Pentecost and pointed out that the celebration of Whitsunday had numerous possibilities for a parish. These included the celebration of baptism, recognition of all those baptized or confirmed during the preceding year, and the renewal of vows by all baptized and confirmed persons.[48]

In 1961, a member of Associated Parishes described the way his parish had observed Pentecost. Each day between Ascension Day and Pentecost, home prayer services were scheduled with emphases relating to mission and evangelism. On the day of Pentecost, the congregation processed to the baptismal font and read from the prayer book their baptism and confirmation vows. During the week following Pentecost, calls were made on lapsed Episcopalians and persons known to be unchurched, and reports of these visitations were presented as part of the offertory on the Sunday after Pentecost.[49] Here Pentecost was celebrated as an opportunity for renewal of baptism and connected to evangelism and the mission of the Church.

These scattered references suggest minimal understanding of the relation between Pentecost and Christian initiation. While it is likely that they did not have a widespread effect on parish life in the Episcopal Church, the latter two articles may have encouraged a few parishes to recognize baptism and/or confirmation on the feast of Pentecost, since they were published at a time when more parishes were celebrating baptism publicly and there was greater awareness of the importance of baptism.

Even less attention was given to the baptism of Jesus as an occasion for baptism. The 1928 revision of the prayer book had introduced the Marcan account of Jesus' baptism as the gospel for the second Sunday after the Epiphany, thus placing one of the traditional Epiphany themes in close proximity with the feast of Epiphany. However, this had gone largely unnoticed. In *The Living Liturgy*, Shepherd pointed out that Eastern churches associated Epiphany with the baptism of Jesus and suggested that the day be revitalized "by drawing it into closer relation to the characteristic notes" of the feast, including baptism. Yet he did not mention that a gospel account of Jesus' baptism now appeared in the lectionary, nor did he have any concrete suggestions for associating Epiphany with baptism.[50] The Associated Parishes pamphlet on baptism gave prominence to the baptism of Jesus as the pattern and example for Christian baptism but did not mention that this was the gospel appointed on the second Sunday after Epiphany.[51]

In 1959, a proposal for keeping the second Sunday after Epiphany as a baptismal day was presented by Boone Porter in *Sharers*, the quarterly publication of Associated Parishes. Porter called attention to the gospel appointed for this day and made several suggestions for ceremonial and music appropriate to the feast. Public baptism should be celebrated. But if there was no baptism, the congregation could process to the font after the Creed, the point at which the prayer book allowed authorized prayers and intercessions. These prayers could include prayers for worthy reception of baptism and confirmation, found in the Form of Consecration of a Church or Chapel, and a thanksgiving for the congregation's baptism, using the concluding thanksgiving from the baptismal rite. The sermon must explain the significance of the celebration.[52] Here was a creative use of the prayer book in combination with ceremonial that would call people's attention to the significance of their baptism. There is no indication of the extent to which Porter's suggestions were followed, yet given the openness of Associated Parishes members and others to liturgical experimentation, it is likely that at least a few parishes experienced some form of the proposed rite.

Baptism and Ministry

The Offices of Instruction in the 1928 prayer book stated that one became a member of the Church at baptism. With this membership came responsibility: one's "bounden duty" as a member of the Church was "to follow Christ, to worship God every Sunday in his Church; and to work and pray and give for the spread of his kingdom." To help Christians fulfill these responsibilities, the Church provided confirmation, "wherein, after renewing the promises and vows of my baptism, and declaring my loyalty and devotion to Christ as my Master, I receive the strengthening gifts of the Holy Spirit."[53]

Yet the affirmation of baptism as the basis of membership in the Church was essentially lip service. For most Episcopalians, confirmation was the primary rite and was frequently described as "the ordination of the laity." Shepherd noted the danger in this analogy: "it might mislead people into thinking that in baptism they did not become fully members of Christ's Body and sharers in His eternal Priesthood." Nevertheless, he suggested, the analogy with ordination could be used profitably, particularly with regard to the ceremonial of confirmation.[54]

The Associated Parishes pamphlet on the eucharist began by identifying participation in the priesthood of believers, but attributed this to baptism *and* confirmation: "these people [those who compose the parish] through Baptism and Confirmation have undertaken a new relationship with God.... [T]he people are to be a 'holy priesthood to offer up spiritual sacrifice acceptable to God through Jesus Christ.'"[55] The meaning of this priesthood was not spelled out. Christian ministry was described broadly: "*Every job, vocation, or profession is a means of Christian Stewardship and ministry,* when it is performed to the glory of God and the service of man." Full-time Christian ministry might include the work of medical professionals, teachers and social workers. But the "supreme opportunity" for a life of service was available to men in the ordained ministry.[56] None of these opportunities for ministry, lay or ordained, were related to the baptismal priesthood.

As baptism gradually was given more prominence in the life of the Church, there began to emerge a new understanding of baptism as a sacrament of ministry. This perception arose from the liturgical movement teaching that the Church is the body of Christ. At the 1959 Associated Parishes conference, Frank Cellier, a lay person who was a member of the Standing Liturgical Commission, argued that there are not three orders of ministry—bishop, priest and deacon—but four, the fourth being the laity. Cellier did not, however, relate the ministry of the laity to baptism. Instead, he identified participation in the eucharist as the primary source of empowerment for the laity and spoke passionately of the need for the Church to equip the laity for their ministry in the world.[57] Citing Cellier's paper, Massey Shepherd commented in 1964:

> The laity is the fundamental Holy Order in the Church, and all of us are made laymen in our Baptism. We must rid ourselves of all the common parlance that

suggests that Confirmation is the so-called "ordination of the laity." Baptism is the layman's ordination.[58]

Shepherd's remarks indicate a shift from his willingness two decades earlier to make use of an analogy of confirmation to ordination. There is no waffling in his later statement; baptism is unequivocally described as the basis for full participation in the body of Christ.

This perspective was more fully discussed in *Baptized into the One Church*, a pamphlet issued in 1963 by the Department of Christian Education of the national Episcopal Church. The author was Chauncie Kilmer Myers, a leader in the liturgical movement who was vicar of the Chapel of the Intercession at Trinity Parish, New York City, when he wrote the pamphlet, and who became Bishop of California in 1966. Describing the Church as "a strange colony in an alien land," Myers emphasized that baptism is incorporation into the body of Christ, a community which transcends the divisions of the world. All those baptized into this body are called to participate in Christ's ministry of service to the world. Myers concluded with a call to Christians to rediscover the meaning of baptism and thus rediscover the Church's ministry to the world.[59] While Myers' views do not seem to have been widely shared at that time in the Episcopal Church, they anticipate a shift to a *baptismal ecclesiology* appropriate in a post-Christian era.

Toward a Baptismal Ecclesiology

As the liturgical movement gained momentum in the Episcopal Church, new understandings and practices of baptism evolved. A growing practice of public baptism at the main Sunday service gave baptism more dignity and importance in the life of the Christian community. Some attention was given to ceremonial, namely, the placement of the font in clear view of the congregation and the use of a significant amount of water. Emphasis was placed upon the selection of sponsors who were active and committed Christians and upon the careful instruction of parents and godparents of infant candidates for baptism. Easter Eve was recognized as an appropriate time for the celebration of baptism. As Easter vigil services with the celebration or renewal of baptism were introduced in Episcopal parishes, the paschal dimensions of baptism received greater importance.

These changes gave baptism in the 1960s far greater significance in the life of the Church than it was accorded in the early decades of the twentieth century. Nevertheless, baptism was not generally understood as the basis of Christian identity. The liturgical movement had facilitated the development of a eucharistic ecclesiology, and by the 1960s the eucharist was increasingly seen as central to the life and mission of the Church. It is a further step to perceive the life of the Church to be rooted in baptism. The changes in baptismal practice advocated by the liturgical movement set the stage for such an understanding. But it is only with the use of the 1979 prayer book that this perspective is coming to be widely shared, part of the common parlance of the Episcopal Church. The changes instigated by the liturgical movement paved the way for a new baptismal rite and a prayer book which articulates a baptismal ecclesiology.

NOTES

1. Parsons and Jones, *The American Prayer Book*, pp. 224-7. While the majority of scholars have accepted the position that *Apostolic Tradition* originates from Rome, is the original work of Hippolytus, and was written *circa* 215, this is far from certain, since no original text of the document is extant and no existing manuscript includes a title or author for the work. Moreover, the description of the baptismal vigil does not specify that it is an Easter vigil, although it is often interpreted as such. For a summary of scholarship on the document and the sections treating baptism, see Paul F. Bradshaw, *The Search for the Origins of Christian Worship*, pp. 89-92, 175-8.

2. Parsons and Jones, *The American Prayer Book*, pp. 236-7.

3. Ladd, "Easter and Baptism," *The Witness*, Apr. 14, 1938, pp. 5-6; cf. *Prayer Book Interleaves*, pp. 75-6.

4. "Jersey Rector Writes about Baptism," *The Witness*, May 19, 1938, pp. 13-14.

5. Thomas E. Jessett, "Ministering Holy Baptism," *The Witness*, Apr. 20, 1944, pp. 8-9.

6. "Holy Baptism," *The Living Church*, Nov. 29, 1942, p. 12.

7. "Baptism Administered At 11 O'clock Services," *The Living Church*, June 20, 1943, p. 20.

8. Francis C. Lightbourn, letter to the editor, *The Living Church*, Oct. 10, 1943, p. 3.

9. "Public Baptism Requested," *The Living Church*, Sept. 26, 1948, p. 6.

10. Reuel L. Howe, "Personal and Social Implications of Baptism," *Anglican Theological Review* 27 (1945): 264-74.

11. Kenneth Worthington, "Liturgical Reception of Communicants," *The Living Church*, Mar. 25, 1945, p. 13.

12. Wilfred T. Waterhouse, "Holy Baptism Is Not a Private Affair!", *The Southern Churchman*, Apr. 15, 1950, p. 5.

13. Lane W. Barton, "Thoughts on Christian Baptism," *Anglican Theological Review* 30 (1948): 213.

14. Angus Dun, "Holy Baptism: A Pastoral Letter," *The Living Church*, Oct. 26, 1952, p. 9.

15. Associated Parishes, *Christian Initiation: Part I—Holy Baptism*, pp. 4-5.

16. Howe, *Man's Need and God's Action*, pp. 59-60.

17. Associated Parishes, *Christian Initiation: Part I—Holy Baptism*, pp. 10-11.

18. Barton, "Thoughts on Christian Baptism," pp. 213-14.

19. Dun, "Holy Baptism: A Pastoral Letter," *The Living Church*, Oct. 26, 1952, p. 9.

20. Associated Parishes, *Christian Initiation: Part I—Holy Baptism*, p. 4.

21. *Journal of the General Convention*, 1949, pp. 190-1.

22. Ladd, *Prayer Book Interleaves*, p. 76.

23. Shepherd, *The Living Liturgy*, p. 96.

24. Howe, "Personal and Social Implications of Baptism," p. 273.

25. Boston Clergy Group of the Episcopal Evangelical Fellowship, *A Prayer Book Manual* (Louisville: The Cloister Press, 1943), pp. 47-8, 56; 4th ed. (n.p., n.d.; library notation reads "196-?"), pp. 62, 70-1.

26. BCP 1928, p. 161.

27. Shepherd, *The Oxford American Prayer Book Commentary* pp. 161-2; Marion J. Hatchett, *Commentary on the American Prayer Book* (New York: Seabury, 1980), pp. 238-9.

28. *The American Missal. Being the Liturgy from the Book of Common Prayer According to the Use of the Church in the United States of America. With Introits, Graduals, and Other Devotions Proper to the Same, Together with Propers for Additional Holy Days and Saints' Days and for Requiem and Votive Masses* (Milwaukee: Morehouse, 1931), pp. 163-90.

29. *Prayer Book Interleaves*, p. 76.

30. "The Observances of Holy Week," *The Living Church*, Mar. 23, 1929, pp. 723-4.

31. Morton C. Stone, "Prayer Book Holy Week Ceremonies," *The Living Church*, Mar. 31, 1946, p. 11.

32. Shepherd, *The Living Liturgy*, p. 93.

33. *An American Holy Week Manual: The Liturgy from Palm Sunday through Easter Day Together with Tenebrae* (Cambridge, MA: Society of Saint John the Evangelist, 1946), p. 273.

34. Ibid., p. 330.

35. Ibid., p. 281.

36. Ibid., p. 325.

37. Wilfred F. Penny, "Easter the New Way," *The Living Church*, Apr. 5, 1953, pp. 12-15. For the Roman Catholic rite see Godfrey L. Diekmann, *The Easter Vigil: Arranged for Use in Parishes* (Collegeville, MN: Liturgical Press, 1953), pp. 31-2.

38. Frank M. McClain, letter to the editor, *The Living Church*, May 3, 1953, p. 3.

39. *The Order for Holy Saturday When the Restored Vigil Is Observed* (London: Church Literature Association, 1953).

40. Massey Shepherd, review of *The Order for Holy Saturday When the Restored Vigil Is Observed*, *The Living Church*, Feb. 15, 1953, p. 27.

41. Massey H. Shepherd (ed.), *Holy Week Offices* (Greenwich, CT: Seabury, 1958), pp. ii-iii.

42. Ibid., pp. 87-100.

43. *The Book of Offices: Services for Certain Occasions Not Provided in the Book of Common Prayer*, 3rd ed. (New York: Church Pension Fund, 1960), pp. 99-102.

44. Henry Breul, "Paul Dombey's Baptism," *The Anglican*, n.s. 6 (Spring 1976): 20.

45. "For Whitsunday: An Act of Affirmation," *The Southern Churchman*, June 6, 1935, p. 7.

46. "Come Holy Spirit," *The Southern Churchman*, May 30, 1936, p. 3.

47. Barton, "Thoughts on Christian Baptism," p. 213.

48. Richard Upsher Smith, "The Meaning of Whitsunday," *Findings*, May 1958, pp. 12-13.

49. Howard R. Kunkle, "Observing Pentecost in a Parish Church," *Sharers* VII (Late Trinity, 1961), pp. 1-3.

50. Shepherd, *The Living Liturgy*, p. 81.

51. Associated Parishes, *Christian Initiation: Part I—Holy Baptism*, p. 2.

52. H. Boone Porter, "Commemorating Our Lord's Blessed Baptism," *Sharers* V (Fall 1959): 5-7, as summarized in Moriarty, "Associated Parishes," pp. 174-5, n. 168.

53. BCP 1928, pp. 290-1.

54. Shepherd, *The Living Liturgy*, p. 98.

55. Associated Parishes, *The Parish Eucharist*, p. 1.

56. Ibid., p. 12 (emphasis in original).

57. Frank Stephen Cellier, "The Liturgical Movement and the Ministry of the Laity," in Shepherd (ed.), *The Eucharist and Liturgical Renewal*, pp. 87-114.

58. Massey H. Shepherd, *Liturgy and Education* (New York: Seabury, 1965), p. 106. The substance of this book was originally given in the Bradner Lectures, General Seminary, Feb. 1964.

59. Chauncie Kilmer Myers, *Baptized into the One Church* (New York: Seabury, 1963).

Chapter 4

The Dilemma of Confirmation

Changes in baptismal practice were essentially noncontroversial and so were gradually implemented in more and more parishes in the Episcopal Church. But confirmation was a far more perplexing matter. Certainly confirmation was regarded as an important milestone in Christian life. But a chronic problem of postconfirmation lapsing was widely lamented. How might the Episcopal Church best encourage continued commitment by those confirmed? The appropriate age for confirmation was also debated. Should children be confirmed before adolescence, to give them the strengthening grace of the Spirit before the turbulent teen years? Or should the sacrament be deferred until a young person was fully able to make a true commitment?

Underlying such pastoral concerns was the ambiguity inherent in the traditional Anglican confirmation rite. In the late nineteenth century, debate erupted in the Church of England as to the relation of baptism to confirmation. Was confirmation to be understood as a sacramental completion of baptism? Or was it primarily a renewal of baptismal vows, the occasion for personal affirmation of the commitment made on one's behalf in infancy? How was the work of the Holy Spirit to be understood in baptism and in confirmation?

Although these issues were not widely discussed in the Episcopal Church in the United States, the positions that were staked out had some influence on the teaching of leaders of the liturgical movement. Perhaps more importantly, when the time came for prayer book revision, the debate about Christian initiation was a significant factor in shaping radically new rites of baptism and confirmation.

The Meaning of Confirmation in Relation to Baptism

Until the nineteenth century, confirmation was of little significance in the life of the Church. This was true not only in the United States, where the absence of bishops precluded confirmation throughout the colonial period, but also in

England, where confirmation was typically administered perfunctorily with little enthusiasm. But when bishops began in the nineteenth century to administer confirmation with great zeal, theological reflection took on greater significance.[1]

The traditional Anglican confirmation rite served two different though complementary functions. On the one hand, confirmation was understood as a bestowal of the gifts of the Holy Spirit, indicated by inclusion of the prayer for the sevenfold gifts of the Spirit:

> Strengthen them...with the Holy Ghost, the Comforter, and daily increase in them thy manifold gifts of grace: the spirit of wisdom and understanding, the spirit of counsel and ghostly strength, the spirit of knowledge and true godliness; and fill them, O Lord, with the spirit of thy holy fear.

On the other hand, confirmation was an occasion for the renewal of baptismal promises, a personal acceptance of the commitment made by sponsors on behalf of an infant: "Do ye...renew the solemn promise and vow that ye made, or that was made in your name, at your Baptism; ratifying and confirming the same...?"[2] This dual meaning of confirmation was sometimes expressed as "God confirms, and we confirm."

In the latter half of the nineteenth century, attention focused on the nature of the gift of the Spirit bestowed at confirmation. The theologians of the Oxford Movement had been largely silent on the topic of confirmation, perhaps reflecting the low estate of confirmation in England at that time. Later Anglo-Catholic theologians suggested that the indwelling presence of the Spirit was bestowed at baptism while confirmation provided an increase of the gifts of the Spirit.[3] A significant theological shift began in 1880 with the publication by F. W. Puller, vicar of Roath (in Great Britain), of a monograph entitled *What Is the Distinctive Grace of Confirmation?* Puller answered this question by asserting that in confirmation, not in baptism, the indwelling presence of the Spirit was bestowed.[4]

Puller's thesis was given a much fuller exposition by A. J. Mason, former fellow of Trinity College, Cambridge, in *The Relation of Confirmation to Baptism.* Mason argued that confirmation in the New Testament and the early Church was a distinct rite customarily administered in conjunction with baptism. Each sacramental action conferred a distinctive grace: the water of baptism provided cleansing from sin, while the gift of the Holy Spirit was imparted at confirmation. To support his claim, Mason cited Acts 8:14-17 and Acts 19:1-6, passages which describe an imposition of hands that bestows the Spirit subsequent to water baptism. On the basis of these two passages and Hebrews 6:1-2 ("the foundation:...baptisms, laying on of hands..."), Mason asserted that the water bath "was normally accompanied by the imposition of the Apostles' hands, and that the gift of the Holy Spirit is expressly said to be conveyed by the second act and not by the first."[5] Mason supported this argument by citing other passages from the New Testament and by an extensive survey of patristic sources.

The position taken by Puller and Mason was strongly rebutted by A. Theodore Wirgman, rector and vice-provost of St. Mary's Collegiate Church, Port Elizabeth, South Africa. Wirgman maintained that the true Catholic doctrine, that the objective personal indwelling of the Holy Spirit is received in baptism, was set forth in the prayer book. The gifts given in confirmation were gifts with a specific purpose, for "equipping and endowing the members of Christ for the exercise of their royal priesthood" and for strengthening "the soldiers of Christ for their spiritual combat." Thus in the stories in Acts 8 and 19, the persons had received the *indwelling* gift of the Spirit when they were baptized but had not received the *strengthening* gifts of confirmation. Wirgman supported his argument by a thorough survey of scriptural and patristic evidence, in many instances using the same texts as Mason but providing a different interpretation.[6]

Wirgman's conclusions were supported by Darwell Stone, principal of Pusey House, Oxford. Stone found it difficult to comprehend a distinction "between the operation of the Holy Spirit upon the human spirit from outside it and His personal dwelling within it." After reviewing scriptural and patristic evidence, he concluded that "in baptism there is a gift of God the Holy Ghost to the souls of the baptized."[7]

Such effort to determine when and how the Holy Spirit is bestowed may appear to be an esoteric theological argument akin to debating the number of angels able to dance on the head of a pin. Yet for over a century much ink was spilled in Anglicanism, particularly in the Church of England, in an attempt to define the operation of the Spirit in baptism and confirmation. More significantly, Mason's position gave confirmation new significance as an essential sacrament, the second stage in what had been in the early Church an integrated rite of incorporation into the Church. From this perspective, confirmation was the necessary completion of baptism, not simply strengthening the confirmand but imparting gifts not bestowed at baptism.

The issues do not seem to have been widely discussed in the Episcopal Church.[8] The 1892 revision of the prayer book introduced Acts 8:14-17 as an optional reading at confirmation. But it was intended to provide a scriptural warrant for confirmation, not to imply that the Spirit was not bestowed in baptism, as Parsons and Jones observed:

> Our use of this passage is not intended to assert, and in fact *is not understood to convey the idea*, that Baptism is not both a ministration and an impartation of the Spirit, but rather that there are many gifts of the Spirit in divers measures and for different ends; among which this quasi-ordination of laity has real power for their "vocation and ministry."[9]

In contrast to the practice described in Acts 8 and 19, where an apostolic imposition of hands supplements baptism by providing the gift of the Spirit, Parsons and Jones pointed to Acts 9:17-18 and 10:47, where the gift of the Spirit *precedes* baptism, and to Pauline and Johannine passages, e.g., 1 Corinthians 12:13, Ephesians 1:13, and John 3:5, which suggest that the Spirit is given *in* baptism. They concluded:

> while the Church in practice conformed to the custom recorded in the Acts that Baptism should normally be supplemented with "Confirmation," it did not require Confirmation for any of the rights of membership, but in theory aligned it with Ordination, as a particular enabling gift and grace for a sort of lay priesthood.[10]

Parsons and Jones thus contributed to the popular understanding of confirmation as "ordination of the laity," which they portrayed as the distinctive grace bestowed in confirmation.

In England, pastoral issues brought renewed attention to the debate. To address concerns about postconfirmation lapsing as well as the considerable disparity between numbers of children baptized and those coming to confirmation, Joint Committees of the Convocations of Canterbury and York were appointed in 1942. An interim report, *Confirmation Today*, asserted that the Holy Spirit is operative in both baptism and confirmation. The Spirit bestowed at baptism effects redemption and incorporation into the body of Christ, while at confirmation, the ordination of the laity, an increase in the gifts of the Spirit is imparted to commission and strengthen Christians for their ministry. Although recognizing the traditional sequence of baptism, confirmation, communion, the committee suggested that children might be admitted to communion prior to confirmation, or that the laying on of hands could be administered prior to first communion and the ratification of baptismal vows postponed to a later age.[11]

The report engendered renewed debate as to the operation of the Holy Spirit in baptism and confirmation. The Puller/Mason line was adopted by Gregory Dix in a 1946 lecture at the University of Oxford. Dix argued that baptism of water, into the death and resurrection of Christ, and baptism of the Spirit are two distinct events which together constituted a single rite in the New Testament and early Church. The two elements had gradually come to be separated, and the theological content of confirmation shifted to water baptism. Confirmation then came to be understood as an increase of grace. Dix called for a return to the "primitive" understanding of confirmation as the bestowal of the Spirit which completed initiation. While not opposed to the continuation of infant baptism, he emphasized that it is an abnormality, "wholly incomplete by itself and absolutely needing completion by the gift of the Spirit and the conscious response of faith." Thus for those baptized as infants, baptism and confirmation should remain separate in time in order that the conscious response of faith could be made at confirmation.[12]

With the renewed controversy came awareness that the issues extended beyond the question of confirmation. Acknowledging the complexity of the practical and theological issues, Michael Ramsey, then professor of divinity at the University of Durham, called for a broadening of the discussion:

> Neither the practical nor the doctrinal problems of the two rites [i.e., baptism and confirmation] can be solved in separation.... What is now vital is that the discussion of the two rites should be drawn together, on both the practical and the doctrinal levels, and that there should be in the Church *a theological study of Christian initiation as a whole*, a study properly theological and yet enriched by considerations of pastoral experience.[13]

Ramsey's recommendation is evidence of a shift to the more comprehensive topic of "Christian initiation." While this shift cannot be attributed to Ramsey alone, his proposal was a harbinger of the future shape of the debate.

In 1946 a Theological Commission was appointed to consider the theology of baptism and confirmation and in light of their conclusions to consider possible variations in the administration of these rites. Although Dix was a member of the commission, the report rejected his distinction between baptism in water and baptism in the Holy Spirit. At the same time, the report emphasized the necessity of both laying on of hands and personal response in Christian initiation. Admission to communion before confirmation would obscure the initiatory aspect of confirmation; the separation of vows from the imposition of hands would eliminate the essential link between baptism and confirmation in Anglican practice. Hence the proposals in *Confirmation Today* to alter the initiatory sequence were rejected.[14]

The questions addressed in the report were taken up by the 1948 Lambeth Conference. Although the Lambeth report was entitled "Baptism and Confirmation," the term "Christian initiation" was frequently employed. Drawing upon the work of the Theological Commission, the Lambeth report asserted that full Christian initiation includes baptism, confirmation and admission to communion; that the activity of the Spirit cannot and must not be dissociated from any part of Christian initiation; and that personal response is an essential component of confirmation. The resolutions of the conference upheld the traditional sequence of baptism, confirmation, admission to communion, and suggested that opportunities be given for periodic reaffirmation of vows by those confirmed.[15]

Although these reports did not adopt the extreme position of Dix that the Spirit is not bestowed in any manner at baptism, they nevertheless viewed baptism and confirmation as successive stages of Christian initiation. A quite different interpretation of the patristic evidence was presented in 1951 by Geoffrey Lampe, professor of divinity at Cambridge University, in *The Seal of the Spirit*. Finding no evidence for Dix's distinction between water-baptism and Spirit-baptism, Lampe argued that the "seal of the Spirit" in the New Testament and in patristic writers was properly understood as one aspect of water baptism. The passages in Acts (8:14-17 and 19:1-6), usually interpreted as descriptions of a distinct rite of confirmation, were said by Lampe to describe not an initiatory bestowal of the Spirit, but rather a symbol of fellowship and solidarity with the Christian community and its apostolic mission.[16]

According to Lampe, as the baptismal rite became increasingly complex in the patristic Church, there was a gradual disintegration of the primitive doctrine of the seal of the Spirit. The gift of the Spirit came to be associated variously with the water-baptism, the pre- or postbaptismal anointing, and the imposition of hands. When the initiatory rite began to break into two parts, the consignation and imposition of hands acquired an independent meaning. A doctrine of confirmation developed to rationalize the division of the rite of initiation, and the initial gift of the Spirit was assigned to baptism while confirmation was understood as a gift of the Spirit for strengthening.[17]

Lampe concluded that the indwelling of the Spirit is "one aspect of the sharing of the resurrection life of Christ which is begun in baptism." For those baptized as infants, confirmation provides a "fuller realization and actualizing of what has already been given and undertaken proleptically." A person baptized as an adult "receives [in confirmation] the blessing of God through the representative leader of the Church and is commissioned for service in the Church's spiritual warfare." Confirmation is thus valuable for adult initiates, although it loses much of its force when separated from their baptism.[18]

In response to Lampe, Lionel Thornton defended confirmation as an essential aspect of the baptismal mystery. Claiming that Lampe's interpretation of scripture was faulty, he found evidence that initiation includes two crucial moments, baptism in water and a ceremony of anointing and consignation. Although the Spirit is the creative agent of all that is effected in baptism, the indwelling gift of the Spirit is reserved to the second stage of initiation. Through this anointing with the Spirit, now known as confirmation, Christians come to share in the fulfillment of Christ's mission.[19]

The ongoing debate was reflected in *Baptism and Confirmation Today*, the final report of the Church of England Joint Committees on Baptism, Confirmation, and Holy Communion. The majority report, following Lampe, found no distinction in the New Testament between water baptism and Spirit baptism. In contemporary practice confirmation imparts divine strength and additional gifts of the Spirit. Contrary to the interim report *Confirmation Today*, the final report maintained that confirmation should not be called the "ordination of the laity," since "baptism makes us all partakers of the corporate priesthood of the Church, the *laos*."[20] The minority report, signed by T. G. Jalland, R. O'Gorman, and J. D. C. Fisher, closely followed the Mason/Dix line: the original apostolic pattern of Christian initiation included the remission of sins through baptismal washing; the gift of the Spirit through imposition of hands, anointing, and consignation; and participation in communion.[21]

The reports and surrounding theological controversy in England attracted little attention in the United States.[22] However, a two-stage process of initiation is evident in the Associated Parishes pamphlets entitled *Christian Initiation: Part I—Holy Baptism* and *Christian Initiation: Part II—Confirmation*. The pamphlet on baptism avoided the extremes of the Mason/Dix line by stating clearly that the Holy Spirit is given in baptism.[23] But this clarity was lacking in the pamphlet on confirmation, which identified the gifts of baptism as forgiveness of sins and incorporation into the body of Christ but spoke of the gifts of the Spirit only in association with confirmation. These were described as "strengthening" gifts of the Spirit, but nowhere was there an indication of the Spirit having been bestowed at baptism.[24] This had the advantage of justifying stages of initiation, first forgiveness of sins and incorporation through baptism, then the ratification of baptismal vows and the blessing of the Spirit in confirmation, and finally admission to communion. But it did not explain how baptism could convey the gift of the Spirit and membership in the Church while not being full initiation into the Church.

Postconfirmation Lapsing

While scholars explored the meaning and practice of initiation in Christian history and debate raged in England as to the relation of confirmation to baptism, attention in the Episcopal Church was focused on concern about the loss of confirmed persons from active membership. In response to concerns voiced to the 1925 General Convention about postconfirmation lapsing, the House of Bishops had appointed a committee to study the cause and prevention of communicant losses. Noting that 20,000 to 40,000 communicants were lost each year by removal from Episcopal Church records, the report to the 1928 General Convention recommended renewed emphasis on pastoral care, more careful regard for letters of transfer, more thorough confirmation instruction, and a reawakening of the Church's call to evangelism.[25] Nine years later, a report from a laymen's commission in the Diocese of Colorado found that the Episcopal Church each year was losing the equivalent of forty-two percent of those confirmed. Claiming that "the greatest weakness of the Church today (both locally and nationally) is the loss on account of lapsed communicants," the commission recommended actions similar to those proposed to the 1928 General Convention, including "more complete and thorough instruction for confirmation."[26]

A call for better confirmation preparation was repeated for several decades. However, there was no consensus as to the content or length of that preparation. For example, a 1929 article by a parish priest recommended that one of the chief means to bring people back into active membership should be "confirmation, preceded by thorough preparation." Preparation required not only instruction in the faith, but even more importantly, the "inculcation of pious habits."[27] In contrast, the author of a manual for confirmation instruction emphasized the teaching of facts about the Church.[28]

Several writers argued that preparation should emphasize to the candidates the importance of worship. D. Robert Bailey, a parish priest from Massachusetts, commented in 1930: "Confirmation too often serves as an opportunity to break with the church school without understanding the real significance of confirmation or having an adequate idea of the church services." Apparently children spent most of their time in Sunday school and began regular attendance at worship only after they had been confirmed. Bailey argued that children ought to be firmly established in the worship of the Church, making Christian education secondary to worship.[29]

A similar approach was advocated in 1938 by Lane Barton, then a parish priest. Observing that "many of those who are eager to be confirmed are not in the habit of attending church," he urged that attendance at worship be made integral to confirmation preparation.[30] A few years later, Barton reported on his efforts to prevent postconfirmation lapsing. He found some value in intensifying instruction, encouraging attendance at worship and teaching individuals how to compose their own prayers. Recognizing that no single remedy prevented lapses, he suggested that the primary goal of improved preparation should be "to make stronger, more effective disciples for Christ."[31]

The problem continued. A 1947 review of a curriculum for confirmation acknowledged disagreement as to the educational method and length of instruction and noted a recent trend to include confirmation instruction as a one-year course in the regular curriculum of the Sunday school, taught by a competent lay teacher with occasional assistance from clergy.[32] In contrast, a committee of clergy and laity in the Diocese of Michigan prepared a workbook for clergy to use in training young candidates for confirmation.[33]

The wide variation in preparation was evident in responses to a survey conducted in 1960 by the national Episcopal Church Department of Christian Education. Confirmation classes met from four to forty times. With regard to the materials used, the report noted, "no one confirmation manual, reader, or workbook has found general acceptance throughout the Episcopal Church for use with confirmation classes." Over half the clergy who responded had developed their own course of instruction.[34]

A variety of suggestions for preparation were included in *Confirmation: History, Doctrine, and Practice*,[35] edited by Kendig Brubaker Cully, professor of religious education at Seabury-Western Theological Seminary. Cully stated in the preface that recent changes in educational methods necessitated a review of approaches to confirmation instruction. Articles by different contributors, all from the Episcopal Church, discussed classes for children and for adults, methodology, curriculum materials, and the role of clergy and of laity. The collection also included several articles discussing the history and doctrine of confirmation, notably an article by Lampe explaining the errors of the Mason/Dix/Thornton school. Although the historical and theological material might provide insight into the nature of confirmation, a reviewer commented that the section addressing practical concerns would be most popular among clergy because "it provides information that is widely sought."[36]

To reduce lapsing, questions were raised about the appropriate age for confirmation. In a 1941 article, Cyril Richardson, professor at Union Theological Seminary, pointed to objections that adolescence, that is, ages thirteen to fifteen, is a psychologically unsuitable age for making the commitment required by confirmation. He observed two types of recommendations: either to delay instruction and the profession of baptismal vows to a later age, or else to administer the rite at the age of ten and adapt the teaching accordingly. Richardson concluded that the imposition of hands and chrismation, which he identified as confirmation, should be restored to baptism and a rite should be developed for the profession of faith at the age of discretion, although he did not specify what that age should be.[37] Richardson's article had no noticeable impact in the Episcopal Church.

A few years later Shepherd addressed the question in his column in *The Witness*. Raising the age for confirmation would permit a more mature decision by the confirmand and hence would be more lasting. Lowering the age to seven or eight would permit children to receive the strengthening of sacramental grace through the turbulent period of adolescence. Shepherd reached no conclusion, suggesting only that the vast differences in children's aptitude and temperament made it unwise to generalize.[38]

A 1954 survey in the Diocese of California found wide variation between parishes in the minimum age for confirmation.[39] The same diversity was found in a 1960 survey by the national Department of Christian Education: the age of confirmation ranged from eight to sixteen, the average age being twelve. As Shepherd had observed and as Bradner had noted in 1920, those who desired confirmation at an early age stressed the sacramental grace bestowed in confirmation, while clergy recommending a later age emphasized the need for maturity when making a personal commitment at confirmation.[40]

A system of sponsorship was suggested as a means of giving more personal attention to confirmands and so preventing lapsing. A parish priest reported to *The Churchman* in 1934 that he had begun asking for a sponsor, preferably one of the godparents from baptism, to accompany each confirmand at the confirmation service. His intent was to encourage laity to take seriously their promise to see that the child they presented for baptism was brought to confirmation.[41] In 1943 *The Living Church* reported that John Hines, then rector of Christ Church in Houston, Texas, had begun to appoint a sponsor for each new confirmand "in an effort to cement the new communicants more closely to the life of the parish and to prevent the drain of communicant strength which national and parochial statistics indicate is a major loss."[42] A similar proposal was made by Roswell Moore, rector of Christ Church in Exeter, New Hampshire, in an article included in Cully's 1962 book on confirmation. Moore recommended that godparents sit with their godchildren at the confirmation service and stand behind them when they came forward to the bishop. Additionally, sponsors could keep in touch with confirmands after the confirmation and encourage the newly confirmed to take their place in the congregation.[43]

Another means proposed to address lapsing was improved pastoral care. In 1946 the rector of a large parish observed that members of confirmation classes frequently drifted away after the period of instruction. He urged the use of personal consultations by the rector with each confirmand during the months following instruction and confirmation. These consultations, as he practiced them, were informal, to continue encouragement and instruction in the faith.[44] Other writers stressed that confirmation must be seen as a beginning, not an end. One suggestion was to give greater attention to preparation for reception of communion.[45] Another recommendation was to continue classes appropriate for adolescents.[46]

Similar advice was given by Roswell Moore, who noted that follow-up to confirmation "is certainly the weakest of all present efforts in the Episcopal Church."[47] Cully urged that the entire congregation accept responsibility for the continuing nurture of the newly confirmed, including incorporation into the life of the parish and ministry to the world.[48] A 1962 article in *Findings* stated that "young people must be made to see that confirmation, though an important milestone, is not the destination." The Church should help those confirmed to grow in their personal devotion, understand the relevance of the Gospel to their daily lives, and participate in service to the world.[49]

There were occasional reports of bishops' efforts to address the problem of lapsing. A 1938 article reported that Eugene Seaman, Bishop of North Texas, had instituted a program of calling the roll of all those he had confirmed during his fourteen-year tenure. His method was to send a postcard to each parishioner, using a list checked by the rector. After the service, members of the congregation were asked to provide information about all those who did not respond to their name. A high percentage of response was reported, even though the diocese had a highly mobile population.[50] In another diocese the bishop asked those confirmed during the previous year to attend and sit together as a body "so that he may again meet them and enquire as to their progress and loyalty to the church."[51]

Clinton Quin, Bishop of Texas, had several recommendations: a presentation, given by lay people during confirmation instruction, on the subject of membership transfers; a "membership audit" committee responsible for the lost and strayed in each parish; a diocesan officer charged with pastoral care of "the isolated"; and a diocesan list of the "lapsed and lost" for the bishop's review and action. Quin did not report the success of his program in reducing communicant loss.[52]

In 1958 Horace Donegan, Bishop of New York, attributed the problem of lapsed communicants to inadequate instruction and lack of follow-through and interest on the part of the congregation. To seek remedies, he appointed a diocesan commission on confirmation preparation. The commission's report emphasized "allegiance," the act of commitment to God and the Church. Instead of mastery of factual data, preparation should elicit personal response and commitment to Christ, and concern for the Christian community. The report made no specific recommendation for the age of confirmation but presented several outlines, each appropriate for a different age.[53]

In these various attempts to address the problem of postconfirmation lapsing, emphasis was placed upon the human response made at confirmation, whether by better preparing candidates for confirmation, introducing a system of sponsorship, or improving methods of follow-up. Only in discussions of the appropriate age for confirmation was there significant attention given to the action of God in confirmation, that is, the bestowal of sacramental grace. For the Episcopal Church's children, confirmation was treated primarily as a rite requiring their active commitment to Christ and only secondarily as a bestowal of sacramental grace.

Affiliation with the Episcopal Church

Although confirmation was commonly viewed as an adolescent rite of affirmation of baptismal vows and strengthening with the Holy Spirit, it was also used in some cases to receive non-Episcopalians into the communion of the Episcopal Church. The confirmation rubric mandated confirmation as a prerequisite to communion. However, this was not always interpreted to mean the Episcopal Church rite of confirmation, since many adults seeking admission to the Episcopal Church had already been confirmed in another denomination.

In 1936 the House of Bishops, noting great diversity in the manner of receiving Christians confirmed in other communions, unanimously authorized the appointment of a committee to study the Episcopal Church's understanding and practice of confirmation. The theological discussion in the report, presented to the House of Bishops one year later, reflected the contemporary theological discussion. Citing Acts 8:14-17, Acts 19:1-7 and Hebrews 6:1-2 as the scriptural warrant for confirmation, the report asserted, "from apostolic times confirmation has been understood to be the completion of baptism and an instrument for the conveying of special gifts of the Holy Spirit." Confirmation was "a kind of lesser ordination to the 'priesthood of the laity,'" and the administration of confirmation was the prerogative of the bishop. While acknowledging variations outside the Anglican Communion as to the minister authorized to preside, the method of administration, and the age of the recipient, the report upheld for the Episcopal Church the requirement that the rite be administered by a bishop and the necessity of confirmation prior to admission to communion. The bishops agreed that persons who had been confirmed in the Roman Catholic Church, the Eastern Orthodox Church, the Old Catholic Church (e.g., the Polish National Church), and the Reformed Episcopal Church could be received into the communion of the Episcopal Church without additional laying on of hands. Persons confirmed in other communions "where the historic episcopate does not obtain" were expected to receive confirmation at the hands of a bishop in the Episcopal Church if they desired to become a communicant therein.[54]

According to the bishops' resolution, the primary criterion for acceptance of confirmation administered in another denomination was episcopacy, specifically bishops in churches which claim apostolic succession. The crucial dimension of confirmation in this context is the sacramental bestowal of the Spirit. The reaffirmation of baptismal vows could even be entirely lacking for persons baptized in the Eastern Orthodox Church. Individuals baptized as infants in an Orthodox Church would not necessarily have made any formal affirmation of their faith, since the Orthodox practice of presbyteral chrismation using episcopally blessed chrism at baptism was considered by the Episcopal Church to be the equivalent of confirmation.

Despite the bishops' agreement, practice was not uniform and confusion continued, as is evident in a 1950 issue of *The Living Church*. Addressing questions from laity regarding confirmation and reception into the Episcopal Church, a columnist explained that persons coming from the Orthodox Church were received and not reconfirmed because they were confirmed at the time of baptism. Likewise, those who had been confirmed in the Roman Catholic Church were received and not reconfirmed. However, those from the Lutheran and Presbyterian traditions, even if they had been confirmed in one of those churches, were required to be confirmed if they wished to become communicants in the Episcopal Church since they had not been confirmed in the Catholic faith.[55] The answers indicate that the pertinent aspect of confirmation is the bestowal of the Holy Spirit through imposition of hands by a bishop. The questions reflect bewilderment caused by the inconsistency of accepting confirmation administered in some denominations but not others.

Further confusion arose when the bishops acted in contradiction to the policy adopted in 1937. A 1950 study of "conversions" from Roman Catholicism found that some bishops were confirming in the usual manner persons who had already been confirmed by a Roman Catholic bishop. Some of the bishops interviewed indicated that "converts" from Roman Catholicism were requesting confirmation.[56] Used in this way, confirmation functioned not only as a bestowal of the Holy Spirit and a ratification of baptismal vows but also as a disciplinary rite of affiliation with the Episcopal Church.

An editorial comment in *The Living Church* a few years later lends support to this interpretation. A footnote in an article had stated that baptism was the only means of receiving people into the Church, although confirmation added some emphasis to an adult's entry from another tradition. In response to criticism that this understated the meaning of confirmation, the editor explained that the purpose of the comment had been "to correct the misconception, based on the analogy of the public profession of faith used in the Reformed Churches, that Confirmation is a rite for making non-Episcopalians into Episcopalians."[57] It is apparent from the editor's comment that people were indeed viewing confirmation as a rite of entry into the Episcopal Church.

As an alternative to the use of confirmation to mark entry into the Episcopal Church, several rites were developed to receive persons whose confirmations were recognized by the Episcopal Church. At their 1935 meeting, the House of Bishops adopted a suggested liturgical form for the reception of persons already confirmed. Since a number of bishops objected to the use of imposition of hands with the sign of the cross because of its primary significance in connection with baptism, the form recommended that the reception be effected by taking the right hand of the candidate (the biblical precedent being Galatians 2:9, "when James and Cephas and John...recognized the grace that had been given to me [Paul], they gave to Barnabas and me the right hand of fellowship"). This action would be preceded by two brief questions regarding the person's previous confirmation and desire to be received into the communion of the Episcopal Church.[58]

Since the House of Bishops declined to mandate this form for reception of those confirmed in other branches of the Catholic Church, a variety of customs continued. Provisions for admission to communion in the Episcopal Church appeared in *A Manual for Priests*, an unofficial handbook published by the Society of St. John the Evangelist in 1944. The rubrics reflect the diversity of practice in the Episcopal Church: local or diocesan custom should dictate whether there should be a formal ceremony of reception; persons who had shared in confirmation preparation could be blessed by the bishop and admitted to communion, "but it should be made clear that the Sacrament of Confirmation is not being repeated." A service of reception to be administered by the parish priest or another priest designated by the bishop was also provided. In addition to a formula of reception, it included several questions addressed to the candidates as well as prayers. The only action indicated was the sign of the cross at the invocation of the Trinity; it is likely that this was a gesture made over or in front of the candidate without actually touching the candidate.[59]

A simpler rite of admission to communion appeared in the second edition of *The Book of Offices*, published in 1949. Although commended for use by the General Convention, its provisions were not mandatory. The rite was similar to that recommended by the bishops in 1935: two brief questions were addressed by the bishop to the candidates, after which the bishop took each person's right hand and said a formula of admission to communion. The rite could take place either at a service of confirmation or as a separate office. It was to be used only for persons confirmed in another part of the "holy Catholic Church," that is, in a denomination where the historic episcopacy obtained.[60] For those not so confirmed, confirmation continued to serve as the rite of affiliation with the Episcopal Church.

The Meaning and Purpose of Confirmation

The wide discrepancies in practice reflect multiple and sometimes conflicting meanings of confirmation. The role of the bishop and the bestowal of the Holy Spirit were the operative factors in determining who could be received into the Episcopal Church without being confirmed by a bishop of the Episcopal Church. Persons already confirmed "by a bishop in apostolic succession" were not required to make the formal public ratification of their baptismal vows that was part of the rite of confirmation. In the eyes of the Episcopal Church, they had received the grace of confirmation and nothing further need be supplied.

But persons entering the Episcopal Church from denominations without the historic episcopate were required to participate in the full Episcopal Church rite of confirmation. Although those who had been confirmed in a denomination such as the Lutheran Church would have made a public profession of faith, they were required to make yet another ratification of their baptismal promises in order to receive episcopal imposition of hands and thereby receive the distinctive grace of confirmation. Such persons would thus make a mature affirmation of faith on at least two separate occasions.

The practice of confirming "Protestants" who had already been confirmed in their former denomination served to make confirmation a rite of reception into the Episcopal Church. This perception was underscored by the inclusion in confirmation classes of non-Episcopalians seeking reception (including those coming from churches with the historic episcopate), a practice serving to equate the requirements for membership with the requirements for confirmation.

The official stance with regard to baptized persons seeking to affiliate with the Episcopal Church was to determine whether the person had received the strengthening gifts of the Spirit associated with confirmation. But with regard to the Church's own children, emphasis was placed upon the ratification of baptismal vows at confirmation. To deal with the problem of postconfirmation lapsing, better preparation and/or aftercare was recommended, an approach that stresses human commitment much more than divine empowerment by the Spirit.

Even those who viewed confirmation primarily as a bestowal of sacramental grace and thus preferred confirmation at an early age considered preparation to be important. The report of the 1960 survey by the Department of Christian Education stated that clergy desiring early confirmation not only stressed the need of sacramental grace as early as possible but also pointed to "the ability to memorize and the willingness to study before the distractions of high school set in."[61] An article discussing the age for confirmation recommended pre-adolescence, with proper preparation, and then concluded, "our guiding consideration must be how best to bring the individual, at any stage in life, to that life in God, through Jesus the Lord, in his Body the Church."[62] The implication is that confirmation includes not only a sacramental bestowal of grace but also human response to God.

As the Episcopal Church approached prayer book revision in the 1960s, there was no clear consensus about the meaning of confirmation. The rite included both a ratification of baptismal vows and prayer for the gifts of the Spirit with imposition of hands by a bishop, but these two dimensions were given different weight by different people and in different situations. In addition, confirmation came to function as a rite of affiliation with the Episcopal Church. Further complicating the picture was the confirmation rubric with its requirement of confirmation before admission to communion.

NOTES

1. S. L. Ollard, "Confirmation in the Anglican Communion," in *Confirmation or the Laying on of Hands*, Vol. I: *Historical and Doctrinal* (London: SPCK, 1926), pp. 60-203, especially pp. 212-22; Peter J. Jagger, *Clouded Witness: Initiation in the Church of England in the Mid-Victorian Period, 1850-1875* (Allison Park, PA: Pickwick Publications, 1982), pp. 101-8, 148-66.

2. BCP 1928, pp. 296-7.

3. "Primitive Teaching on Confirmation and Its Relation to Holy Baptism," *Church Quarterly Review* 34 (1892): 2-5; "The Relation of Confirmation to Baptism," *CQR* 45 (1898): 357-8.

4. F. W. Puller, *What Is the Distinctive Grace of Confirmation?* A Paper Read before the Chapter of the South-Eastern Division of the Upper Llandaff Rural Deanery (London, 1880).

5. Arthur James Mason, *The Relation of Confirmation to Baptism as Taught in Holy Scripture and the Fathers* (New York: E. P. Dutton, 1891), p. 34.

6. A. Theodore Wirgman, *The Doctrine of Confirmation Considered in Relation to Holy Baptism as a Sacramental Ordinance of the Catholic Church; with a Preliminary Historical Survey of the Doctrine of the Holy Spirit* (London: Longmans, Green and Co., 1897), especially pp. 63-6.

7. Darwell Stone, *Holy Baptism* (London: Longmans, Green, and Co., 1899), pp. 67-82.

8. Samuel Hart, *The Book of Common Prayer* (Sewanee, TN: University Press, 1910), the standard American textbook prior to Parsons and Jones, includes both Mason and Wirgman in a short bibliography on confirmation. Confirmation is described as a bestowal of the Spirit, but there is no mention of the relation of this gift of the Spirit to baptism.

9. Parsons and Jones, *The American Prayer Book*, p. 245, n. 36 (emphasis added).

10. Ibid., p. 224.

11. Convocations of Canterbury and York, *Confirmation Today: Being the Schedule attached to the Interim Reports of the Joint Committees on Confirmation, setting forth certain major issues before the Church, as presented to the Convocations of Canterbury and York in October, 1944* (London: Press and Publications Board of the Church Assembly, 1944). For further discussion of the concerns in the Church of England, see J. B. M. Frederick, "The Initiation Crisis in the Church of England," *Studia Liturgica* 9 (1973): 137-57; Dale Moody, *Baptism: Foundation for Christian Unity* (Philadelphia: Westminster, 1967), pp. 162-216.

12. Gregory Dix, *The Theology of Confirmation in Relation to Baptism: A Public Lecture in the University of Oxford delivered on January 22nd 1946* (Westminster: Dacre Press, 1946), pp. 30-1.

13. A. Michael Ramsey, "The Doctrine of Confirmation," *Theology* 48 (1945): 200 (emphasis in original).

14. *The Theology of Christian Initiation: Being the Report of a Theological Commission appointed by the Archbishops of Canterbury and York to advise on the relations between Baptism, Confirmation and Holy Communion* (London: SPCK, 1949).

15. The Lambeth Conference 1948, *The Encyclical Letter from the Bishops; together with Resolutions and Reports* (London: SPCK, 1948), Part I, pp. 50-2; Part II, pp. 106-10, 115-17.

16. Geoffrey W. H. Lampe, *The Seal of the Spirit: A Study in the Doctrine of Baptism and Confirmation in the New Testament and the Fathers* (London: Longmans, Green, and Co., 1951; 2nd ed., London: SPCK, 1967), pp. 3-93.

17. Ibid., pp. 97-231, 308-10.

18. Ibid., p. 318-21.

19. Lionel S. Thornton, *Confirmation: Its Place in the Baptismal Mystery* (Westminster: Dacre Press, 1954).

20. Convocations of Canterbury and York, *Baptism and Confirmation Today: Being the Schedule attached to the Final Reports of the Joint Committees on Baptism, Confirmation, and Holy Communion, as presented to the Convocations of Canterbury and York in October, 1954* (London: SPCK, 1955), p. 44.

21. *The Schedule Presented by Three Members of the Canterbury Joint Committee and Entitled by Them "Baptism, Confirmation, and Communion (Christian Initiation Today),"* appended to *Baptism and Confirmation Today*.

22. Arthur Vogel, professor of theology at Nashotah House, observed that "American theologians have been conspicuous by their absence from public discussion of the problematic issues involved": "Note on the Gifts in Baptism and Confirmation," *Anglican Theological Review* 38 (1956): 276.

23. *Christian Initiation: Part I*, p. 2.

24. *Christian Initiation: Part II*, especially pp. 1, 2, 9, 12-13.

25. *Journal of the General Convention*, 1928, pp. 77-9.

26. "Trends in Church Membership Studied: Laymen's Commission Makes Report," *The Southern Churchman*, Dec. 4, 1937, p. 12.

27. Harold G. Willis, "Where Do We Go From Here?", *The Living Church*, Dec. 7, 1929, pp. 193-5.

28. Daniel Arthur McGregor, review of A. G. O. Pfaffko, *Catechetical Outline of Confirmation Instructions* (Milwaukee: Morehouse, 1931), in *Anglican Theological Review* 14 (1932): 108.

29. D. Robert Bailey, "Where Is the Leakage?", *The Living Church*, July 19, 1930, pp. 403-4.

30. Lane Barton, "The Parson's Lost Sheep," *The Witness*, May 12, 1938, pp. 6-7.

31. Lane W. Barton, "Lapsed Communicants Problem Is Faced by Parish," *The Witness*, Oct. 26, 1944, pp. 5-6.

32. Review of Vernon C. McMaster, *I Prepare for Confirmation*, revised ed. (Louisville: Cloister Press, 1946), in *Anglican Theological Review* 29 (1947): 56.

33. "P. E. Confirmation Workbook," *The Churchman*, Mar. 1, 1950, p. 27.

34. Edric A. Weld, "The Church Reports on Confirmation Instruction," *Findings*, Oct. 1960, p. 10.

35. Greenwich, CT: Seabury Press, 1962.

36. Charles E. Batten, review of Cully (ed.), *Confirmation*, in *Findings*, June 1962, p. 21.

37. Cyril C. Richardson, "What Is Confirmation?", *Anglican Theological Review* 32 (1941): 224-30.

38. Massey Shepherd, "The Living Liturgy: The Age of Confirmation," *The Witness*, Apr. 15, 1948, p. 9.

39. "Confirmation Practices Vary Widely in California," *The Witness*, Apr. 1, 1954, p. 6.

40. Edric A. Weld, "The Church Reports on Confirmation Instruction," *Findings*, Oct. 1960, pp. 10-11.

41. Thomas E. Jessett, letter to the editor, *The Churchman*, July 15, 1934, p. 3.

42. "Confirmation Sponsors," *The Living Church*, June 20, 1943, p. 20.

43. Roswell O. Moore, "The Role of Laymen in Teaching and Follow-Up," in Cully (ed.), *Confirmation*, pp. 195-6.

44. John Heuss, "Following Up Confirmation," *The Living Church*, June 9, 1946, pp. 18-19.

45. Martha C. Pray, "Defend, O Lord, This Thy Child," *The Southern Churchman*, Mar. 24, 1945, p. 8.

46. Dora Chaplin, "After Confirmation—What?", *Episcopal Churchnews*, Nov. 13, 1955, pp. 40, 44.

47. Moore, "The Role of Laymen," in Cully (ed.), *Confirmation*, p. 196.

48. Kendig Brubaker Cully, "Membership Instruction as Continuing Nurture," in Cully (ed.), *Confirmation*, pp. 200-5.

49. Chad Walsh, "Confirmation of Children and Youth," *Findings*, May 1962, p. 10.

50. "Bishop Seaman Calling Roll of Fourteen Years' Confirmations," *The Living Church*, Oct. 5, 1938, p. 330.

51. "A Good Plan," *The Living Church*, Feb. 2, 1938, p. 128.

52. Clinton S. Quin, "Where Are the Lost?", *The Witness*, Sept. 30, 1943, pp. 10-11.

53. *Ready and Desirous: Being the Report of the Commission on the Preparation for Confirmation of the Diocese of New York 1958-1962* (New York: Morehouse-Barlow, 1962).

54. "Confirmation," report of House of Bishops Committee on Confirmation, presented to the House of Bishops at General Convention, Oct. 8, 1937, Record Group 122, Archives of the Episcopal Church, Austin, TX. This report was omitted from the 1937 *Journal of the General Convention*.

55. "The Question Box," *The Living Church*, May 7, 1950, p. 6.

56. Frank L. Carruthers and S. Harrington Littell, "Conversions from Roman Catholicism," *The Living Church*, Sept. 17, 1950, p. 11.

57. "Editor's Comment," *The Living Church*, Apr. 23, 1953, p. 4.

58. "Special Meeting of the House of Bishops," November 1935, in *Journal of the General Convention*, 1937, pp. 63-5.

59. *A Manual for Priests of the American Church, Complementary to the Occasional Offices of the Book of Common Prayer* (Cambridge, MA: Society of St. John the Evangelist, 1944), pp. 27-9.

60. *The Book of Offices*, 2nd ed. (New York: Church Pension Fund, 1949), pp. 1-2.

61. Edric A. Weld, "The Church Reports on Confirmation Instruction," *Findings*, Oct. 1960, p. 11.

62. James Joseph, "At What Age Should Children Be Confirmed?", in Cully (ed.), *Confirmation*, pp. 124-5.

Chapter 5

Admission to Communion

As long as confirmation was not widely administered, the confirmation rubric ("And there shall none be admitted to the Holy Communion, until such time as he be confirmed, or be ready and desirous to be confirmed"[1]) had no real force in the lives of Episcopalians. No doubt being "ready and desirous to be confirmed" satisfied the intent of the rubric for generations of Anglicans, throughout the colonial years when there were no bishops and in the early years of the nascent Episcopal Church when dioceses were large, travel difficult, and access to confirmation almost as restricted as it had been during the colonial period. The extent to which the confirmation rubric was noticed cannot be known, that is, whether there was any requisite preparation or other measure to determine when a person was ready and desirous to be confirmed. Regardless, the vast majority of persons received communion without having first been confirmed. The exception permitted by rubric became the norm.

The situation was reversed during the nineteenth century as confirmation became widely available. Once confirmation became normative and its sacramental dimension emphasized by Anglo-Catholics, the confirmation rubric took on greater importance. It was applied to children baptized in the Episcopal Church, and some argued that it should also apply to those of other denominations wishing to receive communion in the Episcopal Church. During the twentieth century, each of these positions came under attack, the latter as a result of the ecumenical movement and the former in response to concerns about confirmation and changes introduced by the liturgical movement.

Ecumenism and Admission to Communion

Until the latter half of the nineteenth century, a practice of "occasional conformity" was widely accepted in England. Members of dissenting church bodies were welcomed on occasion at communion for two primary reasons: a desire to maintain communion with the established church and political necessity, namely the requirement for all office holders in England to receive communion in the Church of England. But beginning in the 1870s the confirmation rubric was enforced with more vigor. Owing largely to the Anglo-Catholic movement, confirmation came to be viewed as an absolute requirement for admission to communion, and in England occasional conformity all but disappeared.[2]

The situation in the United States was similar, with "spiritual need" being the principal reason for members of other church bodies to receive communion in the Episcopal Church. Even when the confirmation rubric came to be more rigorously applied, the English practice of occasional conformity was recognized by some as an appropriate precedent. Parsons and Jones opined:

> Properly speaking, this rubric has no bearing on the practice of what was known in England as "occasional conformity"; it defines admission to the full and permanent privileges of the *status* of a communicant in the Church.[3]

Others were less lenient. As the ecumenical movement gathered momentum, with a growing desire for intercommunion on at least some occasions, debate raged as to the proper interpretation of the confirmation rubric.

In the decade following the 1927 World Conference on Faith and Order, at Lausanne, Switzerland, there was much enthusiasm for immediate church union, including intercommunion. At the 1930 Lambeth Conference, the Anglican bishops discussed the question of intercommunion in light of the Lausanne Conference. The general principle established was that intercommunion should be seen as the goal of union rather than a means to union. Bishops could permit exceptions in areas "where the ministrations of an Anglican Church are not available for long periods of time or without traveling great distances." A bishop could also authorize baptized communicant members of other churches to receive communion in Anglican churches "when the ministrations of their own Church are not available, or in other special or temporary circumstances."[4]

At the conclusion of the World Conference on Christian Life and Work, held in Oxford, England, in summer 1937, the Archbishop of Canterbury, Cosmo Gordon Lang, presided at a eucharist and invited all baptized Christians to receive communion. The explanation provided was that such "exceptional services" at conferences working toward Christian unity were permitted by resolutions of the Lambeth Conference and the Convocation of Canterbury.[5] The archbishop's interpretation of the Lambeth resolution was disputed by Frank Wilson, Bishop of Eau Claire, Wisconsin, who had been present at the Lambeth Conference and participated in the discussion. In his column in *The Witness*, Wilson presented his recollection of the Lambeth resolutions: that exceptions to the confirmation rubric were permissible under extraordinary circumstances in the mission field, not at interdenominational conferences.[6]

In the wake of the archbishop's action, debate about interpretation of the confirmation rubric came to the fore. Numerous articles, editorials and letters to the editor appeared in popular Episcopal Church periodicals. Other services with open communion were reported. Petitions from opposing camps were circulated and presented to the House of Bishops. In May 1938 a convention of Liberal Evangelicals, numbering about 100 and claiming to represent 1,000 clergy, unanimously adopted the following resolution:

> Resolved, that, in our judgment, the rubric at the close of the confirmation office is a disciplinary rule, intended solely to apply to members of the Anglican Communion, and having no reference whatsoever to the occasional reception of the Holy Communion by baptized members of other Christian bodies who come as guests to what is not "Our Table" but the Table of the Lord.
>
> The admission of these guests is to be regarded as fully warranted historically, as in accord with the liberality of the Anglican tradition, as approved by the overwhelming majority of our people, and as avoiding a legalism which would reduce the catholicity of this church. Moreover, it is in accordance with the spirit of what our Lord said when His disciples sought to exclude from fellowship those who, though they followed Him, were following "not with us"![7]

At the convention, debate on this resolution included consideration of whether the word "occasional" should be removed from the first paragraph. Although the word remained, the discussion is evidence of an even more liberal interpretation of the confirmation rubric by some clergy.

The Evangelical resolution expressed the essence of the controversy over the application of the confirmation rubric to intercommunion. In this ongoing dispute Evangelicals and Anglo-Catholics took opposing stands. The Evangelicals argued that the confirmation rubric was a matter of internal discipline, applying only to members of the Anglican Communion. Furthermore, they emphasized that baptism is the sacrament by which individuals become members of the body of Christ. Finally, they insisted that the eucharist is the *Lord's* Supper and as such should not exclude Christians who were not Episcopalians. In a 1944 statement of purpose the Episcopal Evangelical Fellowship included among their immediate objectives: "The exclusion of any adult baptized Christian from the Communion is not required by the rubric at the end of the confirmation service."[8]

An editorial in *The Living Church* the following year took the opposite point of view: "The confirmation rubric, though designed originally for a different situation, exactly applies to the situation of today." It claimed, albeit erroneously, that one of the original reasons for the rubric was to provide the gift of the Holy Spirit to help dispose the communicant to receive communion worthily. The editorial was on firmer ground in pointing out that the rubric was also introduced in order to emphasize the importance of confirmation. Both reasons continued to be valid in an ecumenical context, since members of Protestant denominations were as much in need of the gifts of the Holy Spirit conferred in confirmation as were Episcopalians. Furthermore, the Reformation requirement of education prior to confirmation and reception of communion was particularly important for Protestants who had no idea of the Anglican understanding of the real presence and the necessity of proper preparation.[9]

The debate continued in popular Episcopal Church periodicals during the late 1940s and early 1950s. Although the stances of the opposing parties remained unchanged, more and more clergy were welcoming baptized and unconfirmed persons to receive communion. In his 1950 commentary on the prayer book, Shepherd noted with approval that the admission of non-Episcopalians to communion was in general "left to the discretion of the priest, acting under the advice and counsel of his bishop."[10] A 1950 letter to the editor of *The Living Church*, decrying this practice, listed several forms of invitation he had heard given, including, "all baptized persons," "all those who are communicants in their own Church," "all lovers of the Lord Jesus," and "all who do truly and earnestly repent of their sins."[11]

Controversy erupted in 1950 when Angus Dun, Bishop of Washington, presided at a eucharist and invited all Christian ministers of Washington to receive communion. The Maryland Branch of the American Church Union presented a formal protest to the Presiding Bishop and the House of Bishops. Although the bishop was not officially censured, debate raged in *The Southern Churchman* for several months.

A 1952 statement from the House of Bishops, addressing the question of communion at ecumenical gatherings, observed, "Bishops of the Anglican Communion have not infrequently been the celebrants at such services according to the use of our Book of Common Prayer." This statement was careful to address itself only to intercommunion during conferences whose purpose was to further the ecumenical movement. The bishops stated their objection to "joint" communion services, at which ministers of two or more separated churches shared in the celebration and administration of the sacrament, on the grounds that churches and not committees rightfully celebrate the Lord's Supper. On the question of intercommunion, that is, extending an invitation to all baptized Christians at a gathering for "responsible ecumenical purpose," the bishops recognized that the bishop in whose jurisdiction such a gathering took place might properly issue such an invitation. The invitation was to be contingent upon proper preparation for and interpretation of the sacrament, emphasizing penitence for the separation of Christian bodies.[12]

The House of Bishops' statement gave official recognition to a practice which was gaining widespread acceptance. Their argument was that the ecumenical movement created an unprecedented situation not foreseen by earlier rubrics and canons of the Church. While they sought to limit their exceptions to official ecumenical gatherings, much wider latitude was given in actual practice.

A decade later, at the 1964 General Convention, the House of Bishops approved a resolution to:

> recognize as a fundamental principle that all Christians duly baptized by water in the Name of the Holy Trinity and qualified to receive the Holy Communion in their own churches, should be welcomed as guests at the Lord's Table in all Christian Churches.

To this end, the resolution proposed that the Standing Liturgical Commission consider rubrical and other changes necessary in the prayer book, and the Committees on Constitution and Canons review requisite constitutional and canonical amendments. Both groups were to present appropriate recommendations to the 1967 Convention. When the resolution reached the House of Deputies, the Deputies voted instead to refer the matter to the Joint Commission on Ecumenical Relations for study and proposal for action at the 1967 Convention.[13]

When the Commission on Ecumenical Relations considered the question, they concluded that no rubrical or canonical changes were necessary to permit "those who in other Christian traditions than ours have by personal profession of faith and personal commitment affirmed their status as members of the Body" to receive communion in the Episcopal Church, not only at ecumenical gatherings but also in circumstances of individual spiritual need. The commission expressed its hope that this recognition of common baptism into the body of Christ would further Christian unity. When this report was presented to General Convention, the House of Deputies amended the conclusion, declaring that it "does not authorize what is commonly called 'open communion' [an invitation by the celebrant for non-Episcopalians to share the eucharist]," but did permit an individual non-Episcopalian to receive communion at his or her own initiative.[14]

Although the resolution adopted in 1967 focused attention on the ecumenical issues, the bishops in 1964 had introduced the question of confirmation and its relation to baptism. Their resolution (which was subsequently rejected by the House of Deputies) explained their intent in welcoming Christians baptized in other denominations to receive communion in the Episcopal Church:

> That in so altering our discipline, the General Convention intends to clarify and emphasize this Church's understanding of Confirmation as a response to and fulfillment of Holy Baptism and not a mere prerequisite to the Holy Communion.[15]

Further explanation was offered by Gerald Burrill, Bishop of Chicago. He claimed that the most important reason for the nearly unanimous support of the bishops (only eleven bishops voted against the resolution) was their agreement that:

> Confirmation should no longer be thought of simply as a disciplinary barrier to admittance to Holy Communion.... In their minds [most laity and some clergy], the Bishop comes on his visitation to "make them members of the Church." This notion has tended to reduce Confirmation to a sentimental "graduation" from instruction classes, a ceremonial "coming out," a religious "debut" before proud parents and curious friends.

Burrill pointed out that the resolution was based upon traditional catholic sacramental theology. The basic requirements for reception of communion were baptism in the triune name and "that one be prepared and desirous of making one's communion." Confirmation was to be understood as conveying the gift of the Holy Spirit and as a kind of ordination to lay ministry, not simply as an admission ticket to communion. Burrill proposed that all baptized members of the Episcopal Church be admitted to communion following proper instruction from the parish priest and preceding their confirmation. He asserted that this would emphasize the proper relationship of the sacraments.[16]

As is apparent from Burrill's article, the growing practice of admitting non-confirmed non-Episcopalians to communion eventually raised questions as to the meaning of confirmation for Episcopalians. Originally the issue was one of ecumenism, a desire to share the fundamental Christian act of communion amongst persons normally separated by denominational affiliation. Despite objections, primarily from Anglo-Catholics, it moved rather quickly from open communion at ecumenical gatherings to invitations extended at regular Sunday services. As non-Episcopalians received communion in the Episcopal Church with increasing frequency, it highlighted the anomaly of excluding baptized but unconfirmed Episcopalians. Increasing dissatisfaction was expressed with the definition of confirmation as the completion of Christian initiation and hence requisite for admission to communion.

Children and Communion: Challenges to the Confirmation Rubric

In a 1953 article, Theodore Ferris, rector of Trinity Church, Boston, argued that confirmation should be postponed until a person was able to make an adult commitment to Christ, perhaps between the ages of eighteen and twenty-five. Following the practice of the Roman Catholic Church, "first communion" should occur when children were quite young, after instruction comparable to what was then being given prior to confirmation. For Ferris, this would mean that "the whole question of who is and who is not entitled to receive the communion would then be put back upon the primary Christian rite of baptism where it belongs."[17]

The same year, Cyril Richardson, professor at Union Seminary in New York City, proposed that confirmation and admission to communion be separated. Richardson defined baptism as the sacrament of "conversion" and confirmation as pertinent to the "assimilation of Christian truth." This meant that it was appropriate to separate the rites of baptism and confirmation for both children and adults. Richardson then proposed that children and adults be admitted to communion after baptism and prior to confirmation, although the only reason he offered was that the eucharist should not be associated with "the years of discretion implied in confirmation."[18]

Questions about the confirmation rubric were raised a few years later by Harlow Donovan, vicar of St. Paul's Church in Sikeston, Missouri. Donovan's article took the form of an imaginary conversation between a rector and a layperson who had been received from the Roman Catholic Church. Discussing the inconsistencies in confirmation practice, the layperson claimed that the confirmation rubric effectively made "second class Church people out of our baptized children who aren't yet confirmed." No definitive recommendations were made for a change in Episcopal Church practice, but the article concluded with the rector's statement, "I've heard other clergymen talk about it once or twice. Perhaps it should be talked about more often."[19]

When Donovan's concerns are viewed together with Richardson's and Ferris' proposals, it is apparent that questions about the necessity and appropriateness of the Anglican sequence of initiation were beginning to emerge. While it is difficult to know the extent to which the issues were discussed during the 1950s, common themes are evident in the arguments. All three writers understood baptism to be the primary sacrament of Christian conversion and initiation. Confirmation was interpreted as a rite of mature commitment. The writers objected to the traditional Anglican practice by which this rite of mature faith also functioned as the rite of admission to communion.

A similar stance was taken by James Pike, Bishop of California, in a 1959 memorandum to his diocesan clergy on the subject of open communion. Pike stated that confirmation required commitment and decision, hence children should be at least twelve years of age before being confirmed. Recognizing that much younger children were often "ready and desirous" insofar as receiving communion was concerned, he suggested that being regular communicants might develop in them a greater desire to make a serious commitment at the time of their confirmation and to maintain that commitment. He then asked whether the confirmation rubric could be interpreted in a manner permitting earlier admission to communion, although he admitted that he was less certain of this interpretation and that it lacked the authority of Anglican scholars. He deferred judgment on this question until a clergy committee could study the issue and make recommendations.[20]

The possibility of admitting children to communion prior to their confirmation was discussed further during the early 1960s. Daniel Stevick, who taught liturgy and homiletics at Philadelphia Divinity School during that period, recalls discussion by Christian educators from the Lutheran, Anglican and Roman Catholic traditions. Papers were circulated at Christian education faculty conferences, and many informal conversations took place. According to Stevick, there were two primary issues: desire for confirmation to "interpret and ritualize adulthood" and desire to "capitalize on the ability of young children to use and understand things of a sacramental and symbolic nature." One suggestion was to admit children to communion at an early age while administering confirmation at a much later age (perhaps a minimum age of twenty) and only at a person's own initiative.[21]

In 1960, the report of the national Episcopal Church Department of Christian Education noted a tension between the desire for children to participate in the sacramental grace of communion, leading to confirmation at an early age, and the desire for confirmation to be a meaningful rite of personal commitment, resulting in confirmation at a much later age. The report commented:

> Admission to the Holy Communion early, with Confirmation later as an act of decision and commitment, seems to several of the clergy to be the only way by which one group of values may be secured without the sacrifice of the other.[22]

It is unclear how widespread this opinion was in 1960, but it is apparent that the possibility of communion before confirmation was being discussed in a number of places.

A 1960 letter to the editor of *The Living Church* suggested that the eucharist be offered to every member of the congregation so that "participation in the eucharist becomes to [our two-year-olds] as natural as breathing."[23] In response, a letter to the editor reported that the problem had been discussed "several years ago" in the Diocese of Western Massachusetts. A group of clergy concluded that the primary problem with confirmation was that it was linked to communicant status. Confirmation should instead be a rite of admission to adult membership in the church. Children would then receive communion either from infancy or from the age of discretion, depending on whether Orthodox or Roman Catholic practice was adopted. Because this proposal was so radical, it had not been acted upon.[24]

In these discussions about admitting children to communion before they were confirmed, the meaning of confirmation was an important factor. Proponents of "early" admission to communion emphasized the commitment made at confirmation and argued that this commitment could best be made if confirmation did not also function as a disciplinary rite of admission to communion. The concurrent scholarly discussion of Christian initiation seems to have gone unnoticed; baptism was viewed as the primary rite of Christian initiation, while confirmation was a rite of mature commitment. There was little or no discussion of the interpretation of confirmation as the bestowal of the indwelling gifts of the Spirit and hence the completion of sacramental initiation.

However, another factor does seem to be at work, although it was not commented upon at the time. In a survey of Anglican eucharistic practice, David Holeton concluded:

> Whenever the church has come to see itself as a small, gathered, eucharistic community, the communion of all the baptized quickly becomes a real question.... [W]hen the church sees itself as established, encompassing the whole of society, there is little question of communicating all the baptized. In the former it is the regular reception of the eucharist that sustains and nurtures the Christian community; in the latter it is social structure, rather than the sacraments, that maintains the fabric of the church.[25]

In the Episcopal Church, discussion about admitting young children to communion arose at a time when the eucharist was becoming more central. As the liturgical movement swept through the Episcopal Church, the eucharist was more commonly the principal act of worship on Sunday and was understood to be a corporate celebration forming the body of Christ, not just an act of individual devotion. It was in this context that questions began to be asked about the exclusion of children from communion. The issue was particularly pressing when family services became common and parishes were faced with the regular presence of baptized but unconfirmed children at the Sunday eucharist.

As family services evolved during the 1950s, parents began bringing their unconfirmed children forward to the altar rail to receive a blessing at the time of communion. Randolph Crump Miller, professor of Christian education at Yale Divinity School, explained:

> Our practice has been to dismiss nursery and kindergarten after the ante-communion, and to let all unconfirmed children come to the altar rail, placing their hands behind their backs. As the priest comes by, he places a hand on the heads of the unconfirmed, perhaps with a word of blessing. If this is not done, the primary department should be dismissed with the younger children, but primaries like this act of blessing and belonging.[26]

Miller's statements offer no insight as to the genesis of this tradition.

Episcopal Churchnews reported in 1957 that at his annual diocesan convention the Bishop of California, Karl Block, had spoken strongly against the practice of unconfirmed children coming to the communion rail because it might lead children to seek privileges that should await greater maturity.[27] A response from a lay woman rejected Block's rationale. She suggested:

> The only thing a small child might "desire" (and usually does, I believe) is "some of what you're eating." That query gives the parents a perfect opportunity to tell them as much as they can understand about what the eucharist means.[28]

However, she did not recommend that the child actually be given communion. This letter suggests that the practice of bringing children to the communion rail for a blessing was already in 1957 leading children to ask about communion.

The question of blessing unconfirmed children was discussed in 1962 in a series of articles in *The Witness* entitled "Issues in Dispute." George Mosley Murray, Bishop Coadjutor of Alabama, gave his reasons for discouraging the practice in his diocese: the rubrics did not call for a blessing during the administration of communion; the individual blessing of children interrupted worship; at a large service it caused undue delay; and the practice created confusion and embarrassment for visiting priests and bishops who did not know which children intended to receive communion.[29]

A response to Murray was given by H. Arthur Doersam, rector of Church of the Epiphany in Glenburn, Pennsylvania, who observed the custom in his parish. Doersam had found that the practice "helped to emphasize the importance of the family worshiping together" and gave "the child a feeling of participation and importance." Cautioning against introducing the practice merely because it was a novel "gimmick," he urged that proper instruction be given to help children understand what was happening at communion.[30]

As it became more and more common for unconfirmed children to receive a blessing at the time of communion, their exclusion from the central act of receiving communion became increasingly apparent. Pike commented on the naturalness of children coming forward to the altar rail with their parents. However, he saw the giving of a blessing as a less satisfactory alternative to their receiving communion.[31] Doersam noted that one objection to blessing unconfirmed children was "that it could lead to the practice of having a child confirmed long before the proper age."[32] He did not explain this, but it seems to reflect the tension between administration of confirmation at an early age to permit earlier admission to communion and concern that confirmation as the ratification of baptismal vows should be administered at a much later age.

In a 1964 letter to the editor of *The Witness*, J. Robert Zimmerman, rector of Calvary Church, Danvers, Massachusetts, expressed his support for admitting children to communion. He pointed out that family services meant that children were required to attend a service in which they could not fully participate. The liturgical movement, with its stress on the centrality of the eucharist, meant that children were growing up with eucharistic worship. The practice of blessing children rather than communicating them was unsatisfactory: "It is unrubrical, it is meaningless, and it, too, becomes boring. How much better to let these children receive their Lord at a level they can understand!" Zimmerman concluded by suggesting that first communion occur at age eight, after some instruction, and confirmation be administered at age sixteen, to provide the strengthening of the Spirit necessary for adult Christian life.[33]

Experimentation: "Early" Admission to Communion

In 1964 the newly elected bishop of Central New York, Ned Cole, concerned about the chronic problem of lapsed communicants, called for a committee to examine the method of the bishop's visitation and confirmation, as well as confirmation instruction. The committee found tremendous dissatisfaction with confirmation instruction and large attrition of newly confirmed youths. In their report they declared that baptism was the complete rite of Christian initiation, while confirmation was a sign of adult participation in the Christian community. On that basis they suggested that admission to communion follow appropriate instruction and confirmation be delayed until adulthood. Their recommendations included:

1. ...Confirmation be seen as an adult commitment...

2. Confirmation is debased when it is seen as a "ticket" to the Holy Communion. We therefore believe that admission to the Holy Communion need not wait upon mature understanding of the full life of the Church...

3. The interval between Baptism and Confirmation we see as a period of growth within the life of the Christian community...

4. The separation of Confirmation and Holy Communion frees Confirmation instruction from the limitation of being only a preparation for Communion and allows it to be an exploration of life and witness as the Church, understood in its ecumenical dimension.[34]

These statements reflect dissatisfaction with confirmation as a rite of membership. Although the committee proposed to separate confirmation from admission to communion, it did not eliminate the requirement of education prior to first communion.

With the authorization of the bishop, five parishes agreed to participate in a pilot project to implement these recommendations. The committee developed materials for communion instruction for children in the fourth grade and a service of admission to communion. A 1968 statement of the Committee on Confirmation reported favorably on parochial and parental response and the faithfulness of the children admitted to communion. A primary difficulty encountered was a tendency to think of admission to communion as simply "confirmation without confirmation." The instructional materials were seen as a different type of confirmation preparation. A further problem was a fear that children admitted to communion would never be confirmed. The committee recommended continuing a course of instruction prior to admission to communion with some revision of the materials.

The Central New York committee had begun by addressing the problem of postconfirmation lapsing. Discussion of these concerns led to consideration of the meaning of baptism and confirmation, and an experimental revision of the initiatory sequence. A similar committee formed in the Diocese of Missouri in 1967 began with authorization to consider possible alternatives to the present practice. The committee of seven clergy consulted with theologians, educators and psychiatrists and took a random sampling of forty laity in six parishes. Their report identified four primary issues which challenged the traditional sequence of Christian initiation:

The Issue of Integrity: If baptism is the basis for full membership in Christ's church...and if, on this basis, all baptized persons (adults) are invited to receive communion, then we are saying, by not including children, that they are less than Christian persons.

The Issue of the Learning Process: By insisting that confirmation (almost always associated with a didactic teaching process) *precede* the experience of receiving Holy Communion, we are flying directly in the face of Twentieth Century learnings about the educational process—to wit, that real learning consists of experience which is shared and then reflected upon...

The Issue of Gnostic Heresy: The view that only intellectual knowledge will produce meaning in terms of Holy Communion is widely held... Basic to our theological understanding of Holy Communion is the affirmation that the meaning and power of Holy Communion is not exhausted by our intellectual understanding of it.

The Issue of Unity:...receiving of Holy Communion together as a family with all ages included, is a force for unity and meaning... [A]n educational program should be designed which is directed toward parents even more than toward the children.[35]

The theological presuppositions are in many respects similar to those of the Central New York committee. Both committees viewed baptism as full Christian initiation and criticized the requirement of confirmation prior to admission to communion. However, the Missouri committee also called into question the necessity of intellectual knowledge before a person could receive communion. Their concerns were both pedagogical and theological. While not recommending complete elimination of instruction, they urged that this be addressed particularly to parents. They recommended a pilot program of admitting children to communion in not less than five selected parishes and missions for at least five years.

A similar program was implemented in the Diocese of Southern Ohio beginning in 1969. A questionnaire on confirmation preparation had indicated that a primary issue was the question of the relation between confirmation and communion and that most people felt that children should receive communion prior to being confirmed. The members of the diocesan Executive Education Committee agreed that children, perhaps as young as eight, should be admitted to communion and that confirmation and first communion should be separated. The committee's report to their diocesan convention in May 1969 acknowledged discussions in the Dioceses of Central New York, Missouri, Washington and Massachusetts. They proposed that children who were baptized but not confirmed "be permitted to receive the Holy Communion as soon as they desire to participate and have received appropriate preparation."

This preparation was the responsibility of the parents with the guidance of the parish priest.[36]

One year later, the Southern Ohio committee reported a very positive response to a pilot program implemented in thirteen parishes:

> The best way to characterize what has been happening in the project is with such words as enthusiasm, joy and excitement. Another way to communicate would be to see a young child in reverence and happiness receiving the sacrament. A very alive spirit has captured the imagination and hearts of church members, as young children are admitted to the Holy Communion.[37]

The theological convictions of the Southern Ohio committee echoed those of Central New York and Missouri. Baptism is full Christian initiation. Confirmation is a mature acceptance and ratification of the baptismal promises. The bestowal of the Holy Spirit was not mentioned explicitly as an aspect of confirmation, although the Southern Ohio report stated that confirmation "enables one to accept and perform for himself the obligations accepted in his name by his sponsors at his Baptism."[38] This occurred through a conferral of grace, although the particular character of this grace was not defined.

These experiments with admission to communion before confirmation reflect a growing dissatisfaction with the meaning and practice of confirmation. Confirmation was a ratification of baptismal vows, a bestowal of sacramental grace, a rite of admission to communion and a rite of full membership in the Episcopal Church. By separating confirmation from admission to communion, the pilot projects emphasized baptism as the rite of full Christian initiation. The earliest proposals continued to require preparation prior to admission to communion and hence did not admit the youngest members of their congregations. Even this began to change as people recognized that the meaning of communion was not fully contained in intellectual understanding. This led to the admission of even younger children to communion and efforts to focus preparation on their parents.

It is likely that these experiments with "early" admission to communion arose not only from theoretical discussion but also from pastoral reality. The liturgical movement was giving new importance to the eucharist as the principal Sunday celebration in a parish, and because of the religious education movement unconfirmed children were more frequently present at celebrations of the eucharist. While these children were at first encouraged to come to the communion rail for a blessing, no doubt some began to ask, "Why can't I have some, too?" and some adults may also have questioned their exclusion. As clergy began to give communion to older unconfirmed children, their younger brothers and sisters doubtless began to ask why they, too, could not receive communion.[39] Once the requirement of confirmation was removed, even on an experimental basis, it became difficult to justify the exclusion of children on the basis of an arbitrarily determined age.

Support for this change was given by the Council of Associated Parishes, which in 1968 called upon bishops of the Episcopal Church to support clergy who wished to communicate baptized but unconfirmed children:

> We believe that our children should not be able to remember when they had not received communion. When they were baptized they were admitted to the church or *koinonia* and the *koinonia* expresses its commonness in the eucharistic meal.

The statement also pointed out the anomaly of the decision by the 1967 General Convention to permit baptized members of other churches to receive communion in the Episcopal Church while baptized children of the Episcopal Church did not have the same opportunity. Further problems were emerging as baptized but unconfirmed children were admitted to communion in one parish and then refused communion in another.[40]

This statement by Associated Parishes reflects the enormous shift that had taken place in little more than a decade. Communion of baptized but unconfirmed children, a revolutionary concept in the 1950s, was rapidly moving from the realm of discussion to officially sanctioned experiments and even wider acceptance. The traditional Anglican pattern of initiation was coming unraveled, although a new and cohesive pattern had not yet emerged in its place.

NOTES

1. BCP 1928, p. 299.

2. Colin Buchanan, "Confirmation," in David Holeton (ed.), *Growing in Newness of Life: Christian Initiation in Anglicanism Today* (Toronto: Anglican Book Centre, 1993), pp. 106-7; James Arthur Muller, "The Confirmation Rubric: A Historical Sketch," *The Southern Churchman*, May 7, 1938, pp. 5-7.

3. Parsons and Jones, *The American Prayer Book*, p. 246 (emphasis in original).

4. Roger Coleman (ed.), *Resolutions of the twelve Lambeth Conferences 1867-1988* (Toronto: Anglican Book Centre, 1992), p. 81.

5. Norman B. Nash, "Oxford Meeting Concludes Tasks; Adopts Reports," *The Witness*, Aug. 19, 1937, p. 8; W. Russell Bowie, "Impressions: Dr. Bowie on the Life and Work Conference," *The Churchman*, Sept. 1, 1937, pp. 26-8; "The Holy Communion at Oxford," *The Southern Churchman*, Sept. 18, 1937, p. 3.

6. Frank Wilson, "Let's Know—Why This?", *The Witness*, Sept. 2, 1937, pp. 6-7.

7. "Liberals Meet; Strong Statements Made on Open Communion," *The Churchman*, June 1, 1938, p. 17; "Vote to Open Door to Other Faiths at the Communion," *The Witness*, June 2, 1938, p. 7.

8. "Statement of Purpose of the Episcopal Evangelical Fellowship," *The Living Church*, June 25, 1944, pp. 10-11.

9. "'Ready and Desirous,'" *The Living Church*, Apr. 15, 1945, pp. 12-14.

10. Shepherd, *Oxford American Prayer Book Commentary*, p. 299.

11. Spencer Ervin, letter to the editor, *The Living Church*, Oct. 15, 1950, pp. 2-3.

12. "A Statement of the House of Bishops Regarding Holy Communion at Ecumenical Gatherings," *Journal of the General Convention*, 1952, pp. 40-2.

13. *Journal of the General Convention*, 1964, p. 338-40.

14. *Journal of the General Convention*, 1967, pp. 370-3.

15. *Journal of the General Convention*, 1964, p. 338.

16. Gerald F. Burrill, "What's All This about 'Open Communion'?", *The Episcopalian*, July 1965, p. 24-6.

17. Theodore P. Ferris, "What about Confirmation?", *Episcopal Churchnews*, June 21, 1953, p. 13.

18. Cyril C. Richardson, "The Proposed Revision of Our Liturgy: II. Confirmation," *Anglican Theological Review* 35 (1953): 179-80.

19. Harlow Donovan, "The Riddle of Confirmation," *The Witness*, Nov. 14, 1957, pp. 10-12.

20. James Pike, "Communion—Open or Closed?", *The Living Church*, Aug. 23, 1959, p. 13.

21. Daniel Stevick, *Baptismal Moments; Baptismal Meanings* (New York: Church Hymnal Corporation, 1987), pp. 105-6; interview with Daniel Stevick, Cambridge, MA, May 25, 1990.

22. Edric A. Weld, "The Church Reports on Confirmation Instruction," *Findings*, Oct. 1960, p. 11.

23. Theodore A. Heers, letter to the editor, *The Living Church*, Oct. 30, 1960, p. 18.

24. Archer Torrey, letter to the editor, *The Living Church*, Mar. 12, 1961, p. 7.

25. "Communion of All the Baptized and Anglican Tradition," in Ruth A. Meyers (ed.), *Children at the Table: The Communion of All the Baptized in Anglicanism Today* (New York: Church Hymnal Corporation, 1995), pp. 35-6.

26. Randolph Crump Miller, "Family Worship in the Church," *The Witness*, Nov. 24, 1955, p. 10; cf. Miller, "The Family Service," *The Living Church*, Aug. 7, 1955, p. 23.

27. "Bishop Urges That Children Be Kept from Communion Rail," *Episcopal Churchnews*, Mar. 17, 1957, p. 10.

28. Edith M. Purrington, letter to the editor, *Episcopal Churchnews*, May 26, 1957, p. 6.

29. George Mosley Murray, "What about Blessing Children? Poor Liturgical Practice," *The Witness*, Apr. 12, 1962, p. 8.

30. H. Arthur Doersam, "What about Blessing Children? Adds to Worship," *The Witness*, Apr. 12, 1962, pp. 8-9.

31. Pike, "Communion—Open or Closed?", *The Living Church*, Aug. 23, 1959, p. 13.

32. Doersam, "What about Blessing Children?", p. 9.

33. J. Robert Zimmerman, letter to the editor, *The Witness*, Dec. 3, 1964, p. 19.

34. Dorothy J. Brittain, "Confirmation:...Rite for Adults?", *Findings*, Sept. 1968, p. 14.

35. "Report of the Committee on Admission of Baptized, But Not Yet Confirmed, Children to Communion," n.d., Record Group 122, Archives of the Episcopal Church, Austin, TX (emphasis in original).

36. Report of the Executive Education Committee to the Diocese of Southern Ohio, May 1969, Record Group 122, Archives of the Episcopal Church, Austin, TX.

37. Report of the Executive Education Committee to the Diocese of Southern Ohio, May 1970, Record Group 122, Archives of the Episcopal Church, Austin, TX.

38. Ibid.

39. Holeton, "Communion of All the Baptized," in Meyers (ed.), *Children at the Table*, pp. 33-4.

40. Associated Parishes, "Statement Issued by the Council of Associated Parishes On the Admission of Children to Communion," Nov. 15, 1968, cited by Moriarty, "The Associated Parishes," pp. 319-21.

Chapter 6

Turning Points: Toward Prayer Book Revision

Revision of the prayer book was officially authorized by the 1967 General Convention. But as we have seen, in the three decades preceding the official commencement of revision, the liturgical movement was fostering renewed understandings of the eucharist and baptism and was encouraging significant change in parish worship life. This liturgical renewal laid the groundwork for the 1979 Book of Common Prayer. The rites of this book are a revolutionary departure from the language and patterns of worship inherited from the Reformation. Rather than minor adjustments in existing rites and the addition of a few new prayers, wholly new rites were created with new structures and new language. Yet in many ways these new texts and rubrics were far more consonant with emerging theological and liturgical understandings and so "caught up" with practices that had already been instituted in parishes influenced by the liturgical movement.

Well before the radically new rites of the 1979 prayer book began to be created, more modest proposals for change were advanced. Only in the late 1950s, as the teachings of the liturgical movement were taking root in a growing number of parishes, did the Episcopal Church and the Anglican Communion begin to consider significant departures from Reformation patterns along with new methods of revising the prayer book.

Early Proposals for Revision

The prayer book had been revised in 1928, but there was continuing dissatisfaction with the office of baptism. During the 1930s and 1940s, several proposals for further revision appeared in popular church periodicals. In addition to simplifying the language and eliminating outmoded words and phrases, these proposals suggested ways to emphasize the responsibilities of parents and godparents. Some of the proposals called for use of the Apostles' Creed (in place of the question "Dost thou believe all the Articles of the Christian Faith, as contained in the Apostles' Creed?"[1]), and some recommended a further reduction in emphasis on original sin.

During this period, the Standing Liturgical Commission began working in earnest on prayer book revision. In 1940, at the request of the commission, the General Convention gave the commission canonical status, so that it no longer required authorization by each triennial General Convention to continue the work of gathering and evaluating material relevant to The Book of Common Prayer. The commission set to work immediately. Pointing to "rich stores of liturgical knowledge contributed by recent research" and "the experience of other Churches of the Anglican Communion with Prayer Books which have appeared since our 1928 revision," it recommended to the 1943 General Convention that a systematic revision be prepared and presented to the Church for study not later than autumn 1949, in conjunction with the four-hundredth anniversary of the first Book of Common Prayer in English.[2] The House of Bishops defeated the motion. One bishop commented that what was needed was "believing in and living the Prayer Book," not prayer book revision which was so unsettling for the Church.[3]

The Standing Liturgical Commission found the reluctance of General Convention puzzling, since the commission had been receiving increasing numbers of suggestions for revision. In order to make church leaders more conscious of the concerns being identified, the commission asked several people to write articles for church periodicals. In a 1946 article Edward Lambe Parsons, then Chair of the Standing Liturgical Commission, observed:

> The baptismal office seems more unpopular than any other in the book. Its content, its structure, its theology are all attacked... The confirmation service, apparently satisfactory in the main, needs polishing.[4]

The discussion which ensued in *The Living Church* and *The Witness* indicated resistance to revision of the prayer book.

At its March 1946 meeting, when the Standing Liturgical Commission discussed further its plan for a proposed prayer book, a guest was Earle Maddux, a member of the Society of St. John the Evangelist, an Anglican monastic community with a ministry in South Africa. Maddux described for the commission the South African church's procedure of publishing revisions of separate prayer book offices for study and trial use. Favorably impressed, the Standing Liturgical Commission voted to propose a series of studies in the Episcopal Church. Publication would begin in 1949 to commemorate the four-hundredth anniversary of the first Book of Common Prayer in English. In its report to the 1946 General Convention, the Standing Liturgical Commission presented its proposal, but instead of asking explicit Convention approval of its plan, requested only the funds to carry out the proposed prayer book studies.[5]

Although funds were not allocated for the project, the Standing Liturgical Commission continued work on prayer book revision during the next triennium. In June 1945 the various prayer book offices had been assigned to different members. Charles Hill had agreed to study and report on confirmation, and Henry Ogilby had begun study on baptism with the assistance of Massey Shepherd, who was not then a member of the Standing Liturgical Commission. The minutes of March 1946 recorded Ogilby's report of opinions regarding the baptismal service:

> He finds dissatisfaction with outmoded phrases, the baptismal promises, the fact that the service provides so little for the sponsors or the family in the way of either teaching or prayers. There is widespread desire to make Baptism a public service.[6]

These concerns reflect the then-current efforts at renewal of baptismal practice, that is, calls for public baptism and renewed attention to the role of parents and godparents. Not only did the Standing Liturgical Commission consider these concerns, but at its March 1946 meeting Shepherd presented a proposed revision of the baptismal rite, in structure and content quite similar to the 1928 rite. After discussion, the commission asked Ogilby and Shepherd to revise their proposal and circulate it among the members. When Hill presented his revision of confirmation, he too was asked to rework his material and disseminate it among commission members. The following year the revisions of baptism and confirmation were presented at a Standing Liturgical Commission meeting and approved for publication as the first *Prayer Book Study*.

The commission took no further action until 1949, when the Church Pension Fund offered to publish the series of *Prayer Book Studies* if a guarantee of $2,000 was forthcoming. Accordingly, the Standing Liturgical Commission proposed to the 1949 General Convention the publication of a series of *Prayer Book Studies*, this time with a contingency fund of $2,000 to guarantee the Church Hymnal Corporation (the publishing subsidiary of the Church Pension Fund) for any losses incurred. This proposal was approved, and the series of *Prayer Book Studies* was launched.[7]

Prayer Book Studies I: A Dixian Proposal

The first two studies were issued in 1950 in a single pamphlet, *Prayer Book Studies: I—Baptism and Confirmation; II—The Liturgical Lectionary.*[8] The preface stated unequivocally that the Standing Liturgical Commission was not proposing any immediate revision, although they expected it at a future date:

> we believe that there ought to be a period of study and discussion, to acquaint the Church at large with the principles and issues involved, in order that the eventual action may be taken intelligently, and if possible without consuming so much of the time of our supreme legislative synod.

The preface emphasized that the studies were issued not for public use but for discussion, and invited readers to submit comments.[9]

The introduction to *Prayer Book Studies I* included a rationale for revision of the offices, a brief history of Christian initiation, and a review of the changes proposed for baptism and confirmation. Although virtually all the discussion in popular church periodicals focused on revisions needed in the baptismal rite and the commission's preliminary work had acknowledged numerous criticisms of baptism but little concern about confirmation, the introductory material in *Prayer Book Studies I* dealt primarily with confirmation and its relation to baptism. The name Gregory Dix never appeared, yet his theological position, set forth in 1946, was evident throughout.

The rationale recognized divergence of opinion in Anglicanism regarding the meaning of confirmation, although in the Episcopal Church these differences had "not as yet been so openly and sharply evident" as in the Church of England. Nonetheless there was "widespread dissatisfaction with the provisions of the traditional services."[10] The historical section began with a description of initiation in the pre-Nicene Church:

> The initiation consisted of two distinct but inseparable stages: 1) the washing with water wherein the candidate received remission of sin, regeneration and adoption by God, and 2) the "sealing" with the Holy Spirit through the laying on of hands and anointing with chrism as an earnest of eternal redemption and inheritance. So far as the evidence goes there was never any restriction regarding the minister of baptism in water. But only an Apostle—and later, after the establishment of mon-episcopacy, only a Bishop—could confer the gift of the Spirit.[11]

These two stages are comparable to Dix's baptism of water and baptism of the Spirit.

The division of Christian initiation into two distinct rites, water baptism which conferred regeneration and remission of sins, and imposition of hands which conferred the Holy Spirit, was the basis for the revisions proposed for both baptism and confirmation. The introduction to the baptismal rite identified three principles for the suggested changes: "the length of the service, the clarification of rubrics to meet modern needs and demands, and the simplification of the ritual text."[12] Careful examination of the text reveals a fourth unstated principle: the omission of all explicit references to the gift of the Holy Spirit in baptism. For example, the opening exhortation in both the 1928 rite and *Prayer Book Studies I* stated: "None can enter into the Kingdom of God, except he be regenerate and born anew of Water and of the Holy Ghost." The 1928 Exhortation then directed the congregation to call upon God to grant that the child "may be baptized with Water and the Holy Ghost, and received into Christ's holy Church," but in *Prayer Book Studies I* the phrase was reworded: "that he, being baptized, may be received into Christ's holy Church."[13] The concluding prayer of thanksgiving in the 1928 rite gave thanks to God, "that it hath pleased thee to regenerate this child with thy Holy Spirit." In *Prayer Book Studies I* the prayer gave thanks, "that thou hast vouchsafed to call thy people to the knowledge of thy grace, and faith in thee."[14] The alternatives for the gospel in *Prayer Book Studies I* excluded the reading of John 3:1-8 ("no one can enter the kingdom of God without being born of water and Spirit") on the grounds that it was not readily intelligible and that its basic teaching was contained in the opening exhortation.[15] The overall effect of these changes was to diminish considerably any teaching that the Spirit is active in baptism.

Noting that Anglican theology was ambiguous as to the work of the Holy Spirit in baptism and confirmation, the rationale for the baptismal rite was equivocal on this point. It acknowledged that it would be inappropriate to deny that the Holy Spirit is given in baptism or to claim that the Spirit acts upon the baptized only externally. Yet it did not state definitively that the Holy Spirit is bestowed in baptism, although it admitted that the Spirit must be capable of "influencing the growth in grace of a child after baptism." As to the rite in *Prayer Book Studies I*:

> All that the present revision claims for itself is that it has sought to avoid any phraseology which would foster an interpretation of baptism with water in such a way that it usurps or makes superfluous the normative and necessary place of confirmation in the perfecting of the Christian, or would reduce the meaning of confirmation to a mere strengthening of what has been received in baptism.[16]

In this refusal to state explicitly that the Holy Spirit was given in baptism, the Mason/Dix line is evident. Confirmation was defined as a necessary completion of baptism, and the indwelling presence of the Spirit was not said to be bestowed at baptism.

Beyond these significant revisions, the baptismal rite also reflected contemporaneous concerns to restore the public nature of baptism, as suggested by the opening rubrics:

> [Baptism] should be administered upon Sundays and other Holy Days, when the most number of people come together: as well for that the Congregation there present may testify the receiving of them that be newly baptized into the number of Christ's Church, as also because in the Baptism of infants every man present may be put in remembrance of his own profession made to God in his Baptism.[17]

This explanation had appeared in the 1662 English Book of Common Prayer but not in the prayer books of the Episcopal Church. To facilitate public baptism, *Prayer Book Studies I* modified the stipulation of both the English and American books that baptism be administered after the second lesson at Morning or Evening Prayer, and permitted as well the administration of baptism after the gospel at Holy Communion, since many parishes now had Holy Communion as their principal service on Sundays. (Nonetheless, the rubric continued to allow the minister to "appoint such other time as he shall think fit.") This did not, however, reflect a new understanding of the relation of baptism and eucharist, since the confirmation rubric remained in its customary place at the end of the confirmation rite.[18]

In addition to encouraging public baptism, preparation of parents and sponsors was expected. Sponsors were to be baptized, and it was desirable for them to be communicants of the Church. In the interrogations, the question about belief in the Apostles' Creed was replaced by a paraphrase of the creed in interrogatory form: "Dost thou believe in God the Father Almighty, Maker of heaven and earth; And in Jesus Christ his only Son our Lord; And in the Holy Ghost?" The full creed was not restored to the baptismal service because it was assumed that baptism would be part of a service which included the full recitation of the creed.[19]

The revisions proposed for confirmation were "designed to restore the primitive view of confirmation as the gift of the indwelling Spirit in all His fullness to the baptized, and not merely as an added, strengthening grace." In a new introductory rite, provided so that confirmation could be a more complete service of common worship, the collect and lesson (Ezekiel 36:25-28, "I will put my Spirit within you") emphasized the gift of the Spirit. The lesson from Acts 8 was also retained. The prayer for the gifts of the Spirit restored the 1549 prayer book wording, "*Send* into their hearts thy Holy Spirit," in place of

"*Strengthen* them with thy Holy Ghost." Likewise in the formula at the imposition of hands "Confirm" replaced "Defend" in order to emphasize God's
action in confirming.[20] By presenting that confirmation as an explicit bestowal
of the indwelling Spirit, these changes adhered to the Mason/Dix line.

The response of faith was also included in the proposed confirmation rite
in a separate section entitled, "The Renewal of the Vows of Baptism." This
accorded with Dix's understanding of the need for a conscious affirmation of
faith by those baptized as infants. It also addressed the popular association of
confirmation with the ratification of baptismal vows. For those baptized as
adults, a rubric directed that baptism and confirmation could be combined by
proceeding from the signing with the cross at baptism immediately to the
prayer for the gifts of the Spirit at confirmation. This emphasized the interrela-
tion of baptism and confirmation while eliminating the duplication of baptismal vows. The relation between baptism and confirmation was also
underscored by rephrasing the questions at the renewal of vows so that they
conformed to the vows taken by candidates or their sponsors at baptism.[21]

The introduction to *Prayer Book Studies I* addressed the question of signing with chrism in conjunction with the imposition of hands at confirmation,
since several bishops were using chrism at confirmation. According to the
introduction, "They justify this additional ceremony on the ground that in the
paucity of ceremonial directions in the Prayer Book some actions not
expressly ordered by the present rubrics must necessarily be added." However, it was important to distinguish between an embellishment which in no
way affected the essence of a rite, for example, the use of incense, and an
action such as chrismation which might be interpreted as the "matter" or
essential ceremony of the rite. The traditional Anglican understanding was
that the essential ceremony of confirmation was laying on of hands, not chrismation. Present scholarship was divided as to whether New Testament references to "sealing" in the context of initiation were metaphorical or indicative
of an actual anointing. Given these uncertainties and the Anglican emphasis
on the imposition of hands, the Standing Liturgical Commission "considered
it unwise to introduce into the proposed revision of the Confirmation Service
any specific reference to 'signing and sealing.' This would leave the question
of the added ceremony of the use of chrism on exactly the same basis that it is
at present," that is, at the discretion of each bishop.[22]

The Standing Liturgical Commission reported that 2,246 copies of *Prayer
Book Studies I* were sold by 1952, 5,402 copies sold by 1955, and 10,786 copies by 1964.[23] The study was read and pondered not only by individual clergy
and laity but by groups both formal and informal, and many of them submitted

responses to the Standing Liturgical Commission. None of these responses addressed directly the theological issue of the work of the Holy Spirit in baptism and confirmation, although some respondents objected to the omission of particular references to the Holy Spirit in baptism. The truncated creedal question was not well received; requests were made to include the full Apostles' Creed or to restore an explicit reference to the creed. Various other comments were received, ranging from recommendations for particular changes in wording, to concerns regarding the length of the service, to suggestions for additional congregational participation. Several requests were made for the permissive use of chrism at confirmation since this was already a practice in several dioceses.

Response in the church press was muted, and little attention was given to the theological issues. The only substantive criticism of the Mason/Dix position in *Prayer Book Studies I* was made by Cyril Richardson in *Anglican Theological Review*. Richardson pointed out that the baptismal rite omitted any reference to the gift of the Holy Spirit in baptism and that the confirmation service implied that the Spirit is bestowed for the first time at confirmation. He argued that "confirmation is a sacramental action whereby the baptized are strengthened for the mature Christian life by the grace of the Holy Spirit which is received in baptism."[24] Since confirmation provided strengthening grace after an individual had grown in Christ, Richardson reasoned, it should not immediately follow baptism, either for infants or for adults.

While Richardson challenged the absence of any reference to the work of the Spirit in baptism, he seems to have been a minority voice in the Episcopal Church in the early 1950s. Both *Prayer Book Studies I* and the Associated Parishes pamphlets entitled *Christian Initiation* (Parts I and II) reflect the predominant view of liturgical leaders in the Episcopal Church, including Massey Shepherd, during the early 1950s: baptism and confirmation are two stages of Christian initiation, and the indwelling gift of the Spirit is bestowed in confirmation. This position is evident as well in Shepherd's commentary on the 1928 prayer book and in his contribution to *The Church's Teaching Series*, *The Worship of the Church*, where he presented what was essentially a Dixian two-stage view of initiation, albeit in a less extreme presentation that acknowledged that baptism included rebirth with the Holy Spirit.[25] Yet within a decade, Shepherd was to admit to the Standing Liturgical Commission that his position had changed, and his 1964 Bradner Lectures at the General Theological Seminary would present a quite different view.

However, with the publication of *Prayer Book Studies I* in 1950, official discussion of Christian initiation ceased for nearly a decade. Responses were gathered and noted, but there was no substantive discussion of theological issues by the Standing Liturgical Commission, nor were any further revisions proposed. For several years the commission gave its attention to the other rites of the 1928 prayer book and the publication of additional *Prayer Book Studies*. When work on the initiatory rites resumed in the early 1960s, the commission had new material and new approaches to consider from the 1958 Lambeth Conference and the Church of England Liturgical Commission.

Lambeth 1958:
New Possibilities for Prayer Book Revision

The Lambeth Conference of 1958 gave considerable attention to the question of prayer book revision in the Anglican Communion. The report of a subcommittee on The Book of Common Prayer affirmed the process of revision underway in different parts of the Anglican Communion and the consequent variety in prayer books, while also pointing to the dangers posed to unity in worship and faith. To permit further revision while preserving the integrity of the Anglican Communion, it established several principles as the basis for further revisions by provinces and dioceses. Of especial importance was the effort to recover the character of worship of the "primitive church," a goal for which Cranmer had striven, but which he had not fully achieved due to a lack of available historical material. The principles enumerated by the committee were summarized in a resolution in which the conference:

(a) calls attention to those features in the Books of Common Prayer which are essential to the safeguarding of our unity: i.e. the use of the canonical Scriptures and the Creeds, Holy Baptism, Confirmation, Holy Communion, and the Ordinal;

(b) notes that there are other features in these books which are effective in maintaining the traditional doctrinal emphasis and ecclesiastical culture of Anglicanism and therefore should be preserved;

(c) and urges that a chief aim of Prayer Book revision should be to further that recovery of the worship of the primitive church which was the aim of the compilers of the first Prayer Books of the Church of England.[26]

The committee report identified several specific features in relation to item (b) and suggested modifications and additions that might help recover elements of the worship of the "primitive church."[27]

This resolution of the Lambeth Conference was a watershed for the Anglican Communion. No longer would the 1662 Book of Common Prayer be the standard for worship and a hallmark of Anglicanism. True, the Episcopal

Church had departed from the 1662 prayer book with its first book in 1789, most notably in the structure of the eucharistic prayer, but many similarities remained and the language and patterns of thought had not changed substantially even with subsequent revisions in 1892 and 1928. Furthermore, as the Anglican Communion grew during the nineteenth and twentieth centuries, the 1662 Book of Common Prayer was adopted, often without any revision at all, as new provinces were established in communion with the Church of England. As early as 1867, the Lambeth Conference had permitted adaptations and additions as necessitated by local circumstances but required that "no change or addition be made inconsistent with the spirit and principles of the Book of Common Prayer."[28] Subsequent Lambeth Conferences had not modified the intent of this resolution. For Anglicans, The Book of Common Prayer was the bond of unity, setting forth standards of doctrine and worship. The 1958 Lambeth Conference marked a significant departure and set the stage for far more radical revision of the prayer book.

When the Standing Liturgical Commission in 1959 discussed further revision of the prayer book, Shepherd, quoting the Lambeth report, stated that the 1662 Book of Common Prayer could no longer be retained as the standard for the Anglican Communion. He suggested that new perspectives made possible by recent historical study called for more radical proposals that would challenge the Church to rethink liturgical principles. As the Episcopal Church inched forward to official revision of the prayer book, the Lambeth 1958 resolution encouraged a far more thoroughgoing approach to revision than the Standing Liturgical Commission had thus far been prepared to consider.

Lambeth 1958:
Recommendations for Christian Initiation

In addition to considering the overall revision of The Book of Common Prayer, the Lambeth subcommittee on the prayer book reviewed the components of the prayer book. Baptism and confirmation were treated together under the heading "Christian initiation," by then a commonly accepted term understood to include baptism, confirmation and first communion. Although no resolutions addressed specifically the topic of Christian initiation, the conference adopted a resolution commending "to the study of the whole Anglican Communion the counsel on Prayer Book Revision given in the Report of the subcommittee on the Book of Common Prayer."[29]

Acknowledging the recent scholarly debate regarding the theology of Christian initiation, the subcommittee stated that "the stage has not yet been reached where the new knowledge can be assimilated and fresh conclusions can be put forward that would be generally accepted." Nonetheless, they recommended the development of services of adult baptism that would combine baptism with confirmation and first communion. This pattern was more closely related to the primitive pattern and would allow the three stages to be seen as one process of Christian initiation. They also listed the elements they thought should be contained in any baptismal service:

1. The Ministry of the Word declaring the teaching of Scripture concerning baptism, e.g. Matt. 28:19; John 3:5; Acts 2:38; Rom. 6:3,4; 1 Cor. 12:13; Col. 2:12.

2. A renunciation of the former way of life, the putting off of the old man (Col. 3:8-10).

3. A profession of faith in Christ with the reciting of the baptismal creed.

4. The promises:
   to hold fast to the Christian faith;
   to obey God's commandments;
   to bear witness to Christ.

5. Blessing of the Water, with a thanksgiving for Christ's baptism and the benefits of his redeeming work and prayer for the fruits of baptism in those to be baptized, which might well be expressed in litany form.

6. Baptism with water in the threefold Name, thereby uniting the baptized person to Christ (John 15:1-8).

7. The signing with the Cross as a sign that we have been bought with a price, that we belong to Christ (1 Peter 1:18,19).

8. The reception of the baptized person into the fellowship of the Church (Gal. 3:26-28).

9. Thanksgiving for having been sealed by the Holy Spirit for ever unto the day of redemption (Eph. 4:30; cf. 2 Cor. 1:21,22 and Eph. 1:13,14)...

10. Prayer for growth in the Christian life.

11. An Exhortation to the congregation reminding them that the newly baptized person has been brought into the life of the family of God and is to be encouraged by its fellowship, supported by its prayers, and strengthened by its example.

12. An Exhortation to the baptized person to live the new life in the power of the Holy Spirit (Col. 3:1).[30]

In its assertion that the baptismal rite should include thanksgiving for having been sealed by the Spirit, the Lambeth report implicitly accepted Lampe's position rather than that of Dix. However, instead of a discussion of theological issues, the committee called attention to several other reports: the work of the

1948 Lambeth Conference; *Baptism and Confirmation Today*, the 1955 report of the Church of England Joint Committees on Baptism, Confirmation and Holy Communion; current work of the Church of England Liturgical Commission; *Prayer Book Studies I*; and the Church in Wales's *Revised Services for Experimental Use: Holy Baptism and Confirmation*.[31]

The Church of England Liturgical Commission

Most of the elements of the baptismal service listed in the Lambeth report can be found in the later revisions proposed for the Episcopal Church. But this report appears to have been much less influential than a 1958 report, *Baptism and Confirmation*, produced by the Church of England Liturgical Commission.[32] Charles Smith reported to the Standing Liturgical Commission that he had attended a special meeting at which the Church of England Liturgical Commission and representatives of the two Convocations reviewed the report. Smith gave an account of the main features of the proposed rites and described "demonstrations" of baptism and confirmation held in various churches in England.

The introduction to the report established two principles as the basis of the proposed rites: the recovery of the worship of the early Church as called for by the 1958 Lambeth resolution, and an understanding of baptism and confirmation as parts of one whole which must further be associated with Holy Communion. This was particularly evident in the rite for baptism and confirmation of adults, which was described as the "archetypal" service and hence was printed first. The rite for "The Ministration of Baptism and Confirmation to those who are of Age to Answer for Themselves" was divided into separately titled sections:

    I.   The Ministry of the Word
   II.   The Procession to the Font
  III.   The Blessing of the Water
  IV.   The Promises
   V.   The Baptism
  VI.   The Ceremonies after Baptism
 VII.   The Confirmation
VIII.   The Holy Communion
  IX.   The Prayers [for use if there was no communion]

The integral connection of baptism, confirmation, first communion was emphasized in a rubric directing that "the newly-confirmed and their witnesses, with others, shall communicate with" the bishop presiding at the service. At the same time, the traditional sequence of rites was maintained; those baptized but not confirmed were not to receive communion, and adults to whom baptism was administered without confirmation should be confirmed as soon as possible in order to be admitted to communion.[33]

The identification of adult baptism and confirmation as the archetypal service marks a dramatic shift for a church in which infant baptism had been the normative practice for centuries. The Liturgical Commission explained its decision: "In the New Testament Adult Baptism is the norm, and it is only in the light of this fact that the doctrine and practice of Baptism can be understood." The Christendom model of infant baptism and adolescent confirmation was not rejected altogether, but these latter rites were seen as derivative from the archetypal pattern of adult baptism. Accordingly, a rite for infant baptism was printed after the adult rite, and confirmation followed "as a corollary of infant baptism."[34] While the provision of a separate rite for infant baptism may seem peculiar to Episcopalians accustomed since the 1928 prayer book to a single rite of baptism for use with candidates of all ages, the Church of England Liturgical Commission was simply continuing the pattern of separate rites introduced in the 1662 prayer book (although the title was modified to describe adult candidates as "those who are of age to answer for themselves," in place of the quaint term from the 1662 book, "such as are of riper years").

While those responsible for prayer book revision in the Episcopal Church never considered returning to a pattern of separate rites for infants and adults, the understanding that adult baptism is theologically normative helped shape the 1979 baptismal rite, as did the effort to restore the so-called primitive unity of baptism, confirmation and communion. The work of the Church of England Liturgical Commission also influenced the Episcopal Church in the provision of a full ministry of the word, with a reading from the Hebrew scriptures, an epistle reading and a psalm in addition to the gospel and a sermon. Moreover, the order of the rite, particularly the close association between the profession of faith and the administration of the water, was the basis for initial proposals advanced in the Standing Liturgical Commission, although ultimately a slightly different structure was adopted for the baptismal rite.

The Standing Liturgical Commission Discusses Christian Initiation

The Standing Liturgical Commission resumed substantive discussion of Christian initiation in the 1960s. While not authorizing a new *Prayer Book Study*, in 1962 the commission appointed a committee, chaired by John Ashton, Vice President at Indiana University and a commission member, to review the correspondence received in response to *Prayer Book Studies I* as well as more recent scholarly work and the work being done in the Church of England.

The committee's report, presented to the Standing Liturgical Commission but not published, took the form of a list of principles and an outline of a rite. The influence of the 1958 report of the Church of England Liturgical Commission was evident in virtually every aspect of the committee's work. Baptism, confirmation and first communion were understood to be normatively one act, though separable on occasion, and the structure of the proposed Church of England rite for adult baptism and confirmation was suggested as a model. The recommendations for infant baptism and confirmation of those baptized in infancy were likewise similar in many respects to the rites proposed for the Church of England.

Minutes from the Standing Liturgical Commission discussion of this report and from subsequent meetings of the committee suggest that members grappled with theological and pastoral issues but reached no conclusions. By proposing a unified initiatory rite for adults, the committee was calling for a pattern that was defined as "normative" and yet did not reflect the actual experience of the vast majority of Episcopalians. How could new rites best incorporate the insights of liturgical scholars while also being effective and appropriate in the average parish? How should theory and pastoral reality intersect?

In its consideration of the issues, the Standing Liturgical Commission introduced additional possibilities—the bishop as the minister of baptism and the establishment of a catechumenate—possibilities that were not addressed in the 1958 Church of England report. Subsequently the committee drafted a statement proposing a new norm: admission to the catechumenate in infancy, followed by baptism, confirmation and first communion at years of discretion. This adaptation of the normative adult pattern would retain a unified initiatory rite, although the committee recognized that the prevailing pattern of infant baptism and adolescent confirmation and communion was likely to remain customary.

While the committee and the Standing Liturgical Commission had wrestled with many significant issues, no further action was taken regarding the work of this committee. Instead, a new committee was appointed for the 1964-1967 triennium, with Bonnell Spencer, a member of the Episcopal Church Order of the Holy Cross, to serve as chair. Spencer enlisted the assistance of Leonel Mitchell, who in 1964 had just completed his Th.D. at General Seminary. The subject of Mitchell's dissertation was baptismal anointing in the liturgies of the early Church up to the tenth century.

In an appendix to the published version of his dissertation, Mitchell concluded that the Anglican churches should restore to baptism the anointing with chrism.[35] He argued this more fully in a 1965 article. Based upon his understanding of the practice of the early Church, Mitchell concluded that any revision of the baptismal liturgy should emphasize the unity of the initiatory rite. He proposed the adoption of the pattern presented by the Church of England Liturgical Commission, in which the normative rite, however infrequently celebrated, would be a rite for the baptism, confirmation and first communion of adults. To conform to the classical "shape" of initiatory rites, Mitchell recommended that such a rite should comprise:

1. The blessing of the font...

2. Renunciation of the devil, accompanied by a confession of the candidate's sinfulness...

3. Acceptance of Jesus Christ as Lord and Savior and assent to the Apostles' Creed...

4. Baptism with water in the Name of the Trinity...

6. The anointing with chrism and signing with the cross...

7. Presentation to the bishop, with the laying on of hands...

8. The welcoming of the new member into the Christian fellowship...

9. Participation in the Eucharist and the reception of Communion.

For infants, a more radical procedure would "maintain the unity of the rite and admit infants to Communion." Since it was not likely that the Anglican Communion would readily abandon its traditional practice, Mitchell proposed a rite for infants that was an adaptation of the normative adult form. This rite omitted both imposition of hands by the bishop and admission to communion, but included anointing and signing with the cross. Children so baptized would then renew their vows, receive laying on of hands by the bishop and be admitted to communion in the context of adult baptism. However, the confirmation service would not include anointing and signing with the cross. Mitchell explained: "As Professor Lampe has pointed out, the anointing and signing with the cross refer to what is done at baptism, not confirmation."[36] What Mitchell did not say is that Lampe viewed chrismation to be at best of minor importance, an edifying symbol, illustrating the effect of baptism in bestowing union with Christ and the indwelling presence of the Spirit. Lampe did not advocate a restoration of chrismation in Anglican baptismal rites. Nonetheless, Mitchell brought to his work with the Standing Liturgical Commission the strong conviction that anointing with chrism should be a normative component of the baptism both of adults and of infants:

> The restoration to the Anglican rite of the anointing after baptism, with its rich Biblical and patristic symbolism, would be a substantial gain, and would place our liturgy in the company of the other historic rites of both Eastern and Western Christendom, without our giving up the tradition of episcopal confirmation.[37]

This view would prove to be a significant contribution as the Episcopal Church began to reshape its initiatory rites.

In a series of reports presented to the Standing Liturgical Commission over the course of the 1964-1967 triennium, both theological issues and the structure of the initiatory rite were considered. The premise of a unified initiatory rite comprising baptism, confirmation and communion was fundamental to much of the committee's work. However, unlike earlier discussion, consideration was given to providing such a rite for young children or even infants, in response to the increasing desire in the Church to admit younger children to communion. Spencer and Mitchell presented several alternatives to the commission: the bishop administering baptism and confirmation to infants of church families; the bishop administering the rites to children of about age six; the priest administering baptism and confirmation to infants, using oil blessed by the bishop; and maintaining the current pattern. When the Standing Liturgical Commission discussed these options, they decided to request guidance from the House of Bishops, but there are no records indicating that any further action was taken in this regard.

Not surprisingly, the question of the operation of the Spirit in baptism and confirmation was a significant dimension of the committee's work. In their first report they suggested a new approach: the Spirit is not *initially* bestowed either in baptism or in confirmation, but has been present since the beginning of creation and breathes life into every human being. When the work of the Spirit is viewed in this manner, the committee reasoned, one can understand baptism as a surrender of faith allowing the already present Spirit to take possession of the soul in an objective and sacramental way, while confirmation can be seen as a ratification of a surrender made by proxy (for those baptized as infants) and thus a deepening of commitment and receptivity to the Spirit.

There is no record of response by members of the Standing Liturgical Commission to this novel approach. However, a subsequent report of the committee distinguished the "seal of the Spirit," associated with chrismation and/or imposition of hands, from baptism with water, and still later a proposed rite called for baptism in water to be followed by "The Seal of the Spirit," specified as anointing and marking the sign of the cross on the forehead. Members of the commission objected strenuously to this proposal. Given the primary scriptural sign of water and the absence of unequivocal evidence of the use of chrism in New Testament times, concern was voiced about the prominence given to the symbol of chrism and its intimate relation to the "seal of the Spirit." While rejecting the proposed rite, the commission eventually accepted the basic underlying premise of the proposal: a distinction between "sacramental" and "pastoral" aspects of confirmation. The sacramental aspect was understood as a sealing which completes the work of baptism and is associated with the gift of the Spirit. The pastoral aspect included personal renewal of baptismal vows and commissioning for ministry.

It is at this point that the work of the committee ceased. The attention of the Standing Liturgical Commission turned to final preparations for the 1967 General Convention and proposals for a formal process of prayer book revision. Yet even as the commission and its subcommittee wrestled with the knotty theological and pastoral issues of Christian initiation, new approaches were being advanced outside the Standing Liturgical Commission.

New Approaches

In the Bradner Lectures given at General Theological Seminary in February 1964, Massey Shepherd proposed a radically new approach to Christian initiation:

> A Christian should be fully initiated once for all, for at whatever age he undergoes this experience...he will need Christian nurture for the rest of his life. It is spiritually healthy for a child to grow up in the household of faith with the full privileges of the family, and eat and drink at the family table. We learn the significance of the Eucharist by experience of its communal integrity before we are capable of understanding its implications by any analytical instruction.... Practically considered—and we can learn something here from our Roman Catholic and Orthodox brothers—we would not lose any more, and would probably lose less of our confirmands from continuing responsible witness, if

we incorporated them at a much earlier stage, if not in infancy, into the fullness of life of the Church.

The lovely custom of the bishop as chief pastor visiting all his flock to participate with them in the liturgy could be made the appropriate time for Baptism, Confirmation, and Eucharist all in one. Whatever the day or hour, whether Sunday or a holy day or some other day, this fullness of the liturgy of the people of God with their chief apostolic pastor would point to and manifest the Easter-Pentecost reality.[38]

Shepherd acknowledged that this might not be the definitive solution, but he argued that pressing pastoral concerns required new ways of thinking and acting. These issues included "divisions of teaching about the meaning and significance of Confirmation, both as it relates to the grace of Baptism and as it relates to the privilege of communicant status" and "decisions as to what infants of what parents to baptize, and the age when such baptized infants should be confirmed and admitted to the Eucharist." A primary concern for Shepherd was to restore the proper significance and dignity of baptism, since Anglican practice effectively magnified confirmation at the expense of baptism.[39]

Shepherd proposed a unified initiatory rite that would conclude with reception of communion. Similar proposals for a single rite of Christian initiation appeared a few years later in a 1968 report, *Confirmation Crisis*, issued by the Executive Council of the Episcopal Church. Having spent several years discussing what constituted satisfactory preparation for confirmation, the Council realized that it must evaluate these issues in light of "the meaning and place of Confirmation in our modern technological society." By coincidence, a Church of England study, *Crisis for Confirmation*, was published in 1967 to address similar concerns in England. Permission was received to reproduce historical and theological chapters from the English study since they concerned matters common to all Anglicans.[40]

Of particular note in the essays reprinted from the English study is an article by the liturgical scholar J. D. C. Fisher. Summarizing the historical development of the rites of Christian initiation, Fisher defined confirmation as a sacramental bestowal of the Holy Spirit, integral to Christian initiation. He argued that in the early Church this postbaptismal ceremony was part of a unified initiatory rite that culminated in communion. It was the sixteenth-century reformers who introduced the novel idea that confirmation was a ratification of baptismal vows:

[The Reformers] were themselves the innovators, because the evidence now available, not all of it known to the Reformers, shows beyond all doubt that in primitive times Confirmation, as it is now called, was an integral part of Baptism, and was administered to candidates of any age from infancy upwards; and since the Confirmation of infants continued to be permitted until the late middle ages, it was impossible up till then to demand that all candidates for Confirmation should have received a course of instruction beforehand.

Although Fisher insisted that ratification of baptismal vows was not part of confirmation, he saw value in the custom for those baptized in infancy. However, this ratification need not precede confirmation or admission to communion. Fisher acknowledged that a major stumbling block was the common Anglican understanding that some degree of personal commitment was essential to confirmation. But he concluded hopefully with a proposal:

> Once it is realized that this is not so [i.e., that some degree of personal commitment is indispensable to Confirmation], the way becomes clear to giving Baptism, Confirmation, and Communion in that order to children of a tender age, and to postponing the ratification of vows to an age which is considered pastorally and psychologically expedient.[41]

Fisher's proposal is virtually identical to that advanced by Shepherd a few years earlier. Implicit in both is a sacramental definition of confirmation, that is, that confirmation is an integral component of initiation and does not require personal ratification of baptismal promises. Both Fisher and Shepherd had thus moved a step beyond proposals which called for a unified initiatory rite for adults but continued to separate infant baptism and adolescent confirmation.

In addition to Fisher's article and other historical and theological essays from the English collection, *Confirmation Crisis* included chapters discussing issues relevant to the Episcopal Church. Frederick Warnecke, Bishop of Bethlehem, Pennsylvania, complained that much confusion arose from the multiple meanings of confirmation:

> [A] number of ill-assorted matters are packaged together in the grab-bag that we call Confirmation. There is the concept that Confirmation is the fulfillment of the commitment of Holy Baptism. There is the imagery of the reception of the sevenfold gifts of the Holy Spirit symbolized by the Laying on of Hands. There is the practical use of the service of Confirmation as a discipline of admission to the Holy Communion. Finally, this is all made the occasion of an episcopal visitation to a congregation and a church. These unlikely matters are intertwined in utter theological and practical confusion![42]

To deal with this confusion, Warnecke proposed separating these different theological and pastoral dimensions. Baptism would provide full and complete membership in the Church and would include the use of chrism blessed by a bishop. Chrismation at baptism would emphasize the gifts of the Holy Spirit, often associated with confirmation, and would further point to the presence of the bishop in baptism. Since baptism would make children full members of the Church, they could be admitted to communion between ages eight and ten after a course of instruction. Confirmation would then be a "serious act of personal commitment to Christ at maturity" and usually would be administered at an age no less than eighteen. Adults coming from denominations without episcopal confirmation would be received and admitted to communion by the parish priest, then subsequently confirmed as a sign of their rededication to lay ministry. Both children and adults would be confirmed at a diocesan service; the bishop's regular parish visitation could then be an occasion of pastoral interaction with the clergy and laity of the parish, including presiding at the regular Sunday services.[43]

By requiring instruction prior to admission to communion and so delaying admission to communion for those baptized in infancy, Warnecke's proposal was less revolutionary than those of Shepherd and Fisher. Yet all three proposals, seeking to untangle the pastoral and theological confusion surrounding confirmation, insisted that baptism be full Christian initiation and that confirmation cease to function as a disciplinary rite of admission to communion. Shepherd and Fisher defined confirmation as a sacramental bestowal of the Spirit and so included confirmation as part of a unified initiatory rite that culminated in communion. Warnecke was unwilling to relinquish the ratification of baptismal vows that was part of confirmation and so called for it to be administered in later adolescence. He was also unwilling to forego cognitive preparation for communion, unlike Shepherd, who suggested that children would come to understand the significance of communion through their experience of participation in the eucharist.

These were not isolated proposals but reflect a rethinking of patterns of Christian initiation that may be attributed to several factors: the shift to a post-Christian world view; the liturgical movement with its emphasis on the eucharist as a corporate action forming the body of Christ; scholarly insights into the historical development of Christian initiation; the ecumenical movement. Such issues encouraged the Anglican bishops at the 1968 Lambeth Conference to consider new approaches to initiation:

> The Conference recommends that each province or regional Church be asked to explore the theology of baptism and confirmation in relation to the need to commission the laity for their task in the world, and to experiment in this regard.[44]

This resolution originated not as an explicitly liturgical matter but in a sub-committee charged with considering the ministry of the laity. Pointing out that local congregations must examine themselves to determine whether they were "able to meet the demands of the twentieth century," the report described the eucharist as "focusing the work of the laity in the world in thanksgiving, offering, and reconciling." Concerned about the lack of any form of commissioning of laity analogous to ordination of clergy, alternative possibilities for experimentation were recommended:

(a) Admission to Holy Communion and confirmation would be separated. When a baptized child is of appropriate age, he or she would be admitted to Holy Communion after an adequate course of instruction. Confirmation would be deferred to an age when a young man or woman shows adult responsibility and wishes to be commissioned and confirmed for his or her task of being a Christian in society.

(b) Infant baptism and confirmation would be administered together, followed by admission to Holy Communion at an early age after appropriate instruction. In due course, the bishop would commission the person for service when he or she is capable of making a responsible commitment.[45]

As Leonel Mitchell has noted, these are not so much two very different proposals as they are different definitions of confirmation.[46] The first proposal would define confirmation as a ratification of baptismal vows (the definition used by Geoffrey Lampe) and hence postpone the rite until a person was prepared to make an adult commitment. This is essentially the definition adopted by Warnecke in his proposal in *Confirmation Crisis*. The second proposal adopted the view of confirmation held by Fisher and Shepherd, that confirmation is the initiatory bestowal of the Holy Spirit and properly belongs with baptism. In this latter case, the Lambeth Conference suggested, an adult rite of commissioning would be appropriate, though it would not be called "confirmation."

Regardless of the definition of confirmation used, the Lambeth recommendations continued to insist on the necessity of instruction prior to admission to communion. A cognitive approach had become such a part of Anglican practice that it was not readily set aside even as new approaches to Christian initiation were being considered. Nevertheless, the preparation necessary for admission to communion was distinguished from that needed for ratification of the baptismal commitment: younger children were capable of being instructed sufficiently to be admitted to communion, but commissioning for responsible Christian living was essentially an adult act.

The separation of admission to communion from a rite of ratification of baptismal vows would not fully resolve the issues surrounding Christian initiation. What, if any, instruction was to be required before admission to communion? Since the sixteenth century, the requirement of catechesis before confirmation coupled with the confirmation rubric had served to link cognitive preparation with admission to communion, and Anglicans seemed reluctant to relinquish this. The Lambeth recommendations viewed instruction as normative, as did Warnecke. But both Shepherd and Fisher proposed a unified initiatory rite culminating in communion, even for young children, and Shepherd suggested that children would come to comprehend the eucharist through participation in it.

What would prove to be more intractable was the definition of confirmation. Was confirmation an initiatory bestowal of the Spirit, properly a component of the baptismal rite, or was it a ratification of baptismal vows and so appropriately postponed until a mature adult commitment would be possible? What should be the role of the bishop in baptism and confirmation? As the Episcopal Church moved to official prayer book revision, this issue would present an enormous stumbling block.

A Method for Revising the Prayer Book

The early *Prayer Book Studies* were published for the purpose of study and discussion in the Church prior to undertaking formal revision of the prayer book. Proposals for the Church to begin official revision of the prayer book were considered and rejected by the 1958 and 1961 General Conventions. At the same time, the Standing Liturgical Commission was urging amendment of the constitution of the Episcopal Church to permit a new method of revision: trial use.

After failing to get such an amendment approved by the 1955 and 1958 conventions, the commission in 1961 published *Prayer Book Studies XV: The Problem and Method of Prayer Book Revision.*[47] This pamphlet began by identifying factors which were stimulating significant interest in prayer book revision in many parts of the Anglican Communion: massive social and cultural changes throughout the world since the revisions of the 1920s; the liturgical and ecumenical movements; advances in liturgical scholarship, particularly in study of the New Testament and patristic eras; contemporary biblical theology; the needs of younger churches in Asia and Africa to adapt liturgy to their own cultures. Although the commission was not calling for the immediate commencement of a formal revision process (no doubt a politically astute assertion, serving to maintain a focus on their proposal for a constitutional amendment), they were concerned that there were significant limitations inherent in the procedures used for previous revisions of the prayer book in the Episcopal Church. The size of General Convention, which continued to grow as the number of dioceses increased, and the amount of business considered by each convention made it difficult for proposals for prayer book revision to receive adequate consideration. Moreover, previous proposals for revision had been considered piecemeal, each change voted upon separately, with the result that it was not possible to review the entirety of a revised prayer book prior to its adoption.

As an alternative, the commission was proposing "trial use," a new method of prayer book revision which had already been used in several provinces of the Anglican Communion. The pamphlet described the primary advantage of trial use:

> It removes the task of liturgical revision from the realm of purely theoretical discussion and provides a basis of judgment on proposed forms from concrete experience.... One learns to worship and pray by doing it far more than by considering and discussing it.... The whole purpose of trial use is summed up in the consideration that we cannot really tell what we ought to say and to do until we try it out under the provident assistance of the Spirit of God working in us.[48]

The pamphlet concluded by urging the 1961 General Convention to approve a constitutional amendment allowing any meeting of the General Convention to:

> Authorize for trial use throughout the Church, as an alternative at any time or times to the established Book of Common Prayer or to any section or Office thereof, a proposed revision of the whole Book or of any portion thereof, duly undertaken by the General Convention.[49]

This amendment passed both Houses of General Convention in 1961 and consequently was brought for a second reading to the 1964 convention, where it was finally adopted.[50]

The 1964 convention, noting "growing desire in various parts of the Church for revision," also directed the Standing Liturgical Commission to develop a plan for revising the prayer book "with a special view to making the language and the form of the services more relevant to the circumstances of the Church's present ministry and life."[51] Approving the strategy proposed by the Standing Liturgical Commission, the 1967 convention initiated the formal process of revision.

The design called for drafting committees to work on separate sections of the prayer book. Each drafting committee was chaired by a member of the Standing Liturgical Commission, and additional members were appointed to each committee by the commission. Baptism and confirmation were treated together by a drafting committee on Christian initiation. The materials produced by the drafting committees were circulated at each stage of their work to 260 reader-consultants, chosen to represent a cross-section of the Episcopal Church, including bishops, priests and lay persons in several different occupations, in addition to a few consultants from other denominations who provided an ecumenical perspective. After a drafting committee reviewed the consultants' responses and revised its work, a draft was submitted to the Standing Liturgical Commission. Frequently the commission would direct the drafting committee to make further revisions. When each drafting committee's work was finally approved by the commission, their report was reviewed by a separate editorial committee for publication as a new *Prayer Book Study*.

Each diocese was asked to form a liturgical commission to assist in distributing questionnaires and compiling the results of trial use. Because these commissions proved to be a useful link between the "person in the pew" and the Standing Liturgical Commission, the chairpersons were eventually included as reader-consultants.

To facilitate the work of the various committees, Leo Malania was employed by the national Episcopal Church as Coordinator for Prayer Book Revision. A skilled diplomat who had served at the United Nations prior to his ordination as a priest, Malania did much to win acceptance of the new Book of Common Prayer through his ability to interpret proposals to the Church. Malania was assisted from 1969 until 1979 by Howard Galley, who was particularly helpful in the editorial work by ensuring consistent style in proposals from the different drafting committees.

A first round of revision, published in *Prayer Book Studies* 18 through 24, was presented to the 1970 General Convention and, with a few modifications, authorized for trial use for the triennium commencing January 1, 1971. The approved texts were published in a single volume for use in worship: *Services for Trial Use*,[52] commonly referred to as "the Green Book," a reference to its olive-green cover. Revisions of these rites and other new materials were approved by the 1973 General Convention for trial use during the triennium beginning on the first Sunday of Advent, 1973. A new pew edition, to be used along with other proposed materials, was published: *Authorized Services 1973*,[53] "the Zebra Book" (another reference to the cover design). The 1973 convention also approved a proposal by the Standing Liturgical Commission to conclude the process of revision. Accordingly, the *Draft Proposed Book of Common Prayer*[54] was circulated to all bishops and deputies six months prior to the opening of the 1976 convention. When that convention approved the draft, with minor amendments, the *Proposed Book of Common Prayer*[55] was authorized for trial use beginning on the first Sunday of Advent, 1976. After ratification by the 1979 convention, the new book became the official Book of Common Prayer of the Episcopal Church.[56]

In addition to the elaborate formal process, the Standing Liturgical Commission found a powerful ally in Associated Parishes. Several of its members served on the commission or on drafting committees, and the meetings of the Associated Parishes Council served as a forum for exchange of information about the work of various committees and as a sounding board for the consideration of ideas and proposals. Additionally, Associated Parishes decided in 1968 to devote all its resources to the success of trial use. Through its publications and through a system of field consultants funded by the national Episcopal Church, Associated Parishes helped congregations understand the purposes of liturgical revision and learn to celebrate the new rites. Another dimension of education emerged when in January 1970 Associated Parishes convened a meeting of the chairs of the diocesan commissions. In the initial stages of its work with the diocesan commissions, Associated Parishes offered assistance in the basic principles of liturgical renewal, principles which Associated Parishes had been developing since its inception in the 1940s. Associated Parishes also nurtured the fledging organization of diocesan liturgical chairs as it emerged as a distinct entity. Moreover, at each successive General Convention which considered revision of the prayer book, Associated Parishes was an active presence, lobbying deputies and bishops, addressing hearings, distributing literature, contributing to an unofficial daily news and opinion sheet, and hosting celebrations of the eucharist.[57]

The process of trial use provided an opportunity for significant liturgical education in many parishes and facilitated widespread participation in the revision of the prayer book. For the first time in the history of the Episcopal Church, the ordinary "person in the pew" was able to experience proposed liturgies at various stages in their development and to offer critique which could help shape the rites of the new prayer book. This was particularly important in the area of Christian initiation. The proposals advanced in the 1960s endeavored to take account of both liturgical scholarship and pastoral concerns. But inevitably these proposals were theoretical, presented as a structure or process of initiation rather than as fully developed rites. Such proposals could only become a practical reality as they came to be more widely discussed and as rites based upon these newly emerging principles were celebrated and then evaluated.

Some dimensions of the proposals were readily accepted with only minimal opposition. Owing to the liturgical and religious education movements, many parishes had already come to accept public baptism at the principal

Sunday service and the need for significant preparation and commitment of sponsors, and baptism was more frequently administered with a richer use of ceremonial. Some parishes and dioceses were beginning to experiment with "early" admission to communion, and there was growing agreement that confirmation should not continue to function as a disciplinary rite of admission to the eucharist. In these areas, agreement was rapidly reached on principles of ritual practice. But, as we have seen, there was no consensus about the meaning of confirmation. It is most especially in this latter area that trial use and the accompanying widespread discussion of prayer book revision enabled the Church to grapple more fully with the issues. In the end, a compromise was achieved, but it was a compromise that has resulted in continuing ambiguities and no small confusion.

NOTES

1. BCP 1928, p. 276.

2. *Journal of the General Convention*, 1943, pp. 404, 434.

3. "Revision Proposal Defeated," *The Living Church*, Oct. 10, 1943, p. 7.

4. Edward L. Parsons, "What about the Prayer Book?", *The Living Church*, Jan. 20, 1946, p. 10.

5. *Journal of the General Convention*, 1946, pp. 271, 439-41.

6. Minutes of the Standing Liturgical Commission, Mar. 12-14, 1946, p. 3, Record Group 10, Archives of the Episcopal Church, Austin, TX.

7. *Journal of the General Convention*, 1949, pp. 434-5.

8. New York: Church Pension Fund (hereafter cited as *PBS* I).

9. Ibid., p. vi.

10. Ibid., p. 5.

11. Ibid., p. 6.

12. Ibid., p. 12.

13. BCP 1928, pp. 273-4; *PBS* I, p. 25.

14. BCP 1928, p. 280; *PBS* I, p. 29.

15. *PBS* I, pp. 13-14.

16. Ibid., p. 19.

17. Ibid., p. 24.

18. Ibid., pp. 15, 24, 35.

19. Ibid., pp. 14-16, 24, 27.

20. Ibid., pp. 20-1, 31-5.

21. Ibid., pp. 19-21, 30-4.

22. Ibid., pp. 22-3.

23. *Journal of the General Convention*, 1952, p. 374; ibid., 1955, p. 377; ibid., 1964, p. 670.

24. Cyril C. Richardson, "The Proposed Revision of Our Liturgy: II. Confirmation," *Anglican Theological Review* 35 (1953): 176.

25. Shepherd, *The Oxford American Prayer Book Commentary*, pp. 271-81, 296-9, especially p. 271; idem, *The Worship of the Church* (Greenwich, CT: Seabury, 1952), pp. 166-86.

26. The Lambeth Conference 1958, *The Encyclical Letter from the Bishops together with the Resolutions and Reports* (London: SPCK; Greenwich, CT: Seabury Press, 1958), p. 1.47.

27. Ibid., pp. 2.80-1.

28. Coleman (ed.), *Resolutions of the twelve Lambeth Conferences*, pp. 2-3.

29. The Lambeth Conference 1958, *The Encyclical Letter...*, p. 1.47.

30. Ibid., pp. 2.85-7.

31. Ibid., p. 2.86.

32. *Baptism and Confirmation. A Report submitted by the Church of England Liturgical Commission to the Archbishops of Canterbury and York in November 1958* (London: SPCK, 1959).

33. Ibid., pp. 2-18.

34. Ibid., p. x.

35. Leonel L. Mitchell, *Baptismal Anointing*, Alcuin Club Collections 48 (London: SPCK, 1966), p. 190.

36. Leonel L. Mitchell, "The 'Shape' of the Baptismal Liturgy," *Anglican Theological Review* 47 (1965): 416-18 (the original text does not include an item number 5 in the outline of the rite).

37. Ibid., p. 419.

38. Shepherd, *Liturgy and Education*, pp. 106-7.

39. Ibid., pp. 104-5.

40. Executive Council of the Episcopal Church, *Confirmation Crisis* (New York: Seabury Press, 1968), pp. 5-8; Michael Perry (ed.), *Crisis for Confirmation* (London: SCM, 1967).

41. J. D. C. Fisher, "History and Theology," in *Confirmation Crisis*, pp. 41-2; cf. Perry (ed.), *Crisis for Confirmation*, pp. 45-65.

42. Frederick J. Warnecke, "A Bishop Proposes," in *Confirmation Crisis*, p. 136.

43. Ibid., pp. 137-43.

44. The Lambeth Conference 1968, *Resolutions and Reports* (London: SPCK; New York: Seabury Press, 1968), p. 37.

45. Ibid., pp. 98-9.

46. Leonel L. Mitchell, "Revision of the Rites of Christian Initiation in the American Episcopal Church," *Studia Liturgica* 10 (1974): 28.

47. New York: Church Pension Fund.

48. *PBS* XV, pp. 11-12.

49. Ibid., p. 15.

50. *Journal of the General Convention*, 1961, pp. 349-52; *Journal of the General Convention*, 1964, pp. 260-2. Holmes, "Education for Liturgy" (in Burson [ed.], *Worship Points the Way*, pp. 125, 130), states erroneously that trial use was defeated in 1961, passed on first reading in 1964, and finally adopted in 1967. This is the likely source of these same dates for the passage of the trial use amendment that are given by Stuhlman, *Eucharistic Celebration 1789-1979*, p. 133, and Moriarty, *The Liturgical Revolution*, p. 109.

51. *Journal of the General Convention*, 1964, pp. 348-9.

52. New York: Church Hymnal Corporation, 1971.

53. New York: Church Hymnal Corporation, 1973.

54. New York: Church Hymnal Corporation, 1976.

55. New York: Seabury, 1976.

56. *Journal of the General Convention*, 1979, pp. C-8-10.

57. See further in Michael Moriarty, "Associated Parishes and the 1979 Prayer Book," *Anglican and Episcopal History* 64 (1995): 218-25; idem, *The Liturgical Revolution*, pp. 156-62.

Chapter 7

Toward a New Pattern
of Christian Initiation:
Communion of All the Baptized

Christian initiation had been on the agenda of the Standing Liturgical Commission since 1962, and radically new proposals for the shape of Christian initiation had been advanced in the mid-1960s by the Anglican liturgical scholars Massey Shepherd, Leonel Mitchell and J. D. C. Fisher. Dioceses had begun to experiment with "early" admission to communion and in that context to reflect upon and challenge the traditional Anglican initiatory pattern of baptism, confirmation, first communion. But no clear consensus had emerged in the Church as to how best to resolve the theological and pastoral issues posed by Anglican initiatory practice as it had developed over the centuries.

The authorization of prayer book revision by the 1967 General Convention required the Standing Liturgical Commission to develop rites that would address the pastoral issues despite the lack of agreement in Anglicanism as to the meaning of confirmation and its place in Christian initiation. Moreover, because any new rites needed the approval of the General Convention for trial use, the Standing Liturgical Commission would need to develop sufficient support for its proposals in order to ensure legislative approval. Hence, with regard to baptism and confirmation, the story of prayer book revision is a story of intensive theological debate and continuing modification of rites as responses were received from around the Church. The story begins with the formation of Drafting Committee VI, on Christian initiation.

The Drafting Committee on Christian Initiation

Bonnell Spencer was reappointed as chair of the committee on Christian initiation, and he invited Leonel Mitchell to continue his service on the committee. Spencer expressed his hopes and concerns in a letter to Mitchell:

The recovery of a full realization and experience of the significance of baptism is essential to the renewal of the church and its members. But since there is far less agreement on what this involves and how it is to be accomplished than there is regarding the eucharist, we have our work cut out for us. Before we can even begin to consider the revision of the baptismal and confirmation offices, we must thoroughly discuss the basic principles and strive to reach a common ground from which we can operate.[1]

To begin the search for this common ground, Spencer invited those appointed to the committee to submit position papers to be circulated amongst the members prior to their first meeting, scheduled for May 1968. Focusing on theological principles, these papers presented a diversity of proposals for revising the pattern of Christian initiation in the Episcopal Church.

The Shape of the Initiatory Rite

In a preliminary report summarizing the work of the 1964-1967 committee, Spencer called for "a restoration of the full integrity of Christian Initiation in a single rite." This rite would include renunciation of evil and commitment to Christ; water baptism; the gift of the Holy Spirit; and admission to communion. Spencer defined the "gift of the Spirit" as a separate and distinct component of the initiatory rite, a component he described as the "sacramental aspect" of confirmation:

> By confirmation we must mean theologically...a sacramental element in the process of Christian initiation, a sealing which somehow completes the work of baptism and is associated with the gift of the Spirit... The [sacramental aspect of confirmation] must clearly and unmistakably be included in the initiation rites.[2]

Spencer's distinction between water baptism and the gift of the Spirit is comparable to the Mason/Dix line, which understood the apostolic pattern of Christian initiation to comprise two stages, remission of sins through baptismal washing and the conferral of the Spirit through imposition of hands, consignation and anointing. Unlike Dix, however, Spencer advocated the reintegration of these two stages into a single rite for infants as well as adults.

A similar proposal was presented by William Spilman, Curate at St. John's Church in Cold Spring Harbor, New York, and Associate Professor of History at C. W. Post College. Citing Dix and Thornton, Spilman argued that Christian initiation historically was administered in three successive stages: water baptism, imposition of hands by the bishop, and admission to communion. According to Spilman, each stage proclaimed a particular spiritual reality:

The primary sacramental signs of initiation would proclaim the spiritual realities of death and resurrection (by water baptism), of the bestowal of the Holy Spirit as the essence of the new life of incorporation into Christ (the laying-on-of-hands by the bishop), and of beginning a regular participation in this new Christ-life (reception of the eucharistic sacrament).[3]

Like Spencer, Spilman asserted that these components of initiation should constitute a single rite. However, Spilman insisted that the second phase (the gift of the Spirit) should be reserved to the bishop, while Spencer suggested that the priest could act as the bishop's deputy for the entire trifold initiatory rite.

Mitchell also urged that the sacramental integrity of Christian initiation be restored, but he did not make the sharp distinction between water baptism and the gift of the Spirit that Spencer and Spilman made. In his preliminary paper, Mitchell argued that the separation of initiation into the sacraments of baptism and confirmation had introduced a distinction foreign to the rites. Based upon the historical evidence presented in his *Baptismal Anointing* in addition to Cyril Pocknee's *Water and the Spirit*[4] and J. D. C. Fisher's article in *Crisis for Confirmation*,[5] Mitchell listed the elements he believed should constitute a "normative rite for Holy Baptism." Mitchell's list, first presented in his 1965 article in *Anglican Theological Review*,[6] had some elements in common with those proposed by Spencer. But while Spencer had listed "the gift of the Holy Spirit" following water baptism, Mitchell instead identified the postbaptismal actions as "anointing with chrism and signing with the cross" and "presentation to the bishop with the laying on of hands."[7] Unlike Spencer, Mitchell understood the gift of the Spirit to be effected by the entire initiatory rite, including water baptism, consignation with anointing, and imposition of hands.

Admission to Communion

Spencer, Spilman, and Mitchell each stated that a full rite of initiation should include admission to communion, but they differed in their understanding of the implications of this for infants and young children. Spilman viewed adult initiation as the norm and so did not discuss initiation of infants or young children, while Mitchell argued that the baptism of children should include their reception of communion.

Spencer's preliminary report stated only that some adjustments would be needed in the rite when the candidate was an infant. In a letter to Margaret Mead, a renowned anthropologist who served on the drafting committee, Spencer clarified his opinion:

there should be three steps for a child of practicing Christian parents. 1) Infant baptism... 2) A service of admission to Holy Communion, administered by the priest and parish when the child is six to ten years old... 3) An informed, self-determined adult commitment to Christ after full instruction as to its significance and duties made in the late teens or early twenties.[8]

This initiatory sequence was supported by Mead in her preliminary paper. She viewed each stage as a rite of passage: baptism marked birth and the beginning of early childhood; first communion would conclude early childhood; confirmation would be a personal commitment made in late adolescence or early adulthood. A similar process was proposed by another drafting committee member, George W. Barrett, Bishop of Rochester, New York, although Barrett did not define these as rites of passage.

Neither Barrett nor Spencer presented any theological rationale for separating infant baptism and admission to communion. Spencer clearly stated that baptism as complete Christian initiation was the only sacramental prerequisite to communion, yet he seemed reluctant to accept the full implications of this premise. First communion between the ages of six and ten was described as "early" admission: "It is important...to let the child share in the full experience of communion at the earliest possible age."[9] Similarly, Barrett commented, "There seems no reason why children should not be fed at the Table at a very early age."[10]

Reluctance to admit infants to communion is understandable, if not theologically defensible, when considered in light of the traditional Anglican practice of restricting communion to those who had been confirmed. Admission to communion at age six or ten would no doubt appear to be quite early when compared to the existing practice, and communicating infants might seem too drastic to consider.

Desire for a profession of faith prior to admission to communion may have been an additional factor, since the traditional Anglican sequence of baptism, confirmation, communion meant that Anglicans who were admitted to communion had ratified their baptismal promises at confirmation (or were "ready and desirous" to do so). Spencer suggested to Mead that the child being admitted to communion should express an "intention to follow Christ as his Lord and Master."[11] Baptism, including infant baptism, could be described as full and sufficient sacramental initiation, but admission to communion was still dependent upon a personal profession of faith.

A New Meaning of Confirmation

Although baptism was seen by several drafting committee members as the only sacramental prerequisite to communion, most of the preliminary papers called for the continued use of a rite of "confirmation." Spencer argued that including the sacramental aspect of confirmation in baptism would allow the pastoral dimensions of confirmation to emerge more fully. Confirmation, administered in the late teens or early twenties, would then be "a recognition of what has been accomplished in baptism and a personal recommitment to it."[12] Likewise, Barrett described confirmation as "an adult decision with strong implication for witness and mission, a kind of commissioning for lay ministry,"[13] and Mitchell suggested that confirmation be "a solemn renewal of the baptismal vows made before the bishop at the Eucharist."[14]

Reuel Howe, another member of the drafting committee, suggested that confirmation be viewed as "joining the world," in order to shift the focus of church life and confirmation instruction to the support and training of Christians for their work and witness in the world.

These proposals share the premise that a mature personal affirmation of faith is an important event in Christian life, even though baptism is understood to be full sacramental initiation. The only objection to a separate rite of reaffirmation came from Spilman, who argued that his proposal to restrict Christian initiation to adults obviated the need for an additional non-sacramental rite. Mead saw a need for additional rites of passage, such as a move to a new home, a change of occupation, the death of a marriage which was ending in divorce, and the formation of a new household, including same-sex friendships, although she recognized that these suggestions went far beyond the purview of the drafting committee.

Theological and Liturgical Principles for Initiation

At its first meeting, in May 1968, the drafting committee began with a thorough discussion of theological and liturgical principles, summarized in a two-page "Findings." The "Findings" emphasized that all people are children of God, whether or not they are baptized:

> Man as created is a child of God. He does not have to be baptized to become one.
>
> ...we must acknowledge that, due to the universal action of the Spirit, God also works in men independently of baptism.

Baptism was described as incorporation into the fellowship of the redeemed:

Redemption is the work of God and man in Christ. By it all mankind is brought into a new relationship with God and man. The baptized accept this reconciliation and are made members of Christ's Body, the humanity that is aware of and responsive to its redemption.[15]

These brief statements of theological principles prefaced a somewhat lengthier discussion of the process of Christian initiation. Throughout the "Findings," baptism as incorporation into Christ was stressed, while other aspects of baptism (e.g., dying and rising with Christ, conversion, inaugurated eschatology) were not discussed.[16]

While not a comprehensive treatment of the meaning of baptism, the "Findings" presented a radical proposal for altering traditional Anglican initiatory practice. Drawing upon members' recommendations for a unified initiatory rite, the report stated: "Baptism should administer all aspects of Christian initiation, including the full gift of the Holy Spirit, and should lead directly to the reception of Holy Communion."[17] There was no discussion of whether "the full gift of the Holy Spirit" is a separate and distinct element of the baptismal rite, as Spencer and Spilman maintained, or is effected by the entire initiatory rite, as Mitchell suggested.

The question of admission to communion was also skirted. The committee agreed that infants should be recognized as eligible to receive at their baptism. They would "not ordinarily be communicated because of the difficulty of administration," but they should be permitted to do so as soon as they desired to participate. A course of instruction was not necessary prior to admission to communion, but the committee could not agree whether to provide a rite to be used when children became regular communicants, nor on the process by which those baptized in other denominations could become communicants in the Episcopal Church.[18]

An additional rite of reaffirmation of baptism, suggested by most of the committee in their preliminary papers, was proposed:

> A service should be provided for a baptized person's mature recognition and acceptance of his place and participation as a Christian in the world, and the reception of grace for it through the laying on of hands.[19]

The committee could not agree whether this service should be called "confirmation." They expressed concern that continued use of the term would imply that the service was a sacramental completion of Christian initiation, that it was the culmination and conclusion of Christian education, and that it should be done at a given age regardless of personal response.

These initial proposals engendered a variety of responses from the Standing Liturgical Commission and its consultants. Most consultants supported the development of a unified initiatory rite. However, just as the drafting committee was not in agreement about admission to communion and a service of mature commitment, so also did consultants express a diversity of opinion. A few consultants argued that preparation and a service of admission to communion were desirable, but others agreed that baptism should lead immediately to reception of communion. Some believed that a service of adult commitment was needed; others found it superfluous. The age at which such a rite would be administered and whether it should be called "confirmation" were also disputed. Questions were raised as to the role of the bishop in initiation, a subject not discussed in the "Findings."

The "Findings" were presented by Spencer at a June 1968 meeting of the Central New York Committee on Confirmation, providing an opportunity to discuss the drafting committee's proposal in light of pastoral experience with altering the traditional initiatory sequence. Spencer reported that the Central New York committee "was in enthusiastic agreement with the basics of our [the drafting committee's] position" but believed that preparation for admission to communion was needed in order to give children "some preliminary insights" and that a simple service of admission was desirable. The Central New York committee supported the idea of a service of adult commitment, but insisted that this be optional and not result in any special status or privilege.[20]

The comments received from the consultants were discussed thoroughly by the drafting committee in September. Deciding that the "Findings" had served their purpose and did not need revision, the committee divided the work of drafting services: a baptismal service that included the sacramental aspects of confirmation, a service to admit baptized children to communion, and a service of adult affirmation of the baptismal commitment. They were still debating the merits of the latter two services: "We are not certain in our own minds whether either the service of admission for children or the subsequent affirmation service is necessary or wise."[21]

At the September meeting the committee also reviewed the recommendations of the 1968 Lambeth Conference regarding the sequence of Christian initiation and stated their agreement with the second alternative:

> Infant baptism and confirmation would be administered together, followed by admission to Holy Communion at an early age after appropriate instruction. In due course, the bishop would commission the person for service when he or she is capable of making a responsible commitment.[22]

The drafting committee's support for this alternative suggests that they had come to agree that the subsequent rite of affirmation should not be called confirmation. While the Lambeth provision for appropriate instruction contradicted the committee's earlier statement that readiness for communion did not require a course of instruction, the minutes of the committee meeting did not address the discrepancy.

A Unified Rite:
Holy Baptism with the Laying-on-of-Hands

When the drafting committee met next, in December 1968, they proceeded to draft a baptismal rite. The draft was circulated to consultants for their responses and revised by the Standing Liturgical Commission, the drafting committee, and finally by the Editorial Committee before its publication as *Holy Baptism with the Laying-on-of-Hands (Prayer Book Studies* 18: On Baptism and Confirmation).[23] The *Prayer Book Study* included an introduction prepared by Spencer and emended by the various committees.

The liturgical principles articulated by the drafting committee had called for a single rite of Christian initiation. The proposed rite, "Holy Baptism with the Laying-on-of-Hands," included ministry of the word, renunciation of evil, interrogatory creed, water baptism, imposition of a hand with consignation and optional chrismation, and eucharist. The committee's intent was explained in the introduction to *PBS* 18: "The basic principle of this proposal is the reunion of Baptism, Confirmation, and Communion into a single continuous service, as it was in the primitive Church."[24]

In its first draft, the drafting committee provided no further rites or ceremonies for admission to communion or for reaffirmation of faith. But at the request of the Standing Liturgical Commission, *PBS* 18 included a form of "Admission to Holy Communion" for persons being received into the Episcopal Church from another Christian church and rubrical provision for administering imposition of hands to persons baptized in accordance with the 1928 rite or any other baptismal rite which did not include "confirmation."[25]

Understandings of Confirmation
The introduction to *PBS* 18 distinguished between "confirmation" and medieval or Reformation practices later associated with confirmation. Confirmation was said to have developed from the final baptismal anointing and imposition of hands which at Rome were reserved to the bishop alone. The practices later associated with confirmation were listed as instruction in Christian faith and life, renewal of baptismal vows, and a prerequisite to reception of communion.[26]

In its discussions, the drafting committee had gradually come to the conclusion that these later practices would be better accomplished separate from
a rite of confirmation. Spencer acknowledged to committee members this
development in their thinking:

> The consultants have not shared in our discussions and therefore do not know
> the process by which we have reached the conclusion (*which we did not have
> at the beginning ourselves*) that Communion, commitment and Christian edu-
> cation should all be constant experiences, rather than Communion be the
> "reward" for a once-for-all commitment after an all-inclusive confirmation
> instruction.[27]

This innovative understanding was explained in the introduction to *PBS* 18.
Education and commitment should be seen as lifelong processes:

> The likelihood of fluctuations in faith and commitment underlines the need for
> continuous instruction geared to a person's intellectual growth and experi-
> ence, and for continuous emphasis on the call to commitment.[28]

Rather than a singular personal affirmation of one's baptismal commitment,
regular renewal was desirable. This would occur as the congregation joined in
the baptismal promises each time baptism was celebrated at the Sunday service and at each celebration of the eucharist:

> since baptism is here associated directly with the Holy Communion, that sac-
> rament will come to be understood, even on other occasions, as an opportunity
> for personal and corporate commitment, self-oblation, and reconsecration to
> Christ.[29]

Since the proposed rite permitted all the baptized to receive communion, confirmation would no longer disrupt the connection between baptism and eucharist, and children would not view communion as a reward for attending
confirmation instruction and renewing their baptismal vows.

Having addressed the practices associated with confirmation during the
Middle Ages and the Reformation, there remained the "primitive" meaning,
that is, postbaptismal anointing and imposition of hands. The introduction to
PBS 18 offered only a brief historical discussion. It focused on the role of the
bishop in baptism and the adjustments made in the early Middle Ages when it
was no longer possible for the bishop to be present at every baptism.[30] Anglican debate about the meaning of confirmation was not acknowledged, and in
most places the introduction used the term "laying-on-of-hands," not "confirmation," when speaking of the postbaptismal action.

The drafting committee's intent was to acknowledge different interpretations of confirmation, as Mitchell explained at a 1970 conference:

If we accept Calvin's definition of confirmation [confirmation is ratifying one's baptismal vows], then the proposal is not confirmation, but simply additional baptismal ceremonies. If we accept the more traditional view [confirmation is a postbaptismal imposition of hands with anointing and consignation], the proposal conforms with tradition.

Mitchell then described the committee's decision not to provide a once-for-all rite of reaffirmation. He pointed out that renewal of baptismal vows would take place as baptized persons participated in the baptism of others, and suggested that other liturgical forms could be devised if it was pastorally desirable to mark specific occasions in the lives of individuals.[31]

The Seal of the Spirit

Although *PBS* 18 did not mention Anglican debate about the definition of confirmation, as the drafting committee prepared its first draft of the new initiatory rite they had given special attention to the seal of the Spirit. Acknowledging that in some Anglican schools of thought confirmation was associated with a sacramental gift of the Spirit, the committee expressed its desire "to indicate that this action has been restored to baptism, of which it originally was a part," while avoiding "the introduction of anything that might be considered a new ceremony in the baptismal liturgy." Hence:

the reception into the Church and signing with the cross, already part of the rite, have been given a more precise association with the gifts of the Spirit. The laying-on of hands is included in the action of the consignation and, if desired, it may take the form of a chrismation.[32]

The imposition of hands and chrismation were an innovation in the baptismal liturgy of the Episcopal Church. Laying on of hands, a baptismal ceremony in the early Church, had traditionally been the central symbolic action of Anglican confirmation rites. With regard to chrism, *PBS* 18 explained that it was part of Christian tradition, even though it was not part of mainstream Anglican tradition: "Chrism has been associated with baptism at least since the second century, it was used universally until the sixteenth century, and it is still used today by the majority of Christians."[33] Hence the committee's claim to avoid introducing "new ceremonies" into the baptismal liturgy was based upon its understanding of the whole of Christian tradition, not Anglican tradition more narrowly defined.

The postbaptismal action was closely identified with the seal of the Spirit. The drafting committee's first draft implied that the seal was conveyed by the consignation: "By this sign of the cross, we receive you into the family of God, and seal you with the Holy Spirit, that you may share in the priesthood of

Christ now and forever."[34] However, the Standing Liturgical Commission, wanting more emphasis on the imposition of hands, proposed a revision: "By this laying-on of hands and sign of the cross I seal you with the Holy Spirit, that you may share in the priesthood of Christ now and forever."[35] The formula was further simplified in *PBS* 18: "*Name*, you are sealed by the Holy Spirit." This eliminated any reference to the action by which the sealing was accomplished, but the rubric immediately following, "When all have been sealed..."[36] made it clear that the postbaptismal action of imposition of a hand, consignation, and optional chrismation was considered to be the sealing with the Spirit.

The rite acknowledged the work of the Spirit in the water of baptism as well. The blessing of the water included the phrase, "through [the water of Baptism] we are renewed by the Holy Spirit," and the postbaptismal prayer began, "Heavenly Father, we thank you that by water and the Holy Spirit you have bestowed upon these your servants the forgiveness of sins, and have raised them to the new life of grace." Yet despite this recognition of the work of the Spirit in the water of baptism, the postbaptismal prayer was a prayer for the bestowal of the gifts of the Spirit: "Strengthen and confirm them, O Lord, with the riches of your Holy Spirit."[37] Since this prayer was followed immediately by the consignation and imposition of hands, the structure implied that the gifts of the Spirit were actually bestowed upon the baptizand through the postbaptismal action.

Although the postbaptismal prayer and action were referred to as "laying-on of hands," not "confirmation," the rubric before the prayer directed that it be said over "the newly-baptized and other candidates for Confirmation."[38] The implication that the postbaptismal imposition of hands was indeed confirmation was strengthened by the use of a contemporary version of the prayer for the sevenfold gifts of the Spirit. This prayer, found in the Gelasian sacramentary as a prayer said by the bishop after the baptismal washing, had been included in Anglican rites of confirmation since the 1549 prayer book. When Mitchell presented the proposed rite at a meeting of the Anglican Society in May 1969,[39] they suggested that the prayer be more recognizably that of the 1928 BCP, to emphasize that baptism and confirmation were both included in the rite. Accordingly, the drafting committee's proposed prayer was rewritten by Charles Guilbert, Custodian of the Book of Common Prayer and a member of the Standing Liturgical Commission, during the final editing of *PBS* 18.[40]

Hence, despite Mitchell's claim that the proposal allowed different interpretations of confirmation, the committee's intent was clear. The introduction to *PBS* 18 asserted that "Baptism, Confirmation, and Communion" were reunited "into a single continuous service," a rite which included "burial with Christ in the water...followed by the conferring of the gifts of the Spirit by the Laying-on-of-hands."[41] This was a two-stage rite, water-baptism followed by the seal of the Spirit. Although the introduction was careful to speak of "the laying-on-of-hands," not "confirmation," when describing the postbaptismal rites, the committee had defined confirmation as a postbaptismal imposition of hands that bestowed the Spirit, and rejected the definition of confirmation as the ratification of baptismal vows. They acknowledged that conscious reaffirmation of baptismal faith was pastorally desirable but repudiated the position that it was a component of initiation.

Admission to Communion

PBS 18 included a rubric permitting the newly baptized to receive communion: "Those who have now been christened may receive Holy Communion."[42] The introduction specified that all the newly baptized, including infants, should be communicated at the time of their baptism: "It is anticipated that Holy Communion will be administered to all who have been baptized at this service: by ancient custom, infants are communicated from a spoon or by intinction."[43] However, reception of communion at the baptismal eucharist was distinguished from regular reception of communion by children: "The age at which a child is admitted to communion on a regular basis is a pastoral problem which will require sensitive handling." Acknowledging the concern voiced by several consultants that children ought to be instructed and have some understanding prior to their admission to communion, the introduction asked rhetorically, "How much does an adult understand?" It suggested that reception of communion should be an integral part of even very young children's experience:

> A small child often has a natural recognition of the sacrament; but even when there is little evidence of such recognition, early admission to the altar has this great value: communion becomes an integral part of the child's Christian experience from the beginning. He can never remember when he was not fed at the table of the Lord.[44]

Further clarification of the feasibility of communicating infants and young children was left to be determined by trial use.

The committee had considered developing a service to admit children to communion but had decided against it. When such a service was tried in the Diocese of Central New York, it was perceived as confirmation without the laying on of hands. Spencer explained to a consultant:

to make an occasion out of it [admission to communion] directs the attention to the "first" rather than to the communion. Our feeling is that the more naturally and quietly the child slips into his place at the Lord's Table, the better.[45]

While no rite was provided for admission of children to communion, at the request of the Standing Liturgical Commission the drafting committee developed a brief rite of "Admission to Holy Communion" to receive into the Episcopal Church persons baptized in other churches. The Standing Liturgical Commission was particularly concerned that the laying on of hands be provided. Spilman objected to this request:

> To insist that persons having received water baptism but not the laying on of hands must receive the latter before enjoying full membership in the Episcopal Church is, in effect, to say that their baptism was defective and that episcopal confirmation is necessary for Christian initiation. To take this position seems to undermine what we set out to do.[46]

Although laudable from an ecumenical standpoint, Spilman's argument is inconsistent with the drafting committee's inclusion of the imposition of hands as a postbaptismal action. Spilman seems to say, on the one hand, this new baptismal rite must include these postbaptismal actions because they represent confirmation and the seal of the Spirit, but, on the other hand, we must acknowledge water baptism administered in other traditions without insisting upon imposition of hands. Thus the postbaptismal sealing was necessary for those baptized in the Episcopal Church, but that same action should not be required of those baptized in other communions.

The drafting committee shared Spilman's concern and proposed that the decision to receive laying on of hands be made by the person being admitted into the Episcopal Church.[47] Their hope was that most people would neither desire nor request it. However, several consultants insisted that imposition of hands be mandatory. In the final editing before publication, the Editorial Committee added a concluding rubric to the proposed rite of Admission to Holy Communion: "To receive the Laying-on-of-hands, persons so admitted to Holy Communion shall present themselves at a public service of Baptism."[48] This could be construed as leaving imposition of hands optional, but the force of the rubric strongly encouraged it, if not absolutely requiring it.

However, the purpose of the laying on of hands for persons thus admitted to communion is not readily apparent. The service of admission stated that persons were "officially received into The Episcopal Church," and the concluding rubric implied that people could receive communion after the rite of admission but before receiving laying on of hands.[49] The introduction noted that the admission service did not include laying on of hands "in order to avoid any possible misapprehension that this action is an essential prerequisite for admission to the communion of the Episcopal Church."[50] Thus the laying on of hands did not convey membership or admission to communion. However, a rubric introductory to the baptismal rite equated the laying on of hands with confirmation: "Those who have been baptized in this or any other Christian Church, but have not been confirmed, may receive the Laying-on-of-hands at this Service."[51] By adding to the service of "Admission to Holy Communion" a rubric strongly encouraging or requiring imposition of hands, the Editorial Committee implied that confirmation was still necessary and should be supplied for persons baptized but not confirmed, even if no change in status would result from the additional ceremony.

Just as persons baptized in another Christian church but not confirmed could receive the laying on of hands at a service of baptism, those baptized with the 1928 prayer book rite but not confirmed could receive the laying on of hands at this new rite. This was not required, although Spencer suggested privately that those baptized with the 1928 rite would "all receive the laying-on of hands at the baptismal eucharist of the bishop's first visitation after they reach the age at which in that parish they begin their regular Communions."[52] This suggestion reflects the importance attached by Spencer and other members of the drafting committee to the imposition of hands at baptism. The post-baptismal action was not merely an explanatory ceremony enriching the baptismal rite. Rather, the imposition of hands was an integral part of baptism because it conferred the gift of the Spirit, and so it should be supplied for those who had not received this sacramental action. Spencer did not explain why this would be done by the bishop and not the parish priest, to whom the entire rite of baptism with laying on of hands could be delegated. However, the suggestion is in keeping with the traditional Anglican practice of confirmation by a bishop, although in the *PBS* 18 proposal the episcopal imposition of hands would not necessarily precede admission to communion.

The Role of the Bishop

The proposed rite was revolutionary not only in combining baptism, confirmation and communion in a single service, but also in its understanding that the bishop is the chief minister of baptism and should normally preside over the entire service. The introduction claimed that this would demonstrate the bishop's function as "chief sacramental minister of the diocese, the clergy of the parish joining with him as fellow ministers." No longer would the bishop's role in initiation be limited to confirmation, a small part of the total initiatory action.[53]

The idea that the bishop should preside at baptism was virtually unchallenged. However, the proposal that the bishop could delegate the entire rite to a priest was less favorably received. One consultant commented, "I doubt most seriously that the church or its General Convention is any way near accepting the idea of the priest acting for the bishop and 'confirming.'"[54] Others expressed concern that the delegation of the rite to priests would diminish the bishop's relationship with local congregations.

In addition, a few persons expressed a desire for the bishop to take part in receiving persons into the Episcopal Church. Members of the Anglican Society suggested to Mitchell that reception by the bishop was "the distinctive thing you do to become an 'Episcopal.'"[55] The Anglican theologian John Macquarrie argued that the bishop as representative of the whole Church was "one of our main bulwarks against both individualism and congregationalism."[56]

Consultants proposed various options to strengthen the role of the bishop. Some recommended that the initiatory rite be delegated to a priest only in exceptional circumstances; others urged that the use of chrism blessed by the bishop be mandatory, not optional. However, no provisions were made to enhance the role of the bishop in the rites presented in *PBS* 18.

Reaffirmation of Faith

After much deliberation, the drafting committee had decided not to provide a service for the reaffirmation of faith. While recognizing a pastoral need for those baptized as infants to affirm and renew their baptismal vows, they concluded that this was best done continually, not as a once-for-all recommitment. There were numerous objections to this position. Many consultants emphasized the importance of a mature personal affirmation of the baptismal commitment, and some recommended that the bishop preside over this rite.

Despite resistance to the elimination of a ritual reaffirmation of baptismal vows, most consultants were willing to separate admission to communion from such a rite. The primary concern was not to preserve the traditional Anglican initiatory pattern but rather to provide for a conscious personal affirmation of faith:

> I think that there is still very much a need for personal renewal of baptismal vows, and assumption of adult responsibility on the part of the individual. I don't care whether it is called confirmation or not... The important thing is that it be an adult commitment; and that it not be tied to admission to communion.[57]

At its January 1969 meeting, the Standing Liturgical Commission discussed the requests for a service of affirmation of faith. Rather than assign the development of a "puberty rite" to the Drafting Committee on Christian Initiation, the commission requested that the Drafting Committee on the Catechism consider "the provision of liturgical material for occasional services...connected with...significant turning-points in the lives of individuals (e.g., a 'puberty rite')."[58] By delegating this task to the committee on the catechism, the Standing Liturgical Commission separated reaffirmation of faith from Christian initiation. Nonetheless, although the committee on the catechism gave some attention to the question of rites of reaffirmation and rites of passage, the task of developing a rite eventually fell to Spencer.[59] He produced "A Form of Commitment to Christian Service," which was presented to the Standing Liturgical Commission in July 1970 and published with other rites in Prayer Book Studies 24, *Pastoral Offices*.[60]

The introduction to *PBS* 24 reaffirmed the basic principles of *PBS* 18:

> The Commission has taken the stand that the theological and pastoral integrity of baptism should not be broken or overshadowed by a separated confirmation... [P]ersonal commitment to one's baptismal promises should be made not once and for all at confirmation, but many times over, preferably within the context of a service of baptism with the Laying-on-of-Hands.[61]

The new service was intended as a renewal of a lay person's "commitment to the service of Christ in the world," especially at critical moments such as graduation and change in vocation. The service was simple and flexible. The individual, in consultation with the minister, developed in advance a statement of purpose or a series of questions and answers. Before the offertory at a eucharist, the person came forward to make the statement, and the minister then commended the person to the work and said a prayer. The eucharist continued with the exchange of the peace and the offertory.[62]

The "Form of Commitment to Christian Service" was accepted by the 1970 General Convention and included essentially unchanged in the 1979 prayer book.[63] Yet although intended to fulfill the expressed need for a ritual public commitment to the vows of one's baptism, it did not satisfy demands for a rite of reaffirmation, perhaps because it was completely separate from the initiatory rite and was not administered by a bishop.

The Church's Response to *Prayer Book Studies* 18

The proposed rite of "Holy Baptism with the Laying-on-of-hands" introduced a revolutionary change in Anglican theology and practice. Cognizant of this, the drafting committee and the Standing Liturgical Commission took several steps to introduce the proposed rite.

The process of sending minutes of each drafting committee meeting to consultants allowed some preliminary discussion of the issues. Not only did consultants read and respond to the theological statements and draft rites, some also presented the materials to groups of clergy and laity and reported responses to the drafting committee. At least a few consultants used the proposed rites on an experimental basis. After the Suffragan Bishop of Oklahoma, Frederick Putnam, used a draft of the proposed rite to baptize three adults and confirm about thirty, the rector of the parish reported:

> The service was very well received by members of the parish family, and many expressed their feeling of actually participating in Christian initiation as opposed to the present Prayer Book Baptism and Confirmation Services, in which the congregation are spectators.[64]

The discussions and occasional experimental use of drafts of the new rites offered insights as the drafting committee continued its work and helped affirm the direction taken in the revision. Perhaps more importantly, these discussions encouraged a significant number of people in the Church to grapple with the issues.

At its January 1969 meeting, the Standing Liturgical Commission discussed how to introduce the rite, particularly how to encourage the support of bishops for the "quite-radical treatment of confirmation." They decided that the task should be primarily handled by the bishops on the commission.[65]

When *PBS* 18 was prepared for publication in summer 1969, drafts were sent first to all bishops with a cover letter from Chilton Powell, Bishop of Oklahoma and chair of the Standing Liturgical Commission. Powell encouraged the bishops to comment on the draft and to consult with their diocesan liturgical commissions. A few weeks later, consultants and the chairs of diocesan liturgical commissions also received the draft, with a request for comments and suggestions prior to final review by the Standing Liturgical Commission in September 1969.

This consultation with bishops and diocesan liturgical commissions was an unusual step, one not taken, for example, with revisions of the eucharist or the daily offices. The Standing Liturgical Commission, recognizing the radical nature of the proposal, desired as wide a measure of consultation as possible prior to publication of *PBS* 18. It reported to the 1970 General Convention: "The positive response of Consultants, Diocesan Chairmen, and Bishops, encouraged the Commission to proceed with the publication of this proposal."[66]

PBS 18 was completed nearly a full year prior to the 1970 Convention. This permitted widespread discussion in the Church. Many who read the study accepted the invitation in the preface to "contribute to this consultation by sending comments to the Standing Liturgical Commission."[67] Associated Parishes sponsored two conferences, one for the chairs of diocesan liturgical commissions, to introduce *PBS* 18. Spencer and Mead spoke at these conferences, and the proposed rite was celebrated with candidates for baptism.[68] Mitchell spoke at a conference sponsored by the Church of St. Mary the Virgin in New York City; the proceedings of this conference were published, permitting wider dissemination of the material presented.[69] The proposal was discussed by many diocesan liturgical commissions and other groups of clergy and laity, and in at least a few parishes, the rite was used experimentally. *The Living Church* presented a series of articles and an editorial about *PBS* 18; an editorial also appeared in *The Witness*.

Some respondents stated their enthusiastic support for the proposal and their hope that the rite would be approved for trial use, but others had reservations about the rite or the rationale given. There were numerous calls for some rite of adult affirmation of faith:

> The issue of the later commitment of the fully-initiated infants is not adequately faced by the new rite.[70]

> Is it not also true that at some point there is need for verbal and rational commitment and that this definite commitment is provided by confirmation?[71]

> The first great criticism of the clergy and the lay people to whom I've presented Prayer Book Studies 18...is that it neglects any recognition of adolescence or adulthood.[72]

The "Form of Commitment to Christian Service" was developed in response to these and similar criticisms, but it was not completed until July 1970 and was published only a short time before the General Convention in October 1970. Even after its publication, it was rarely mentioned in articles or correspondence about initiatory practice and theology and thus does not seem to have been widely acclaimed as a rite of affirmation of baptismal vows.

Most of those who called for a rite of adult commitment were willing to separate admission to communion from a such a rite, but objections were made to infant communion. It was argued that communion requires conscious cooperation and rational understanding on the part of the individual, and that admitting infants to communion suggests a "magical" view of sacraments. One article pointed out, "in effect the proposal says that arguments in favor of infant baptism are arguments for infant confirmation and communion as well," but the author did not explain why the arguments for infant baptism should not apply to infant confirmation and communion.[73]

The role of the bishop engendered numerous comments. There were many suggestions that the use of chrism be required in order to provide a link with the bishop. For similar reasons, it was asserted that the imposition of hands should be mandatory for persons being received from other Christian traditions: "it is important for the church to retain a visible sacramental sign of union with the bishop."[74] While some agreed that the use of the new rite would strengthen the bishop's relationship with local parishes, many questioned whether this would be the result: "is it not more likely that the service will evolve upon the parish priest regularly, thus rather *diminishing* the bishop's role in Christian initiation?"[75]

The argument that this was a single continuous rite, "as it was in the primitive Church," was challenged. Should we engage in a particular practice *because* it was done in the early Church? An editorial pointed out that chrism seemed to be introduced into the rite because of its association with baptism in the early Church, not because it was pastorally desirable in the twentieth century.[76] Mitchell responded at a conference on prayer book revision:

> Actually, we began from the other end of the calendar—with the current year and the so-called confirmation crisis... Our intention has been to make pastoral, liturgical, and theological sense. Whether or not we have succeeded will be for you and our fellow churchmen to decide.[77]

In addition to the comments on the rite and its rationale, there were numerous comments about the potential problems of trial use. If the rite was approved for trial use and then used in some parishes but not others, great confusion could result. If a child was baptized and admitted to communion in one parish, would the child be able to continue to receive communion in parishes with a different practice? Should all baptized and unconfirmed persons be immediately admitted to communion? How would the Episcopal Church handle membership statistics, which counted people as "baptized," "confirmed," and "communicant"? If the rite was not finally accepted in a new prayer book, what would be the status of infants and children initiated under trial use? Several respondents recommended that trial use be postponed until more extensive discussion and education could take place throughout the Church.

In response to such concerns the Standing Liturgical Commission appointed a "Special Committee of Advice on the Implications of Prayer Book Studies 18," chaired by Dupuy Bateman, a lay member of the commission. The committee met in May 1970 and made several recommendations to the

Standing Liturgical Commission. A proposal that the use of chrism be mandatory was rejected due to vigorous protests by some commission members, who argued that the practice would be less objectionable if it was optional and not required.[78] The Standing Liturgical Commission agreed that imposition of hands should be required for persons being received from other communions, but because of the expense of a new printing of *PBS* 18, the commission simply noted the suggestion for consideration when the rite was revised in the next triennium. The committee of advice supported the development of a rite of reaffirmation; "A Form of Commitment to Christian Service" was included in *PBS* 24.

Other proposals of the committee of advice were addressed in a resolution presented by the Standing Liturgical Commission for adoption by the 1970 General Convention. The special committee recommended a period of study for clergy to enable them to provide similar training in their congregations; the proposed legislation directed bishops to "arrange a period of intensive study and instruction in their several dioceses until Easter 1971." The special committee urged that priests have the explicit permission of their bishop to administer the full rite with imposition of hands and chrismation; the legislation called for priests to receive a special license, "under the bishop's signature and seal," to administer the rite. Concern about the bishop's contact with parishes was addressed by provisions requiring the bishop to inaugurate trial use in each parish wherein the rite was to be used and to endeavor to visit at least yearly every parish where the priest was so licensed and there preside at Holy Baptism with the Laying-on-of-hands. The legislation also stipulated that adults received from other communions be listed as "communicants" only if they received imposition of hands and that children who received laying on of hands not be termed "communicants" for statistical purposes "until they have reached the age at which it is customary for them to be so counted."[79]

At the 1970 General Convention, the Standing Liturgical Commission proposal proved unsatisfactory when it was discussed in the House of Bishops. A report of the debate summarized the primary issues for the bishops:

> Members expressed concern that having some infants confirmed and some not during the three year trial use would produce insurmountable complications and chaos later when the babies reached the usual confirmation age. In addition, many were uneasy because the resolution proposed that a bishop could specially license clergy to perform the whole rite.[80]

To address these concerns, the proposed legislation was substantially revised. With the concurrence of the House of Deputies, *PBS* 18 was approved for trial use with these stipulations:

1) That the Baptismal Section...be authorized for trial use, subject to the direction and guidance of the Ordinary;

2) That children be admitted to Holy Communion before Confirmation, subject to the direction and guidance of the Ordinary;

3) That the Rite entitled Holy Baptism with the Laying-on-of-hands be authorized for trial use by a Bishop provided that no children under the present age normal for confirmation shall receive the Laying-on-of-hands during the trial use period with a Bishop as the Officiant.[81]

With this resolution, the convention effectively rejected the essence of the proposed rite. The rite could be used for baptism, but a priest could not administer the laying on of hands, and a child under the current "normal" age for confirmation could not receive imposition of hands, that is, confirmation, even from a bishop. The one significant departure from traditional Anglican initiatory practice was the admission of children to communion prior to confirmation.

Some of the resistance to full trial use may have resulted from concerns about the problems of trial use rather than objection to the principles underlying the proposal. However, the challenges to the basic principles continued during the next two triennia, suggesting that the potential difficulty of trial use was no more than a secondary factor in the convention's decision.

The resolution eliminated from the rite not only the imposition of hands and optional chrismation but also the postbaptismal consignation. Immediately after the convention, Mitchell, in a letter to Malania, pointed out that consignation was required according to the 1928 prayer book and that it had been a significant issue for Anglicans in the controversy with the Puritans. Mitchell urged that a rubric restoring the consignation be included in any copies of the rite published for trial use.[82]

Taking up this concern at its February 1971 meeting, the Standing Liturgical Commission proposed a "Schedule of Variations under Special Circumstances" to be authorized by the Presiding Bishop and the President of the House of Deputies. The schedule of variations called for consignation and a postbaptismal prayer to be substituted for the prayer for the sevenfold gifts of the Spirit when baptism was administered without the imposition of hands. In addition, two variations could be used at a bishop's visitation: "Holy Baptism with the Laying-on-of-on-of-hands," and "The Laying-on-of-hands without the ministration of Holy Baptism." This permitted the rite to be used on a trial basis in the fullest possible manner while still conforming to the stipulations of General Convention. The entire rite was printed, without alteration and prefaced by the enabling resolution, in *Services for Trial Use*.[83]

Communion of all the Baptized: Continuing Debate

The 1970 General Convention authorized the admission of children to communion before confirmation, already an experimental practice in some dioceses. Because this was "subject to the direction and guidance of the Ordinary" and because this was trial use, not mandatory in every diocese, the provision was implemented in varying ways.

Many parishes and dioceses responded enthusiastically. The Diocese of Southern Ohio, where a pilot program was already under way, implemented a general diocesan policy of admitting young children to communion as soon as they desired to participate and had received appropriate preparation. An article in *The Living Church* reported:

> For those congregations who have become involved, an exciting spiritual renewal and education growth process has taken place... [W]e've set aside confirmation as a requirement, and have recognized that a child can unconsciously respond to and learn from the Holy Communion.[84]

This article did not specify the preparation expected for young children beyond stating that it was the responsibility of the parents with the guidance of parish clergy.

Others urged more careful instruction and preparation. The argument that cognitive understanding was necessary in order to receive communion was supported by some on the basis of scripture. An article in *The Living Church* interpreted Paul's warning that "all who eat and drink without discerning the body, eat and drink judgment against themselves" (1 Cor. 11:29) as an injunction against communicating infants and young children: "these key words—examine, judge, discern—require a degree of maturity and understanding on the part of a communicant which a child not 'come to the years of discretion' cannot possibly have." The practice of infant baptism was defended on the basis of Jesus' practice of blessing children, but admission to communion was said to require careful preparation, repentance, "a living faith," and the intention to live in obedience to the commandments of God.[85]

Responses to this article pointed out inconsistencies in the author's reasoning:

To waive these requirements [repentance and faith] in one case [baptism] but not the other [communion] would seem to call for more justification than the article gives.[86]

"Suffer little children to come unto me, and forbid them not," can be cited to support infant communion as well as infant baptism.[87]

The debate continued on the pages of *The Living Church* during 1971 and 1972. The validity and merits of infant communion were disputed; others questioned whether admission to communion could properly occur before confirmation.

A 1971 survey of the House of Bishops indicated a diversity of opinion and practice. Of the twenty-seven dioceses represented by the responses, four did not permit admission to communion before confirmation. The remainder authorized communion before confirmation with varying provisions. Only two specified a minimum age for children to receive, in one case age seven, in another age four. Twelve indicated that instruction or some preparation of parents and/or children was required. Two bishops linked admission to communion to a child's taking a place at the family table; one admitted all children who could walk to the rail.[88]

A 1971 survey of trial use by the Standing Liturgical Commission yielded similar results and noted considerable confusion. Some of the dioceses admitted only older children, with minimum ages of nine to eleven. The Diocese of Georgia reported, somewhat contradictorily, that "many congregations were not even informed that this practice exists; however it is 'widespread' in the diocese." Many diocesan commissions were producing bibliographies and guidelines for preparing children for admission to communion, and some had designed rites of admission to communion.[89]

At its October 1971 meeting, the Standing Liturgical Commission discussed this diversity of practice and noted a problem with very young children who had been admitted to communion in one place and were then refused communion when their families visited or transferred to other parishes or dioceses. Pointing out that this was tantamount to excommunication, the commission asked that the House of Bishops address a statement to the Church on the matter.

A few weeks later, the House of Bishops adopted a statement recommending that the action of a congregation in admitting a child to communion be honored whenever the child's family visited or transferred to another congregation. The bishops also recommended that "no child be admitted to Holy Communion unless instructed in the meaning of this sacrament" and agreed that "it is preferable that the reception of the Holy Communion be for children an experience in which the whole family shares."[90] At the same meeting, in a statement on "Holy Baptism and Its Relation to Confirmation," the bishops affirmed that "Confirmation should not be regarded as a procedure of admission to the Holy Communion."[91] (For the full texts of these statements, see Appendix A.) Thus the bishops affirmed the decision of the 1970 convention to admit children to communion before confirmation, although the expectation of instruction precluded infant communion.

A few years later the Evangelical Education Society sponsored a symposium to consider infant communion, described as an "innovative rite" and a "new venture in child rearing."[92] A report of the conference indicated insistence upon the necessity of cognitive understanding and faith, as well as concern about the continuing diversity of practice and the resultant confusion in the Episcopal Church.[93]

Taking an official stand against infant communion, the Board of Managers of the Evangelical Education Society sent to the House of Bishops in October 1974 a resolution expressing "strong disagreement with the theological implications of administering the consecrated elements of Bread and Wine to infants."[94] The matter was taken up by the Theological Committee of the House of Bishops.

The theological committee, noting "the growing custom of administering Holy Communion to young infants," disputed the argument that infant communion was parallel to infant baptism. While infant baptism can be justified as admission to God's covenant people, reception of communion requires a moral response, as stated in 1 Corinthians 11. Full intellectual understanding is not possible, but "a movement of the heart and will in response to Christ's act...is asked for. An unconscious infant is not capable of such a response." The committee concluded that giving communion to young children "is theologically sound and should be encouraged," but infant communion "is theologically questionable" and so was not recommended. Accordingly, the committee called for a rubric stipulating that the baptized could receive communion after appropriate instruction.[95]

When the committee's report was discussed by the Standing Liturgical Commission in June 1975, the commission simply eliminated the rubric stating that the newly baptized could receive communion. In a subsequent letter, Chilton Powell, chair of the commission, explained that a rubric requiring instruction could be interpreted as contradicting the House of Bishops ruling that "guests" from other churches could receive communion in the Episcopal Church. Powell added that the House of Bishops recommendation for instruction prior to first communion was seen to be adequate.[96]

Discussion of admission to communion did not end with approval of the *Proposed BCP* in 1976. Since several dioceses had requested a service of admission to communion, the Standing Liturgical Commission assigned this task to a committee on the revision of *The Book of Offices*. A subcommittee on Christian initiation, chaired by Mitchell, considered the issue in 1977 and recommended that a form for the admission of baptized children to communion not be provided. In October 1977 the Standing Liturgical Commission approved a statement setting forth the rationale for this decision.

In its carefully worded statement, the commission emphasized that baptism is "full initiation by water and the Holy Spirit"[97] and thus is the only sacramental prerequisite for reception of communion. Without explicitly affirming infant communion, the statement acknowledged that many would admit newly baptized persons of all ages to communion at the time of their baptism, a practice differentiated from the "regular reception of communion." The latter was encouraged "upon evidence of [the child's] desire to communicate, and after consultation between the parish priest and the parents." Since the age for beginning regular reception would vary, depending on the pastoral situation, no general provision would be practicable. Artificial norms should be avoided, including a fixed age for "First Communion," and formation of "First Communion classes," since authorized forms for admission to communion would obscure the fully initiatory character of baptism.[98]

Prayer Book Studies 18:
First Step toward a New Initiatory Pattern

Although discussion of infant communion continued for several years, there was little objection to separating admission to communion from confirmation. This was a significant departure from the traditional Anglican initiatory pattern, but this step was not the sole initiative of the drafting committee on Christian initiation or the Standing Liturgical Commission. The idea of communion before confirmation had been proposed by a number of people in the Episcopal Church, and by 1970 several parishes and dioceses were experimenting with this change in the traditional Anglican initiatory pattern. The 1970 General Convention action, that is, the explicit provision that children be admitted to communion before confirmation, thus gave official approval to a practice that was already being implemented in some places and discussed in many more.

Other aspects of the drafting committee's proposal did not fare as well. The committee had recommended a radical change in Anglican initiatory practice, a proposal made on the basis of extensive discussion of the theological and pastoral issues involved in baptism, confirmation and admission to communion. But the committee's conclusions were not widely shared in the Episcopal Church. Many feared that the proposed rite would eliminate a pastorally significant opportunity for personal affirmation of baptismal vows and would diminish the bishop's relationship with parishes. The stipulations imposed on the rite by the 1970 General Convention effectively rejected the essence of the drafting committee proposal for a single unified rite of Christian initiation. When the committee resumed work after the 1970 General Convention, its major task was to respond to the expressed need for a rite of reaffirmation presided over by a bishop and thereby to clarify the meaning of confirmation and its relation to baptism.

NOTES

1. Personal correspondence, Bonnell Spencer to Leonel Mitchell, Dec. 4, 1967.

2. "Progress Report on Baptism-Confirmation," n.d., p. 4 (Archives of the Episcopal Church, Record Group 122, box 7, file 26; hereafter references to archival material will be cited as Rev. Files and numbered according to Record Group, box number, and file number, e.g., Rev. Files 122-7-26).

3. William Spilman, "A Proposal for Christian Initiation," Mar. 10, 1968, p. 1 (Rev. Files 122-7-9).

4. London: Darton, Longman and Todd, 1967.

5. "History and Theology," in *Crisis for Confirmation*, pp. 45-65.

6. "The 'Shape' of the Baptismal Liturgy," p. 416.

7. Mitchell, "Thoughts on Christian Initiation," May 2, 1968 (Rev. Files 122-7-12).

8. Spencer to Margaret Mead, n.d. (reply to letter, Mead to Spencer, Feb. 19, 1968) (Rev. Files 122-7-9).

9. Ibid.

10. Barrett, "Christian Initiation," n.d., p. 5 (Rev. Files 122-7-12).

11. Spencer to Mead, n.d. (reply to letter, Mead to Spencer, Feb. 19, 1968) (Rev. Files 122-7-9).

12. Spencer, "Christian Initiation: Preliminary Report," n.d., p. 3 (Rev. Files 122-7-12).

13. Barrett, "Christian Initiation," n.d., p. 5 (Rev. Files 122-7-12).

14. Mitchell, "Thoughts on Christian Initiation," May 2, 1968, p. 4 (Rev. Files 122-7-12).

15. "Findings," Committee on Christian Initiation, First Meeting, General Theological Seminary, New York, N.Y., May 2-3, 1968, p. 1 (Rev. Files 122-7-12).

16. The file from the first meeting of the drafting committee contains a document entitled "Elements in Christian Initiation" (n.d., Rev. Files 122-7-12). Among the

items listed are "death and resurrection into Christ," "regeneration as new creature," "sealed in new age to everlasting life—eschatological aspect." There is no indication as to whether this list was prepared prior to the meeting or generated during the meeting. The existence of the list suggests that the drafting committee did not ignore entirely the theological richness of initiation, even though the subject was not explored thoroughly in the summary presented in the committee's "Findings."

17. Drafting Committee VI (hereafter DC VI) Minutes, May 2-3, 1968 (Rev. Files 122-7-12).

18. Ibid.

19. Ibid.

20. Spencer, "Central New York Experiment," n.d. (Rev. Files 122-7-25).

21. Spencer to Frederick Warnecke, Sept. 26, 1968 (Rev. Files 122-7-9).

22. Lambeth Conference 1968, *Resolutions and Reports*, p. 99.

23. New York: Church Pension Fund, 1970 (hereafter cited as *PBS* 18).

24. Ibid., p. 19.

25. Ibid., pp. 24, 32, 46-7.

26. Ibid., p. 16.

27. Spencer to George Barrett, Jan. 25, 1969 (Rev. Files 122-7-14) (emphasis added).

28. *PBS* 18, p. 14.

29. Ibid., p. 18.

30. In a letter to Spencer (Aug. 11, 1969; Rev. Files 122-7-10), the British liturgical scholar Colin Buchanan pointed out the weakness of the historical argument: "The evidence is surely of no 'confirmation' anywhere until around 180-190 A.D., and of none long after that in the East?" Buchanan's concern did not result in any revision of the introduction, perhaps because his letter was not received until after the Editorial Committee had completed its work on *PBS* 18.

31. Leonel L. Mitchell, "The Eucharist and Christian Initiation," in Donald Garfield (ed.), *Worship in Spirit and Truth; Papers from a Conference Entitled Worship in Spirit and Truth* (New York: Jarrow Press, 1970), p. 40.

32. DC VI Minutes, Dec. 16-17, 1968, p. 1 (Rev. Files 122-7-14).

33. *PBS* 18, p. 23.

34. DC VI Minutes, Dec. 16-17, 1968, p. 9 (Rev. Files 122-7-14).

35. "Revision of the Liturgy," n.d. (Rev. Files 122-7-15); DC VI Minutes, Apr. 21-22, 1969, p. 17 (Rev. Files 122-7-15). The formal reception into the Church ("we receive you into the family of God") was separated from the sealing and included in a formula said immediately following the imposition of hands.

36. *PBS* 18, pp. 39-40.

37. Ibid., pp. 37, 39.

38. Ibid., p. 39.

39. Mitchell, "What Shall We Do about Baptism and Confirmation?", *The Anglican* 25 (1969-70): 1-6.

40. Interview with Spencer, West Park, NY, May 22-23, 1990. For further discussion of the history of the prayer for the sevenfold gifts of the Spirit, see Marion Hatchett, *Commentary on the American Prayer Book*, pp. 278-9.

41. *PBS* 18, p. 19.

42. Ibid., p. 40.

43. Ibid., p. 24.

44. Ibid., p. 21.

45. Spencer to Thomas A. Fraser, June 12, 1969 (Rev. Files 122-7-16).

46. Spilman to Spencer, Mar. 8, 1969 (Rev. Files 122-7-10).

47. "If the person has not received the Laying-on of Hands or its equivalent, and if that person desires to receive it, he may do so in the manner prescribed above for those baptized in the Anglican Communion without receiving it": DC VI Minutes, Apr. 21-22, 1969, p. 20 (Rev. Files 122-7-15).

48. *PBS* 18, p. 47.

49. *PBS* 18, pp. 46-7.

50. Ibid., p. 24.

51. Ibid., p. 32.

52. Spencer to Thomas Fraser, June 12, 1969 (Rev. Files 122-7-16).

53. *PBS* 18, p. 20.

54. Custis Fletcher, "Consultant's Comments on DC-VI 4," received July 7, 1969 (Rev. Files 122-6-21).

55. Mitchell to Spencer, May 20, 1969 (Rev. Files 122-7-10).

56. John Macquarrie to DC VI, May 31, 1969 (Rev. Files 122-7-10).

57. J. Robert Zimmerman to DC VI, Jan. 7, 1969 (Rev. Files 122-6-20).

58. SLC Minutes, Jan. 17-21, 1969, pp. 12-13 (Rev. Files 122-1-22).

59. Malania to Spencer, May 15, 1970 (Rev. Files 122-6-10).

60. New York: Church Hymnal Corporation, 1970.

61. Ibid., p. 10.

62. Ibid., pp. 40-1.

63. BCP 1979, pp. 420-1.

64. Charles Brown to Malania, May 14, 1969 (Rev. Files 122-6-20).

65. SLC Minutes, Jan. 17-21, 1969, p. 12 (Rev. Files 122-1-22).

66. Report of the SLC, *Journal of the General Convention*, 1970, p. 499.

67. *PBS* 18, p. 9.

68. "Infant Initiatory Rite Used," *The Living Church*, Nov. 16, 1969, p. 8.

69. Garfield, ed., *Worship in Spirit and Truth*.

70. W. Francis Maguire, "Christian Initiation: 3," The Living Church, July 26, 1970, p. 9.

71. Gardiner M. Day, "Critique of Unified Rite," *The Witness*, II Apr. 1970, p. 8.

72. Henry Louttit, Chairman, Diocese of Georgia Liturgical Commission, to Malania, May 20, 1970, p. 1 (Rev. Files 122-6-10).

73. F. Washington Jarvis, "Questions about *PBS* 18," *The Living Church*, July 12, 1970, p. 13.

74. John H. Heidt for the Theological Commission of the American Church Union, to SLC, Apr. 21, 1970 (Rev. Files 122-6-22).

75. F. Washington Jarvis, "Questions about *PBS* 18," *The Living Church*, July 12, 1970, p. 15 (emphasis in original).

76. Gardiner M. Day, "Critique of Unified Rite," *The Witness*, II Apr. 1970, p. 9.

77. Mitchell, "The Eucharist and Christian Initiation," in Garfield (ed.), *Worship in Spirit and Truth*, pp. 37-8.

78. Mitchell later pointed out that it is difficult to defend the position that chrism is necessary to full Christian initiation because of the scarcity of scriptural evidence for its use and because it has not been a part of Anglican baptismal practice: Leonel L. Mitchell, "The Place of Baptismal Anointing in Christian Initiation," *Anglican Theological Review* 68 (1986): 206.

79. Minutes of the "Special Committee on Advice," May 14, 1970 (Rev. Files 122-9-27); Memorandum, Dupuy Bateman to Members of Special Committee on PBS 18, July 20, 1970 (Rev. Files 122-9-27).

80. Martha C. Moscrip, "Surprises Coming in the Prayer Book Rack," *The Episcopalian*, Dec. 1970, pp. 17-18.

81. *Journal of the General Convention*, 1970, pp. 342-5. The legislation also directed that the proposal be referred to the Anglican Consultative Council meeting in February and March, 1971, for "its consideration and council," and that the bishops arrange for a period of intensive study and instruction in their dioceses.

82. Mitchell to Malania, Nov. 6, 1970 (Rev. Files 122-7-11).

83. *Services for Trial Use*, pp. 21-35.

84. Jack C. Burton, "Children's Communion," *The Living Church*, Mar. 14, 1971, pp. 17-18.

85. Henry Summerall, "Children and Communion," *The Living Church*, June 20, 1971, p. 9.

86. William D. Loring, letter to the editor, *The Living Church*, Aug. 29, 1971, p. 3.

87. Robert B. Dunbar, letter to the editor, *The Living Church*, Sept. 5, 1971, p. 5.

88. "House of Bishops Questionnaire—October 1971" (Rev. Files 122-7-18).

89. "Admission to Communion," in "Trial Use Progress Report," Oct. 5, 1971, appended to SLC Minutes, Oct. 8-11, 1971 (Rev. Files 122-1-23).

90. Report of the Special Meeting of the House of Bishops, Pocono Manor, PA, Oct. 24-29, 1971, in *Journal of the General Convention*, 1973, p. 1063.

91. Ibid., p. 1073.

92. "Re: Infant Reception of Holy Communion," *The Evangelical Outlook*, Oct. 1974, p. 3.

93. *The Evangelical Outlook*, June 1975, pp. 1-3.

94. "Re: Infant Reception of Holy Communion," *The Evangelical Outlook*, Oct. 1974, p. 3.

95. Statement of the House of Bishops Theological Committee, cited by John Burt, letter to Chilton Powell, June 13, 1975 (Rev. Files 122-7-24).

96. Powell to Burt, June 24, 1975 (Rev. Files 122-7-24).

97. *Proposed BCP*, 1976, p. 298.

98. "Admission to 'First Communion,'" Oct. 27, 1977, Appendix D, SLC Minutes, Oct. 9-13, 1977 (Rev. Files 122-2-4).

Chapter 8

Toward a New Pattern
of Christian Initiation:
Redefining Confirmation

The General Convention's refusal fully to accept the proposals in *Prayer Book Studies* 18 was a blow to the drafting committee. Daniel Stevick, professor of liturgics at Philadelphia Divinity School when he joined the drafting committee in 1971, later reflected on the committee's response to the convention's action:

> When I joined the committee...the committee was to some extent licking its wounds... The thing they had most sought, which was to have a rite which brought together baptism, the postbaptismal blessing, anointing, Spirit-moment and the communion...had not been gained. So they felt more defeated than pleased by what had happened.[1]

The drafting committee had envisioned a revolutionary change in Christian initiation, a proposal arrived at after extensive discussion of theological and pastoral questions. But the committee's vision was not widely embraced, despite their efforts and the efforts of the Standing Liturgical Commission to provide a compelling theological and pastoral rationale for the proposal. Louis Weil, professor of liturgics at Nashotah House and a member of the drafting committee from 1974 to 1976, summarized the Church's response to *PBS* 18:

> The general reaction of the Church to PBS 18 was not merely that it was too radical, but rather more that a rite of profound pastoral importance in the Anglican tradition had been lost. It was not so much a question that the sacramental clarification implied by the rite was rejected, but rather that the significance of confirmation as an occasion of personal profession of faith and pastoral contact with the bishop had been cast aside.[2]

As the committee's work proceeded, they struggled to maintain their vision of a single unified initiatory rite while also responding to the deeply felt need for a rite of personal profession of faith. Throughout the triennia from 1970 to 1973 and 1973 to 1976 the drafting committee listened to responses from around the Church and continually refined its proposals. In this ongoing dialogue, bishops and the nascent organization of chairs of diocesan liturgical commissions played significant roles by articulating theological and pastoral issues.

The Pocono Statement
on Baptism and Confirmation

At its 1971 meeting in Pocono Manor, Pennsylvania, the House of Bishops took up the question of Christian initiation. In addition to their statement on the admission of children to communion, the House of Bishops Theological Committee prepared "A Statement on Holy Baptism and Its Relation to Confirmation"[3] (see Appendix A).

Although intended to give "theological clarification," the statement was ambiguous. On the one hand, it affirmed that baptism is full Christian initiation: "in Holy Baptism a person is made fully and completely a Christian and a member of Christ's Body, the Church." Nevertheless, a rite of personal profession of faith, presided over by a bishop, is a significant component of Christian life. This is confirmation, "one's personal and public commitment to the implications of his baptism." While not a rite of admission to communion or joining the Church, confirmation is necessary for those baptized as infants: "For many of us, infant baptism can only be defended when at a later date a person makes his own personal decision for Jesus Christ."[4] The statement did not explain how baptism could be full Christian initiation, and yet those baptized as infants must at some point undergo a further rite.

The work of the Holy Spirit in initiation was explained by asserting that the Spirit is bestowed in baptism, is "continually a presence in the life of every baptized person," and further intervenes "in particular ways as a person lives out his Christian life." Confirmation in the Anglican tradition was described as "liturgically and sacramentally a significant occasion of such intervention." The statement was emphatic in expressing the bishops' desire for a separate rite of confirmation presided over by a bishop.[5]

The bishops' assertion that baptism is full Christian initiation and includes the bestowal of the Holy Spirit is in accord with the proposal in *PBS* 18. But the bishops indicated significant disagreement by insisting on the importance of a distinctive rite that included public profession of faith and episcopal laying on of hands. By defining this subsequent rite as "confirmation," the bishops rejected the drafting committee's view that confirmation is a postbaptismal laying on of hands integral to the baptismal rite. Moreover,

the bishops' emphasis on a rite of personal commitment to one's baptism contradicted the drafting committee's understanding that renewal of the baptismal commitment was best seen as an ongoing lifelong process punctuated by
regular opportunities for reaffirmation.

Responses to the Pocono Statement

The bishops' statement was discussed at a conference of the chairs of diocesan liturgical commissions held soon after the 1971 House of Bishops meeting. A resolution adopted unanimously advocated a different approach, one
more in keeping with the *PBS* 18 proposal. The resolution called upon the
Standing Liturgical Commission to develop "additional liturgical forms for
the expression of personal and public commitment to Christian discipleship."
But this would not be confirmation, which "is not generally an effective
expression of Christian commitment." Furthermore, while the bishops
emphasized the role of the bishop in confirmation, the liturgical commission
chairmen expressed their hope that emphasis would instead be given to "the
bishops' role as chief liturgical officers of Baptism and Laying-on-of-hands
and of the Eucharist."[6]

The Pocono Statement was criticized more directly at a colloquium on confirmation in the life of the Church. A transcript of this colloquium, along with
the text of the Pocono Statement, was published in *Anglican Theological
Review*.[7] Urban Holmes, a member of the drafting committee from 1974 to
1976, argued that the bishops' description of confirmation as an adult affirmation of baptism was not consistent with the typical practice of confirmation at
ages nine through twelve, and he characterized this adult affirmation as
"Pelagianism" and "a kind of modern individualism."[8] After a lengthy discussion of rites of passage and Christian commitment, Taylor Stevenson, editor of *ATR*, concluded:

> the only viable place for confirmation seems to be in conjunction with the bap-
> tismal rite. And secondly, that the efforts to make confirmation into some kind
> of rite of passage are hopeless. Thirdly, that there may be a place for a repeat-
> able rite of passage of some sort in the life of the Church.[9]

The rite of passage suggested by Stevenson was an adult rite affirming one's
vocation. It would not mark passage to a new status as a Christian but rather
passage to a new stage in one's life. Because of the extended length of adolescence in twentieth-century American culture and because of the diversity of
roles and high mobility of individuals in this culture, this rite of passage
should be repeatable.[10]

The concept of a repeatable rite of affirmation of faith was new for the Episcopal Church. *PBS* 18 suggested that regular renewal of baptismal commitment would occur through participation in the corporate affirmation of faith during the baptismal liturgy and through celebration of the eucharist. "A Form of Commitment to Christian Service" introduced a repeatable rite for individual commitment to the service of Christ in the world. The theologians' discussion and the resolution of the liturgical commission chairs, calling for "liturgical forms for the expression of personal and public commitment to Christian discipleship," mark the beginning of churchwide consideration of a repeatable rite of Christian commitment.

A recommendation for a repeatable rite of commitment was made in a statement entitled "Confirmation and Commitment," a response to the Pocono Statement presented at the April 1972 Standing Liturgical Commission meeting. The statement pointed out that understanding confirmation to be unrepeatable implies that confirmation conveys "an indelible spiritual character." If baptism is the sacrament of full Christian initiation, as the bishops acknowledged, then any sacramental character attributed to confirmation should be restored to baptism, and any subsequent act of commitment to Christ must be clearly distinguished from sacramental initiation. Therefore such an act of commitment should not be called "confirmation" because "confirmation" has traditionally been a sacramental completion of baptism; it should be seen as repeatable, not bestowing indelible character; it should be entirely optional, with no further status dependent upon it; and the prayer for the sevenfold gifts of the Spirit should not be used. Even with such precautions, a service of commitment might be "spiritually harmful": making a solemn commitment at a mature age could imply that one need not make any commitment at an earlier age, emphasizing a particular act of commitment could obscure the need for ongoing commitment, and such a service could produce two classes of Christians. To determine whether such a rite would be helpful or harmful, a rite of "Affirmation of Christian Discipleship" was proposed for use by those bishops who felt that a service of commitment was pastorally desirable.[11]

After discussion of "Confirmation and Commitment," a representative of the Anglican Church of Canada Task Force on Christian Initiation reported to the Standing Liturgical Commission their proposal to separate the two aspects of confirmation. The sacramental completion of Christian initiation would be expressed through the imposition of hands as part of the baptismal rite for both infants and adults, a proposal similar to *PBS* 18. But in addition to this unified initiatory rite, the second aspect of confirmation, the renewal of baptismal vows, would constitute a service of "Christian Commitment and Commissioning."[12]

Following the Canadian report, the commission agreed on several propositions:

1. Baptism is a complete act of Christian initiation.
2. Holy Baptism, the Laying-on-of-Hands, and the Eucharist form one continuous action.
3. The recognition of the intimate relation of the act of initiation with the paschal mystery is crucial....
4. It is desirable that there should be multiple opportunities for Christians to renew their baptismal covenant, including one such occasion at "confirmation age."[13]

The first two propositions correspond to the principles established in *PBS* 18, and the third is a more explicit statement of the theology implied in *PBS* 18. The fourth proposition acknowledges the bishops' insistence upon confirmation as a rite of public commitment to baptism but asserts that renewal of the baptismal commitment should repeatable. It became the task of the drafting committee to provide a rite for this renewal.

A New Proposal: "A Form for a Bishop's Visitation"

When the drafting committee met in May 1972, they had before them the Pocono Statement, the resolution of the chairs of diocesan liturgical commissions, and the reports from the April Standing Liturgical Commission meeting, as well as a report from the Worship Commission of the Consultation on Church Union (COCU) and a report from the Louvain meeting of the Commission on Faith and Order of the World Council of Churches. The COCU report had used *PBS* 18 as a model for a baptismal rite but did not address the question of confirmation. In contrast, the report of the Commission on Faith and Order provided support for a repeatable rite of reaffirmation: "we also wish to lay emphasis upon repentance, renewal of baptismal vows and personal profession of faith, whether on a single or on repeated occasions."[14]

At its meeting, the drafting committee developed "A Form for a Bishop's Visitation with the Laying-on-of-Hands." Citing the Pocono Statement, the rationale for this new rite explained that the title "confirmation" was not used because "the word has several connotations which the bishops have rejected," including the completion of Christian initiation, joining the Church, and admission to communion. The rite was suggested for a variety of purposes since, "as the bishops have pointed out, the Holy Spirit 'intervenes again and again in particular ways as a person lives out his Christian life.'"[15]

The proposed rite was quite simple. An introductory rubric stated that a bishop's visitation should normally include the celebration of baptism and eucharist. Following the baptism and before the peace, the candidates for laying on of hands were presented by their sponsors. The bishop asked the candidates, "Do you seek and affirm membership in this parish (or mission, or community) of Christ's Church and do you commit yourself to our Life and Mission?" After the candidates answered affirmatively, they knelt before the bishop, who laid hands on each of them and said, "*Name*, by this Laying-on-of-Hands we confirm your Baptism and we welcome you into this community of Christ's Church and we share our ministry and mission with you." After the imposition of hands, the congregation joined the bishop in saying the traditional confirmation formula, "Defend, O Lord..."[16]

The new rite was sent immediately to members of the House of Bishops Theological Committee to seek their support. Richard Emrich, Bishop of Michigan and chair of the committee, and John Burt, Bishop of Ohio and a member of the committee, opposed the proposal. They expressed concern that the proposed rite stressed the candidates' affiliation with a parish, rather than requiring candidates to renew their baptismal vows. Moreover, Burt and Emrich complained that the proposal diminished the distinctive nature of confirmation. Emrich wrote:

> You belittle [confirmation] by spreading the laying on of hands to "serve a variety of purposes;" you belittle it by saying that its basic function is "to strengthen a bishop's pastoral relations with his people." I don't want people to be related to me by confirmation, for I will be soon gone; I want them related to Christ by their decision.[17]

Burt was more amenable to a repeatable rite but nonetheless wanted to preserve a unique rite of personal commitment:

> While there is nothing wrong with inviting people to renew their baptismal vows again and again, the need for one special, self-conscious occasion when a person takes his religious obligations off his sponsors' shoulders on to his own is something quite different—and precious. I happen to believe it is absolutely essential, if personal discipleship is to mean anything.

According to Burt, this rite of personal discipleship should be distinct from baptism: "baptism takes us into the Church; confirmation sends us out."[18]

At its August 1972 meeting, the drafting committee reconsidered the proposed "Form for a Bishop's Visitation" in light of Burt's and Emrich's comments. Despite the bishops' requests for a unique rite of confirmation, the committee retained the basic premise of their proposal: the reaffirmation of baptismal promises with imposition of hands by a bishop is voluntary and is appropriate at several different times in Christian development. In response to the concern that the rite was too congregational, the examination of the candidates was expanded to three questions. The first question asked, "Do you renew the promise made at your Baptism?" to which the candidates were to respond, "I do, and I intend to follow Jesus Christ as my Lord and Savior," a declaratory form of the question to the candidates in the 1928 confirmation rite: "Do ye promise to follow Jesus Christ as your Lord and Savior?" A focus on the local community was retained in the second and third questions, which asked if the candidates desired to share "in the common life of this Christian community" and to exercise their mission "through this community of [Christ's] Church." A new formula at the imposition of hands eliminated the explicit welcome into the community and instead invoked the blessing of the Holy Spirit without implying that the Spirit was being bestowed for the first time: "*Name*, may the Holy Spirit strengthen you in faith, hope, and love, and make you fruitful in all good works."[19]

The following month at the Standing Liturgical Commission meeting, the discussion on initiation began with the reading of a "Statement on Holy Baptism" prepared by a Committee on Theological Statements chaired by Virginia Harbour, a member of the Department of Christian Education of the national Episcopal Church and a member of the Drafting Committee on Christian Initiation from 1968 to 1970. The statement did not mention any rite of renewal or recommitment to baptismal vows but emphasized that the baptized must be nurtured in Christian life through the celebration of the eucharist, preaching, and the support of the Christian community. While Burt had asserted that confirmation sent Christians into the world, the statement claimed that baptism is "the foundation of new relationship...to human society" and concluded, "the sacramental act of baptism is at the heart of the Church's charter of existence and its catholic mission to the world."[20]

This conclusion made explicit an understanding of baptism as the foundation for Christian mission, a view implicit in the baptismal rite in *PBS* 18 but not given particular attention in the theological rationale for that rite. In articulating this perspective, the Standing Liturgical Commission contributed to an emerging baptismal ecclesiology, an ecclesiology which views baptism as the basis for all Christian life and ministry. This was still a new perspective in the Episcopal Church, and as the commission began to emphasize that baptism was commissioning for ministry, it would find itself opposing those who had been taught that confirmation was the "ordination of the laity."

After discussing the statement on baptism, the commission reviewed the correspondence from Burt and Emrich and decided to invite the members of the House of Bishops Theological and Prayer Book Committees to participate in a discussion of the initiatory rites at its December meeting. The "Form for a Bishop's Visitation" was approved after the second and third questions to the candidates had been emended to eliminate the congregational focus. The new drafts of "Holy Baptism" and "The Bishop's Visitation" together with the "Theological Statement on Holy Baptism" were distributed to bishops, consultants and chairs of diocesan liturgical commissions, with a request for comments and suggestions to be considered at the December meeting.

Several consultants acknowledged the value of a repeatable reaffirmation of faith but objected to the elimination of confirmation. One person commented: "What is wrong with the name, and the idea, of confirmation?... To eviscerate the few [rites of passage] we have does not represent a very perceptive response to human needs and the human situation."[21] Another consultant remarked, "I agree that such a repeatable service and rite [should] be made available, but don't think confirmation should be dropped by pushing it out the back door."[22] In contrast, Massey Shepherd complained that the rite of confirmation was being "brought in by the back door again." He expressed concern that much confusion would result from having two rites of laying on of hands, one in infancy by a priest and one at a later age by a bishop.[23]

Shepherd defended the basic premise of PBS 18 at the October 1972 House of Bishops meeting, where he led a discussion on the proposed rites for baptism and "The Bishop's Visitation." The draft rites were also presented by Spencer to the October 1972 conference of the chairs of diocesan liturgical commissions. The conference passed a resolution reaffirming its 1971 stance that baptism is complete Christian initiation and commending the Standing Liturgical Commission for upholding this position in its most recently proposed revisions.

Agreed Theological Positions

Prior to the December 1972 meeting of the Standing Liturgical Commission with the Theological and Prayer Book Committees of the House of Bishops, Burt prepared a paper entitled "Some Reflections on the Future of Confirmation as the Rite of Holy Baptism is Revised." While affirming that baptism is full Christian initiation, Burt asserted that confirmation marks the moment of subjective human response to the act of God in baptism. The need for a rite of personal commitment did not imply that baptism is incomplete but rather that "what is objectively given should also be subjectively received." He emphasized the importance of a distinctive rite of confirmation, which he understood as "lay ordination":

> there is a special quality, so we have believed, to that special moment when for the first time in a public assemblage of the gathered Church and in the presence of the bishop, the personal commitment to "follow Jesus Christ as Lord and Savior" is made and the confirming blessing to that commitment given by God through his Church.

Burt made several specific recommendations for liturgical revision, including: 1. The proposed baptismal rite should not include the imposition of hands, since this had been associated in Anglicanism with a rite of maturity. Additionally, it was unrealistic to expect the bishop to be the chief minister at baptism. 2. A revised rite of confirmation should retain the title "confirmation" and should emphasize Christian commitment and commissioning for lay ministry. The bishop should be designated chief minister of confirmation, although this is not a "doctrinal necessity." Confirmation should "be encouraged" for all Christians, not merely offered to "those 'who *may* desire' it." 3. An alternative formula at the imposition of hands should be provided to permit those confirmed in another denomination to be received into the Episcopal Church as part of the rite of confirmation. This should include both those confirmed by a bishop and those confirmed by a presbyter or pastor; "to continue our present tradition of honoring only the episcopal confirmations of other Churches involves us in some untenable theology respecting the validity of certain reformed ministries."[24]

At the Standing Liturgical Commission meeting, Burt presented thirty-three responses by bishops to his paper, of which thirty-two supported his position. Several expressed frustration that the commission seemed to be ignoring the bishops' views outlined in the Pocono Statement. A few bishops who agreed with most of Burt's argument opposed his suggestion that the Episcopal Church recognize confirmation by a presbyter or pastor in another church tradition.

In addition to Burt's paper and the responses thereto, a letter was read from Charles Price, professor of theology at Virginia Theological Seminary and member of the Standing Liturgical Commission, who was on sabbatical in England and did not attend the meeting. Price argued that the claim by some bishops that confirmation is an unrepeatable sacrament assigned to the bishop was untenable in light of the practice of the Orthodox and Roman Catholic Churches. However, Price was sympathetic to the bishops' desire for the pastoral relationship with people in their dioceses afforded by confirmation and recommended that the repeatable reaffirmation of baptism with episcopal imposition of hands be explained as increasing rather than decreasing a bishop's pastoral relationships. He further proposed that this expanded rite be entitled "confirmation":

> Then instead of saying that we have "done away" with confirmation, or that we have "put confirmation and baptism together again," we would say that we have restored laying on of hands to baptism and have revised and enlarged the theology and practice of confirmation so that: 1. In no sense can it be thought to complete baptism; 2. It is no longer a once-and-for-all occurrence... 3. It is not an admission ticket to the eucharist...[25]

Agreeing that baptism in water and in the triune name constitutes full Christian initiation, the bishops and commission members at the meeting discussed three fundamental questions regarding reaffirmation of baptismal vows:

> [I]s such a rite voluntary or obligatory? if obligatory, it perpetuates the confusion involved in the concept, "completion of baptism."
>
> Is such a rite repeatable? for, if it is not, the implication is that it confers sacramental "character."
>
> Is a bishop's action necessary for its validity? if so, and Baptism in its entirety can be delegated, then "confirmation" is made to seem more prestigious than baptism.

The most difficult question was that of repeatability. This is not surprising, given the insistence of Burt and Emrich on the uniqueness of the act of commitment in the traditional Anglican rite of confirmation. Eventually a compromise was reached. A distinction was made between the first moment at which a person baptized in infancy personally affirms the baptismal promises and receives the strengthening gift of the Spirit through the imposition of hands, and subsequent affirmations of faith. The first rite of affirmation was said to be unrepeatable "in the sense that one cannot turn the clock back to an earlier stage in one's life." However, the same rite was also deemed suitable for other occasions in Christian life, in particular for the recommitment of a lapsed Christian.[26]

After reaching agreement on basic principles, a subcommittee comprising four of the six members of the Theological Committee (including Burt and Emrich) and four members of the Standing Liturgical Commission (including Spencer and Shepherd) was appointed to write a statement of "agreed positions" (see Appendix B). This statement began by affirming the sufficiency of baptism as full Christian initiation, a rite in which the "essential element" was "baptism by water and the Spirit, in the name of the Holy Trinity, in response to repentance and faith" and which normatively included as well

> the laying-on of hands, consignation (with or without Chrism), prayer for the gift of the Holy Spirit, reception by the Christian community, joining the eucharistic fellowship, and commissioning for Christian mission.[27]

This list accepts all the elements in the initiatory rite proposed in *PBS* 18, including the postbaptismal prayer and imposition of hands with consignation not approved by the 1970 General Convention. Contrary to Burt, it designates baptism, not confirmation, as the rite of commissioning for mission. Burt's concern that it was unrealistic to expect the bishop to be the chief minister of baptism was addressed by the statement "when the bishop is present, it is expected that he will preside at the rite," a statement that acknowledges the bishop's role in baptism but allows a priest to administer the rite without explicit authorization by the bishop.

The "agreed positions" also included a section "concerning a postbaptismal affirmation of vows." It began by asserting: "An act and occasion for (more or less) mature personal acceptance of promises and affirmations made on one's behalf in infancy is pastorally and spiritually desirable." Although this was termed "voluntary," it was to be "strongly encouraged as a normal component of Christian nurture, and not merely made available." Nonetheless, it was not to be seen as the completion of baptism, a requirement for admission to communion, or the bestowal of a "special status of church membership." The affirmation of baptismal vows by those baptized in infancy was said to be "a significant and unrepeatable event," but the statement also asserted that the rite "is suitable, and should be available, for other occasions in the lives of Christian people." As Burt and others had insisted, the rite was assigned to the bishop, who "should recall the applicants to their Christian mission" and give a blessing through the laying on of hands and prayer. The rite of reaffirmation was not given the title "confirmation," but the occasion of affirming the baptismal vows made on one's behalf in infancy was identified as one's "Confirmation Day."[28]

Prayer Book Studies 26

After achieving theological consensus at its December 1972 meeting, the Standing Liturgical Commission reviewed the drafts of "Holy Baptism" and "The Bishop's Visitation." Spencer then prepared revised rites in accordance with the recommendations made at the meeting, and these were distributed to the drafting committee, the Standing Liturgical Commission, and the bishops on the Theological and Prayer Book Committees. The rites were given further scrutiny by the full drafting committee, the Editorial Committee, and the Standing Liturgical Commission, then published as *Holy Baptism, together with A Form for the Affirmation of Baptismal Vows with the Laying-On of Hands by the Bishop, also called Confirmation* (*Prayer Book Studies* 26).[29]

Postbaptismal Actions

The postbaptismal actions in the *PBS* 18 rite—prayer for the gift of the Spirit followed by imposition of a hand with consignation and optional chrismation—required little change, since the "agreed positions" identified these elements as normative components of Christian initiation. However, the prayer for the sevenfold gifts of the Spirit was revised to read, "*sustain* them, O Lord, with the riches of your Holy Spirit,"[30] rather than the wording in *PBS* 18, "*strengthen and confirm* them,"[31] an emendation which eliminated the implication that the postbaptismal actions constituted "confirmation."

Perhaps the most controversial of the postbaptismal actions was the optional use of chrism. Many respondents to *PBS* 18 had urged that the use of chrism be mandatory, but Spencer suggested that it would be more readily accepted if it were optional. To support his argument, he told this anecdote: A preacher of the Reformed tradition was to preach in the chapel at Princeton University. A preaching gown was laid out for him, but he paid no attention to the garment. Finally the president of the college asked if the preacher wanted to wear the gown. The preacher asked if he was required to wear it, and when told it was not required, replied that he would wear it.[32]

The official introduction to the *Draft Proposed BCP* (*PBS* 29) explained that allowing the use of chrism to be optional respected different opinions:

> Some hold that the sacramental character of the sealing with the Spirit, and the role of the bishop in the whole rite of initiation, can be safeguarded only if oil blessed by him is used during the sealing. Others hold that the ceremonial use of oil is now meaningless because oil is no longer widely used in everyday life after bathing, and the Old Testament connection between oil and the Spirit has been largely forgotten... For these persons oil has become a "dead symbol." They would resist being required to use it, and would point out that the sacramental presence of the bishop at a rite of initiation is better safeguarded by a presbyter on whom he has laid his hands than by oil on which he has laid his hands.[33]

Mitchell, who preferred that the use of chrism be mandatory, was amenable to optional use: "there are enough early rites which do not use chrism for this signing that there can be no real question of its being essential."[34]

The formula for the sealing continued to be revised. In December 1972 the bishops and Standing Liturgical Commission approved this formula: *"Name, child of God and inheritor of the Kingdom of Heaven, you are sealed by the Holy Spirit of promise, marked as Christ's own for ever and ever."*[35] The verb tense was changed in *PBS* 26: "you *have been* sealed by the Holy Spirit."[36] This allowed different interpretations—that the sealing is the inward part of the sacrament of baptism, or that the sealing occurs at the postbaptismal consignation. The formula was further amended at the 1973 General Convention by the House of Bishops: *"by the water of baptism* you have been sealed by the Holy Spirit."[37] The additional phrase implicitly adopts Lampe's thesis that the seal of the Spirit occurs in the water of baptism and gives no room for other interpretations.

The Affirmation of Baptismal Vows

The proposed "Form for the Affirmation of Baptismal Vows" was based upon the same principles as "The Bishop's Visitation": both forms were repeatable rites of affirmation of baptismal vows with prayer and imposition of hands by the bishop. However, the wording differed significantly. Many of the changes altered the rite to conform more closely to the understanding of confirmation articulated by Burt and other bishops.

The title "confirmation" was given increasing precedence as the rite was revised. At their December 1972 meeting, the bishops and the Standing Liturgical Commission agreed upon the title "A Form for the Affirmation of Baptismal Vows with a Blessing by a Bishop, also called Confirmation."[38] Burt, Emrich and Stanley Atkins, Bishop of Eau Claire and a member of the Standing Liturgical Commission, later objected to the use of the term "blessing" because it omitted direct reference to the sacramental act of imposition of hands.[39] The title was then changed to "A Form for the Affirmation of Baptismal Vows with the Laying-On of Hands by the Bishop, also called Confirmation."[40] At the 1973 General Convention the title was further amended to "A Form for Confirmation or the Laying-on-of-Hands by the Bishop, with the Affirmation of Baptismal Vows."[41]

The understanding of baptism as full initiation was articulated in the preface to the rite of reaffirmation:

> Holy Baptism is full initiation by water and the Holy Spirit into Christ's body the Church. The bond which God establishes in Baptism is indissoluble.[42]

The identification of baptism as full Christian initiation was not altered in the successive revisions of the rite of reaffirmation. This constancy reflects widespread acceptance of the fundamental principle of a single unified initiatory rite, a principle set forth in *PBS* 18 but not accepted by the 1970 General Convention.

The principle of a repeatable rite of affirmation was acknowledged in the preface with a list of events for which such an affirmation would be appropriate: a mature public commitment to the responsibilities of baptism, the renewed commitment of a person who had lapsed from Christian life, and entering the Episcopal Church from another denomination. However, successive revisions set forth ever stronger expectations for the use of the rite. "The Bishop's Visitation" suggested "in the course of their Christian development, baptized members of the Church *may desire* to reaffirm their baptismal promise."[43] In conformity with the agreed positions, the language was revised to read "baptized members of the Church *should be encouraged* to reaffirm..."[44] and further strengthened to say "baptized members...*are* encouraged..."[45] Even this was not sufficient for the bishops. At the 1973 General Convention the House of Bishops deleted the word "encouraged" and substituted a phrase specifying that baptized members are "*expected* as a normal component of their Christian nurture" to reaffirm their baptismal commitment.[46]

The central ritual action of the reaffirmation was entitled "Dedication to Mission." A brief address by the bishop emphasized commitment to mission and asked the candidates to renew that commitment. In response, the candidates promised to "follow Jesus Christ as my Savior and Lord," and to "work and pray and give for the spread of his kingdom," a compilation of answers from "The Bishop's Visitation." This was followed by a tripartite prayer: an introductory prayer over all the candidates, a prayer with the imposition of the bishop's hand on each candidate, and a concluding petition by the bishop. The first portion of the prayer, newly formulated for this rite, linked commitment to Christian service with the covenant God has made with the people of God:

> Almighty God, we thank you that by the Cross of your Son Jesus Christ you have overcome sin and brought us to yourself, and by the sealing of your Holy Spirit have bound us to your service. Renew in *these* your *servants* the covenant you made with *them* and all your people, and send *them* in the power of that Spirit to perform the tasks you set for *them*.[47]

The second portion of the tripartite prayer, also a new text, was a petition for strengthening by the Holy Spirit and empowerment for mission: "Strengthen, O Lord, your servant, *Name*, with the riches of your Holy Spirit; sustain *him*, and empower *him* for your service."[48] When all the candidates had been "commissioned" by use of this formula, the prayer concluded with the traditional Anglican confirmation formula in plural form ("Defend, O Lord, these your servants...."), said over all the candidates. The emphasis on mission is unmistakable, although the rite does not imply that this is the first occasion of commissioning, a position which would contradict the assertion, set forth in the "agreed positions," that the initiatory rite includes commissioning for Christian mission.

Apologetic for *Prayer Book Studies* 26

In retrospect, the introduction to *PBS* 18, a brief twelve pages, was woefully inadequate. The Standing Liturgical Commission was proposing a revolutionary change in the Anglican initiatory pattern, and the rationale offered in *PBS* 18 was but a cursory summary of theological and pastoral conclusions achieved after substantial discussion by the drafting committee and the Standing Liturgical Commission. It was insufficient for its purpose of convincing the Church that the proposed rite was a necessary and appropriate resolution of the complex issues in Christian initiation in the Anglican tradition.

To provide a more thorough introduction, Spencer invited Stevick to prepare a separate supplement to *PBS* 26. The Standing Liturgical Commission took the unusual step of publishing the supplement under Stevick's name rather than as an official rationale or position statement. They explained that they wanted to permit Stevick to express his views without needing to accommodate other opinions held by members of the commission, and to eliminate any possible confusion between Stevick's work and the agreed positions, printed in a preface to *PBS* 26.[49] Despite this disclaimer, a draft of Stevick's paper was presented at the December 1972 Standing Liturgical Commission meeting and reviewed by the drafting committee. Subsequently, Spencer, Mitchell and Thomas Talley, professor of liturgics at General Theological Seminary and member of the drafting committee from 1971 to 1976, worked with Stevick in final revision and editing for publication.

In the supplement, Stevick traced the historical development of initiatory rites from the New Testament era to the twentieth century. He argued that the breakdown of Christendom was redefining the relationship between Church and society and hence required reevaluation and revision of rites of Christian initiation:

> The two-stage pattern [infant baptism, adolescent confirmation and first communion] seems to assume, for its best operation, social conditions and ways of personal development which cannot be taken for granted today.[50]

With regard to the reaffirmation of faith that so many Episcopalians understood to be an essential Christian rite, Stevick asserted that the complexities of modern society precluded a single identifiable point of entry into adulthood. Because response to baptism was a lifelong process, a repeatable rite might be a more suitable liturgical expression than the common practice of confirmation as a once-for-all puberty rite.[51]

While justifying a repeatable rite of reaffirmation, Stevick's primary contribution was to identify two primary strands in Anglican understanding and practice of confirmation:

> (1) One line of ancestry of confirmation is the postbaptismal blessing, which traces to the early Church... (2) Another line of ancestry came from the Reformation. It is the ratification of baptismal promises.[52]

This was not a new insight. Spencer had described confirmation as having two distinct aspects, "sacramental" and "pastoral." A similar distinction was made in the report of the Canadian Task Force on Christian Initiation. Stevick's contribution was to articulate this understanding in a quasi-official document introducing a significant change in Anglican initiatory practice. Later Stevick began to identify the two clusters of meaning as "Confirmation A" (the postbaptismal blessing) and "Confirmation B" (ratification of baptismal promises), and this terminology gained currency in explanations of the revision of the Anglican initiatory pattern.

Stevick explained that the rites proposed in *PBS* 26 did not have the two-stage structure familiar to Anglicans but had a different relationship to each other. The new rite of baptism was a sacramentally complete rite of initiation. Nonetheless, baptism "must always be considered the beginning of a process of response." Liturgical response occurs through participation in the eucharist, through participation in the baptism of others, and in the proposed "Form for the Affirmation of Baptismal Vows with the Laying-on of Hands by the Bishop, also called Confirmation." The latter rite was not a completion of baptism but a solemn renewal of the baptismal covenant with imposition of hands by the bishop. As a repeatable rite, with no resultant special status or privilege, it had the flexibility to meet the varying circumstances of human and Christian experience.[53]

The Church's Response to *Prayer Book Studies* 26

The proposals in *PBS* 26 were widely discussed in the Episcopal Church. Members of the Standing Liturgical Commission and the drafting committee spoke at numerous events around the country, and the new approach to confirmation was discussed in articles and letters to the editor in various church periodicals. A 1973 meeting of the chairs of diocesan liturgical commissions, at which Stevick, Malania and other leaders in the revision process were present, provided opportunity for discussion of the rites in *PBS* 26 and for response to General Convention actions. Chilton Powell, chair of the Standing Liturgical Commission, sent to all bishops a questionnaire asking their opinions of the rites in *PBS* 26, and the House of Bishops meeting in October 1974 included substantial discussion of initiation.

The Meaning of Confirmation

Stevick had identified two primary clusters of meaning in the traditional Anglican practice of confirmation and asserted that the proposed rites separated these two strands. But there was continuing disagreement.

With regard to the postbaptismal rites, one writer found that they were used and understood in varying ways by different parish clergy: "Some used oil, others did not; and of the former some thought they were confirming, others simply doing baptism with bells on." Bishops had disparate opinions: some viewed the anointing as confirmation, but others did not, even when it was administered by a bishop; others "acknowledge 'essential' confirmation in such a rite, but of a sort that needs augmenting later on"; still other bishops forbade their clergy to use the anointing.[54] Some respondents argued, for various reasons, that the postbaptismal actions were not equivalent to confirmation: the addition of the phrase "by the water of baptism" denied that the sealing was a sacramental act; the use of chrism was not mandatory; the postbaptismal rites could be administered by a priest.

There were also different responses to the proposed rite of affirmation. Some argued that a mature affirmation should be required and should be understood as a completion of baptism, while others complained that the new "Form of Affirmation" did not suffice as a sacrament. There was support for the proposed rite of affirmation as a mature reaffirmation of baptismal vows, but some expressed a need for a rite of passage for adolescents similar to the traditional rite and practice of confirmation. In some places, the use of the rite for those already confirmed was referred to as "reconfirmation." This terminology caused some to question whether confirmation could be used for occasions in Christian life such as return of a lapsed member or reception from another Christian communion. There were also questions about how the new rites related to the canonical definition of a "confirmed communicant" of the Episcopal Church.

The New York Proposal

Concerted opposition to *PBS* 26 came from the bishops of the Diocese of New York. The diocesan bishop, Paul Moore, refused to authorize the use of *PBS* 26 in his diocese because the "sacramental essence" of confirmation, incorporated into the baptismal rite, could be administered by a priest. Furthermore, Moore opposed the concept of a repeatable rite of affirmation. To buttress his opposition, Moore asked faculty from General Theological Seminary in New York to prepare papers addressing historical and pastoral issues. In August 1974 these papers and a proposed revision of *PBS* 26 were sent to all bishops.

In a paper addressing pastoral and psychological issues, John Romig Johnson, professor of pastoral theology at General Seminary, concluded that the nonrepeatable sacrament of confirmation was a crucial element of the Church's response to twentieth-century culture and thus needed to be strengthened.[55] Walter Roland Foster, Dean of General Seminary, contributed a historical survey of confirmation and episcopacy in the Episcopal Church. He suggested that confirmation by the bishop "may still be a very important way in which the reality of the diocese is sustained" and urged careful consideration of "any revisions which would disassociate the bishop and confirmation."[56]

The major response to *PBS* 26 was prepared by J. Robert Wright, professor of church history at General Seminary. Wright defined confirmation as:

> a nonrepeatable sacramental act, not of dominical institution, which strengthens the baptized Christian with a further gift of the Holy Spirit sufficient to the pledges he has made, and which (in the Anglican tradition mediated by the pastoral practice of the Episcopal Church) is normally expected of all persons at an age of maturity.[57]

While he had no objections to the proposed postbaptismal rites, Wright urged that the "status" of the revised rite of confirmation be "heightened so that it no longer seems merely a liturgical afterthought."[58]

Wright presented his paper at the May 1974 annual meeting of the Anglican Society, and his paper was subsequently published in both *The Anglican* and *Anglican Theological Review*.[59] In a response in *ATR*, Urban Holmes suggested that confirmation should be described as a "rite of intensification" rather than a rite of passage because confirmation did not convey a change in role or status in the Church: "What other change in the role and status of a Christian as church member can there be but in baptism?" As a rite of intensification, confirmation is a repeatable rite of strengthening and renewal.[60]

Revision of *Prayer Book Studies* 26

The actions of the 1973 General Convention and the New York proposal were primary factors in the revision of *PBS* 26. The drafting committee made several revisions at meetings in March and September 1974. These revisions were presented to the House of Bishops in October 1974, and the bishops' responses were taken into account at a meeting of the drafting committee with the Standing Liturgical Commission in November 1974. The revised rites were then authorized by the Presiding Bishop and the President of the House of Deputies for trial use during 1975-1976 and published as a separate pamphlet without introduction.[61] The work was urgent because the 1973 General Convention had agreed to conclude the process of prayer book revision at the 1976 convention; lack of agreement on a matter as central as Christian initiation could jeopardize approval of a new prayer book.

The Seal of the Spirit

The phrasing of the formula at the postbaptismal consignation continued to be problematic. Soon after the 1973 convention, the chairs of diocesan liturgical commissions expressed their concern about the addition of the words "by the water of Baptism" to the formula:

> Whereas, in Anglican tradition the sacramental rites have attempted to express something of the richness of God's acts for us in these sacraments, rather than to define the exact moment and limits of that action, this conference...finds inconsistent the House of Bishops' addition to the "consignation."[62]

In a paper presented at the January 1974 Standing Liturgical Commission meeting, Spencer pointed out that the phrase "by the water of baptism" reflected the "entirely respectable theological position [of Lampe] that the gift of the Spirit is effected solely and fully by the water action of baptism." However, the phrase eliminated the Mason/Dix school of thought, that the gift of the Spirit is associated with a second action of chrismation or imposition of hands. Persons holding this latter view would be forced to look elsewhere for the sacramental bestowal of the Spirit, and the most likely place would be the separate rite of "confirmation."[63]

In response, the Standing Liturgical Commission agreed to delete the words "the water of" from the phrase "by the water of baptism" and to change tense of the verb to "you are sealed."[64] The drafting committee proposed a simplified formula: "*Name*, you are sealed by the Holy Spirit and marked as Christ's own forever."[65] After the 1974 House of Bishops meeting, the formula was modified by the addition of the words "in Baptism": "*Name*, you are sealed by the Holy Spirit in Baptism and marked as Christ's own for ever."[66]

The phrase "in Baptism" introduces ambiguity. While not as explicit as "by the water of baptism," it can be interpreted in the same manner, that is, that the seal of the Spirit is given through the water bath. It can also be understood as a reference to the entire complex baptismal action.[67] When considered in light of the structure of the rite, in which the consignation follows the prayer for the gift of the Spirit, the consignation and accompanying formula can be understood as the seal of the Spirit.[68] However, Gerard Austin points out that from a Roman Catholic perspective "the sealing formula...might cause difficulty by implying that this act of sealing is not a distinct sacramental rite, separate from the water-bath itself," although he recognizes that the final wording "represents a compromise that was only grudgingly accepted."[69]

In addition to the wording of the formula, the order of the postbaptismal ceremonies was debated. Several consultants and bishops complained that it was awkward to do the water bath, return the child to a parent or sponsor, say the prayer, then go back to each baptizand for the consignation. Shepherd insisted that placing the consignation immediately after the water bath and before the prayer for the gifts of the Spirit would cause confusion in the interpretation of the ceremonies: "Either they are just ceremonies like the present signing with the cross in the Prayer Book baptismal rite, or they are a true laying on of hands in the ancient sense." The prayer preceding the consignation functioned as an explication of the action to follow and thus served to distinguish the liturgical action of laying on of hands from the water bath.[70] In essence, Shepherd was arguing that the baptismal rite should clearly comprise two stages, even though the components, that is, water bath and imposition of hands, were part of a single rite. The Standing Liturgical Commission and the drafting committee considered altering the sequence, but the order was unchanged in *PBS* 26 Revised.

A Rite of Reaffirmation

Revising the "Form for Confirmation" was a delicate and complex task. The drafting committee and the Standing Liturgical Commission needed to balance demands for an unrepeatable rite of confirmation with their desire to uphold the principle of a single unified initiatory rite and a repeatable rite of affirmation of baptismal vows.

In its March 1974 revision, the drafting committee proposed that the title "confirmation" refer to the "confirmation of baptismal vows" by persons in a variety of circumstances. Several alternative formulas were provided for the bishop to use at the laying on of hands, but the occasion for which any of them should be used was not specified. One was the formula at the imposition of hands in *PBS* 26 ("Strengthen your servant..."); one was especially suitable for persons coming to the Episcopal Church from other denominations: "*Name*, we receive you into the fellowship of this Communion, and we acknowledge you as a member of the Holy Catholic Church, in the name of God, Amen"; the others were prayers for blessing and strengthening through the Spirit. The traditional confirmation formula was not included, although rubrical permission for the bishop to use "other suitable words" would allow the traditional words to be said if desired.[71]

This proposal met with considerable objection because it retained the title "confirmation" for various affirmations of faith. At the September 1974 drafting committee meeting, a compromise was reached. The rite would permit both "confirmation" and "reaffirmation of baptismal vows." The preface no longer specified occasions at which confirmation or reaffirmation was appropriate. Candidates were presented "to receive the laying-on of hands." The first portion of the tripartite prayer in *PBS* 26 ("...renew in these your servants the covenant...") was said prior to the imposition of hands. Formulas "For Confirmation," "For Reaffirmation" and "For Reception" were provided for the laying on of hands. For confirmation there were two alternatives, the wording from *PBS* 26 ("Strengthen your servant...") and the traditional confirmation formula. The formula for reception used the wording developed in the March 1974 draft, and another formula from the March draft was offered for reaffirmation.[72]

Although the new draft distinguished "confirmation" from "reaffirmation" and "reception," it did not define these, nor did it specify that confirmation was not repeatable. Several bishops requested that the categories be more clearly distinguished. The House of Bishops recommended that the reaffirmation be moved to a different place in the rite and the term "laying on of hands" be used only in connection with confirmation.[73] Spencer was particularly concerned that the reaffirmation not be separated from confirmation:

> Please KEEP Confirmation, Reception, and Reaffirmation as we have them.
> This is essential to the proposal. We have made Confirmation a unique event,
> but keep it from being considered theologically unrepeatable and the completion of baptism by putting Receptions and Reaffirmations in the same service.[74]

Spencer urged that the preface to the rite define confirmation, reception and reaffirmation, but this clarification was never provided.

At their November 1974 meeting the drafting committee and the Standing Liturgical Commission endeavored to respond to the bishops' concerns without abandoning the basic principles of a unified baptismal rite and a repeatable rite of reaffirmation. Confirmation, reception and reaffirmation were retained in a single rite entitled "A Form for Confirmation, for Reception, and for the Reaffirmation of Baptismal Vows." Confirmation was given precedence through the use of larger typeface in the title and in the subheadings for the three occasions, and by being listed first among the three. Candidates were presented specifically "for confirmation," "to be received into this communion," or as persons "who desire to reaffirm their baptismal vows." Immediately following their presentation, they were asked, "Do you affirm your renunciation of evil and your commitment to Jesus Christ?", to which they responded, "I do, and with God's grace I will follow him as my Savior and Lord." The rubrics directed the laying on of the bishop's hand for confirmation. No action was specified for reception and reaffirmation, although no action was precluded. The formula for the reaffirmation was modified to read, "*Name*, may the Holy Spirit, who has begun a good work in you, direct and uphold you in the service of Christ and his kingdom."[75]

Among its revisions earlier in 1974, the drafting committee had deleted the prefatory rubric stating that baptized persons were expected to reaffirm their baptismal promises. In response to the bishops' request to restore the rubric, a new rubric specified that "those baptized at an early age" were expected to make a "mature public affirmation of faith...and to receive the laying-on of hands by a bishop."[76] Nothing was said of expectations for those baptized as adults.

The *Proposed Book of Common Prayer*

Although in the revision of *PBS* 26 the essential compromises had been made, there were a few additional changes before the *Draft Proposed Book of Common Prayer* (*DrPrBCP*) was distributed to bishops and deputies to General Convention. Several changes requested by the Theological Committee of the House of Bishops were approved at the June 1975 Standing Liturgical Commission meeting. The bishops of New York continued to protest what they perceived as a weakening of the Church's doctrine of confirmation, and in response the Standing Liturgical Commission made further revisions at its May 1976 meeting. Those dissatisfied with the revisions brought by the Standing Liturgical Commission to the General Convention proposed changes at the convention, and a few of these resolutions were adopted before the rites of "Holy Baptism" and "Confirmation with forms for Reception and for the Reaffirmation of Baptismal Vows" were accepted as part of the *Proposed Book of Common Prayer*.

The order of the new prayer book was the subject of significant debate. A Committee on the Contents and Order of the Draft Proposed Book favored retaining the order of the 1928 prayer book, but other opinions were offered. Eventually it was agreed that Holy Baptism would follow the Great Vigil of Easter and precede Holy Eucharist, and Confirmation, Reception and Reaffirmation would be included in a newly titled section of "Pastoral Offices" for use when there was no baptism. Rather than grouping baptism with other rites for particular occasions in the lives of individual Christians, where baptism had been placed in every Anglican prayer book since 1549, the *DrPrBCP* linked baptism with eucharist and thus implied that baptism is a major sacrament. Confirmation as a separate rite remained among the pastoral offices. The New York bishops asked that confirmation be included with the "Episcopal Services" (ordinations, Celebration of a New Ministry, and Consecration of a Church) since it is an episcopal ministry, but their motion was defeated by the House of Bishops at the 1976 General Convention.[77]

There was continued resistance to the sequence of the postbaptismal ceremonies. Several bishops simply ignored the rubrics and did the consignation immediately after the water bath and before the prayer for the gifts of the Spirit. At the suggestion of the Theological Committee of the House of Bishops, the Standing Liturgical Commission added a rubric after the consignation: "Or this action may be done immediately after the administration of water and before the preceding prayer."[78] This retained the sequence of prayer followed by action, which Shepherd and other liturgists maintained was the correct liturgical structure, while acknowledging that others did not hold the same position.

The New York bishops argued that the words "A Form for" prefixed to "Confirmation" weakened the sacramental status of the service. Since Holy Baptism and most other rites in the proposed prayer book did not use such a prefix, the bishops asked that the prefix be omitted. In the *DrPrBCP* the Standing Liturgical Commission acceded to this request.[79]

The New York bishops also requested a return to the 1928 confirmation question, "Do you promise to follow Jesus Christ as your Lord and Savior?", which they saw as "stronger and more direct" than the question "Do you affirm your renunciation of evil and your commitment to Jesus Christ?" At its May 1976 meeting, the Standing Liturgical Commission separated the questions, so that the candidates were first asked, "Do you reaffirm your renunciation of evil?" and then, "Do you renew your commitment to Jesus Christ?" The candidates responded to the latter question, "I do, and with God's grace I will follow him as my Savior and Lord."[80] Still unsatisfied, the New York bishops proposed a return to the 1928 question with the simple answer "I do," but their motion was defeated by the House of Bishops at the 1976 Convention.[81]

In the new confirmation rite, the actions of confirmation, reception and reaffirmation were followed immediately by the exchange of the peace, a rather abrupt ending. The New York bishops asked that the traditional prayer for the sevenfold gifts of the Spirit be added as a concluding prayer. Instead, at the request of the House of Bishops Theological Committee, a revised form of the postconfirmation prayer in the 1928 rite was added. The new prayer omitted reference to apostolic laying on of hands and asked that the Spirit be with the candidates and that the candidates might serve God in this life and dwell with God in the life to come.[82]

At the General Convention, several attempts were made to emphasize the importance of confirmation. The theological committee and the New York bishops succeeded in adding to confirmation an introductory rubric:

> Those baptized as adults, unless baptized by a bishop, are also expected to make a public affirmation of their faith and commitment to the responsibilities of their Baptism in the presence of a bishop and to receive the laying on of hands.[83]

This rubric meant that all persons, not just those baptized as infants or young children, would be expected to make a public affirmation of faith and receive imposition of hands by a bishop. In the case of adults, this undermines an understanding of baptism as full Christian initiation, since adults who make a public affirmation of faith at their baptism are nonetheless expected to present themselves for another rite.

The New York bishops sought several revisions to underscore the responsibility of parents and godparents to bring their children to be confirmed. The House of Bishops rejected a proposal to add a statement to this effect to the preface to baptism, but they approved an amendment adding this expectation in the form of a question to parents and godparents in the baptismal rite and an amendment to the catechism stating that those baptized as infants were expected "when ready and duly prepared" to make a mature public affirmation of faith and receive imposition of hands by the bishop in confirmation. These latter two amendments were rejected by the House of Deputies.[84] Hence, unlike earlier Anglican prayer books, the 1979 prayer book does not mention any responsibility of parents and godparents to bring their children to be confirmed.

The *DrPrBCP* was deliberately ambiguous regarding reception. Although it was customary to receive and not confirm persons who had been confirmed "by a bishop in apostolic succession" and to confirm all other baptized persons affiliating with the Episcopal Church, this distinction was not spelled out. The New York bishops proposed a revised sentence for the presentation of candidates for reception: "I present these persons, already confirmed by episcopal laying on of hands or chrismation, to be received into this Communion." This was rejected by the House of Bishops, which also refused a proposal to specify that the bishop should take a person's right hand while saying the formula of reception and should "bless" each person reaffirming baptismal vows.[85] Thus the 1979 prayer book does not define reception or reaffirmation, nor does it specify or prohibit any ritual action to accompany the formulas.

A New Initiatory Pattern: Clarification and Ambiguity

When the Drafting Committee on Christian Initiation began its work in 1968, they faced a complex set of pastoral and theological issues posed by the traditional Anglican initiatory pattern of infant baptism and adolescent confirmation and admission to communion. Their first proposal, *Prayer Book Studies 18*, attempted to reunite these separated components in a single rite that included the water bath, imposition of a hand with consignation and optional chrismation, and communion. They recognized that the traditional Anglican rite of confirmation comprised both a postbaptismal sacramental sealing associated with the gift of the Spirit and a pastoral reaffirmation of the baptismal commitment. But in the course of their discussions, they had concluded that the reaffirmation was best seen as a continuous lifelong process effected not by a distinctive rite of reaffirmation but by participation in the baptism of others and by regular participation in the eucharist.

The Episcopal Church was not prepared for such a revolutionary proposal. Communion before confirmation was accepted with little dispute, the primary issue in debate being the necessity and appropriateness of infant communion. But many Episcopalians, lay and clergy alike, objected to the elimination of a separate rite of commitment to baptism presided over by a bishop.

As the drafting committee and Standing Liturgical Commission wrestled with these issues and listened to the debate around the Church, a new initiatory pattern emerged: a single rite of Christian initiation, described as "full initiation by water and the Holy Spirit into Christ's Body the Church,"[86] and a repeatable rite of reaffirmation of baptismal vows.

Yet while baptism is said to be full Christian initiation, ambiguity remains in the rite of reaffirmation. The revisers believed that they were separating what had been two aspects of Anglican confirmation rites, with one aspect, the sacramental sealing, now included in the baptismal rite. But the use of the title "Confirmation..." for only the second aspect, the rite of affirmation of the baptismal commitment, permits an interpretation in keeping with earlier Anglican initiatory patterns, that is, that this rite of confirmation is the final and necessary stage of incorporation into the Christian community and the Episcopal Church. Such a view is supported by the rubric added to the confirmation rite by the 1976 General Convention: "those baptized as adults, unless baptized with laying on of hands by a bishop, are also expected to make a public affirmation of their faith...in the presence of a bishop and to receive the laying on of hands."[87] If baptism is full Christian initiation, it is difficult to see what such a rite adds for adults who make a profession of faith at their baptism.

The lack of definitions adds further ambiguity. How does the rite of reception relate to confirmation? When baptized persons affiliate with the Episcopal Church, is a distinction to be made between those "confirmed" in a denomination having the historic episcopate and those baptized or confirmed in denominations without the historic episcopate?

Despite these ambiguities in the rite of confirmation, a radically new initiatory pattern is evident in the 1979 prayer book. Baptism includes significant components previously associated with confirmation in Anglicanism. While earlier rites expected that the parish priest would be the minister of baptism and the bishop administer confirmation, the 1979 prayer book specifies that "the bishop, when present...is expected to preach the Word and preside at Baptism and the Eucharist."[88] The prayer for the sevenfold gifts of the Spirit, part of every Anglican confirmation rite since 1549, follows the water bath in the 1979 baptismal rite. The confirmation rubric, "and there shall none be admitted to the Holy Communion, until such time as he be confirmed, or be ready and desirous to be confirmed," is no longer in the prayer book, and baptism normatively concludes with the celebration of the eucharist. It had become popular in the mid-twentieth century to speak of confirmation as the "ordination of the laity," but the 1979 prayer book understands baptism to include commissioning for ministry.

These changes—and more—accepted in the 1979 baptismal rite reflect revolutionary change for the Episcopal Church. With this rite, the newly emerging baptismal ecclesiology could take root and begin to transform the Church.

NOTES

1. Interview with Daniel Stevick, Cambridge, MA, May 25, 1990.

2. Louis Weil, "Christian Initiation: A Theological and Pastoral Commentary on the Proposed Rites," *Nashotah Review* 14 (1974): 206.

3. Report of the Special Meeting of the House of Bishops, Pocono Manor, PA, Oct. 24-29, 1971, in *Journal of the General Convention*, 1973, p. 1072.

4. Ibid., pp. 1072-3.

5. Ibid.

6. "Resolution, adopted unanimously on November 6, 1971, by A Conference of Chairmen of Diocesan Liturgical Commissions held at St. Louis, Missouri," with letter, Malania to all bishops, Feb. 7, 1972 (Rev. Files 122-6-23).

7. "Documentation and Reflection: Confirmation Today," *ATR* 54 (1972): 106-119. Participants in the colloquium included W. Taylor Stevenson and John H. Heidt of Marquette University, Milwaukee; Mason Knox of Sacred Heart Monastery, Milwaukee; and O. C. Edwards, Urban T. Holmes, and Louis Weil of Nashotah House.

8. Ibid., p. 112.

9. Ibid., p. 118.

10. Ibid., pp. 112-15.

11. "Confirmation and Commitment," in SLC Minutes, Apr. 19-21, 1972, pp. 11-13 (Rev. Files 122-1-24).

12. "Report of the Doctrine and Worship Committee's Task Force on Christian Initiation," in SLC Minutes, Apr. 19-21, 1972, pp. 18-21.

13. SLC Minutes, Apr. 19-21, 1972, p. 21.

14. "Commission on Faith and Order, Louvain, Belgium, August 2-13, 1971, Report of Committee III" (Rev. Files 122-7-18).

15. "Drafting Committee on Christian Initiation, Seventh Meeting, May 1-2, 1972, at General Theological Seminary, New York, N.Y.," pp. 1, 5 (Rev. Files 122-7-18).

16. Ibid., p. 6.

17. Emrich to Spencer, July 31, 1972 (Rev. Files 122-7-19).

18. Burt to Wolf, Aug. 21, 1972, p. 2 (Rev. Files 122-7-19).

19. "Drafting Committee on Christian Initiation, Eighth Meeting—August 31-September 1, 1972, at General Theological Seminary, New York, N.Y.," pp. 1, 4-7 (Rev. Files 122-7-19).

20. "Theological Statements: Holy Baptism (Accepted by the Standing Liturgical Commission September 27, 1972. This Draft incorporates the Commission's comments and suggestions)" (Rev. Files 122-2-1); SLC Minutes, Sept. 25-27, 1972, p. 7 (Rev. Files 122-2-1).

21. Mary McDermott Shideler, "The Bishop's Visitation, draft of Sept. 1972," Nov. 7, 1972 (Rev. Files 122-7-1).

22. Robert B. Meyers to Malania, Nov. 4, 1972 (Rev. Files 122-7-1).

23. SLC Minutes, Sept. 25-27, 1972, p. 8 (Rev. Files 122-2-1).

24. John H. Burt, "Some Reflections on the Future of Confirmation as the Rite of Holy Baptism is Revised" (Rev. Files 122-7-7).

25. Charles Price to Spencer, Nov. 18, 1972, p. 2, Appendix C, SLC Minutes, Dec. 6-9, 1972 (Rev. Files 122-2-1).

26. SLC Minutes, Dec. 6-9, 1972, pp. 4-5 (Rev. Files 122-2-1).

27. "Report of a Consultation on Christian Initiation," Apr. 5, 1973, p. 2 (Rev. Files 122-7-7).

28. Ibid., pp. 2-3.

29. New York: Church Hymnal Corporation, 1973 (hereafter referred to as *PBS* 26).

30. Ibid., p. 15 (emphasis added).

31. *PBS* 18, p. 39 (emphasis added).

32. Interview with Spencer, West Park, NY, May 22-23, 1990.

33. Charles P. Price, *Introducing the Draft Proposed Book: A Study of the Significance of the Draft Proposed Book of Common Prayer for the Doctrine, Discipline, and Worship of the Episcopal Church, Prayer Book Studies* 29 (New York: Church Hymnal Corporation, 1976), pp. 69-70 (hereafter cited as *PBS* 29).

34. Leonel L. Mitchell, "By Water and the Holy Spirit," *The Anglican*, n.s. 5 (1974): 3.

35. SLC Minutes, Dec. 6-9, 1972, p. 6 (Rev. Files 122-2-1).

36. *PBS* 26, p. 15 (emphasis added).

37. *Journal of the General Convention*, 1973, p. 455 (emphasis added).

38. SLC Minutes, Dec. 6-9, 1972, p. 6 (Rev. Files 122-2-1).

39. Burt to Chilton Powell, Dec. 28, 1972 (Rev. Files 122-8-4); "A Form for the Affirmation of Baptismal Vows with a Blessing by a Bishop, also called Confirmation," Revised Draft, Dec. 1972, with handwritten emendations and comments by Emrich, received Jan. 11, 1973 (Rev. Files 122-8-4); Atkins to Malania, Jan. 4, 1973 (Rev. Files 122-8-4).

40. *PBS* 26.

41. *Journal of the General Convention*, 1973, pp. 455-6.

42. *PBS* 26, p. 22.

43. "Draft: The Bishop's Visitation," Sept. 1972, p. 2 (Rev. Files 122-8-2) (emphasis added).

44. "A Form for the Affirmation...," Revised Draft, Dec. 1972, p. 2 (Rev. Files 122-7-20) (emphasis added).

45. "Holy Baptism," revised draft, Jan. 19, 1973, p. 21 (Rev. Files 122-8-5) (emphasis added).

46. *Journal of the General Convention*, 1973, p. 455 (emphasis added).

47. *PBS* 26, p. 26. Marion Hatchett, *Commentary on the American Prayer Book*, p. 282, attributes the prayer to Spencer.

48. *PBS* 26, p. 26. Hatchett, *Commentary on the American Prayer Book*, p. 282, attributes this formula to Urban Holmes; Holmes was not present at the Standing

Liturgical Commission meeting at which the formula was introduced, although he may have submitted the prayer to a member of the SLC prior to their meeting.

49. Daniel Stevick, *Holy Baptism, together with A Form for the Affirmation of Baptismal Vows with the Laying-On of Hands by the Bishop also called Confirmation*, Supplement to Prayer Book Studies 26 (New York: Church Hymnal Corporation, 1973), p. 6 (hereafter cited as *Supplement to PBS 26*).

50. Ibid., p. 10.

51. Ibid., pp. 65-70, 102-4.

52. Ibid., p. 49.

53. Ibid., pp. 86-92.

54. Harold R. Brumbaum, "Confirmation," *The Living Church*, Jan. 11, 1976, p. 21.

55. John Romig Johnson, "Several Pastoral Psychological Observations on the Proposed Confirmation Rite," in "PBS 26—An Alternative Proposal; A statement by the Bishop of New York with papers prepared at his request, together with a Proposed Alternate Service to PBS 26 and a Resolution prepared for submission to the House of Bishops; In preparation for the meeting of the House of Bishops, in Mexico, October 1974; New York: August 1974," pp. 1-2 (Rev. Files 122-7-23).

56. Walter Roland Foster, "Confirmation and Episcopacy in the Tradition of the American Episcopal Church," in "PBS 26—An Alternative Proposal," pp. 24-7; cf. Foster, "Some Notes on Confirmation and Episcopacy," *The Anglican*, n.s. 5 (1974): 18-21.

57. J. Robert Wright, "Prayer Book Studies 26: Considered Objections," in "PBS 26—An Alternative Proposal," p. 6.

58. Ibid., p. 19.

59. "Prayer Book Studies 26: An Objection, Some Observations, and a Proposed Alternative," *The Anglican*, n.s. 5 (1974): 7-18; "Response: Prayer Book Studies 26: Considered Objections," *ATR* 57 (1975): 60-71.

60. Urban T. Holmes, "Confirmation as a Rite of Intensification: A Response to J. Robert Wright," *ATR* 57 (1975): 73.

61. *Holy Baptism; A Form for Confirmation, for Reception, and for the Reaffirmation of Baptismal Vows* (New York: Church Hymnal Corporation, 1975) (hereafter cited as *PBS* 26 Revised) (*Holy Baptism* and *A Form for Confirmation...* are paginated separately in this pamphlet).

62. Resolutions of the Conference of Diocesan Liturgical Commission Chairmen, Nov. 6-8, 1973 (Rev. Files 122-2-6).

63. "Some Theological Issues in Christian Initiation," pp. 1-2, "Exhibit B," SLC Minutes, Jan. 14-17, 1974 (Rev. Files 122-2-2).

64. SLC Minutes, Jan. 14-17, 1974, p. 7 (Rev. Files 122-2-2).

65. DC VI Minutes, Sept. 27-28, 1974, p. 7 (Rev. Files 122-7-23).

66. *Holy Baptism, PBS* 26 Revised, p. 14.

67. Stevick makes this argument in *Baptismal Moments; Baptismal Meanings*, p. 163.

68. This is the position presented by Mitchell in *Praying Shapes Believing: A Theological Commentary on the Book of Common Prayer* (Minneapolis: Winston, 1985), pp. 110-11.

69. Austin, *Anointing with the Spirit*, p. 76.

70. Shepherd to Malania, Oct. 30, 1974 (Rev. Files 122-7-5).

71. DC VI Minutes, Mar. 20-21, 1974, p. 5 (Rev. Files 122-7-21).

72. DC VI Minutes, Sept. 27-28, 1974, pp. 9-10, 16-17. The prayers and formulas for the laying on of hands were printed both at the conclusion of the baptismal rite and as part of a separate rite for use when there was no baptism.

73. "Special Meeting of the House of Bishops, Oaxtepec, Mexico," Oct. 1974, in *Journal of the General Convention*, 1976, pp. B-268-9.

74. Spencer to DC VI, Nov. 12, 1974, p. 1 (Rev. Files 122-6-11) (emphasis in original).

75. *A Form for Confirmation...*, *PBS* 26 Revised, pp. 1-3, 5, 8.

76. *A Form for Confirmation...*, *PBS* 26 Revised, p. 2.

77. *Journal of the General Convention*, 1976, p. B-111.

78. BCP 1979, p. 308.

79. Ibid., p. 415.

80. Ibid., pp. 303, 415.

81. *Journal of the General Convention*, 1976, p. B-110.

82. BCP 1928, p. 298; BCP 1979, pp. 310, 419.

83. *Journal of the General Convention*, 1976, p. B-112.

84. Ibid., pp. B-109, C-25, D-122.

85. Ibid., pp. B-109-10.

86. BCP 1979, p. 298.

87. Ibid., p. 412.

88. Ibid., p. 298.

Chapter 9

The 1979 Baptismal Rite: Foundation for a Baptismal Ecclesiology

The baptismal liturgy in the 1979 prayer book was the result of thorough consideration of theological principles for Christian initiation. The drafting committee examined not only the pattern of initiation but also the nature and meaning of baptism. This theological discussion established the foundation of the new baptismal rite, which bears little resemblance to the rite in the 1928 Book of Common Prayer and other earlier Anglican baptismal rites. A few phrases, including the baptismal formula, remain, but the rite and its underlying principles represent a radical revision of baptismal practice and theology for the Episcopal Church.

The rite in *PBS* 18, *Holy Baptism with the Laying-on-of-Hands*, was the basis of the baptismal rite given final approval in 1979. Although there were numerous changes in wording as theological reflection continued and as the rite was used for the celebration of baptism, the structure of the new baptismal rite underwent few changes between 1970 and 1976. In this aspect of its work, the drafting committee largely succeeded in its original attempt to provide an initiatory rite suitable for the Episcopal Church in the late twentieth century.

Context of the Baptismal Rite: The Eucharist

Unlike the 1928 prayer book, which directed that baptism take place after the second lesson at Morning or Evening Prayer or at another time appointed by the minister, the introduction to the 1979 baptismal rite specifies that "Holy Baptism is appropriately administered within the Eucharist as the chief service on a Sunday or other feast" (p. 298). An alternative ending, similar to the ending of the 1928 rite, is provided for occasions when the eucharist is not celebrated, but the rubrics "Concerning the Service" (p. 298) and "Additional Directions" (pp. 312-13) point to the eucharist as the normative context for baptism.

The new rubric marks a significant change for the Episcopal Church, but there was little opposition to this, even when first introduced in *PBS* 18. The general acceptance of this principle was, in all likelihood, the result of the liturgical movement. As a eucharistic ecclesiology emerged, celebration of the eucharist was increasingly viewed as central to the life and mission of the Church and as a corporate expression of faith, an understanding expressed in the 1979 prayer book statement that the Holy Eucharist is "the principal act of Christian worship on the Lord's Day and other major Feasts" (p. 13). The structure of the eucharist as revised in 1979 allows other rites, baptism as well as most of the pastoral offices and episcopal services, to serve as the liturgy of the word at the eucharist. Thus baptism and eucharist can easily be combined in a single celebration.

Moreover, the baptismal renewal that was part of the liturgical movement, albeit a secondary emphasis, had encouraged the public celebration of baptism at the main Sunday service. Thus the new rubric made explicit a change in baptismal practice that was already occurring.

Context of the Baptismal Rite: The Liturgical Year

A new feature of the 1979 rite is the designation of baptismal days: "Holy Baptism is especially appropriate at the Easter Vigil, the Day of Pentecost, on All Saints' Day or the Sunday after All Saints' Day, and on the Feast of the Baptism of our Lord (the First Sunday after the Epiphany). It is recommended that, as far as possible, baptisms be reserved for these occasions or when a bishop is present" (p. 312). An outline for the Easter vigil, including the celebration of baptism, was developed by a Drafting Committee on the Calendar, Eucharistic Lectionary, and Collects, chaired by Massey Shepherd, and was approved by the 1970 General Convention.[1] The additional baptismal days were first specified in the draft of baptism developed in December 1972, and the list was then included in *PBS* 26.[2]

The Easter vigil adopted in 1970, based upon the revised Roman Catholic vigil, included baptism but, unlike the Roman rite, made no provision for a renewal of baptismal promises when there was no baptism. In response to recommendations of the Drafting Committee on Christian Initiation and at least one consultant, a renewal of vows was added to the vigil. When the decision was made to print the Easter vigil in full in the new prayer book, "The Renewal of Baptismal Vows" was included for use "in the absence of candidates for baptism or confirmation" (pp. 292-4). An introductory address by the celebrant makes explicit the relation between baptism and the paschal mystery celebrated in the Easter vigil. The renewal is verbal; in contrast to the Roman rite, there are no directions for sprinkling the congregation with water from the font, although such action is not precluded.

After *PBS* 26 was approved, the Drafting Committee on the Church Year recommended that the renewal of baptismal vows be used in place of the Nicene Creed at the eucharist on other baptismal days when there were no candidates for baptism. Although no introductory addresses were provided parallel to the address at the Easter vigil, the use of the baptismal covenant highlights the baptismal character of the other feasts.

The baptismal dimension of the paschal cycle is evident from Ash Wednesday through Pentecost. The Ash Wednesday liturgy includes an exhortation (adapted from the 1959 Canadian prayer book) which announces: "This season of Lent provided a time in which converts to the faith were prepared for Holy Baptism" (pp. 264-5). Lent is then a time of preparation for baptism (and renewal of baptism) at the Easter vigil. This is emphasized in the lessons appointed for the third, fourth and fifth Sundays in Lent Year A—John 4 (the woman at the well), John 9 (the healing of the man born blind), and John 11 (the raising of Lazarus)—lessons which many scholars believe to be the ancient core of a three-week period of final preparation for baptism. These lessons were introduced as part of the Episcopal Church's adaptation of the three-year Roman Catholic lectionary developed in the late 1960s. The Episcopal Church lectionary adds John 3 (rebirth by water and Spirit) on the second Sunday in Lent. Emphasis on baptism continues during the season of Easter. From the second through the seventh Sundays of Easter in Year A, the lectionary appoints 1 Peter, portions of which some scholars believe to be an ancient baptismal liturgy. The paschal cycle concludes with Pentecost, a baptismal day which underscores the work of the Spirit in baptism. Lessons are provided for a vigil of Pentecost, with a structure similar to that of the Easter vigil (rubrics sketching the outline of the vigil are include with the collects for Pentecost, pp. 175, 227): a service of light, using An Order of Worship for the Evening (p. 109); the collect of the day; three or more lessons, each followed by a psalm or canticle; gospel; sermon; and baptism, confirmation, or Renewal of Baptismal Vows (p. 292).

The baptism of Jesus has historically been celebrated on Epiphany by Eastern churches, and the 1928 prayer book introduced the baptism on the second Sunday after the Epiphany (although this was largely unnoticed). In accord with the revised Roman lectionary, the baptism was shifted to the First Sunday after the Epiphany.

A suggestion that All Saints' Day be a baptismal day was made by Boone Porter in a 1968 article in *Worship*.[3] But the identification of All Saints' Day (or the Sunday following) as a baptismal day also had a practical purpose. With the shift to public baptism at the main Sunday service, in large parishes baptism potentially could occur on virtually every Sunday of the year. Designated baptismal days would limit the number of celebrations of baptism. Easter, Pentecost and the baptism of Jesus were obvious choices because of their traditional associations with baptism. The drafting committee on initiation suggested that the feast of All Saints would provide an additional occasion for baptism between Pentecost and Epiphany and would be appropriate because it would emphasize baptism as incorporation into the body of Christ and the communion of saints.[4]

The designation of baptismal days is a unique feature of the 1979 prayer book. The provision for baptism or the renewal of vows on particular days acknowledges the baptismal character of those feasts: "the location of Baptism within the Christian Year can say something valuable about both Baptism and the Church's expressive use of time."[5] Each feast highlights a different aspect of the theological richness of baptism.

A Diversity of Ministries

A key teaching of the liturgical movement was the active participation of all the people in the liturgy, a concept articulated in the 1979 prayer book:

> In all services, the entire Christian assembly participates in such a way that the members of each order within the Church, lay persons, bishops, priests, and deacons, fulfill the functions proper to their respective orders, as set forth in the rubrical directions for each service. (p. 13)

This is a statement of the corporate nature of liturgy: liturgy is an action involving God's people gathered in a particular place and time.

The provision for *public* baptism is an important corollary of this principle. Placing baptism in a primary public celebration makes it less a ministry of the Church provided for the baptizand and immediate family and friends, and more a rite affecting and involving the entire community of God's people. Removing baptism from the section of pastoral offices in the prayer book also suggests that it is of a different character than those offices provided for significant occasions in the lives of individual Christians. Portions of the baptismal rite continue to focus on the individual, but this is balanced by the involvement of the entire community.

The baptismal rite includes the diversity of ministries that is part of every rite in the 1979 prayer book. Lay persons (sponsors if desired) read the lessons and lead the prayers for the candidates; a deacon or priest reads the gospel; an assisting priest or deacon may administer the water. The congregation makes responses throughout the rite, unlike the 1928 rite, in which, except for an occasional "amen," the only persons who spoke in addition to the presiding minister were the adults to be baptized and/or the godparents of children being baptized.

Perhaps the most significant change from 1928 and earlier Anglican rites is that the bishop, when present, is expected to be the celebrant, including preaching and presiding at baptism and the eucharist. No longer is the bishop's role in initiation restricted to the rite of confirmation, a concluding fragment separated from what had once been a single initiatory rite. Instead, the bishop presides throughout the initiatory rite, giving new emphasis to the centrality of baptism in the life of the Church. Underscoring the importance of the bishop as chief minister of baptism is the recommendation that, in addition to four designated feasts of the liturgical year, baptism be reserved for occasions "when a bishop is present" (p. 312).

Although the 1979 prayer book sees the bishop as the primary minister of baptism, a priest presides at baptism in the absence of a bishop. The requirement that chrism, if used, be consecrated by the bishop suggests to some a concrete link with the bishop when the bishop is not present at a baptism. Others, however, have suggested that a link with the bishop might better be seen in the priest who presides. This interpretation is supported by the Celebration of a New Ministry, at which the bishop presents a vessel of water to the new minister (usually the new rector of a congregation) and says, "help me baptize in obedience to our Lord" (p. 561). Such an explicit connection is not made when chrism is consecrated by a bishop.

A deacon may also preside at baptism, although this is limited to baptismal days when "the ministry of a bishop or priest cannot be obtained." In such circumstances, the deacon must be "specially authorized" by the bishop to preside (p. 312). While such an arrangement would permit the observance of a baptismal day, the rite would be diminished by the rubrically required omission of the prayer for the gifts of the Spirit and the laying on of a hand with consignation and optional chrismation. The distinctive ministry of the diaconate is far better recognized by utilizing the ministry of a deacon in more customary places: reading the gospel, leading the prayers of the people, preparing the table for eucharist, giving the dismissal. In addition, an assisting deacon may administer the water.

While a priest may preside at baptism, the bishop is the sole minister authorized to preside at confirmation and the related forms for reception and reaffirmation. Rubrics introduced in the House of Bishops and supported by the House of Deputies at the 1973 and 1976 General Conventions describe this as a rite "expected" of members of the Episcopal Church and identify the requisite liturgical action as a public affirmation of faith and laying on of hands by the bishop. The bishop's presidency at confirmation is a deeply cherished dimension of Anglicanism, and Episcopalians were unwilling to accept alternatives. Baptism may be full Christian initiation, but the actions of the General Convention suggest that this tangible association with the bishop in conjunction with a personal profession of faith is an important hallmark of Christian life for those in the Episcopal Church.

The Candidates for Baptism

The 1979 prayer book provides for the baptism of adults and older children who are able to answer for themselves and of infants and younger children unable to answer for themselves. The practice of infant baptism was carefully considered at the first meeting of the drafting committee in 1968 as part of their comprehensive review of the theology and practice of baptism.

The question of infant baptism becomes particularly crucial in the shift to a post-Christian worldview. In the Christendom model, the entire society is presumed to be Christian and infants are baptized as a matter of course, with the expectation that Christian nurture will occur as part of daily living as well as through participation in the life of the Church. But as Christendom crumbles and the broader societal supports for a Christian worldview disappear, increasing emphasis is placed upon individual decision and commitment. This may be one factor in the recurring concerns expressed about postconfirmation lapsing. It has also led to questions about infant baptism.

When the Drafting Committee on Christian Initiation was formed in 1968, William Spilman called for adult initiation as the norm. He later changed his position, a shift he attributed to Margaret Mead, who taught him about the "unconscious, psychological impact of sacramental action and symbolism."[6] This perspective was included in the rationale for infant baptism in the introduction to *PBS* 18: because infants and young children could be shaped by the symbolic, nonverbal dimension of liturgy, it was appropriate for them to be baptized. But it was therefore critical that these children participate regularly in the worship of the local congregation and that the congregation be "a true family of God, with a personal concern on the part of all its members for the nurture of its children."[7]

The primary rationale given for infant baptism was that it permits incorporation into the body of Christ. Since infants cannot respond consciously, they are baptized on the basis of the corporate faith of the Church. The introduction to *PBS* 18 suggested that this corporate faith is significant for adults as well as infants:

> Although in [believers' baptism] the candidate can declare his faith, it may or may not reflect a true commitment. Far more important is the response of faith of the Church into which one is sacramentally incorporated by Baptism. This is true both for an adult and for an infant.[8]

To emphasize the corporate nature of the baptismal commitment, the rite in *PBS* 18 directed that all questions of renunciation and commitment, including the Apostles' Creed in interrogatory form, be asked of the entire congregation.[9]

Commenting on this congregational affirmation of faith from the perspective of the Disciples of Christ (a believers' baptist tradition), Keith Watkins, professor of worship at Christian Theological Seminary, noted:

> When a rite is made into a pleasant act of infant dedication, that classical doctrine is compromised. Yet when the parents are made to speak on behalf of the child, the rite always has an artificial character. But in the promises that your rite has developed, promises said by the entire congregation, both of these great difficulties are overcome.

Nonetheless, Watkins expressed concern that the individual aspect of baptism was "unduly restricted" by the emphasis on corporate faith.[10] Colin Buchanan, a member of the Church of England Liturgical Commission, also questioned the stress given to the faith of the Church: "Does this mean that the child of unbelievers is as well qualified for baptism as those of believers?" He pointed out that the corporate affirmation of faith "drowns" the part of the candidates and recommended that candidates "be interrogated visibly."[11] To provide both an individual affirmation of faith and a corporate statement of belief, subsequent revisions separated the congregational affirmation of faith in the baptismal covenant from questions of renunciation and commitment to Christ, made only by candidates who can speak for themselves and by parents and sponsors of infants and younger children.

While some members of the drafting committee continued to maintain that adult baptism should be seen as a norm, a different approach was taken by Stevick in the *Supplement to PBS 26*. He argued that both infant baptism and believers' baptism had shortcomings as well as positive aspects. Baptism of the infant children of believers witnesses to the continuity of the generations and brings the children into the community of faith, but these children do not always grow up to take responsibility for commitments made on their behalf. Believers' baptism encourages adult conversion and commitment, but in communities where this is the practice, the adult decision tends to occur predictably at the expected age in the children of believers. Stevick concluded:

> It may be that the specific meaning and vocation of adult baptism and of infant baptism within the Christian fellowship would be enhanced, if both were real possibilities and were common enough in practice to have to endure the corrective of one another.[12]

Stevick's argument is not made explicit in the 1979 prayer book. Some interpreters of the rite give priority to adult baptism on the basis of the placement of the presentation of adults and older children before the presentation of infants and younger children. However, the use of a common rite for adult and infant baptism suggests that both approaches are equivalent.

The Role of Sponsors

The preface to the 1979 baptismal rite directs that each candidate for baptism be sponsored by one or more baptized persons. This provides more flexibility than previous stipulations that every boy have two godfathers and one godmother, and every girl have two godmothers and one godfather,[13] while introducing the expectation that at least one sponsor be baptized. This new stipulation is another reflection of the emergence of post-Christendom; as the Church comes to be seen as an institution separate from the surrounding society, sponsors have a more distinctive role in representing and interpreting the Church to the candidates and the candidates to the Church. For such a weighty responsibility, the requirement that the sponsor be baptized, that is, at least formally a member of the church community (if not an actively participating member), is a minimal expectation.

The provisions for sponsors were modified several times as the baptismal rite was developed. Because the baptismal renewal that began before prayer book revision had emphasized the responsibilities of sponsors, the issues in revision centered on how these responsibilities were best expressed liturgically.

In *PBS* 18, sponsors signed the baptismal register "as the expression of their assent," but their only specific role during the service was to present the candidates.[14] Unlike earlier rites, sponsors of children did not make promises on their behalf but instead joined in the congregational affirmation of faith. By this the drafting committee intended to show "that the candidates are being enveloped in the faith of the whole Church, and that the sponsors are representatives of the congregation."[15] However, consultants objected that the congregational affirmation of faith obscured the particular commitment of sponsors of infants to fulfill their responsibilities. In response to this criticism, the drafting committee added questions to the parents and godparents of infants, although there is no question exacting from the godparents the promise to bring their child to be confirmed, and the House of Deputies in 1976 rejected the attempt of the bishops to introduce such a question.

Unlike the 1928 rite, the godparents are not asked to respond on behalf of the infant to the question "Wilt thou be baptized in this Faith?"[16] They do, however, speak "on behalf of the infants and younger children" in response to the questions of renunciation of evil and adherence to Christ (p. 302).

PBS 18 directed that sponsors be "instructed about baptism and their duty to help the Candidate grow in his Christian privileges and responsibilities" but did not differentiate between sponsors of adults and sponsors of infants. John Burt, a member of the House of Bishops Theological Committee, asked that a distinction be made between sponsors of adults, who simply present a candidate, and sponsors of infants, who make promises on behalf of a child.[17] In *PBS* 26, revised prefatory rubrics specified that sponsors of adults "present their candidates...and thereby signify their endorsement of the candidates and their intention to support them by prayer and example in their Christian life," while sponsors of infants "present their candidates, make promises in their own names, and also take vows on behalf of their candidates."[18]

Preparation for Baptism

The "Findings" from the first drafting committee meeting acknowledged the importance of preparation: "The sacrament of baptism should not be administered without undertaking adequate preparation of the candidates if mature enough, or of the parents and sponsors of infants."[19] However, the 1979 prayer book speaks only of the instruction of parents and godparents. Mitchell suggests that preparation of adults was assumed, while preparation of sponsors of infants was sufficiently novel that the drafting committee thought it important to stipulate this requirement.[20] Although the rubrical provision for instruction of parents and godparents was a new addition to the prayer book, there was virtually no objection. This change in baptismal practice had been given increasing emphasis for at least two decades before *PBS* 18 introduced it in a rubric.

For the preparation of adults, a few suggestions for a catechumenate were made during the revision process, and Mitchell, in consultation with Thomas Talley, drafted a rite for the enrollment of catechumens. The proposal was not pursued, according to Spencer, because baptism was rarely administered to adults and thus there was little need for a catechumenate. Mitchell recalls that the catechumenate was considered to be of secondary importance, and hence the committee devoted its efforts to crafting rites for baptism and reaffirmation of faith.[21]

The Entrance Rite and Ministry of the Word

The baptismal rite begins with the opening acclamation from the Holy Eucharist, followed by versicles and responses based upon Ephesians 4:4-6. This dialogue, proposed by William Spilman during the development of *PBS* 18, sets the tone for the baptism that is to occur.

When baptism is celebrated as the principal service on a Sunday or other feast, the collect and lessons "are properly those of the day" (p. 300). Additional rubrics permit the collect and/or lessons for baptism to be used "when a bishop is present, or on other occasions for sufficient reasons" (p. 312).

In the first draft of *PBS* 18, a collect and lessons for baptism were given, but there was no provision for the use of the proper of the day. Since this conflicted with the efforts of the Drafting Committee on the Calendar, Eucharistic Lectionary, and Collects to reestablish the precedence of Sunday in the liturgical calendar, *PBS* 18 and subsequent revisions directed that the proper of the day be used.[22] Although not all Sunday propers are explicitly baptismal, the celebration of baptism on the specified baptismal days permits the use of lessons closely related to baptism.

The 1979 lectionary principle of two lessons in addition to the gospel is a significant enrichment. The 1928 prayer book had provided only gospel readings at baptism, and although there would be additional readings when baptism was celebrated in the context of Morning or Evening Prayer, those readings would not necessarily relate directly to baptism.

When the baptismal lessons are selected rather than those of the day, Ezekiel 36:24-28 is designated as the Old Testament lesson, but permission is given to substitute any other Old Testament lesson from the Easter vigil. The epistle lections, Romans 6:3-5, Romans 8:14-17, and 2 Corinthians 5:17-20, speak of different theological aspects of baptism. The gospels differ from those provided in the 1928 rite. Matthew 28:18-20 was eliminated because it had been incorporated into the Thanksgiving over the Water. The selection from John 3 concludes at verse 6 instead of verse 8. A new option, Mark 1:9-11 (the baptism of Jesus), is given. Mark 10:13-16 ("let the children come to me") was eliminated by the drafting committee, but at the request of the Standing Liturgical Commission it was restored as an option for the gospel, in spite of objections by the Council of Associated Parishes and several consultants that this selection is not appropriate for baptism.

The lessons are followed by the sermon. During the course of revision, concern was expressed that restless children and crying babies would disrupt the sermon. Repeated suggestions that the sermon be shifted to a place immediately following the peace led eventually to the inclusion of rubrical permission for this.

Presentation of Candidates and Affirmation of Faith

The most extensive changes from 1968 to 1975 were in the presentation of candidates and affirmation of faith. One reason for these changes was the need expressed for an individual profession of faith in addition to the community's affirmation of faith. The crafting of a new rite for Christians in the United States in the late twentieth century required language that gave vivid expression to the commitments made in baptism. In addition, new structures were needed to allow the new rite of reaffirmation to be celebrated in combination with baptism when a bishop was present.

The Relation of the Profession of Faith and the Water Bath

The rite proposed by the drafting committee in December 1968 placed the examination of the candidates, including the renunciation, interrogatory Apostles' Creed, and questions of commitment, just prior to the water bath. In this order of service, similar to that proposed in the 1958 report of the Church of England Liturgical Commission[23] and subsequently recommended by Mitchell and by Spencer, affirmation of faith and water baptism in the triune name are closely linked.

However, the Standing Liturgical Commission directed that the presentation of candidates and the examination be placed directly after the ministry of the word and prior to the litany and blessing of the font. This order was intended to parallel that of the rites of ordination and marriage. Candidates would be presented and examined before they were prayed for and the font blessed for them. Spencer explained to the drafting committee that the commission did not find the link between affirmation of faith and water baptism to be essential: "it was felt that since we use the baptismal formula, the Act of Faith between the blessing and the formula interrupts the dramatic action."[24]

The change in order occasioned little response from consultants, although Colin Buchanan noted: "our pundits here [England] would criticize the separation of vows and baptism."[25] Despite Buchanan's objection, the revised order remained in the 1979 rite.

Renunciations

In *PBS* 18 a single question of renunciation, "Do you renounce evil in all its forms?" followed three questions of commitment. Marion Bingley, the drafting committee member assigned to this portion of the rite, had suggested that the baptismal vows would be stronger if the affirmation of faith was made first, followed by the renunciation. The question of renunciation proved to be unacceptable. An editorial in *The Living Church* described the proposed renunciation as "about as drastic and heroic as coming out fearlessly for motherhood."[26] Some consultants requested the traditional renunciation of the world, the flesh and the devil.

The drafting committee then proposed three questions of renunciation, to be asked immediately following the presentation of candidates and before any affirmation of faith. The committee agreed that these questions should be answered only by the adult candidates and by the sponsors of infants speaking on behalf of those candidates. However, the wording of the renunciations underwent significant revisions in the drafts leading up to *PBS* 26.

Of particular concern was whether "the devil" or "Satan" should be used. A September 1972 revision did not include these terms but asked candidates to renounce "all demonic powers that rebel against God," "all evil forces that despoil the creatures of God," and "all sinful desires that draw us from the love of God."[27] A consultant responded, "The reference to demonic powers rebelling and evil forces despoiling conjures up comic-book images of devils in red suits with horns, pointed tails, and pitchforks."[28] In the January 1973 draft and in *PBS* 26, "Satan" was named: "Do you renounce Satan and all the powers of wickedness that rebel against God?"[29]

Although the question was retained in essentially the same form in the 1979 prayer book, the meaning and use of the term "Satan" continued to be discussed by the Standing Liturgical Commission. The official introduction to the *Draft Proposed BCP* argued that it was important for the Christian faith to recognize a personal spirit of evil: "Satan stands for a reality in the Christian understanding of evil, the reality of an evil beyond human control though not beyond God's control."[30]

Commitment to Christ

In *PBS* 18, the presentation of the candidate was followed by three questions of commitment: "Will you obey and follow Jesus Christ as your Savior and Lord?" "Will you seek and serve Christ in all men, loving your neighbor as yourself?" "Will you strive for justice, peace, and dignity among all men?" Next came the question of renunciation, followed by the Apostles' Creed in interrogatory form. As the triple renunciation was developed, the drafting committee experimented with different structures for an act of adherence and the Apostles' Creed following the renunciations.

In the 1972 drafts, the three renunciations were followed by a single, rather verbose question eliciting the candidate's commitment "to obey and follow Jesus Christ as my Savior and Lord." This affirmation was followed by prayers for the candidates; the interrogatory Apostles' Creed and additional questions of commitment came after the prayers. Shepherd and others objected to placing the prayers between the renunciations and the profession of faith. Otis Charles, Bishop of Utah and a member of the House of Bishops Prayer Book Committee, recommended that three short questions be used for the act of commitment, parallel to the renunciations. Hence in *PBS* 26 the three questions of renunciation were followed by three questions of adherence addressed only to candidates and to sponsors of infants and young children. Although different wordings and structures were subsequently proposed, the Standing Liturgical Commission eventually returned to the structure and wording similar to the questions in *PBS* 26.

The Congregation's Support of the Candidates

As *PBS* 18 was being revised, several consultants suggested that the baptismal rite should include a question asking the congregation to support those being baptized. Such a question would parallel the question to the congregation in the proposed rite for the Celebration and Blessing of a Marriage: "Will you who witness these vows do all in your power to support and uphold this marriage in the years ahead?"[31] A question to the congregation was finally introduced when *PBS* 26 was revised in late 1974.[32]

When first proposed, the question was placed immediately after the presentation of candidates for baptism and confirmation and before the renunciations. This meant that the focus moved from candidates presented for baptism, to candidates presented for "confirmation of baptismal vows," to the congregation, then back to candidates for baptism (for the renunciation and adherence), then back to the congregation (for the baptismal covenant). This order was revised in order to provide a more coherent structure. The structure accepted in the 1979 prayer book permits a focus first on candidates and sponsors for baptism, as candidates are presented, questions are asked of the sponsors of infants, and adult candidates and the sponsors of infants respond to questions of renunciation and adherence. Then the focus moves to the other candidates, who are presented and asked to affirm their renunciation of evil and commitment to Christ. Finally the focus shifts to the congregation, first for the question asking their support and then to the baptismal covenant.

The Baptismal Covenant

The Baptismal Covenant developed gradually over the course of revision. *PBS* 18 used the version of the Apostles' Creed recommended by the International Consultation on English Texts in October 1969, in keeping with the Episcopal Church's participation in this ecumenical endeavor. In the first draft of *PBS* 18, the Creed was followed by two queries: "Will you then obey and follow Christ as your Lord and Savior?" and "Will you in Christ seek and serve him in all men, loving your neighbor as yourself?"[33]

After this first draft was distributed to consultants, Henry Breul, a long-time member of Associated Parishes, recommended the inclusion of a social action question.[34] The committee added "Will you strive for justice, peace, and human dignity among men and nations?" a modification of a question proposed by Breul.[35] The question reflects the heightened emphasis on social justice in the Church of the late 1960s, and there were a few objections that this question catered to a passing fad.

After *PBS* 18 was completed in summer 1969, a respondent pointed out that seeking and serving Christ in all people and striving for justice could be done without participating in the eucharist. To incorporate this concern, the drafting committee turned to Acts 2:42: "Will you continue in the apostles' teaching and fellowship, in the breaking of bread and the prayers?"[36]

At the December 1972 meeting of the Standing Liturgical Commission with the Theological and Prayer Book Committees of the House of Bishops, another question was added: "Will you, by word and example, proclaim the good news of God in Christ Jesus?" No rationale was given for this question.[37]

As *PBS* 26 was being revised, a theology committee of the Standing Liturgical Commission, chaired by Charles Price, recommended that expressions of penitence be strengthened in the draft rites. At Spencer's suggestion, the drafting committee proposed: "Will you persevere in resisting evil in all its forms and, if you sin, return to the Lord in penitence?"[38] When the House of Bishops reviewed the proposal, they asked that "if you sin" be changed to "when you sin," but Spencer insisted that persons about to be baptized should not be told that they would certainly sin, as implied by "when you sin."[39] The issue was resolved by the use of the word "whenever": "Will you persevere in resisting evil, and whenever you fall into sin, repent and return to the Lord?"[40]

When in revising *PBS* 18 the drafting committee separated the candidates' renunciations and affirmation of faith from the corporate response by the congregation, they titled the latter section "Profession of Faith and Commitment." This title reflected the content: profession of faith in the form of the interrogatory creed, followed by profession of commitment in response to a series of questions. In *PBS* 26, the "Profession of Faith and Commitment" also included the questions of adherence addressed to the candidates and sponsors of infants; a bidding then invited the congregation to renew their "baptismal covenant." In *PBS* 26 Revised, the title "Profession of Faith and Commitment" was eliminated, and the addition of the title "The Baptismal Covenant" made a clearer separation from the presentation and examination of the candidates.

Although the baptismal covenant was not conceived as such when the drafting committee began its work in 1968, the use of questions of commitment is not a novelty in Anglican baptismal rites. In the 1662 English prayer book and previous prayer books of the Episcopal Church, the interrogatory creed has been followed by the question, "Wilt thou then obediently keep God's holy will and commandments, and walk in the same all the days of thy life?"[41] The questions that developed in the 1979 rite are the result of the drafting committee's efforts to express the intent of this question in contemporary terms. What is new for Episcopalians is the use of the covenant as a corporate affirmation of faith during the baptismal liturgy and at baptismal days when there are no baptisms.

Prayers for the Candidates

The litany for the candidates, initially drafted by Weil and then edited by the drafting committee, touches upon several baptismal motifs, including redemption, incorporation, mission and eschatological hope.

In the first draft of *PBS* 18, the litany included the petition "Strengthen them against temptation and all evil."[42] Several consultants lamented that throughout this draft references to baptismal regeneration and remission of sins were lacking. Spencer acknowledged this to the committee:

We have omitted any reference to forgiveness of sin. I think we felt it inappropriate to infants. Any reference to original sin will inevitably be for the average laymen interpreted as original guilt. We also were primarily concerned with a positive emphasis. But in view of adult baptism and the traditional concepts, perhaps the phrase remission of sin or redemption from sin should be introduced at a few places.[43]

One response of the committee was to revise the first petition of the litany to read: "Redeem them, O Lord, from all evil, and rescue them from the way of sin and death."[44]

When *PBS* 26 was revised, a new petition was added: "Fill them with your holy and life-giving Spirit,"[45] emphasizing the bestowal of the Spirit in baptism. A concluding collect, an adaptation of the 1928 collect for Easter Even,[46] was also added in the revision of *PBS* 26.

The use of a litany with a concluding collect said by the celebrant provides a structure parallel to the intercessions in the eucharist, but the focus on the candidates for baptism is markedly different from the content of the intercessions at the eucharist. In this respect the litany for the candidates is akin to the prayers in the pastoral offices of marriage and burial. However, unlike the pastoral rites, the baptismal rite offers the option of including the prayers of the people after the peace and before the offertory of the eucharist, an option introduced in *PBS* 18. The difficulty with this structure is that it does not conform to the usual flow of the eucharist, since the prayers of the people ordinarily precede the peace. Nevertheless, no significant attention was given during the revision process to this structural variation.

Thanksgiving over the Water

The Thanksgiving over the Water was a new prayer composed by Mitchell, who drew upon the 1958 proposal of the Church of England Liturgical Commission and medieval western material. The prayer is of particular importance in its recovery of biblical typology—creation, the Exodus, Jesus' baptism.

When the first draft was presented to the Standing Liturgical Commission, Shepherd insisted that the typology of the flood (Genesis 6-9) be removed from the blessing of the water. Margaret Mead assured the drafting committee that anthropological and archaeological evidence of the flood appeared in various traditions and was taken quite seriously by anthropologists, but the committee did not attempt to reintroduce any reference to the flood in the blessing of the water.[47]

In response to the requests for mention of the forgiveness of sins in baptism, several changes were made. Redemption was explicitly connected to Jesus' death and resurrection: "who would lead us by his death and resurrection from the bondage of sin into everlasting life." The water of baptism was also linked to redemption: "in which we are buried with Christ in his death that we may share in his resurrection." The first draft had associated the baptismal water with being "born again"; in *PBS* 18, cleansing from sin was added to this phrase: "that those who here are cleansed from sin may be born again."[48]

Although only minor changes in wording were made after *PBS* 18, the title was changed from "The Blessing of the Water" to "Thanksgiving over the Water." A consultant responding to *PBS* 18 had argued that water is already blessed by the act of God's creation; in baptism it is set aside for sacramental use, not changed into holy water.[49] As *PBS* 26 was revised, the theology committee of the Standing Liturgical Commission recommended that the prayer be given a title parallel to that of the Great Thanksgiving at the eucharist, and "Thanksgiving over the Water" was thereby introduced.

Consecration of the Chrism

The prayer for the consecration of chrism, newly composed in the drafting process, was revised several times as the drafting committee explored images suggested by the reintroduction of chrism into the baptismal rite. In April 1969, Spilman suggested that the anointing indicated that baptism "is an ordination of the laity into the servant ministry of the Lord."[50] The prayer in *PBS* 18 introduced this interpretation, calling upon God "whose Son Jesus Christ was anointed by the Holy Spirit to be the servant of all men" and asking God to consecrate the oil "that those who are sealed with it may have a share in the ministry of our great High Priest and King."[51] In *PBS* 26 Revised, the latter phrase was altered to read "that those who are sealed with it may share in the royal priesthood" of Jesus,[52] wording which gives the chrism a more explicit association with the biblical image of Christians as members of the royal priesthood (1 Peter 2:5,9; 1 John 2:20,27; Revelation 1:6, 5:10). The depiction of Jesus as an anointed servant alludes to Acts 4:27.

The prayer was entitled "The Blessing of Oil" in *PBS* 18 and "The Blessing of Chrism" in *PBS* 26. The theology committee of the Standing Liturgical Commission recommended that the term "consecrate" be used to "designate not the communion of Spirit and spirit involved in a blessing, but the identification of an object as God's possession." Accordingly the prayer over the oil was retitled "Consecration of the Chrism."[53]

Water Baptism and Postbaptismal Ceremonies

The provisions for the central core of the baptismal rite—the administration of water in the triune name—are essentially unchanged from earlier Anglican prayer books. The quaint term "dip" has been updated, and the rubrics now direct the celebrant to "immerse" or pour water upon the candidate, but this is the same order in which the actions were previously listed. The Trinitarian formula continues to be pronounced in the active voice, "I baptize you..."

As *PBS* 18 was being refined, the drafting committee asked consultants whether a passive construction should be used: "you are baptized..." Although there was some favorable response, no change was made.[54] Mitchell recalls that the committee decided not to alter the baptismal formula because the remainder of the rite was such a radical change for Episcopalians.[55]

A few consultants suggested that the rite include the giving of a candle to the newly baptized. A rubric introduced in the "Additional Directions and Suggestions" in *PBS* 26 permitted a candle, which could be lit from the paschal candle, to be given to the newly baptized or their godparents.

The most significant changes—and among the most controversial issues in the revision process—are the postbaptismal ceremonies. The prayer for the sevenfold gifts of the Spirit, historically part of Anglican confirmation rites, follows the water rite. The language of the prayer has been significantly modified from its original form, in keeping with efforts to use language and imagery that resonate with the experiences of twentieth-century Christians. As we have seen, the formula at the sealing was repeatedly revised throughout the drafting process, and the final form was a hard-fought compromise.

Following the prayer for the gifts of the Spirit and the sealing, the newly baptized are welcomed by the congregation. The first draft of *PBS* 18 had combined the sealing and reception into the congregation, in a manner similar to the formula at the postbaptismal consignation in the 1928 prayer book ("we receive this child into the congregation of Christ's flock; and do sign *him*..."). The Standing Liturgical Commission directed that the reception be done through the peace, comparable to the rites proposed for marriage and ordination. Instead, the drafting committee separated the sealing from a statement of welcome and placed the exchange of the peace immediately after the welcome. In response to requests from consultants, *PBS* 18 and subsequent drafts directed that this formula of welcome be recited by the entire congregation. While there was little opposition to this structure, the phrasing of the welcome was revised several times as the drafting committee and Standing Liturgical Commission worked to find appropriate liturgical language for this new formula.

Inclusive Language

During the revision process, the Standing Liturgical Commission formed a subcommittee, convened by Virginia Harbour, on "sensitivity relating to women," to address questions concerning the language of the prayer book. The subcommittee report, given at the June 1974 Standing Liturgical Commission meeting, began by asserting that women were finding "that the language of Prayer Book and Hymnal is couched to affirm man at the expense of woman." The generic use of masculine nouns and pronouns "reinforces the concept of maleness as the human norm, femaleness as the exception or the psychological 'other'" and so does not affirm the full human dignity of women.[56]

The subcommittee urged that the commission eliminate the generic use of masculine nouns and pronouns in liturgical texts and rubrics. They were prepared to recommend rewordings of draft texts to the chairs of each drafting committee, work which had already begun with a review of the proposed baptismal rite. Detailed comments with suggested revisions had been sent to Spencer. Careful comparison of successive drafts indicates that the subcommittee's comments had been incorporated into the rites of baptism and affirmation of baptismal vows prior to the publication of *PBS* 26.

The subcommittee on sensitivity relating to women also pointed out that masculine images of God were overemphasized in the liturgy, and they recommended greater use of terms denoting God's actions, for example, "the creative, saving/redeeming, sustaining, loving, empowering activities of the Godhead."[57] However, no changes seem to have been introduced in response to this suggestion.

Foundation for a Baptismal Ecclesiology

As the rite of Holy Baptism was developed, every aspect was carefully reviewed by the Drafting Committee on Christian Initiation and the Standing Liturgical Commission. They worked to formulate a rite in which the language, images and ritual structure and action would be suitable for the Episcopal Church as it moved into the post-Christian era in the late twentieth century and at the same time would maintain a theology of Christian initiation solidly rooted in biblical principles and the Christian tradition.

In some ways, the new rite built upon the baptismal renewal already under way as a result of the liturgical movement—public baptism at the principal Sunday service, the importance of preparation of sponsors of infants and young children, the active participation of the entire community in its liturgy. Moreover, the rite was consciously shaped by substantial theological discussion of twentieth-century biblical and liturgical scholarship. Thus the rite contains the seeds of a *baptismal ecclesiology*, a vision of baptism as fundamental to Christian identity and, with the eucharist, central to the life and mission of the Church.

Nevertheless, the revisers could not have envisioned the full ramifications of the new rite. Like all liturgy, the rite also shapes those who celebrate it. Thus the implications of this revolutionary new rite have only gradually been comprehended as worshiping communities in the Episcopal Church have celebrated the rite and continued to reflect on its meaning for their life and mission.

NOTES

1. *The Church Year: The Calendar and the Proper of the Sundays and Other Holy Days throughout the Church Year*, *Prayer Book Studies* 19 (New York: Church Hymnal Corporation, 1970), pp. 189-92 (hereafter cited as *PBS* 19).

2. *PBS* 26, p. 18.

3. "Baptism: Its Paschal and Ecumenical Setting," *Worship* 42 (1968): 208.

4. Interview with Leonel Mitchell, Evanston, IL, Apr. 23, 1992.

5. *Supplement to PBS 26*, p. 106.

6. Spilman to Spencer, Mar. 22, 1969 (Rev. Files 122-7-10).

7. *PBS* 18, pp. 15-16.

8. Ibid., p. 14.

9. Ibid., pp. 22, 35-6.

10. Keith Watkins to Malania, May 19, 1970 (Rev. Files 122-7-15).

11. Colin Buchanan to Spencer, Aug. 11, 1969 (Rev. Files 122-7-10).

12. *Supplement to PBS 26*, p. 47.

13. BCP 1928, p. 273.

14. *PBS* 18, pp. 32, 34.

15. Ibid., p. 22.

16. BCP 1928, p. 277.

17. John Burt to Chilton Powell, Dec. 28, 1972, p. 2 (Rev. Files 122-8-4).

18. *PBS* 26, p. 8.

19. DC VI Minutes, May 2-3, 1968, p. 2 (Rev. Files 122-7-12).

20. Interview with Mitchell, Evanston, IL, Apr. 23, 1992.

21. Interview with Spencer, West Park, NY, May 22-23, 1990; interview with Mitchell, Evanston, IL, Apr. 23, 1992.

22. *PBS* 18, p. 32.

23. *Baptism and Confirmation* (London: SPCK, 1959), pp. x-xi, 3-14.

24. "Revision of Liturgy" (Rev. Files 122-7-15).

25. Buchanan to Spencer, Aug. 11, 1969 (Rev. Files 122-7-10).

26. "Holy Baptism Bowdlerized," *The Living Church*, Sept. 12, 1971, p. 17.

27. "Draft: Holy Baptism," Sept. 1972, p. 5 (Rev. Files 122-8-2).

28. Thomas G. P. Guilbert, "Comments on: Initiatory Rites and Program of Prayer Book Revision," received Nov. 14, 1972 (Rev. Files 122-8-2).

29. *PBS* 26, p. 11.

30. *PBS* 29, p. 72.

31. *PBS* 24, p. 27.

32. *Holy Baptism*, *PBS* 26 Revised, p. 9.

33. DC VI Minutes, Dec. 16-17, 1968, pp. 7-8 (Rev. Files 122-7-14).

34. "Revision of the Liturgy" (Rev. Files 122-7-15).

35. DC VI Minutes, Apr. 21-22, 1969, p. 15 (Rev. Files 122-7-15).

36. DC VI Minutes, May 1-2, 1972 (Rev. Files 122-7-18).

37. SLC Minutes, Dec. 6-9, 1972, p. 6 (Rev. Files 122-2-1).

38. DC VI Minutes, Sept. 27-28, 1974, p. 5 (Rev. Files 122-7-22).

39. Spencer to DC VI, Nov. 12, 1974, p. 1 (Rev. Files 122-6-11).

40. *Holy Baptism*, *PBS* 26 Revised, p. 11.

41. Marshall, *Prayer Book Parallels*, Vol. 1, pp. 250-1.

42. DC VI Minutes, Dec. 16-17, 1968, p. 6 (Rev. Files 122-7-14).

43. "Revision of Liturgy" (Rev. Files 122-7-15).

44. *PBS* 18, p. 36.

45. *Holy Baptism*, *PBS* 26 Revised, p. 11.

46. BCP 1928, p. 161.

47. Interview with Spencer, West Park, NY, May 22-23, 1990; DC VI Minutes, Apr. 21-22, 1969, p. 16 (Rev. Files 122-7-15).

48. *PBS* 18, pp. 37-8.

49. John Spong to Malania, Aug. 20, 1969 (Rev. Files 122-6-21).

50. Spilman to Spencer, Easter Even, 1969 (Rev. Files 122-7-10).

51. *PBS* 18, p. 38. Spilman's phrase "ordination of the laity into the servant ministry of the Lord" was incorporated into the explanation for the use of chrism (ibid., p. 23).

52. *Holy Baptism*, *PBS* 26 Revised, p. 13.

53. "Theological Committee of the Standing Liturgical Commission: Proposed New Prayers over Material Objects" (Rev. Files 122-10-2).

54. DC VI Minutes, Apr. 21-22, 1969, p. 21 (Rev. Files 122-7-15).

55. Interview with Mitchell, Evanston, IL, Apr. 23, 1992.

56. "Committee on Sensitivity Subcommittee Relating to Women," SLC Minutes, June 24-28, 1974, pp. 6-7 (Rev. Files 122-2-2).

57. Ibid.

Chapter 10

Enriching the Prayer Book:
The Book of Occasional Services
and *The Hymnal 1982*

Materials to support the implementation of the new rites of Holy Baptism and "Confirmation with forms for Reception and for the Reaffirmation of Baptismal Vows" have been included in *The Book of Occasional Services*. Because the texts in this book are considered optional and require the approval of just one General Convention, new materials are added on a regular basis. (The preceding collection, *The Book of Offices*, underwent three editions between 1940 and 1961.) This encourages the continual growth and development of liturgy and allows worshiping communities to use new materials in a manner suited to their particular characteristics and needs. Materials that are widely used may be incorporated into a subsequent revision of the prayer book, just as forms for the adoption of a child and for the Easter vigil were added to *The Book of Offices* and then revised for inclusion in the 1979 prayer book.

The Consecration of Chrism
Apart from Baptism

PBS 8 included the "blessing of oil" in the context of baptism. When a separate rite of imposition of hands by the bishop was developed, a rubric was introduced to permit the consecration of chrism during the rite of confirmation, using the prayer in the baptismal rite. However, there were no directions explaining how to incorporate this consecration into the confirmation rite; since chrism is not used at confirmation, there is no inherently logical place for its consecration in the rite.

After the *Proposed BCP* was approved in 1976, the question of the consecration of chrism apart from baptism was taken up by the Committee on the Revision of *The Book of Offices* and its Subcommittee on Christian Initiation Materials. The committees rejected the incipient custom of a chrism mass and reaffirmation of ordination vows on Maundy Thursday, an imitation of contemporary Roman Catholic practice. (Although the consecration of chrism had been part of Maundy Thursday celebrations since the Middle Ages, the reaffirmation of ordination vows was an unprecedented innovation introduced in the Roman Catholic Church in the late 1960s. Its introduction seems to have been a reaction to challenges to clerical celibacy voiced in the Roman Catholic Church during the 1960s, and thus the rite can be understood as an effort to enforce priestly celibacy and obedience to the bishop.)[1]

The committees recommended that bishops be encouraged to consecrate chrism during their visitations to parishes and that the Standing Liturgical Commission clarify the rubric regarding the consecration of chrism when there was no baptism. The commission assigned this task to a Committee on Holy Week, which developed the "Consecration of Chrism Apart from Baptism" for inclusion in the 1979 *Book of Occasional Services*.

Following medieval precedent, the rite directs that chrism be consecrated immediately after the postcommunion prayer. Although the committee considered revising the consecration prayer in order to enrich the biblical imagery, they decided to maintain consistency with the prayer book form for the consecration of chrism. However, expanded imagery is provided by an introductory address relating baptismal anointing to the gift of the Holy Spirit, the use of oil to anoint priests and kings in ancient Israel, and Jesus' anointing by the Holy Spirit at his baptism. This is followed by the baptismal prayer for the consecration of chrism. In addition, introductory rubrics explain that chrism traditionally consists of olive oil to which oil of balsam or other fragrant oil is added; such practical guidance was not included in the prayer book despite Episcopalians' unfamiliarity with chrism.

Although the Committee on the Revision of *The Book of Offices* had opposed a separate rite for the consecration of chrism, a collect and lessons are provided for use "if there is a need to consecrate chrism at a separate, diocesan service," with no mention of when such a diocesan service should or could occur. In addition, a form for "Reaffirmation of Ordination Vows" was developed, thus providing separate rites, each with proper collect and lessons, that offer a parallel to the Roman Catholic consecration of chrism and reaffirmation of ordination vows. While there are no rubrical directions for combining the rites, the forms follow one another in *The Book of Occasional Services*, and a number of dioceses have introduced such a celebration on Maundy Thursday or another day during Holy Week.

Significant difficulties are created by combining the consecration of chrism and the reaffirmation of ordination vows. The proper for the consecration of chrism, particularly the collect and the lesson from Revelation 1:4-8, suggests that all Christians are anointed by the Spirit to participate in the royal priesthood of Christ. However, the reaffirmation of ordination vows, with propers from ordination or the Celebration of a New Ministry, focuses on ordained ministry. The two emphases are in tension with one another; the particular recommitments made by clergy can easily obscure the commitment of all Christians to the reconciling ministry of Christ. Furthermore, the Reaffirmation of Ordination Vows suggests that it is used "when the clergy are gathered together with the bishop." Nowhere is the presence of the laity specifically mentioned. Yet not only is chrism identified with the baptismal anointing of the laity, ordained ministry is properly understood only in the context of the community of the baptized among whom the clergy serve. Finally, the Reaffirmation of Ordination Vows is focused on presbyteral ministry. The promise "so to minister the Word of God and the sacraments of the New Covenant that the reconciling love of Christ may be known and received" is taken verbatim from the Examination in the Ordination of a Priest;[2] no comparable question points to the ministry of deacons.

Despite these difficulties, some clergy have found the ritual reaffirmation of ordination vows to be deeply meaningful. It seems to address a felt need similar to the demands for a reaffirmation of faith that led to the new rite of Confirmation with forms for Reception and for the Reaffirmation of Baptismal Vows. In a post-Christian age, when membership in the Church cannot be taken for granted and Christian teachings stand in tension with secular values, there is a strong need for expressions of individual faith and commitment. For some clergy, the Reaffirmation of Ordination Vows meets this need and so supports them in their ordained ministry. The challenge for the Episcopal Church is to find expressions of this commitment that are consistent with the baptismal ecclesiology that underlies the 1979 prayer book.

The Development of a Catechumenate

Although during the process of prayer book revision some attention was given to the development of catechumenal rites, work began in earnest only after the *Proposed BCP* was approved. The Subcommittee on Christian Initiation Materials, chaired by Leonel Mitchell, urged the development of a catechumenate because of increasing numbers of persons who were unbaptized and had little or no experience of the Christian faith. Rites for admission to the catechumenate and to candidacy, the final stage of preparation, were adapted from the new Roman Catholic Rite of Christian Initiation of Adults.

The catechumenate provides both a process of adult formation and ritual expression of the gradual incorporation of these adults into the Christian community. However, adult initiation was a new concept for the Episcopal Church. The catechumenate spread slowly, and as it came into wider use, modifications were added to *The Book of Occasional Services.*

A formal catechumenate seems to have been first implemented in the Episcopal Church in 1978 at Church of the Good Shepherd, Granbury, Texas, and All Saints Church, Baytown, Texas, working independently of one another. At the 1979 meeting of Diocesan Liturgy and Music Commissions a slide presentation by Robert Brooks, rector of All Saints, was enthusiastically received and led to further discussion of the catechumenate at the 1980 meeting of the Council of Associated Parishes. A few additional parishes instituted a catechumenate during the early 1980s, but these efforts were scattered and uncoordinated; by 1985, about 150 congregations were using a catechumenal process.[3]

More formal efforts began when the 1985 General Convention directed the Standing Liturgical Commission and the Education and Evangelism Departments of the Episcopal Church to develop "materials and suggested detailed guidelines for the implementation of a practical adult catechumenate with experimental use in pilot parishes."[4] The Diocese of Milwaukee was designated as the pilot diocese. Some parishes and dioceses adopted the Milwaukee model, while others used materials developed for the Roman Catholic Rite of Christian Initiation of Adults. In 1988 a national conference on the catechumenate, sponsored by Associated Parishes, was attended by over two hundred people from thirty-two dioceses.[5] More recently, the Episcopal Church and the Evangelical Lutheran Church in America have worked together to train leaders for the catechumenate in their respective churches.

In the mid-1980s a Standing Liturgical Commission survey of parishes using the catechumenal process found that the rites were used in many places to prepare baptized persons for confirmation, reception or reaffirmation, despite the explicit statement in the *BOS* that the rites are appropriate only for use with persons preparing for baptism. To address this concern, the commission developed more detailed principles for the implementation of the catechumenate and parallel processes and rites for preparation of baptized persons for reaffirmation of the baptismal covenant and for preparation of parents and godparents for the baptism of infants and young children (see Appendix C). These new materials were approved by the 1988 General Convention for inclusion in the *BOS*; further revisions were made in 1991 and 1994 in response to experience with the rites.

The initial stage, a brief period of inquiry for adults seeking baptism or reaffirmation of baptism, paralleled by pregnancy in the case of parents and godparents preparing for the baptism of an infant, concludes with a public rite: Admission of Catechumens, the "welcoming" of baptized persons preparing for reaffirmation, or the blessing of a pregnant woman. The primary period of formation then begins, a time of reflection on scripture, Christian prayer and worship, and ministry. For parents and godparents, this formation includes consideration of the implications of the baptismal covenant for Christian marriage and parenting. A second public rite then introduces the final intensive stage of preparation: catechumens are enrolled as candidates, those preparing to reaffirm their baptismal covenant are enrolled "for Lenten Preparation," and parents and godparents celebrate the Thanksgiving for the Birth or Adoption of a Child. This intensive preparation concludes with the celebration of baptism; those preparing for reaffirmation participate in a "Maundy Thursday Rite of Preparation for the Paschal Holy Days," then reaffirm their baptismal covenant at the Easter vigil, and finally, if the bishop was not present at the Easter vigil, are presented to the bishop to receive the laying on of hands, preferably during the Great Fifty Days.[6]

The implementation of the catechumenate is an important component in a renewed understanding of baptism as central to Christian life. When introduced with the support and involvement of an entire congregation, it can focus attention on the power of baptism and the profound implications of baptism for every aspect of Christian life. Those involved in the catechumenate, whether as candidates, sponsors or catechists, attest to the effectiveness of the catechumenate in facilitating the process of conversion and formation and in revitalizing the life of congregations. However, there are some difficulties, both in ritual structure and in the implementation of the catechumenate and parallel processes.

Introductory rites are provided in each of the three parallel processes, although these are not entirely comparable. The rite of admission to the catechumenate is always appropriate for unbaptized adults, but for those preparing for reaffirmation, the rite of welcoming is suited only for those entering (or reentering) a particular community, that is, "baptized persons who have returned to the life of the Church after a time away" and those baptized in other traditions and now affiliating with the Episcopal Church.[7] No ritual expression is provided for persons who are already active participants in a community and seek to reaffirm their baptismal vows. In the process for parents and godparents, it is far more common for parents to seek baptism after the birth of the child than to begin baptismal preparation when pregnancy is discovered. The rubrics recognize this situation and direct that the first two stages be combined.[8] While there is thus not a true parallel at the beginning of the different processes, continued experience with the rites will no doubt lead to further refinements; the differences in ways of coming to seek baptism or reaffirmation may suggest that different rites are needed, or perhaps that the beginning of the process need not be ritualized in every situation.

Far more serious are the challenges presented by the prayer book stipulations that a bishop preside at the rite of reaffirmation and that those baptized as adults are expected to receive the laying on of hands by a bishop. For those reaffirming baptismal vows and for catechumens seeking baptism, the ritual structure leads to a climax at the Easter vigil, yet these persons must later be presented to the bishop for another affirmation of baptismal vows in order to receive episcopal laying on of hands.

One means of addressing the expectation that adult baptizands receive episcopal imposition of hands is to present adults for baptism at the bishop's visitation, one of the five occasions recommended for the celebration of baptism. However, unless the bishop's visitation coincides with the specified baptismal days, the connection of the final baptismal preparation with the liturgical year is disrupted. A partial solution is to schedule regional services of baptism and reaffirmation during the Great Fifty Days; while this does not provide the ritual climax at the Easter vigil, it allows some link between Lenten preparation for baptism (or reaffirmation) and the final rite of baptism (or confirmation, reception or reaffirmation).

Other questions might be raised about the integration of the rites with the liturgical year. The *BOS* states that the baptism of catechumens "is normally reserved for the Great Vigil of Easter" but permits enrollment at the beginning of Advent for baptism on the Feast of the Baptism of Our Lord,[9] while the process and rites for reaffirmation are designed to come to completion during Lent. The focus on the paschal cycle makes good use of the baptismal emphasis of the Lenten lectionary, particularly when a congregation uses the Year A readings during Lent and Easter if there are candidates for baptism at the Easter vigil, an option the *BOS* offers in any year of the lectionary cycle.[10] But the restriction of adult baptisms to the Easter vigil may also serve to diminish the baptismal dimensions of the other designated baptismal days. The historical evidence suggests that Easter baptism was introduced during the third century and became the predominant practice only during the fourth century. Moreover, the paschal motif of participation in Christ's death and resurrection is but one biblical aspect of baptism; prior to the fourth century, the central themes in eastern baptismal rites were rebirth and participation in Jesus' baptism, not death and resurrection.

The Church's understanding of baptism would be enriched if significant attention were given to all the baptismal days. The materials for the preparation of parents and godparents call for baptism "on a major baptismal day at a principal service of worship."[11] If this were fully implemented along with the prayer book provision for Renewal of Baptismal Vows when there are no candidates on the specified baptismal days, perhaps the richness of the baptismal days would be more fully communicated by the Church's liturgy.

Beyond such questions inherent in the ritual structure and texts are issues of implementation. A highly structured process of stages of formation may not offer sufficient flexibility for candidates from a variety of backgrounds. A couple fully integrated in the life of the Church and preparing for the birth of their third child has needs quite different from parents returning to the Church after the birth of their first child. Likewise, a person raised with Buddhist parents and coming to the Church for the first time requires a very different kind of preparation from a professor who has taught religion at a Quaker college for twenty years and now seeks baptism in the Episcopal Church. The rubrics acknowledge the need for adaptation based upon each candidate's background and current needs, but it is all too easy to develop a set program and expect candidates to fit into that program.

An additional difficulty arises from the related rites for preparation of persons for reaffirmation of the baptismal covenant. These rites make an important distinction between baptized and unbaptized persons, but they draw upon a pool of candidates already within the Church. Many of the "catechumenal processes" implemented in parishes comprise only baptized persons. Participation by these persons in a catechumenal process furthers their Christian formation and may provide some renewal in a congregation. But maintaining a focus on persons already baptized may also prevent a congregation from developing a true catechumenate by evangelizing unbaptized persons.

The catechumenate and related processes have enormous potential for forming individual Christians and Christian communities that comprehend the rigorous demands of baptism in a post-Christian world. However, the implementation of the catechumenate requires sustained commitment and ongoing reflection as Christians are shaped by the liturgies they celebrate.

Baptismal Vigils

Complementing the Easter vigil and the vigil of Pentecost, both included in the prayer book, the *BOS* provides baptismal vigils for the Eve of the Baptism of Our Lord and the Eve of All Saints' Day or the Sunday after All Saints' Day. These parallel the Easter vigil: a service of light, using the prayer book Order of Worship for the Evening, introduces a series of readings from the Hebrew scriptures, each followed by silence and a psalm, canticle or hymn. Unlike the lessons for a vigil of Pentecost, all the proper lessons of the feast are included among the vigil readings (for the Pentecost vigil, only Acts 2 is appointed for both the vigil and the principal service). While the Easter vigil places baptism after the Old Testament readings and before the gospel, the vigils for the Baptism of Jesus and All Saints' Day follow the pattern of the vigil of Pentecost; the gospel is the climax of the vigil readings, and baptism, confirmation, or the Renewal of Baptismal Vows follows the sermon.

In addition to these baptismal vigils, the *BOS* provides a vigil for the eve of a baptism, for use in preparation for baptism at the principal Sunday service. The readings (and homily) are followed by prayers for the candidates about to be baptized, and the service concludes with a blessing or dismissal.

While these forms offer ways to give additional focus to the designated baptismal days, they have not come into common use in the Episcopal Church.

The Hymnal 1982

In addition to *The Book of Occasional Services*, *The Hymnal 1982* provides materials to enrich the celebration of baptism and rites of reaffirmation. The 1928 prayer book, in introductory rubrics "Concerning the Service of the Church," had given general permission to sing "hymns set forth and allowed by the authority of this Church, and Anthems in the words of Holy Scripture or of the Book of Common Prayer...before and after any Office" in the book.[12] But there was no provision to integrate music, be that hymns, anthems or service music, into the offices of baptism and confirmation. Music for the liturgical texts was not provided for either rite in official books of the Episcopal Church, that is, *The Hymnal 1940* or the altar edition of the prayer book, although editions of the American missal included music for the *Exsultet* and the blessing of the font at the Easter vigil.

Instead of general permission for the use of hymns and anthems, the 1979 prayer book specifies the places in each rite at which music may be used. Rubrics for the rites of baptism and confirmation allow a hymn, psalm, or anthem to be sung before the opening acclamation and following the first and second lessons, provisions parallel to the rubrics for the Holy Eucharist. The "Additional Directions" for baptism suggest that a psalm, such as Psalm 42, or a hymn or anthem may be sung if the movement to the font is a formal procession. Likewise, a psalm, e.g., Psalm 23, or hymn or anthem may be sung in procession to the front of the church for the prayer for the gifts of the Spirit and the ceremonies that follow it (pp. 312-313). In addition, the hymnal includes service music for the opening acclamation and baptismal versicles, and a musical appendix to the altar edition of the Holy Eucharist provides music for the Prayers for the Candidates, the Thanksgiving over the Water and the Consecration of Chrism (music for the people's responses to the prayers and the Thanksgiving over the Water is in the hymnal).

The availability of service music offers the possibility for significant enrichment of a congregation's celebration of baptism. As Winfred Douglas noted in 1937, music expresses the shared life of the body of Christ and allows each member of the body to join actively in giving praise and glory to God. While it is not absolutely necessary to sing the baptismal prayers, singing rather than speaking the liturgical texts adds a dimension of festivity and celebration.

Complementing the service music for baptism, *The Hymnal 1982* includes six hymns for baptism and two for confirmation, in contrast to two hymns for baptism and two for confirmation in the 1940 hymnal. The words for five of the six baptismal hymns are recent compositions, dating to the 1960s and 1970s.[13] While each of the hymns in the 1940 hymnal seek a blessing upon the child(ren) to be baptized (a list identified six other hymns suitable for adult baptism), the 1982 hymns give voice to the theological richness of baptism: rebirth, participation in Christ's death and resurrection, bestowal of the Spirit, adoption, entrance into the body of Christ. For confirmation, a hymn that appeared in the 1892 and 1916 editions of the hymnal (but not the 1940 edition) has been revised to emphasize the strengthening gift of the Spirit. There is also a new confirmation hymn that focuses on the commitment renewed at confirmation.[14]

The hymns designated for baptism may be supplemented by hymns for specific baptismal days, especially Easter and the baptism of Jesus. For Easter, hymn 176/177, "Over the chaos of the empty waters" speaks of creation, recreation by the power of the Spirit, and resurrection, as does hymn 213, "Come away to the skies," with allusions to 2 Corinthians 5. Hymn 187, "Through the Red Sea brought at last," is replete with imagery of Passover and resurrection. Several hymns relate the baptism of Jesus to our baptism:

120, "The sinless one to Jordan came"; 121, "Christ when for us you were baptized"; and 116, "'I come,' the great Redeemer cries." However, the hymns for Pentecost and for All Saints' Day do not explicitly make reference to baptism, although there are baptismal hymns that would be particularly appropriate for these days.

Summary: Enriching the Prayer Book

The liturgical materials in *The Book of Occasional Services* and *The Hymnal 1982* complement the rites of baptism and reaffirmation in the 1979 prayer book. The introductory address in the form for consecration of chrism apart from baptism offers much fuller biblical imagery than the prayer for the consecration of chrism that is part of the baptismal rite. Likewise, the hymns for baptism and confirmation and those for the baptismal days contain a rich diversity of biblical images and metaphors for baptism. The process and rites of the catechumenate, and the parallel rites for persons preparing for reaffirmation of baptismal vows or for the baptism of an infant, encourage Christian formation that is rooted in scripture and addresses all dimensions of Christian life—prayer and worship as well as ministry and service. Used thoughtfully, these materials can help build a renewed and deepened understanding of the power and promise of baptism for Christian life and so contribute to the emerging baptismal ecclesiology in the Episcopal Church.

NOTES

1. Niels Rasmussen, "The Chrism Mass: Tradition and Renewal," in *The Cathedral: A Reader* (Washington, DC: US Catholic Conference, 1979), pp. 31-2; see further in Michael Hopkins, "The Renewal of Ordination Vows," in Ruth A. Meyers (ed.), *Baptism and Ministry*, Liturgical Studies 1 (New York: Church Hymnal Corporation, 1994), pp. 48-51.

2. *The Book of Occasional Services* 1994, p. 238 (hereafter cited as *BOS*); BCP 1979, p. 532.

3. Office of Evangelism Ministries, *The Catechumenal Process: Adult Initiation & Formation for Christian Life and Ministry: A Resource for Dioceses and Congregations* (New York: Church Hymnal Corporation, 1990), p. 13.

4. *Journal of the General Convention*, 1985, pp. 195-6.

5. The proceedings of the conference were published in Michael Merriman (ed.), *The Baptismal Mystery and the Catechumenate* (New York: Church Hymnal Corporation, 1990).

6. *BOS* 1994, pp. 114-30, 136-45, 157-62.

7. Ibid., p. 139.

8. Ibid., p. 162.

9. *BOS* 1994, pp. 114, 116.

10. Ibid., p. 128.

11. Ibid., p. 161.

12. BCP 1928, p. viii.

13. Raymond Glover (ed.), *The Hymnal 1982 Companion*, Vol. 3A (New York: Church Hymnal Corporation, 1994), pp. 566-75.

14. Ibid., pp. 347-50.

Chapter 11

Baptism and Reaffirmation of Faith: A Continuing Agenda for the Episcopal Church

The prayer book rites and the materials in *The Hymnal 1982* and *The Book of Occasional Services* represent a significant shift in theology and practice for the Episcopal Church. They are rooted in a baptismal ecclesiology, an understanding of the Church as a community formed by baptism and empowered by baptism and the eucharist to carry out the reconciling ministry of Christ in the world. Yet as parishes and dioceses interpret and implement the rites, a wide range of practice has resulted. Some have readily embraced the new rites, including the introduction of a full catechumenal process leading to baptism at the Easter vigil. In other places the impact of the rites has scarcely been felt as old understandings continue to prevail. Elsewhere, change in attitudes and in liturgical practice has come gradually.

This process of change reflects the gradual breakdown of Christendom. Two very different models of baptism are at work: a Christendom model, which views baptism as a rite of passage marking birth and confirmation as a rite of adolescence, and a post-Christendom baptismal ecclesiology, in which baptism is incorporation into a faith community distinct from secular society. As the Church adapts to a post-Christian era, patterns of initiation and reaffirmation of faith are gradually changing, but current practices reflect a mixture of old and new models.

Efforts to interpret and implement the provisions of the 1979 Book of Common Prayer are evident in the guidelines developed by several dioceses and parishes.[1] Most of them discuss not only baptism but also admission to communion and confirmation, reception, and reaffirmation. The involvement of dioceses in establishing initiatory policy suggests a new understanding of the role of the bishop in baptism as well as confirmation.

The various guidelines emphasize the centrality of baptism in Christian life and set forth an expectation of careful preparation and ongoing Christian nurture. Some of them articulate a radical change in initiatory practice, with emphasis on adult baptism after a full catechumenate. Other guidelines are more modest, addressing primarily infant baptism celebrated on a baptismal day after some preparation of parents and godparents.

An important question is that of terminology. Since the 1940s, "Christian initiation" has been used to refer to a complex of rites: baptism, confirmation and admission to communion. Many dioceses describe their guidelines as "guidelines for Christian initiation." However, to subsume the 1979 rite of confirmation under such a title is misleading. The prayer book defines *baptism* as full Christian initiation. Confirmation, although related to baptism, is a rite of *renewal* or *reaffirmation of faith* and not a rite of initiation. In this concluding chapter, Christian initiation and reaffirmation of faith will be addressed separately.

Christian Initiation: A Baptismal Ecclesiology

Although the 1979 baptismal rite was developed with careful attention both to scholarly research and to pastoral considerations, in many ways the revisers did not and could not know the full implications of their work. For the first time in the history of the Episcopal Church, the prayer book says unequivocally that "Holy Baptism is full initiation by water and the Holy Spirit into Christ's Body the Church" (p. 298). This marks a revolutionary change, one which has enabled the gradual emergence of a baptismal ecclesiology and thus has expanded the eucharistic ecclesiology of the liturgical movement. A baptismal ecclesiology understands the Church to be rooted in baptism and nourished by the eucharist. Baptism forms the body of Christ, a community which is distinct from the surrounding culture and yet is called to participate in Christ's reconciling ministry to the world. As this ecclesiology develops, continuing reform and renewal of baptismal practice is needed, and aspects of the baptismal rite requiring revision become evident.

The Baptismal Covenant
The baptismal covenant is an important component in the renewed understanding of baptism. The five questions of commitment are frequently cited as concrete statements of expectations for Christian life. At its 1985 meeting, the Council of Associated Parishes issued a statement calling upon the Episcopal Church "to re-examine the implications of the Baptismal Covenant in its search for a better understanding of the meaning of discipleship, including all forms of ministry in the contemporary age."[2] The "Mission Imperatives"

adopted by the Executive Council of the Episcopal Church in 1988 include "Imperative V: strive for justice and peace among all people and respect the dignity of every human being," a declaratory form of one of the questions in the baptismal covenant.[3] More recently, the Standing Commission on the Structure of the Church used the final three questions (proclaim by word and example the Good News of God in Christ; seek and serve Christ in all persons, loving our neighbors as ourselves; strive for justice and peace among all people, and respect the dignity of every human being) to define the essence of the ministry and mission of the Church.[4] Such rhetoric suggests that baptism is increasingly viewed as commissioning for Christian mission, an interpretation explicitly articulated in the December 1972 "Agreed Positions" of the Standing Liturgical Commission and the House of Bishops Theological and Prayer Book Committees. This represents a significant shift from earlier understandings of confirmation as "ordination of the laity."

Yet although the questions of commitment receive considerable attention, the Apostles' Creed, the first half of the baptismal covenant, is less frequently discussed. Its content may be reviewed during preparation for baptism and rites of reaffirmation of faith, but it is often overlooked in other discussions of baptismal commitment. That is, the link between faith in the triune God and Christian action is not often expressed in terms of the baptismal covenant. This disjunction between Trinitarian faith and Christian life reflects the abstract approach to Trinitarian theology taken by many western theologians since the early Middle Ages. But some contemporary theologians have begun to assert the practical significance of Trinitarian doctrine for Christian life. Catherine Mowry LaCugna, a Roman Catholic theologian, states that living Trinitarian faith means entering "into a life of love and communion with others."[5] Patricia Wilson-Kastner, an Episcopalian theologian, offers a similar perspective:

> In the Trinity we have an invitation to enter fully and consciously into a relationship of love with each other and the world about us, within the overarching and undergirding exchange of love with the God who is the life of the dance, who is perfect harmony, peace, and love. In Christ, the Trinity becomes known to us and is active among us, and we are invited to share freely in the Trinitarian life itself.

Wilson-Kastner proposes that this participation in the divine life encompasses the values of inclusiveness, community and freedom.[6] As Wilson-Kastner, LaCugna and other contemporary theologians contribute new insights into Trinitarian faith and its practical significance for Christian living, Christians may come to new understandings of the radical consequences of the faith professed in the baptismal covenant. However, discussion of a revitalized Trinitarian theology is currently a predominantly scholarly activity. It remains for this renewed awareness to be more widely embraced.

Not only is there a disjuncture between the Trinitarian faith professed in the baptismal covenant and the questions articulating the practical consequences of that faith, there is also a separation between worship and Christian mission. The final three questions of the covenant, describing Christian commitment to ministry in the world and social justice, are cited far more frequently as a summary of Christian ministry and mission than the first two questions about Christian life—the promises to "continue in the apostles' teaching and fellowship, in the breaking of bread, and in the prayers" and to "persevere in resisting evil, and, whenever you fall into sin, repent and return to the Lord." The commitment to be faithful in worship is not always recognized as integral to Christian mission, although the catechism in the prayer book claims that "the Church pursues its mission *as it prays and worships*, proclaims the Gospel, and promotes justice, peace, and love" (p. 855; emphasis added). In worship, Christians are not only nourished and empowered for ministry in the world, they are actively engaged in Christian mission. They do so by giving praise and glory to God on their own behalf and on behalf of all creation, and by offering intercession for the needs of the world and the Church. To use the language of the catechism, which states that "the mission of the Church is to restore all people to unity with God and each other in Christ" (p. 855), in worship Christians celebrate and renew their union with one another in Christ, and they intercede to God for the restoration of the world and the Church to unity with God, lived out in the establishment of justice and peace. Such missionary activity through worship is as essential to Christian life as active service in the world.

The promise to persevere in resisting evil is another important component of Christian mission. The question tends to be interpreted in an individual sense, no doubt reflecting the promise to repent and return to the Lord whenever one falls into sin. But there is also a corporate dimension to resisting evil. Evil is not only a power affecting individual Christians, it is a force evident in the world around us. Evil is apparent in war and violent civil strife; in humanity's wastefulness and pollution of creation; in the grossly disproportionate use of the world's resources by a few large and wealthy nations; in racism, sexism and other "isms." To resist such evils requires much more than the commitment of individual Christians to work against these and other sinful forces. Resisting evil calls for the active efforts of the body of Christ to confront evil with the reconciling love of Christ.

Certainly, as the foregoing analysis suggests, there are dimensions of the baptismal covenant which have not captured popular imagination in the Church. More attention is needed to the relation between faith in the triune God and the radical consequences of this faith for Christian living. Furthermore, deepened understanding is needed of the implications for Christian mission in the promises to "continue in the apostles' teaching and fellowship" and to "persevere in resisting evil." Yet it is remarkable that in just two decades the baptismal covenant has become such a significant statement of the essence of the ministry to which Christians are called by their baptism. Such widespread use of the baptismal covenant suggests that a baptismal ecclesiology is indeed taking root in the Episcopal Church.

Baptismal Symbolism

While the baptismal covenant is used extensively to assert the importance of Christian ministry begun in baptism, the ritual celebration of baptism remains impoverished. Profession of faith and water baptism in the triune name are the essential elements of baptism. Yet these two aspects are not closely linked in the celebration of baptism. The profession of faith, that is, the baptismal covenant, is followed by prayers for the candidates and the thanksgiving over the water (and, on occasion, the consecration of chrism). The central ritual act of water baptism is thus not associated directly with the faith and commitment professed in baptism.

In future revisions of the prayer book, placing the baptismal covenant immediately prior to the administration of the water would establish more strongly the link between the faith professed in baptism and the act of baptism in water, with its rich symbolic meanings. The connection between the water rite and baptismal faith could also be strengthened by attention to ritual aspects of the reaffirmation of baptismal faith.

The prayer book permits the renewal of baptismal vows (p. 292) in place of the Nicene Creed at the eucharist on designated baptismal days when there are no candidates for baptism. The regular use of the baptismal covenant in this way, in addition to its use by the entire congregation at celebrations of baptism and confirmation, has doubtless helped to establish the baptismal covenant as a core statement of Christian faith and life. But the impact of renewing the baptismal covenant could be enhanced by the use of water, thereby complementing the verbal with the symbolic. Such a renewal might begin with a procession to the baptismal font following the sermon on a designated baptismal day. At the font, water would be poured and the thanksgiving over the water sung or said. The congregation would then be invited to renew their baptismal covenant. When the words of the baptismal covenant have been spoken, the congregation could be sprinkled with water from the font or invited to come forward individually to encounter the water. They might dip a finger or a hand into the font and then make the sign of the cross on themselves or touch their face with their moistened hand.

More attention is also needed to the use of water at celebrations of baptism. A 1978 Associated Parishes pamphlet on baptism states that just before the Thanksgiving over the Water, water should be poured into the font "in enough volume to be heard and seen. There is no need to take pains to avoid splashing... [B]aptism is intended to be a very wet ceremony." At the time of the baptism, "again, water should be seen and heard. It should be poured liberally over the candidate's head, or the candidate should be immersed."[7] Similar suggestions are made in other commentaries and in some manuals of ceremonial.[8] However, baptism by immersion is practiced in very few Episcopal churches.

One difficulty with immersion is that baptismal fonts in many Episcopal churches are placed in obscure corners and are far too small to bathe an infant, much less an adult. In a 1985 "occasional paper" of the Standing Liturgical Commission, Marion Hatchett recommended that as church buildings are built or renovated, the font be set "in a prominent place, so that baptisms are visible, and to be a constant reminder of baptism." Additionally, he suggested that a font large enough for immersion should be considered, since the prayer book gives precedence to baptism by immersion.[9]

Hatchett's recommendations have not been widely adopted. In a study of contemporary liturgical architecture in the Episcopal Church, William Seth Adams, professor of liturgy at the Episcopal Seminary of the Southwest in Austin, Texas, visited a number of parishes which had built new buildings or undergone major renovations since 1980. Adams reported:

> Typically, I found small stone or wooden fonts, sometimes covered, sometimes not, sometimes containing a "candy dish," sometimes not, typically empty of water. Occasionally, it was clear to the observer that the most frequent role played by the font, particularly those near entrances, was as a place to set things, for example, service leaflets.[10]

Even where there is a larger permanent font, there is often a much smaller dish set inside the font, making it very convenient to remove the dish and empty it once the baptism is over.

Adams suggests that the location and size of the font is just one dimension of a pervasive sacramental minimalism in the celebration of baptism. Comparing the typical baptismal celebration with an ordination, he contends that our ritual practice belies our rhetoric. For example, ordinations take place at special times, with attendance by invitation, while baptism is celebrated at the Sunday liturgy, typically without special invitation. At the central moment in the ordination of a presbyter, the moment of transition, there is a hymn invoking the Holy Spirit, corporate silence, and an extended prayer during which the ordinand is "buried" in both presbyteral and episcopal hands. In contrast, in many celebrations of baptism a minimal amount of water is sprinkled on the candidate and then dried off immediately "lest anyone get wet!" Adams concludes, "At no step in our comparison does the action of baptism (as conventionally practiced) speak more loudly than ordination at a comparable point."[11]

While many congregations do not practice baptism by immersion or even use copious amounts of water, the symbol of light has been more widely accepted. As the Easter vigil was restored in the 1950s and 1960s, the use of a paschal candle had become widespread. The paschal candle is customarily lit at the celebration of baptism, and it is common for a candle to be presented to the newly baptized.

The use of chrism has also gained wide acceptance, although there are a variety of episcopal directives regarding its use. A 1983 survey found that fifty-nine percent of the bishops replying approved the use of chrism, an additional twenty-one percent strongly encouraged or required its use, and another eleven percent did not encourage it but provided it for those clergy requesting it. Only one of the sixty-six bishops replying refused to consecrate chrism, and two consecrated it only for their own use.[12] A 1986 survey reported similar results.[13]

As with the administration of water, the tendency is to use a minimal amount of oil. The most common procedure for chrismation is for the priest or bishop to dip a thumb into the oil and then trace the cross on the baptizand's forehead. One pastoral manual recommends as an alternative that the priest or bishop pour oil into the palm, spread it across the person's forehead, then trace a cross on the person's forehead with the thumb.[14]

The preference of many Episcopal parishes for a minimal use of water and oil suggests both discomfort with messiness and reluctance to accept the full implications of baptism as death and resurrection with Christ. In some parishes where the catechumenate is implemented and consequently there has been more education about the radical meaning of baptism, both water and oil are used profusely. For example, pictures accompanying a 1981 article on the catechumenate show an adult being fully immersed and a container of oil being poured over the person's head.[15]

There is great need in the Episcopal Church for a recovery of the fuller use of the symbols of water and chrism. Baptism signifies and effects a profound transformation: we are buried with Christ in his death so that we might also participate in his resurrection (Romans 6); we are washed clean from the stain of sin (Acts 2:38); we are reborn, brought forth from the watery womb of the font (John 3). The use of water can speak vividly about this transformation and enable people to experience viscerally the power of the living God in the baptismal burial, bathing and birth. While some efforts have been made to encourage use of abundant quantities of water in baptism, all too often the celebration of baptism does not vividly communicate the transformation effected in the font.

Likewise, more attention could be given to the use of chrism, which offers a luxurious anointing as well as a distinctive fragrance. A little dab of oil on the forehead, from an oil stock hidden in the palm of a priest's hand, bears little resemblance to the anointing of Jesus by an unnamed woman who poured costly oil over Jesus' head just before his crucifixion and so anointed him as priests and kings were anointed in ancient Israel (Matthew 26:6-13; cf. Mark 14:3-9). Allowing baptismal candidates to luxuriate in the aromatic oil of chrism, rubbed liberally over face and head and arms so that the fragrance lingers for hours, could help convey in a compelling manner the empowerment by God's Holy Spirit that is such an integral part of baptism.

The Seal of the Spirit

Although chrism tends to be used in a minimal fashion, there is increasing agreement in the Episcopal Church that the seal of the Spirit is given in baptism. Marion Hatchett commented in a 1981 interview in *The Episcopalian*: "The historic Anglican view that confirmation is the 'receiving of the Holy Spirit' is falling by the wayside."[16] A 1983 survey of bishops supports this assertion; virtually all the bishops responding agreed that the Holy Spirit is given in baptism.[17] The principle that baptism is "full initation by water and the Holy Spirit" has been widely accepted in the Episcopal Church.

The Anglican Communion may also be moving beyond its disputes about the bestowal of the Holy Spirit. At the 1991 International Anglican Liturgical Consultation on Christian initiation, the long-standing debate about the work of the Spirit in baptism and confirmation was not renewed. Rather, the findings of this consultation assert that "through baptism with water in the name of the Father, and of the Son, and of the Holy Spirit, Christ...seals us with the Holy Spirit."[18] Moreover, while acknowledging that some Anglicans have historically understood confirmation as sealing by the Holy Spirit, the findings maintain that this view "has been firmly set aside in the past two decades in New Testament and liturgical scholarship, where it has been made clear that sacramental initiation is complete in baptism."[19]

Although in the Episcopal Church there is general acceptance of the principle that the Spirit is bestowed in baptism, there are different opinions regarding the baptismal seal of the Spirit. One interpretation of the 1979 baptismal rite holds that the postbaptismal consignation with optional chrismation is equivalent to the ancient rite of "confirmation," that is, a sacramental postbaptismal blessing that in the Middle Ages became a separate rite. This position was articulated by Charles Price in a 1984 occasional paper of the Standing Liturgical Commission.[20] Yet half the bishops responding to a 1983 survey disagreed that the Episcopal Church had intended to include in baptism the sacramental content of the former rite of confirmation.[21] Arthur Vogel, Bishop of West Missouri and a member of the House of Bishops Theological Committee, responded to Price with the assertion that the baptismal sealing refers to the gift of the Spirit through water baptism, but an additional initiatory gift of the Spirit, a strengthening gift for ministry, is conferred at confirmation through the laying on of hands.[22]

If one accepts that baptism does convey fully the initiatory gift of the Spirit, another interpretation, espoused by Stevick, is to attribute to the rite as a whole the sacramental effects of baptism, including the gift of the Spirit.[23] Offering yet another perspective, Mitchell suggests that the postbaptismal consignation and chrismation are particular signs of the inward sealing of the Holy Spirit, but nonetheless water baptism in the Trinitarian name has a "unique central position." Hence consignation and chrismation cannot be considered absolutely necessary elements of Christian initiation, although they are normative.[24]

These varying interpretations of the gift of the Spirit are held together through the celebration of a common rite of baptism. However, to continue to insist that the 1979 rite of baptism includes elements of confirmation is confusing as well as theologically and historically questionable. To say that the ancient rite of confirmation has been reattached to baptism creates confusion because there remains a separate rite entitled "Confirmation." It is historically inaccurate to claim that the "ancient rite" of confirmation is now included in baptism, since a separate rite of confirmation did not develop until the medieval period. To insist upon consignation and/or chrismation as essential to baptism ignores ecumenical agreement that the essence of baptism is the administration of water in the Trinitarian name.[25] That water baptism in the triune name is the essential core of baptism was asserted in the

1972 "Agreed Positions" of the Standing Liturgical Commission and the House of Bishops Prayer Book and Theological Committees. This stance is also articulated in the prayer book form for conditional baptism, which states that baptism "with water 'in the Name of the Father, and of the Son, and of the Holy Spirit'...are the essential parts of baptism" (p. 313).

Mitchell cautions that "to do sacramental theology by inquiring how little is necessary for validity is seriously to impoverish both liturgy and theology and leads to a dangerous minimalism."[26] This is an important caveat, although identification of the essential elements places the remainder of the rite in perspective. Thus, for example, the findings of the 1991 International Anglican Liturgical Consultation note that actions such as anointing and consignation "offer valuable means of explicating the significance of baptism," but the report warns that "they must not obscure the centrality of the baptismal act itself."[27]

Perhaps the 1979 baptismal rite can best be understood as full Christian initiation, including the seal of the Spirit. The administration of water in the Trinitarian name is the central act of baptism. Additional rituals (consignation, chrismation, imposition of hands, and other actions such as giving a lighted candle or clothing in new garments) give further expression to the theological richness of Christian initiation but do not in themselves complete the initiation or add something not conveyed by the central water action. Rather, the seal of the Spirit is effected by the rite as a whole. Vividly expressive use of these associated ritual actions, along with an effusive use of water, can unfold the multiple meanings of baptism, including the bestowal of the Spirit, without diminishing the centrality of baptism by water in the triune name.

Baptism and Eucharist

Since 1970, when General Convention approved admission to communion prior to confirmation, there has been a growing acceptance of communion of all the baptized. Infant communion is practiced in a significant number of parishes, although it is still not the universal custom in the Episcopal Church.

Two surveys conducted in 1986 indicated that the vast majority of parishes admit children to communion before confirmation, but there is a wide range of practice within this broad norm. One survey found that nine percent of the dioceses reported all or almost all of their parishes admitted all persons, including infants, to communion upon baptism; thirty-six percent of the bishops required instruction before admission to communion; and nine percent of the dioceses reported that one-third to one-half of their parishes required confirmation before admission to communion. In approximately one-half of the dioceses, admission to communion was left to the discretion of the local pastor, with a resultant diversity of practice in those dioceses. Overall, this survey concluded that eighty-one percent of parishes in the Episcopal Church admitted children to communion at some point before confirmation.[28] A second survey confirms these results.[29]

The question of children and communion was addressed in 1985 at an International Anglican Liturgical Consultation, which recommended that because baptism is full Christian initiation, all baptized persons should be admitted to communion (see Appendix D).[30] The report of the consultation was distributed informally by Associated Parishes at the 1985 General Convention, and at the 1988 General Convention the report was formally commended to the Church for study.[31] The 1985 recommendations were reaffirmed and endorsed by the 1991 International Anglican Liturgical Consultation.[32]

Infant communion was discussed by the House of Bishops at its 1986 and 1987 meetings. FitzSimons Allison, Bishop of South Carolina, argued against the practice of infant communion on the grounds that it contradicts the biblical injunction against unworthy reception (1 Corinthians 11:27-29) and obscures the importance of a conscious response of faith. Other bishops reported their positive experiences with children receiving communion.[33]

In response to Allison, Louis Weil pointed out that the arguments for infant baptism apply equally to infant communion. Weil suggested that the issue goes beyond the question of the initiatory pattern:

> If we are to consider infants as in any way the appropriate recipients of sacramental grace, at a time when neither the infant's will nor understanding can be a constitutive factor, then we must look at the professing adult community and be much more concerned than we have been about the deepening of adult understanding and also in helping sponsors to see that the promises which they make at a baptism require a mature will if they are to be carried out.

Arguing that Christian initiation is best celebrated in a single liturgical rite of water baptism, consignation and communion, Weil gave his support to the practice of infant communion.[34]

Despite Allison's vigorous objections, the House of Bishops at the 1988 General Convention approved a resolution giving pastoral guidelines for infant communion. The resolution affirmed the growing practice of communicating infants at their baptism, then next offering them communion when they and their parents express a desire for them to receive. This resolution expressed "the mind of the House of Bishops" (see Appendix E). Efforts to seek the concurrence of the House of Deputies were defeated.[35]

Further clarification of the Church's position on infant communion came in the 1988 General Convention action on the order for "The Preparation of Parents and Godparents for the Baptism of Infants and Young Children." As presented by the Standing Liturgical Commission, the rite included the statement, "The infant...*will* receive Holy Communion."[36] This was amended by the convention to read, "*may* receive."[37] Mitchell interpreted the convention action in this way:

> [Infant communion] is no longer an exotic phenomenon. The argument has moved from, "Is it permissible for young children to receive communion?" to "Is it absolutely necessary for them to do so?" The Convention has said that it is not, but it has equally certainly affirmed that it is a reasonable and authorized practice.[38]

The discussion and official actions of the mid-1980s reflect growing acceptance of communion of all the baptized in the Episcopal Church. As it becomes normative to administer communion to all newly baptized persons, including infants, a rubric directing that the newly baptized receive communion should be included when the prayer book is revised again. This would further emphasize the link between baptism and eucharist as the primary sacraments from which all Christian life flows.

Baptism and Ministry:
New Understandings of Leadership and Authority

As indicated by the growing use of the baptismal covenant to articulate the baptismal call to ministry, Episcopalians increasingly understand baptism to be the basis for all Christian ministry. This was already expressed in the statement of the catechism that "The ministers of the Church are lay persons, bishops, priests, and deacons," with the further specification that the laity not only "take their place in the life, worship, and governance of the Church" but also "carry on Christ's work of reconciliation in the world" (p. 855). Ministry takes place not only in the Church but also in the world, and all baptized Christians participate in this ministry. In a thorough review of the canons on ministry presented to the 1988 General Convention, the Council for the Development of Ministry included among the duties of the clergy their responsibility "to ensure that children, youth and adults receive instruction...in the exercise of their ministry as baptized persons."[39] Underlying their proposal was the theological principle that "Holy Baptism is the root of all ministry."[40]

This emerging understanding of baptismal ministry has intersected with dramatic changes in the role of women in the Church. The 1969 Special General Convention permitted women to be licensed as lay readers on the same basis as men. The 1970 convention was the first at which women were officially permitted to be seated as deputies. At the same time, debates about women's ordination were heating up. The 1970 convention repealed the eighty-year-old canon on deaconesses and eliminated all distinctions between women and men as deacons. Eleven women were ordained to the priesthood in 1974, and one year later four more women were ordained to the priesthood. In 1976 an amendment to the canons officially made the provisions of the ordination canons "equally applicable" to women and men.

In assessing the validity of the first ordinations of women to the priesthood, an international group of Anglican theologians concluded:

> There is no ground whatever for supposing that women are intrinsically incapable of entering into the role of the person who sacramentally represents to the Church its identity in Christ. Indeed, it seems that to make this assertion would be implicitly to deny or to qualify the meaning of women's baptism.[41]

By turning to baptism to assert the validity of the ordination of women to the priesthood, the theologians not only suggested a broader understanding of ordained ministry, they also pointed to the importance of baptism as the basis for Christian life. Opening ordination to a new class of people has a profound effect on our understanding of what it means to be Christian, as Pamela Darling concludes in her study of the changing roles of women in the Episcopal Church:

> Standards for ordained members of the church are implicitly held up as the desirable ideal for all members. Changes in the standards represent shifts in the boundary between the sacred and the profane, the whole (holy) and the imperfect, and thus signal changes in the corporate understanding of who can be a real Christian or a real Episcopalian.[42]

Thus the ordination of women, which has gained increasing acceptance at the same time as a baptismal ecclesiology has been developing, has contributed to a new understanding of the significance of baptism. The ordination of women suggests the equal dignity of women and men in the Christian community, a dignity proclaimed in Galatians 3:28 ("there is no longer male and female; for all of you are one in Christ Jesus") but not enacted in the traditional patriarchal structures of Christianity. These traditional structures are being challenged by efforts to include women in all dimensions of leadership, ordained and lay, in the Episcopal Church.

Moreover, as women's ordained leadership is more widely accepted, and in the very struggle for the inclusion of women, new models of authority are being introduced. Whereas traditional models are based upon inequality and subordination, including the subordination of women to men and laity to ordained leaders, the primary models operative for those advocating for the full inclusion of women are based upon equality and mutuality. Certainly ordained women exercise a variety of leadership styles, as do ordained men, and not all ordained women understand the values of mutuality and equality to be the primary basis for their authority. Nonetheless, the ordination of women has fundamentally changed the distribution of power and the exercise of authority in the Episcopal Church. As these changes reverberate through the Church, new theological understandings are emerging, understandings which are at the core of our identity as the people of God.

There is no simple cause and effect between the emergence of a baptismal ecclesiology and efforts to bring about the full inclusion of women in the Episcopal Church. Rather, both are dimensions of the profound transformations taking place in the Church in the late twentieth century. The increasing acceptance of the leadership of ordained women means ever increasing acceptance of the full participation of women in all aspects of the life of the Church and new understandings of God and human nature. If women can embody sacramental power and exercise spiritual authority, as do men, then all women, lay and ordained, share equally with men in the salvation accomplished through the incarnation, life, death and resurrection of Christ. These emerging theological understandings are interwoven with a baptismal ecclesiology which views the Church as rooted in baptism, a baptism which empowers all Christians to carry on the reconciling ministry of Christ in the world.

Rites of Reaffirmation:
The Continuing Dilemma of Confirmation

While there are many signs of a new appreciation of the centrality of baptism in the life of the Church, there are also indications of significant confusion about the new rite of "Confirmation, with forms for Reception and for the Reaffirmation of Baptismal Vows." Because of the compromises made as the rite was developed, the rite can be interpreted in varying and sometimes conflicting ways. The revisers viewed the new rite as a rite of reaffirmation of faith, suitable for use on various occasions in Christian life. But it can also be seen as a revised form of the traditional Anglican rite of confirmation, the expected or even required completion of baptism. The result has been widely divergent practice throughout the Episcopal Church.

The Use of Chrism at Confirmation

Although chrismation is included in baptism, a 1986 survey found that nearly half the bishops responding used chrism "as a normal part of every confirmation."[43] This may be the continuation of Anglo-Catholic practice begun at least several decades prior to the introduction of the 1979 prayer book, a practice imitating the Roman Catholic confirmation rite. The survey does not indicate whether additional bishops began to use chrism at confirmation after it was introduced into baptism.

The use of chrism at confirmation is problematic because it perpetuates confusion about the seal of the Spirit and the meaning of confirmation. In the 1979 baptismal rite, chrismation is part of baptism, where it can be understood as the sign of the baptismal seal of the Spirit or as a ritual gesture giving further expression to the theological richness of baptism. To introduce chrism into confirmation is to suggest an additional sealing with the Spirit in confirmation and thereby to undermine the sufficiency of baptism as full Christian initiation.

If imitation of "catholic" practice is intended by the use of chrism, it should be remembered that chrismation in the Roman Catholic rite of confirmation is equivalent to the postbaptismal chrismation in the 1979 prayer book. In the Roman Catholic confirmation rite the bishop or priest dips his thumb in the chrism, makes the sign of the cross on the forehead of the confirmand, and says "N., be sealed with the Gift of the Holy Spirit." That confirmation is integral to baptism is underscored in the contemporary Roman Catholic Rite of Christian Initiation of Adults: when an adult or child of catechetical age is baptized, the celebrant omits the customary first postbaptismal anointing and instead confers confirmation. So important is the connection of baptism and confirmation that in the absence of the bishop, the presbyter who baptizes also administers this confirmation. The use of chrism in the Episcopal Church rite of confirmation thus does not parallel the Roman Catholic practice of confirmation but instead duplicates the postbaptismal rites of the 1979 Book of Common Prayer. If one argues that chrism must be used because it may not have been administered at baptism, then its use at confirmation suggests that the baptism was incomplete.

If a symbolic link with baptism is what is desired, it is odd to use the secondary symbol of chrism rather than the primary symbol of water. However, use of water for individuals reaffirming their faith might imply rebaptism, and so would not be a desirable alternative. By contrast, imposition of hands is a multipurpose gesture, used to signify strengthening and blessing not only in baptism and confirmation but also in healing, sacramental reconciliation and ordination.

It is not easy to determine whether individual bishops have considered the liturgical principles involved and come to different conclusions, or are continuing the divergent practices of their predecessors, or perhaps are responding to requests from particular parishes or priests. In any event, the power of symbols is such that the use of chrism at confirmation deserves careful reflection and more attention than it has thus far received. Lacking compelling liturgical, theological or historical rationale for its use in confirmation (a rite of reaffirmation, not a rite of initiation), the practice should be discontinued.

The Age for "Confirmation"

Defining confirmation as a rite of mature affirmation of faith has not entirely clarified questions about the age for confirmation. A 1986 survey found that most bishops preferred to assess on an individual basis the appropriate age for confirmation. Most of those responding supported later adolescence as the time for confirmation, and thirty-two percent agreed with a statement that adolescents "should not be encouraged to [make a mature commitment of faith] at least until they have completed their high school education." But one bishop commented, "If we abandon Confirmation as a puberty rite, we will need to create another puberty rite."[44]

In a 1990 article, John Westerhoff, professor of religion and education at Duke University Divinity School, argued that adolescence is an inappropriate stage of life for individuals to make the mature profession of faith required for confirmation. However, he continued, there is need for rites of passage *for* adolescence, to provide opportunity both to move into adolescence at around twelve years of age and to move into adulthood at about age eighteen. Westerhoff recommended that neither of these rites be termed "confirmation" because they would not be rites of mature profession of faith.[45]

One recent response to the profoundly felt need for a rite or rites of adolescence is the Journey to Adulthood program being implemented in a number of parishes and dioceses. Developed in the early 1990s at St. Philip's Episcopal Church in Durham, North Carolina, as a complete formation program for youth in junior and senior high school, Journey to Adulthood is spreading throughout the Episcopal Church. Based upon the concepts that manhood and womanhood are gifts from God and that adulthood must be earned, the program provides an in-depth exploration of self, sexuality, spirituality and society.

The beginning of adolescence is marked by "The Celebration of Manhood and Womanhood," loosely modeled after the Jewish bar mitzvah, which affirms that the young people are men and women (a physiological change), acknowledges that they are moving apart from their families in order to seek out their peer group, and challenges the congregation to support the youth in their journey toward adulthood. At a second ritual, the young people are separated from their families for a eucharist which includes a litany where they affirm their support for each other on the journey. Near the end of the program, the young people make a pilgrimage (for example, groups have gone to Jerusalem, Ireland, and St. Petersburg [Russia]). Upon return from their pilgrimage, they are received back into the church community as young adults.[46]

The approach taken by the Journey to Adulthood program distinguishes confirmation from life-cycle rites designed to ritualize the transitions of the extended period of adolescence. Although the program is so new that its long-term effects cannot be assessed, the concept offers a way forward in addressing the dilemmas about the age of confirmation. By introducing new rituals, the program may respond to the human need for rites of passage to mark significant turning points in the life-cycle, a need which was not originally the purpose of confirmation but which confirmation nonetheless came to fulfill for many. Instead of moving adolescents to an affirmation of faith which all too often is treated as the completion of their formation and thus the occasion for departure from active participation in the life of the Church, the program endeavors to build appreciation for ongoing faith development and periodic reaffirmation of commitment to one's baptismal faith. This may in turn allow confirmation to function more fully as a rite of *mature* affirmation of faith.

Because confirmation has for so many years functioned as a rite of passage for adolescents, there remains a perceived need to ritualize the process of growth and maturation at some point during adolescence. New rites may serve as life-cycle rites, marking the transition from childhood to adulthood and allowing confirmation to be a rite of mature commitment without associating it with a particular moment in the human life-cycle.

Defining Confirmation, Reception and Reaffirmation

Perhaps the most perplexing aspect of the 1979 rites of reaffirmation arises from the lack of clear definition of "confirmation," "reception," and "reaffirmation," and the resultant diversity in the administration of the rites. The issue is further complicated by canonical changes introduced in response to the 1979 rites of baptism and confirmation.

Canonical definitions of membership. The Offices of Instruction in the 1928 prayer book included the statement: "I was made a member of the Church when I was baptized."[47] However, the requirement of confirmation prior to admission to communion created two classes of members, baptized members and communicants, terms used in varying ways, sometimes with the qualification "in good standing." After much debate during the 1950s, the 1961 General Convention amended the canons of the Episcopal Church to define "member," "member in good standing," and "communicant in good standing." A member was defined as anyone baptized with water in the Trinitarian name and whose baptism had been "duly recorded" in the Episcopal Church; members in good standing were required to keep the Lord's Day by regular participation in public worship, by hearing the Word of God read and taught, and by "other acts of devotion and works of charity"; because of the confirmation rubric, to be a communicant in good standing required one to be confirmed.[48]

The prayer book definition of baptism as full Christian initiation and the admission to communion of unconfirmed persons necessitated a revision of the canons. Proposals to the 1982 General Convention from the Standing Liturgical Commission and the Standing Commission on Ecumenical Relations resulted in two changes which are still in effect. A member is now defined as anyone baptized with water in the Trinitarian name, *whether in the Episcopal Church or another Christian church,* and whose baptism has been duly recorded in the Episcopal Church. The added phrase explicitly recognizes baptism administered in any Christian church, provided that the baptism is "with water in the Name of the Father, and of the Son, and of the Holy Spirit" (Canon I.17.1[a]).[49] The second revision adopted in 1982 specifies that all adult members of the Episcopal Church are expected to make a mature public affirmation of faith and be confirmed or received "by a bishop of this Church or by a bishop of a Church in communion with this Church," an expectation in accord with the rubrics introductory to the rite of confirmation. This new canon was to take effect on January 1, 1986, to permit review of canons requiring the status of "communicant in good standing."[50]

"Communicant in good standing" was used in several places in the constitution and canons to specify requirements for those holding office and being ordained. In 1985 the General Convention amended this phrase to read "confirmed adult communicant in good standing," effectively requiring a rite additional to baptism in order for one to serve in various leadership roles in the Episcopal Church. This wording was considered to be the most nearly equivalent to the earlier requirement, since, prior to prayer book revision, all communicants were confirmed. However, this approach did not take into account the radically new definition of baptism in the 1979 prayer book.

It can be argued that it is appropriate to require leaders to have made the conscious affirmation of faith that is part of confirmation, a commitment that the prayer book "expects" of the Church's members. But to *require* confirmation is a step beyond *expecting* it and suggests that confirmation confers additional status. Certainly those who are leaders in the Church should make a conscious commitment to their baptismal faith. Yet confirmation is only one means of making this commitment. The primary recommitment and renewal of baptism occurs each time a person participates in a celebration of the eucharist. Renewed commitment to baptism also occurs when a person participates in the baptism of another, as well as in the renewal of the baptismal covenant at the Easter vigil and on other baptismal days when there are no candidates for baptism. Requiring confirmation for those who hold office emphasizes this specific, one-time rite of baptismal renewal rather than an ongoing deepening of faith and commitment through regular participation in the celebration of the eucharist and the primary feasts of the liturgical year.

A canonical definition of "confirmed." Drawing upon interpretations proposed by Charles Price in a 1984 occasional paper of the Standing Liturgical Commission, the 1985 convention added to the new canon on membership definitions of the ways in which a person can be considered to be "baptized and confirmed" for the purpose of the canons (that is, any canon requiring one to be confirmed):

> Any person who is baptized in this Church as an adult and receives the laying on of hands by the Bishop at Baptism is to be considered...as both baptized and confirmed; also,

> Any person who is baptized in this Church as an adult and at some time after the Baptism receives the laying on of hands by the Bishop in Reaffirmation of Baptismal Vows is to be considered...as both baptized and confirmed; also,

> Any baptized person who received the laying on of hands at Confirmation (by any Bishop in apostolic succession) and is received into the Episcopal Church by a Bishop of this Church is to be considered...as both baptized and confirmed; and also,

> Any baptized person who received the laying on of hands by a Bishop of this Church at Confirmation or Reception is to be considered...as both baptized and confirmed. (Canon I.17.1[d])

The effect of these definitions is to permit a divergence of practice, evident in surveys conducted in 1986 and 1992 and in various diocesan guidelines. Underlying the disparities is the requirement that baptized members of the

Episcopal Church make an affirmation of faith and receive laying on of hands by a bishop in order to be considered "confirmed." The rite at which this happens and the formula used at the imposition of hands vary depending upon the circumstances of the individual and the interpretation of each bishop, diocese or parish.

Those baptized as adults in the Episcopal Church. An adult baptized by the bishop makes an adult affirmation of faith and receives the laying on of hands in the postbaptismal sealing by the bishop. According to the first paragraph cited above, this person can be considered to be baptized and confirmed. Yet a 1992 survey of diocesan practice found that in nineteen percent of the responding dioceses, the bishop administered an additional rite, usually confirmation but in one case reaffirmation. In an additional twelve percent of the dioceses, the bishop administered confirmation or reaffirmation upon request of the parish priest.[51]

An adult baptized in the Episcopal Church by a priest will make a mature affirmation of faith at baptism but will not receive episcopal imposition of hands. Charles Price recommended that such adults "should publicly *reaffirm their baptismal vows* before the bishop, and receive laying on of hands in order to establish symbolically their tie to the whole Church."[52] This interpretation is reflected in the second paragraph of the canon cited above. Guidelines issued in 1990 by the Diocese of Connecticut utilize this approach, but 1988 guidelines of the Diocese of Hawaii state that confirmation is the appropriate rite.[53] A 1986 survey found that eighty-five percent of the responding bishops used the words for confirmation, not reaffirmation. Six years later, sixty-five percent of the respondents indicated that the words for confirmation were used, and an additional twelve percent used the confirmation formula at least some of the time.[54]

Whether the words for confirmation or reaffirmation are used, there is an expectation that adults baptized by a priest appear before the bishop for an additional rite. This undermines the claim that baptism is full Christian initiation. Using the formula for reaffirmation may preserve a theoretical distinction that adults baptized by a presbyter are not being "confirmed." But this "reaffirmation" qualifies a person as "baptized and confirmed," and these adults are expected to participate in a rite identical to "confirmation" in virtually every way, including the imposition of hands. It is arguable whether the difference in the formula is sufficient to support a claim that those baptized as adults do not undergo confirmation. This would be best addressed by eliminating the rubric expecting adults not baptized by a bishop to make another affirmation of faith and receive imposition of the bishop's hands. Short of prayer book change, however, administering reaffirmation rather than confirmation may help facilitate a shift away from the expectation that every Episcopalian must be "confirmed."

Those baptized in other denominations and now affiliating with the Episcopal Church. In his 1984 occasional paper, Price recommended that if adults baptized in another church, whether Roman Catholic, Lutheran, Orthodox or Baptist, had already made a mature commitment to Christ, they should be received by the bishop with imposition of hands "to symbolize that special link to the whole Church which our bishops represent to us."[55] The 1985 canons, in the third paragraph cited above, preserve the peculiar Anglican distinction that those confirmed "by a bishop in apostolic succession" can be received into the Episcopal Church rather than confirmed. But the fourth paragraph permits any baptized person to be "received," provided he or she receives the imposition of hands. This provision does not specify that the person have previously made a mature commitment to Christ, the requirement suggested by Price.

A 1986 survey suggests a diversity of practice. Fifty-eight percent of the bishops responding received Roman Catholics with the laying on of hands, and fifty-six percent received with imposition of hands those coming from the Orthodox churches. The remainder of the bishops received these persons without episcopal imposition of hands. But only twenty-seven percent of these bishops received Lutherans using laying on of hands and the formula for reception, and only eighteen percent received "other Protestants (Presbyterians, Methodists, etc.)" with imposition of hands and the formula for reception. The remaining bishops confirmed these persons. Responses in 1992 were similar.[56]

Similar diversity is evident in diocesan policies. The guidelines of the Diocese of Hawaii are least restrictive: "Reception applies to those who are coming to the Episcopal Church from another Christian communion."[57] The Dioceses of Connecticut and Indianapolis, following Price's recommendation, specify that reception is for persons coming from another tradition who have already made a mature profession of faith.[58] The Connecticut guidelines further stipulate that this applies without distinction to:

> a Southern Baptist who was baptized at age twelve, a Roman Catholic baptized in infancy and confirmed in early adolescence by a bishop..., and a Lutheran baptized in infancy and confirmed as an adolescent by the parish pastor.[59]

Guidelines proposed in 1990 for the Diocese of Chicago required that candidates for reception "have been properly confirmed within another tradition of the Church," although not necessarily by a bishop, and thus the Southern

Baptist in the above example would presumably be confirmed, while the Lutheran and the Roman Catholic would be received.[60] The Diocese of Northern Indiana specifies that persons who have not received the sacramental laying on of hands by a bishop are presented for confirmation.[61]

The distinctions are especially bewildering when the practice of other denominations is considered. In some places in the Episcopal Church, such as the Diocese of Northern Indiana, a distinction continues to be made between, on the one hand, those who, coming from Roman Catholic and Orthodox churches, have been "confirmed by a bishop in apostolic succession," and, on the other hand, those from other Christian denominations. Yet those from the Orthodox churches and some of those from the Roman Catholic Church will not have been confirmed by a bishop. In the Orthodox churches there is no separate rite of confirmation. Episcopalians have considered the postbaptismal presbyteral chrismation to be the equivalent of "confirmation," yet this chrismation is clearly not comparable to the mature profession of faith with imposition of hands that constitutes the 1979 rite of confirmation. In the Roman Catholic Church, the Rite of Christian Initiation of Adults permits designated presbyters to confer confirmation, either in the absence of the bishop or when there are many to be confirmed. Hence the reception of persons coming from the Roman Catholic and Orthodox churches cannot be defended on the basis that they have been confirmed by a bishop in apostolic succession. Lacking this qualification, there is no clear justification for continuing to receive people from the Roman Catholic and Orthodox churches while confirming "Protestants."

The criteria of having made a mature profession of faith, as in the Connecticut and Indianapolis guidelines, or of having been confirmed (although not necessarily by a bishop), as the Chicago guidelines specify, are also unconvincing. The Connecticut guidelines insist that confirmation is a rite of maturity, not puberty, and stipulate that "the criterion distinguishing candidates for reception from those for confirmation is their own maturity at the time they made a public avowal of faith." Yet in the examples given, the affirmations by the Southern Baptist and the Roman Catholic seem to be made at puberty, not maturity. The requirement of "mature profession of faith" is imprecise at best. Moreover, it does not address the situation of persons coming from Orthodox churches, where no such rite exists. The requirement of a previous rite of confirmation fails to consider not only Orthodox churches, but also those churches which practice believers' baptism.

In short, efforts to make distinctions whereby some persons from other denominations are received by confirmation and others by reception, are riddled with inconsistencies. Using the formula for reception with episcopal imposition of hands and without qualification (except perhaps that the person have been a communicant member or an adult member of another Christian church) for all baptized persons affiliating with the Episcopal Church would eliminate the ambiguities and emphasize that baptism constitutes full Christian initiation. To shift to this as a norm in the Episcopal Church would require theological reflection by the wider Episcopal Church community, particularly by bishops.

Confirmation, reception and reaffirmation: the need for further revision. Underlying the confusion about "confirmation" for those baptized as adults and for persons baptized in other denominations and later affiliating with the Episcopal Church, is the continuation of a two-tier system of membership. Baptism is defined as full Christian initiation and thereby admits to communion. Yet confirmation or its equivalent (that is, making a public affirmation of faith and receiving imposition of hands by the bishop) is expected of all adults in the Episcopal Church and is a prerequisite for certain positions, including Deputy to General Convention, Lay Eucharistic Minister, and ordination. These restrictions suggest that the Episcopal Church has not yet fully accepted baptism as complete Christian initiation, or perhaps that Episcopalians do not recognize the significance of the renewal of baptism that takes place in every celebration of the eucharist and every time a community celebrates the sacrament of baptism.

Ultimately the term "confirmation" must be eliminated. It has had too many meanings historically to enable further reinterpretation. The current confusion about the nature and meaning of confirmation indicates that the effort to redefine confirmation in the 1979 prayer book has not been altogether successful. Eliminating confirmation, or any other *expected* rite of mature affirmation of faith, would remove an emphasis on the first occasion of affirmation and suggest that rites of renewal may be appropriate at various times in an individual's life.

Short of eliminating the term "confirmation," several steps can be taken. Changing the canons to emend "confirmed adult communicant in good standing" to "adult communicant in good standing" would emphasize baptism and an active life of faith, rather than confirmation, as the basis for serving in leadership positions and other canonically defined ministries in the Episcopal Church. Encouraging the baptism of adults by a bishop, rather than a presbyter, would avoid the need for an additional rite and thus emphasize their baptism as fully initiatory. For those baptized as adults but not by a bishop, administering reaffirmation rather than confirmation may encourage a shift away from the expectation that every Episcopalian be "confirmed" by a bishop. When the prayer book is revised, the revisers should eliminate the rubric expecting those baptized as adults to subsequently be presented to the bishop for laying on of hands. For those affiliating with the Episcopal Church, anyone who has been a communicant member or adult member of another Christian church should be received rather than confirmed. A definition of "reception" should be added when the prayer book is revised.

The bishop's role in confirmation and other rites of affirmation. Reserving these rites of reaffirmation to the bishop permits individuals to be linked symbolically to the wider Church through the ministry of the bishop. Yet requiring the bishop to administer these rites gives them undue importance and diminishes the primary significance of baptism. The 1991 International Anglican Liturgical Consultation recommended, "The pastoral rite of confirmation may be delegated by the bishop to a presbyter" (see Appendix D). The consultation suggested that the role of the bishop includes being a teacher of the faith, a leader of the community of faith, and a guardian of the unity of the Church. The bishop expresses the unity of the Church by presiding at baptism and eucharist and through delegating or presiding at other rites of commitment, including confirmation, reception of Christians from other communions, and celebrations of reconciliation.[62] The Episcopal Church would do well to consider the recommendations of the Anglican consultation and reflect carefully upon the role of the bishop in baptism and confirmation in the context of a broader vision of episcopacy.

NOTES

1. Some examples of parish and diocesan policies are included in A. Theodore Eastman, *The Baptizing Community: Christian Initiation and the Local Congregation*, 2nd ed. (Wilton, CT: Morehouse, 1991), pp. 111-32.

2. "Church Asked to Review Baptismal Covenant," *The Living Church*, June 23, 1985, p. 7.

3. "Mission Imperatives as Adopted by Executive Council," *The Episcopalian*, Jan. 1988, p. 18.

4. Standing Committee on the Structure of the Church, "Comment Draft Report," June 1996.

5. Catherine Mowry LaCugna, *God for Us: The Trinity and Christian Life* (New York: HarperCollins, 1991), p. 382. The final chapter of this book is an exploration of "Living Trinitarian Faith."

6. Patricia Wilson-Kastner, *Faith, Feminism, and the Christ* (Philadelphia: Fortress, 1983), pp. 129-30.

7. *Ministry I: Holy Baptism* (Alexandria, VA: Associated Parishes, 1978), pp. 5, 8.

8. Eastman, *The Baptizing Community*, pp. 72-5; Howard E. Galley, *The Ceremonies of the Eucharist: A Guide to Celebration* (Cambridge, MA: Cowley, 1989), pp. 176-9; Byron D. Stuhlman, *Prayer Book Rubrics Expanded* (New York: Church Hymnal Corporation, 1987), pp. 111-12, 116-18.

9. Marion J. Hatchett, "Architectural Implications of The Book of Common Prayer," Occasional Paper 7 (March 1985), in *The Occasional Papers of the Standing Liturgical Commission* (New York: Church Hymnal Corporation, 1987), p. 58.

10. William Seth Adams, "Decoding the Obvious," in Ruth A. Meyers (ed.), *Baptism and Ministry*, p. 6.

11. Ibid., pp. 10-11.

12. Paul John Tracy, "Christian Initiation Complete in Baptism? A Continuing Problem for Anglicans" (M.A. Thesis, University of Notre Dame, 1985), pp. 51, 62. The bishops responding to this survey represent slightly more than half of the dioceses of the Episcopal Church.

13. M. Richard Hatfield, "Baptism, Chrismation and Eucharist: Christian Initiation: A Recovery of the Primitive Pattern" (S.T.M. Thesis, Nashotah House, 1988), pp. 84-8.

14. Galley, *Ceremonies of the Eucharist*, p. 180.

15. Robert J. Brooks, "Faith of Our Fathers," *The Living Church*, Jan. 11, 1981, pp. 8-9.

16. David E. Sumner, "An Interview with Marion Hatchett: What Is Confirmation?", *The Episcopalian*, Sept. 1981, p. 14.

17. Tracy, "Christian Initiation Complete in Baptism?", pp. 49-50, 60, 62.

18. "Walk in Newness of Life: The Findings of the International Anglican Liturgical Consultation, Toronto 1991," in Holeton (ed.), *Growing in Newness of Life*, p. 230.

19. Ibid., p. 244.

20. Charles Price, "Rites of Initiation" (Sept. 1984), in *Occasional Papers of the Standing Liturgical Commission*, p. 31 [reprinted in Meyers (ed.), *Baptism and Ministry*, p. 94].

21. Tracy, "Christian Initiation Complete in Baptism?", p. 61.

22. Arthur A. Vogel, "Are You My Type?", *Anglican Theological Review* 69 (1987): 376-84.

23. Stevick, *Baptismal Moments*, p. 163.

24. Leonel Mitchell, "The Theology of Christian Initiation and *The Proposed Book of Common Prayer*," *Anglican Theological Review* 60 (1978): 418; "The Place of Baptismal Anointing in Christian Initiation," *ATR* 68 (1986): 204-10.

25. "Baptism," in *Baptism, Eucharist, and Ministry*, Faith and Order Paper No. 111 (Geneva, Switzerland: World Council of Churches, 1982), sec. 17.

26. Mitchell, "The Place of Baptismal Anointing," p. 206.

27. "Walk in Newness of Life," in Holeton (ed.), *Growing in Newness of Life*, p. 253.

28. Hatfield, "Baptism, Chrismation, and Eucharist," pp. 70-83.

29. Edward W. Jones, "Present Practices of Bishops in the Episcopal Church, with Regard to the Rite of Confirmation," report of survey conducted during sabbatical, Indianapolis, 1986, Part I, "Introduction to a Questionnaire," p. 7, and summary of responses to questionnaire, p. 4.

30. "The Boston Statement: Children and Communion," in Colin Buchanan (ed.), *Nurturing Children in Communion: Essays from the Boston Consultation*, Grove Liturgical Study 44 (Bramcote, Nottingham: Grove Books, 1985), pp. 42-9; reprinted in Meyers (ed.), *Children at the Table*, pp. 127-40.

31. Jim Bethell, "AP at Anaheim," *Open*, Oct. 1985, pp. 1-2; *Journal of the General Convention*, 1988, p. 544.

32. "Walk in Newness of Life," in Holeton (ed.), *Growing in Newness of Life*, p. 228.

33. Interim Meeting of the House of Bishops, San Antonio, TX, Sept. 19-25, 1986, in *Journal of the General Convention*, 1988, pp. 359, 374; Interim Meeting of the House of Bishops, St. Charles, IL, Sept. 25-Oct. 1, 1987, in ibid., p. 429. Allison's objections were presented in a paper, "Anglican Initiatory Rites: A Contribution to the Current Debate," later published in *Anglican and Episcopal History* 56 (1987): 27-43.

34. Louis Weil, "Disputed Aspects of Infant Communion," *Studia Liturgica* 17 (1987): 260-1.

35. *Journal of the General Convention*, 1988, pp. 158-60.

36. *The Blue Book*, 1988, p. 187 (emphasis added).

37. *Journal of the General Convention*, 1988, p. 696 (emphasis added).

38. Mitchell, "Communion of Infants and Little Children," *Anglican Theological Review* 71 (1989): 76-7.

39. *The Blue Book*, 1988, p. 287.

40. Ibid., p. 234.

41. Richard A. Norris, Eugene R. Fairweather, James E. Griffiss and Albert T. Mollegen, "Report on the Validity of the Philadelphia Ordinations," Jan. 15, 1975, cited in Darling, *New Wine*, pp. 133-4.

42. Darling, *New Wine*, p. 227.

43. Edward W. Jones, "Present Practices of Bishops in the Episcopal Church, with Regard to the Rite of Confirmation," Introduction, p. 6, and summary of responses, p. 3.

44. Ibid., Introduction, p. 7, and summary of responses, p. 3.

45. John H. Westerhoff, "Confirmation: An Episcopal Church Perspective," *Reformed Liturgy and Music* 24 (1990): 200-3.

46. Journey to Adulthood is available from LeaderResources. I am indebted to David Crean, a developer of the program, for providing me with information about this program.

47. BCP 1928, p. 290.

48. White and Dykman, *Annotated Constitution and Canons*, Vol. 1, pp. 384, 391, 423.

49. Numberings used here refer to the 1994 *Constitution and Canons* of the Episcopal Church.

50. *The Blue Book*, 1982, pp. 59-62, 153-6; *Journal of the General Convention*, 1982, pp. C-41-4.

51. Ruth A. Meyers, summary of responses to survey of members of the Association of Diocesan Liturgy and Music Commissions, "Present Diocesan Practices in the Episcopal Church with Regard to Baptism and Confirmation, Reception, Reaffirmation of Baptismal Vows," November 1992 (responses were received from 26 dioceses, representing slightly more than one-fourth of the domestic dioceses of the Episcopal Church).

52. Price, "Rites of Initiation," in *Occasional Papers of the Standing Liturgical Commission*, pp. 31-2 (emphasis in original).

53. Diocese of Connecticut, "Revised Diocesan Guidelines," *Open*, Winter 1990, p. 7; "Christian Initiation in Hawaii," *Open*, March 1988, p. 12.

54. Jones, "Present Practices of Bishops," Introduction, p. 4, and summary of responses, p. 1 (responses to this survey were received from 71 bishops); Meyers, "Present Diocesan Practices."

55. Price, "Rites of Initiation," in *Occasional Papers of the Standing Liturgical Commission*, p. 32.

56. Jones, "Present Practices of Bishops," Introduction, p. 5, and summary of responses, p. 2; Meyers, "Present Diocesan Practices."

57. "Christian Initiation in Hawaii," *Open*, Mar. 1988, p. 12.

58. Diocese of Connecticut, "Revised Diocesan Guidelines," *Open*, Winter 1990, p. 7; Episcopal Diocese of Indianapolis, "Guidelines for Rites of Initiation," in Eastman, *The Baptizing Community*, 2nd ed., p. 118.

59. Diocese of Connecticut, "Revised Diocesan Guidelines," p. 7.

60. "Christian Initiation in the Diocese of Chicago: A Draft Proposal Submitted by the Task Force on the Catechumenate and the Commission on Liturgy," Jan. 1990, p. 13.

61. "The Committee on Liturgy of the Diocese of Northern Indiana: Guidelines for the Celebration of the Rites of Christian Initiation" (1989), p. 3.

62. "Walk in Newness of Life," in Holeton (ed.), *Growing in Newness of Life*, pp. 248-9.

Conclusion

Continuing the Reformation

As the Episcopal Church was developing the rites of baptism and confirmation in the 1979 prayer book, other churches were also in the process of revising their rites. There was growing ecumenical understanding of the evolution of rites of Christian initiation from the New Testament to the Reformation and shared appreciation of the pastoral difficulties faced by churches in the shift to a post-Christendom worldview. But as was true in the Episcopal Church, there was no clear consensus as to the resolution to these pastoral challenges in light of the historical development of initiatory rites. The Episcopal Church was slightly ahead of most other North American and other Anglican churches in the timing of its revision process. Consequently, several churches have followed approaches taken by the Episcopal Church in its new rites of initiation and reaffirmation of faith. Representatives of the Doctrine and Worship Committee of the Anglican Church of Canada had met with the Standing Liturgical Commission throughout the period of prayer book revision and contributed to the discussions of the principles underlying the new rites. Hence the rites in the Canadian *Book of Alternative Services* (1985) are markedly similar to those of the 1979 prayer book. But numerous parallels also exist in the rites and patterns of other churches.[1]

New Patterns of Initiation and Reaffirmation of Faith

Baptism as full Christian initiation. The understanding of baptism as full Christian initiation was affirmed by the 1985 International Anglican Liturgical Consultation, which recommended that all baptized persons be admitted to communion because baptism is "the sacramental sign of full incorporation into the church"[2] (see Appendix D). Not only did the 1991 International Anglican Liturgical Consultation reaffirm this understanding of baptism, the consultation also described confirmation as a "rite of affirmation" which has "a continuing pastoral role in the renewal of faith among the baptized but [is] in no way to be seen as a completion of baptism or as necessary for admission to communion"[3] (see Appendix D). Thus these consultations supported the understanding of initiation adopted in the 1979 prayer book, despite the fact that this unequivocal stance had not been taken by the Anglican churches in the British Isles which issued new or alternative liturgical books in the 1980s.

The principle of baptism as full initiation administered in a single rite had been advocated in 1958 by the Church of England Liturgical Commission, which proposed a rite of adult baptism and confirmation, concluding with communion, a pattern adopted in the 1980 *Alternative Service Book*. But in this book baptism and confirmation are clearly separable rites, and children unable to answer for themselves at baptism are neither confirmed nor admitted to communion as part of the baptismal rite. This is the pattern adopted in the revised rites of the Anglican churches in Australia and in Kenya. In contrast, the Canadian rite makes no distinction between infants and adults being baptized. As in the Episcopal Church rite, the Canadian rite includes no explicit direction that the newly baptized receive communion, but nothing suggests that they do not receive.

The context of baptism: the eucharist. Several of the revised Anglican rites place baptism within the context of the eucharist, a significant change from earlier Anglican provisions for baptism to be administered after the second lesson at Morning or Evening Prayer. The Canadian rite is most explicit: there is no provision for any conclusion other than eucharist. Other revised Anglican rites, including those of Australia, New Zealand, Southern Africa and Kenya, suggest or state explicitly that the normative context for baptism is eucharist, particularly in the case of the baptism of adults, but provide as well for the celebration of baptism in Morning or Evening Prayer.

It is not only revised Anglican rites, however, which place baptism in the context of the eucharist. The new rite of the United Methodist Church explicitly states: "It is most fitting that the service continue with Holy Communion, in which the union of the new members with the body of Christ is most fully expressed. The new members, including children, may receive first."[4] Similarly, the United Church of Christ worship book states in its introduction to the baptismal rite, "Baptism is most properly incorporated into a Service of Word and Sacrament, where it follows the sermon and precedes Holy Communion... For the newly baptized, the journey is from the font to the feast of the table." However, the outline of the rite states that it "*may* be incorporated into a Service of Word and Sacrament *or* a Service of the Word."[5] The Presbyterian Church (USA) does not encourage the celebration of communion as strongly but nonetheless recommends the communion of the newly baptized: "When the Lord's Supper is celebrated, it is appropriate for the newly baptized to receive Communion first."[6] These rites thus point to baptism as full Christian initiation.

In contrast, although the Lutheran *Manual on the Liturgy* (designed for pastors) specifies that the eucharist is the normative context for baptism, the congregational edition of the *Lutheran Book of Worship* makes no mention of this.[7] Moreover, the official stance of the Evangelical Lutheran Church in America is to permit admission to communion in the fifth grade, although a number of Lutheran congregations have further lowered the age of communion, and the 1997 Churchwide Assembly will consider a statement on sacramental practice that suggests that the newly baptized, including infants, may be communed for the first time at the service in which they are baptized.[8]

Thus in Anglicanism as well as in American Protestant churches, the eucharist is increasingly seen as the normative context for baptism. Those rites which explicitly permit the communion of all the newly baptized further underscore an understanding of baptism as full Christian initiation.

In the Roman Catholic Church, however, confirmation is understood as an integral component of initiation. Thus the baptism of children does not necessarily take place in the context of the eucharist, since children not of catechetical age are not ordinarily confirmed or admitted to communion at the time of their baptism. The introduction to the rite of baptism for children suggests that baptism might be celebrated during the mass on Sunday, "so that the entire community may be present and the necessary relationship between baptism and eucharist may be clearly seen," but it goes on to caution, without further explanation, "this should not be done too often."[9] However, the Rite of Christian Initiation of Adults expects that adults and children of catechetical age will be baptized, confirmed and admitted to communion as part of a single rite, normally the Easter vigil.

Congregational participation in baptism. Not only is the eucharist becoming the primary context for baptism, many of the new rites specify that baptism most appropriately takes place on the Lord's Day in the presence of the community. Those rites which permit exceptions still urge that baptism be administered when the congregation gathers for worship. In addition, the rites are far more participatory. As in the rites of the Episcopal Church, members of the congregation promise to support those being baptized in their life in Christ, join the candidates and their sponsors in response to the interrogatory Apostles' Creed, and welcome the newly baptized with a formula of welcome and the greeting of peace. All of these actions underscore that baptism forms the Church and candidates are being incorporated into a living body.

The baptismal covenant. A unique feature of the Episcopal Church rite is the series of questions of commitment which with the interrogatory Apostles' Creed comprise the baptismal covenant. Only the Anglican Church of Canada has adopted this covenant. *A New Zealand Prayer Book* uses a revised version of these questions as the "Commitment to Christian Service" that precedes the laying on of hands for confirmation and renewal of faith, but candidates for baptism do not make such an explicit expression of commitment to Christian life. The *Lutheran Book of Worship* also includes in its service of reaffirmation a question asking the candidates if they "intend to continue in the covenant God made with you in Holy Baptism." Specific aspects of Christian life are then enumerated in a list that loosely resembles the questions of the Episcopal Church's baptismal covenant.[10] Similarly, the 1991 draft service of confirmation for the Anglican Church in Kenya provides a series of questions articulating dimensions of Christian life (using language quite different from the New Zealand, Canadian and American forms), but the Kenyan baptismal rite does not include any such questions of commitment.

Other revised baptismal rites—the Anglican prayer books for Southern Africa and Australia and the United Methodist, United Church of Christ, and Presbyterian books—separate commitment to Christian life from the Apostles' Creed. The entire congregation joins the candidates and sponsors in the creedal affirmation of faith, but only the candidates for baptism respond to questions making explicit their promise to live a Christian life. This provides a corporate expression and renewal of baptismal faith for the entire congregation, yet at the same time emphasizes that the candidates are not only turning to Christ as Savior but also making specific promises to lead a Christian life.

The Roman Catholic rites make quite different provision for the profession of faith. Explicit commitment to a Christian life is not part of the baptismal rite, although such commitment is an important dimension of catechumens' preparation for baptism. In the baptismal rite for adults and children of catechetical age, the celebrant addresses three questions to each candidate individually, eliciting their assent to belief in the triune God. Each candidate's profession of faith is followed immediately by her or his baptism. When baptism is celebrated during the Easter vigil, the congregation will renew their baptismal faith in response to the same questions, but after all the candidates have been baptized (and confirmed). When infants and young children are baptized, the same questions are addressed to their parents and godparents, and the celebrant and congregation then acknowledge this profession of faith to be theirs.

In the American and Canadian Anglican rites, the baptismal covenant, with its creedal profession of faith and questions of commitment to Christian life, is used not only for baptism but also on occasions of baptismal renewal, that is, the Easter vigil and other baptismal days. Other books make similar provision for baptismal renewal, and some include a thanksgiving over the water, sometimes with opportunity for sprinkling the congregation or some other means for worshipers to encounter the water. Easter vigil rites with the renewal of baptismal vows appear in a number of denominational worship books, and the American Presbyterian and United Methodist books provide separate services for a congregational reaffirmation of the baptismal covenant, as do the *Alternative Service Book* of the Church of England and the prayer book of the Anglican Church in Southern Africa. This common practice of renewal, which includes renunciation of evil and affirmation of faith, may be traced to the Roman Catholic Easter vigil introduced in 1951. That it has been so widely adopted across denominations suggests a new or renewed understanding of baptism as the basis of life in Christ.

Postbaptismal rites: anointing and prayer for the gifts of the Spirit. For those who drafted the Episcopal Church baptismal rite, the introduction of these postbaptismal rites provided a significant ritual expression of baptism as full Christian initiation. Other North American books—those of the Anglican Church of Canada as well as the American Lutheran, Presbyterian and Methodist churches—include the option of anointing within the text of the baptismal rite. In each of these rites, the formula at the consignation is similar to that of the Episcopal Church prayer book. The Canadian Anglican rite also follows the Episcopal Church by including at this point in the baptismal rite a version of the traditional prayer for the sevenfold gifts of the Spirit, while in the Presbyterian and Lutheran rites prayer for the sevenfold gifts of the Spirit accompanies the imposition of hands, and consignation follows separately. Similarly, in the United Methodist rite the pastor invokes the Holy Spirit (no text for this invocation is included) at the imposition of hands, and an optional consignation with chrismation follows. In the United Church of Christ rite, laying on of hands is accompanied by a formula invoking the Spirit, but consignation and anointing are not included in the rite. Each of these rites thus enriches the baptismal rite with additional symbolic actions.

Although the consignation and optional chrismation in the Episcopal Church rite can be interpreted as a separate sacramental action conveying the gift of the Spirit and thereby completing baptism, other rites lean away from such an interpretation. In the Canadian Anglican rite, the formula at the consignation is "I sign you with the cross, and mark you as Christ's own for ever."

Following this action, the prayer for the gifts of the Spirit is said "over the newly baptized."[11] Nowhere is the "seal of the Spirit" mentioned, and the prayer for the Spirit is clearly a postbaptismal prayer. The rubrics in the *Lutheran Book of Worship* and the United Church of Christ *Book of Worship* also specify that imposition of hands and (in the Lutheran rite) consignation are administered to the "baptized."[12] The *United Methodist Book of Worship* includes consignation and chrismation as optional actions listed along with the giving of new clothing, the presentation of a lighted baptismal candle, and the presentation of the baptismal certificate. The book cautions that "these should not be so emphasized as to seem as important as, or more important than, God's sign given in the water itself."[13]

While these North American rites offer consignation and chrismation as part of the postbaptismal ceremonies and include prayer for the gifts of the Spirit, other Anglican rites which permit chrismation at baptism—Kenya, Australia and New Zealand—are less explicit. These Anglican rites provide directions for the use of chrism in rubrics that preface or follow the baptismal rite, calling much less attention to the option of chrismation. Moreover, none of these baptismal rites includes prayer for the gift of the Spirit. Instead, the rites for confirmation retain the traditional prayer for the sevenfold gifts. These baptismal rites are thus more ambiguous. Anointing is possible, but the ritual texts of baptism do not associate the chrism with the gift of the Spirit. Elsewhere in the Australian and New Zealand books, however, chrism is related to the Spirit: the prayer suggested in the New Zealand book to "set apart" the oil asks God that "those who are signed at their baptism...in this holy oil, may be sealed by your Spirit as yours for ever";[14] the notes in the Australian prayer book explain that the use of chrism "restores an ancient baptismal ceremony...traditionally associated with the Holy Spirit."[15]

These revised Anglican books thus make tentative steps toward the inclusion of a ritual action giving particular expression to the baptismal gift of the Spirit. A different approach was taken in the *Alternative Service Book* of the Church of England and the prayer book of the Anglican Church in Southern Africa. Both books include in confirmation the prayer for the sevenfold gifts of the Spirit as well as the optional use of chrism. In these rites confirmation functions more explicitly as a sacramental bestowal of the Holy Spirit in addition to being an occasion of reaffirmation of faith.

The rites in England and Southern Africa are in this way similar to the Roman Catholic rites. In the latter, confirmation includes prayer for the sevenfold gifts of the Spirit, accompanied by the imposition of hands and followed by consignation with anointing, using the formula, "Be sealed with the gift of the Holy Spirit."[16] Addresses by the celebrant, first to the candidates and then to the congregation, describe this as the outpouring of the Holy Spirit, and this ritual bestowal of the Spirit is explicitly understood as the completion of Christian initiation. While confirmation is a sacrament distinct from baptism and is administered several years later to those baptized as infants, the normative pattern for adults includes both baptism and confirmation, culminating in the celebration of the eucharist. So important is the unity of these initiatory sacraments that when the bishop is absent, the presbyter who baptizes is also expected to confer confirmation.

Although the Roman Catholic Church views baptism and confirmation as separate sacraments, the ritual pattern for adults and older children is identical to the baptismal rite of the Episcopal Church. That is, baptism in water is followed by prayer for the sevenfold gifts of the Spirit and consignation with anointing accompanied by a formula proclaiming that the candidate is sealed with the Holy Spirit. The difference is that the Episcopal Church calls the entire rite "baptism" and administers the same rite to infants and young children.

A repeatable reaffirmation of faith. Another key dimension of the Episcopal Church's rethinking of confirmation was the concept that reaffirmation of faith is repeatable. This is the approach taken by the 1991 International Anglican Liturgical Consultation, which in a summary of Anglican views of confirmation interpreted it as a renewal of baptismal faith and rejected on the basis of contemporary scholarship the view that confirmation is sealing by the Spirit. The consultation suggested that laying on of hands with prayer for strengthening by the Spirit could be used to respond to various pastoral needs, including occasions of renewed or deepened faith, reception from other communions, and reconciliation of the lapsed.[17]

The principle of a repeatable affirmation of faith has been adopted by a number of churches, although the term "confirmation" has generally been retained to refer to the affirmation of baptismal vows by those baptized as infants (of the rites surveyed, only the Presbyterian *Book of Common Worship* does not call this rite "confirmation"). Other occasions recommended for reaffirmation include restoration to active membership and reception into membership in a denomination.

Many of these rites stress that baptism is full initiation. For example, in the introduction to a "combined order" for "Baptism and Reaffirmation of the Baptismal Covenant," the Presbyterian *Book of Common Worship* cautions:

> In including such rites [of reaffirmation] along with Baptism, care should be
> taken to ensure that Baptism is clearly recognized as the means by which per-

sons are received into the church. While a public profession of faith for the first time, by those previously baptized, and a reaffirmation of faith are important occasions in Christian life, neither should encroach upon the centrality of Baptism.[18]

Likewise, the Lutheran *Manual on the Liturgy* advises that "great care must be taken that Confirmation neither implies joining the church nor overshadows Baptism."[19]

While these American rites stress that baptism is full initiation, Anglican rites, which have historically given great value to confirmation by a bishop, continue to insist upon confirmation by the bishop. *A New Zealand Prayer Book* directs that "Either at the same time as baptism, or at a later stage in the person's life, those making a profession of faith for the first time are confirmed by the bishop through the laying on of hands."[20] Presumably this means that those baptized as adults, if not baptized with laying on of hands by a bishop, must subsequently be confirmed. The Australian rite also recommends that when adults are baptized, their confirmation and first communion take place at the same service, implying that confirmation must be supplied if it is not administered at the time of baptism. Like the Episcopal Church, the Australian and New Zealand rites expect a subsequent affirmation before the bishop for those baptized as adults by a presbyter (or deacon), thus introducing inconsistency in implementing the principle that baptism is full Christian initiation. However, the Kenyan and the Canadian Anglican rites are silent as to whether a subsequent reaffirmation is expected of those who are baptized as adults without imposition of hands by a bishop.

The symbolic gestures and ritual texts accompanying the reaffirmation of faith vary widely. The most extensive provisions are found in the American Methodist and Presbyterian books. The Presbyterian rites of reaffirmation take place at the baptismal font. The laying on of hands may be accompanied by consignation, with or without anointing, and the formula used is the same as the formula in the imposition of hands at baptism, that is, a form of the prayer for the sevenfold gifts of the Spirit (or a form of the traditional Anglican confirmation prayer, "Defend, O Lord, your servant N. with your grace..." an alternative both at baptism and at reaffirmation). The Methodist rite suggests the symbolic use of water "in ways that cannot be interpreted as baptism," in addition to imposition of hands.[21] Only pastoral experience will determine whether rites of renewal that make use of water are seen as a kind of rebaptism, a caution sounded as well by the 1991 Anglican liturgical consultation (see Appendix D).

The Anglican rites make the connection with baptism less explicit: like the 1979 prayer book rite, the Canadian Anglican rite directs laying on of hands at confirmation but no ritual gesture is specified for reception or reaffirmation; the Australian and New Zealand rites call for imposition of hands to accompany the formula of reaffirmation said by the bishop. The *Lutheran Book of Worship* is even more restrained, with a separate formula and imposition of hands only for confirmation.

Reception into a denomination. Although the Episcopal Church and Canadian books simply include "reception" as one formula among several alternatives in a rite of reaffirmation, other books make more explicit provisions for reception of baptized Christians into a denomination or a specific congregation. In the *Book of Common Worship* of the Presbyterian Church, the "Reaffirmation of the Baptismal Covenant for Those Uniting with a Congregation" includes not only reception of those coming from another church but also restoration to membership for those returning to active membership after lapsing. Individuals are presented by an elder, respond to questions of renunciation and profession of faith, and join the congregation in the Apostles' Creed. Ritual gesture, however, is not required. Imposition of hands, with optional consignation and chrismation, is permitted but is said to be "especially appropriate for those who have not participated in the life of the church for an extended period of time." The reception concludes with a brief prayer, a sentence of welcome "to this congregation and its worship and ministry" and the peace.[22] The "Order for Reception of Members: Affirmation of Baptism" in the United Church of Christ *Book of Worship* is similar: individuals are presented by a leader of the church, respond to questions of renunciation and profession of faith, and join the congregation in confession of faith in the triune God. Ritual gesture is not required, but the pastor and representatives of the congregation may extend "the hand of Christian love" to each new member.[23]

Whereas the Presbyterian and United Church of Christ rites focus on affiliation with a congregation, the Methodist rite includes forms both for reception into the United Methodist Church and for reception into the local congregation, the latter for those joining the congregation from other United Methodist congregations. Rather than a formula of welcome, with or without ritual gesture, those being received are asked a single question about their intention to participate in the ministries of the United Methodist Church or the congregation. Those received, along any who have been baptized or confirmed in the same rite, are then acknowledged in a statement from the congregation which may be followed by acts of welcome, including the peace.

The "Affirmation of Baptism" in the *Lutheran Book of Worship* likewise provides no ritual gesture for reception. In this rite, as candidates are presented in turn for confirmation, reception into membership, and restoration to membership, the pastor acknowledges the step being taking by each group, for example, "we rejoice to receive you, members of the one holy catholic and apostolic Church, into our fellowship in the Gospel." The rite continues with affirmation of faith, prayers for the candidates, and the prayer for the gifts of the Spirit, said over all those affirming their faith.

In contrast, the Anglican prayer books of Southern Africa and Australia provide distinct rites of reception. These include questions not only about one's profession of the Christian faith but also one's desire to become a communicant member and willingness to accept the teaching of the Anglican church. The rite for Southern Africa includes extension of the right hand of fellowship to those confirmed in other churches, but confirmation, with imposition of hands and optional consignation and chrismation, is required for those not confirmed in another church. The Australian rite also calls for taking the hand of the person being received, followed by imposition of hands with the formula for reaffirmation of faith.

Likewise, the Roman Catholic rites also include a "Rite of Reception of Baptized Christians into Full Communion with the Catholic Church." The person being received recites the Nicene Creed, then makes a statement of belief in the faith and teaching of the Catholic Church. This is followed by a statement of reception and, for those not previously confirmed, confirmation, that is, prayer for the sevenfold gifts of the Spirit and consignation with anointing. Laying on of hands accompanies the statement of reception or, when confirmation follows, the prayer for the gifts of the Spirit. The celebrant then greets the person who has been received and takes that person's hands as a sign of friendship and acceptance.

This diversity of ritual practice suggests a need for a formal reception into membership in a denomination but a lack of clear consensus as to how this is best expressed ritually. Most of the rites of reception may be included in services of baptism and/or reaffirmation of faith, reflecting a common understanding that affiliation with a congregation is also an occasion of renewed commitment to the Christian faith. Several of the rites also include specific questions to the candidates regarding their desire to be received and their intention to participate in the life of their new denomination, thus going beyond the underlying profession of faith. But the books differ in the ritual gesture recommended or required.

A Baptismal Ecclesiology

The revised rites of these different churches indicate a renewed understanding of baptism and reaffirmation of faith. Underlying the revisions is a new model of the Church that is evolving across denominations as a post-Christendom worldview emerges. When it can no longer be assumed that the surrounding culture will provide the necessary environment for Christian nurture, commitment takes on new meaning.

A renewed understanding of commitment is evident as the centrality of baptism is emphasized. Baptism during the principal Sunday service emphasizes that this sacrament involves the entire local community. The community's role is further underscored by promises to uphold the newly baptized in life in Christ and by the congregation's participation in the profession of baptismal faith.

The communion of all the baptized is further evidence of the changing self-understanding of the Church. David Holeton has argued convincingly with regard to Anglicanism that "whenever the church has come to see itself as a small, gathered, eucharistic community, the communion of all the baptized becomes a real question." In such a community, regular participation in the eucharist, including reception of communion, sustains and nurtures the Christian community.[24] In the Episcopal Church and in other churches, the liturgical movement has fostered renewed appreciation for the centrality of the eucharist, and the shift to a post-Christian era is giving new meaning to the Church as a small, gathered community.

A changing understanding of rites of reaffirmation of faith also reflects the emergence of a baptismal ecclesiology. Commitment can no longer be assumed in a largely non-Christian society. A single expression of commitment at baptism, or even one additional occasion at a non-repeatable rite of confirmation, is scarcely adequate for the human experience of failure and repentance throughout one's Christian life, or for moments of reawakening or deepening of Christian faith. The repeatable reaffirmation of baptismal vows is providing opportunities for further expressions of commitment during Christian life. Development of rites of adolescence is another acknowledgment of the need for various opportunities for reaffirmation of faith.

Finally, a shift to a post-Christian era calls for renewed attention to evangelism. The Church cannot assume that it will be perpetuated primarily through the baptism of the children of its members. The Episcopal Church must come to see itself as a "baptizing community," called to go forth into the world, to proclaim the gospel, and to baptize and teach.

NOTES

1. Anglican rites considered here include: Anglican Church of Australia, *A Prayer Book for Australia* (Alexandria, New South Wales: Broughton Books, 1995); Anglican Church of Canada, *The Book of Alternative Services* (Toronto: Anglican Book Centre, 1985); Church of the Province of Kenya, *Modern Services* (Nairobi: Uzima Press, 1991); Church of the Province of New Zealand, *A New Zealand Prayer Book* (Auckland: William Collins Publishers, 1989); Church of the Province of Southern Africa, *An Anglican Prayer Book* (London: Collins Liturgical Publications, 1989). Other Anglican churches have made less substantial revisions: Church in Wales, *The Book of Common Prayer for use in The Church in Wales* (Church in Wales Publications, 1984); Church of England, *The Alternative Service Book* (1980); Church of Ireland, *Alternative Prayer Book* (London: Collins Liturgical Publications, 1984).

North American rites considered include: *Book of Common Worship*, prepared for the Presbyterian Church USA and the Cumberland Presbyterian Church (Louisville: Westminster/John Knox Press, 1993); United Church of Christ, *Book of Worship* (New York: United Church of Christ Office for Church Life and Leadership, 1986); *Lutheran Book of Worship* (Minneapolis: Augsburg; Philadelphia: Fortress, 1978); *The United Methodist Book of Worship* (Nashville, TN: United Methodist Publishing House, 1992).

Also included in this survey are the rites of Christian initiation in *The Rites of the Catholic Church* (study ed., New York: Pueblo, 1976), pp. 1-354.

2. "The Boston Statement: Children and Communion," in Meyers (ed.), *Children at the Table*, pp. 139-40.

3. "Walk in Newness of Life," in Holeton (ed.), *Growing in Newness of Life*, pp. 228-9.

4. *United Methodist Book of Worship*, p. 94.

5. UCC, *Book of Worship*, pp. 131, 132 (emphasis added).

6. *Book of Common Worship*, p. 415.

7. *Manual on the Liturgy—Lutheran Book of Worship* (Minneapolis: Augsburg, 1979), p. 172.

8. Evangelical Lutheran Church in America, "The Use of the Means of Grace" (1996), p. 25.

9. "Rite of Baptism for Children," par. 9, in *Rites of the Catholic Church*.

10. *Lutheran Book of Worship*, p. 201.

11. *Book of Alternative Services*, p. 160.

12. *Lutheran Book of Worship*, p. 124; UCC, *Book of Worship*, p. 143.

13. *United Methodist Book of Worship*, p. 91.

14. *A New Zealand Prayer Book*, p. 382.

15. *A Prayer Book for Australia*, p. 70.

16. "Rite of Christian Initiation of Adults," par. 227-31, 266-70, 361-5, and "Rite of Confirmation," par. 24-7, in *Rites of the Catholic Church*.

17. "Walk in Newness of Life," in Holeton (ed.), *Growing in Newness of Life*, pp. 243-7.

18. *Book of Common Worship*, p. 431.

19. *Manual on the Liturgy—Lutheran Book of Worship*, p. 340.

20. *A New Zealand Prayer Book*, p. 380.

21. *United Methodist Book of Worship*, p. 92.

22. *Book of Common Worship*, pp. 461-2.

23. UCC, *Book of Worship*, p. 164.

24. Holeton, "Communion of All the Baptized and Anglican Tradition," in Meyers (ed.), *Children at the Table*, pp. 34-5.

Appendices

Appendix A:
Statements of the House of Bishops, 1971

A Statement on the Admission of Children to Communion[1]

After the 63rd General Convention authorized "that children be admitted to Holy Communion before Confirmation, subject to the direction and guidance of the Ordinary," it has been noted that children, having been admitted to Holy Communion in one congregation, have been refused the Sacrament when they visited, or transferred to, another.

Since this refusal is equivalent to excommunication, it can obviously give offense to "little ones" in the flock of Christ.

It is the recommendation of this House that, when a family visits, or transfers to, another congregation, the action of its former congregation in admitting the children thereof to Holy Communion be honored.

We further recommend that no child be admitted to Holy Communion unless instructed in the meaning of this Sacrament, and we agree that it is preferable that the reception of the Holy Communion be for children an experience in which the whole family shares.

A Statement on Holy Baptism and Its Relation to Confirmation[2]

It is the understanding of this House that in Holy Baptism a person is made fully and completely a Christian and a member of Christ's Body, the Church. God the Holy Spirit acts, so we believe, to bestow the gift of His grace in response to the affirmation of faith by His Church.

At the same time, it is also our understanding that God the Holy Spirit, while continually a presence in the life of every baptized person, intervenes again and again in particular ways as a person lives out his Christian life.

Confirmation, as Anglicans have practiced it, is liturgically and sacramentally a significant occasion of such intervention. It involves the special moment in a person's life when an individual makes a personal and public commitment to discipleship—a discipleship to which the faith of the Church committed him in Baptism. Confirmation is, thus, one's personal and public commitment to the implications of his Baptism.

Confirmation should not be regarded as a procedure of admission to the Holy Communion; nor is it "joining the Church."

We believe that there is something greatly to be cherished in the historic practice of Anglicanism in authorizing the Bishop to act for the Church when a person publicly makes the faith of his fathers his own and when a special blessing of the Holy Spirit is invoked.

We believe that there is something greatly to be cherished in the Anglican expectation that baptized Christians who live out their lives in this branch of the Church should, at some appropriate moment, be encouraged to make the Confirmation commitment and to receive episcopal laying on of hands.

We do not wish to see the meaning of a public, mature, decision for Christ lost by this Church. We trust the experience of the centuries and feel that it is our duty to deepen and spiritualize the existing service. For many of us, infant baptism can only be defended when at a later date a person makes his own personal decision for Jesus Christ.

Appendix B:
Statement of Agreed Positions

Standing Liturgical Commission and Theological and Prayer Book Committees of the House of Bishops
Joint Meeting, Dallas, Texas, December 6-9, 1972[3]

A. Concerning Baptism

1. There is one, and only one, unrepeatable act of Christian initiation, which makes a person a member of the Body of Christ.

2. The essential element of Christian initiation is baptism by water and the Spirit, in the Name of the Holy Trinity, in response to repentance and faith.

3. Christian initiation is normatively administered in a liturgical rite that also includes the laying-on of hands, consignation (with or without chrism), prayer for the gift of the Holy Spirit, reception by the Christian community, joining the eucharistic fellowship, and commissioning for Christian mission. When the bishop is present, it is expected that he will preside at the rite.

B. Concerning a Postbaptismal Affirmation of Vows

1. An act and occasion for (more or less) mature personal acceptance of promises and affirmations made on one's behalf in infancy is pastorally and spiritually desirable.

2. Such an act and occasion must be voluntary; but it should be strongly encouraged as a normal component of Christian nurture, and not merely made available.

3. It is both appropriate and pastorally desirable that the affirmations should be received by a bishop as representing the diocese and the worldwide church; and that the bishop should recall the applicants to their Christian mission, and, by a laying-on of hands, transmit his blessing, with a prayer for the strengthening graces.

4. The rite embodying such affirmations should in no sense be understood as being a "completion of Holy Baptism," nor as being a condition precedent to admission to Holy Communion, nor as conveying a special status of church membership.

5. The occasion of the affirming of baptismal vows and obligations that were made by godparents on one's behalf in infancy is a significant and unrepeatable event. It is one's "Confirmation Day."

6. The rite itself, however, is suitable, and should be available, for other occasions in the lives of Christian people. For example, (1) when a person who has been baptized in some other fellowship of Christians wishes to become a member of the Episcopal Church, it is desirable and appropriate that this person be presented to the bishop, as representing the worldwide episcopate, and that the new relationship be blessed with the laying-on of hands and a recommissioning to Christian service; and (2) when a person whose practice of the Christian life has become perfunctory, or has completely lapsed, awakes again to the call of Christ and desires to signalize his response publicly, and to receive a strengthening gift of the Spirit for renewal.

Appendix C:
The Catechumenate and Parallel Processes[4]

	The Catechumenate: Preparation of Adults for Baptism	Preparation of Baptized Persons for Reaffirmation of the Baptismal Covenant	Preparation of Parents and Godparents for the Baptism of Children
Stage 1	Pre-catechumenal Period	Inquiry	Pregnancy
Concluding Rite	Admission of Catechumens	The Welcoming of Baptized Christians into a Community	Blessing of Parents at the Beginning of Pregnancy
Stage 2	Catechumenate	Formation	Pregnancy and Birth
Concluding Rite	Enrollment of Candidates for Baptism	Calling of the Baptized to Continuing Conversion	Thanksgiving for the Birth or Adoption of a Child
Stage 3	Candidacy for Baptism	Preparation for Reaffirmation	Birth to Baptism
Concluding Rite	Baptism	Maundy Thursday Rite for Baptized Persons in Preparation for the Paschal Holy Days	Baptism

Appendix D:
International Anglican Liturgical Consultations

Recommendations of the First International Anglican Liturgical Consultation at Boston 1985 on Children and Communion[5]

i. That since baptism is the sacramental sign of full incorporation into the church, all baptized persons be admitted to communion.

ii. That provincial baptismal rites be reviewed to the end that such texts explicitly affirm the communion of the newly baptized and that only one rite be authorized for the baptism whether of adults or infants so that no essential distinction be made between persons on basis of age.

iii. That in the celebration of baptism the vivid use of liturgical signs, e.g., the practice of immersion and the copious use of water be encouraged.

iv. That the celebration of baptism constitute a normal part of an episcopal visit.

v. That anyone admitted to communion in any part of the Anglican Communion be acknowledged as a communicant in every part of the Anglican Communion and not be denied communion on the basis of age or lack of confirmation.

vi. That the Constitution and Canons of each province be revised in accordance with the above recommendations; and that the Constitution and Canons be amended wherever they imply the necessity of confirmation for full church membership.

vii. That each province clearly affirm that confirmation is not a rite of admission to communion, a principle affirmed by the bishops at Lambeth in 1968.

viii. That the general communion of all the baptized assume a significant place in all ecumenical dialogues in which Anglicans are engaged.

Recommendations of the Fourth International Anglican Liturgical Consultation at Toronto 1991 on Principles of Christian Initiation[6]

a. The renewal of baptismal practice is an integral part of mission and evangelism. Liturgical texts must point beyond the life of the church to God's mission in the world.

b. Baptism is for people of all ages, both adults and infants. Baptism is administered after preparation and instruction of the candidates, or where they are unable to answer for answer for themselves, of their parent(s) or guardian(s).

c. Baptism is complete sacramental initiation and leads to participation in the eucharist. Confirmation and other rites of affirmation have a continuing pastoral role in the renewal of faith among the baptized but are in no way to be seen as a completion of baptism or as a necessary for admission to communion.

d. The catechumenate is a model for preparation and formation for baptism. We recognize that its constituent liturgical rites may vary in different cultural contexts.

e. Whatever language is used in the rest of the baptismal rite, both the profession of faith and the baptismal formula should continue to name God as Father, Son, and Holy Spirit.

f. Baptism once received is unrepeatable and any rites of renewal must avoid being misconstrued as rebaptism.

g. The pastoral rite of confirmation may be delegated by the bishop to a presbyter.

Appendix E:
Statement of the House of Bishops on Children and Communion

General Convention, July 1988[7]

Whereas, the Church teaches that Holy Baptism is the sacrament by which God adopts us as children by grace, and makes us, at whatever age we are baptized, members of Christ's Body, the Church; and

Whereas, the practice of the Church has evolved since previous statements by this House on the subject of communion by young children, so that a statement of the current mind of this House may be useful; therefore be it

Resolved, That the mind of the House of Bishops is that:

Those baptized in infancy may, as full members of the Body of Christ, begin receiving communion at any time they desire and their parents permit; and that the following pastoral principles are recommended to guide the church in communicating those baptized as infants:

1. That the reception of communion by young children should normally be in the context of their participation with their parents and other family in the liturgy of the church;

2. That instruction is required for adults and older children before their baptism and first communion; instruction is also essential for young children after they are baptized and have received communion in infancy, that they may grow in appreciation of the grace they have received and in their abil-

ity to respond in faith, love, and thankful commitment of their lives to God;

3. That pastoral sensitivity is always required: in not forcing the sacrament on an unwilling child, in not rejecting a baptized child who is reaching out for communion with God in Christ, and in respecting the position of the parents of a child in this regard; and

4. That the practice of some parishes which customarily give first communion to infants at their baptism, then next offer them communion when they and their parents express a desire that they receive, is seen to be an acceptable practice in the spirit of these guidelines; and be it further

Resolved, that the Committee on Theology be instructed to present a report on this matter to the next House of Bishops meeting.

NOTES TO APPENDICES

1. Report of the Special Meeting of the House of Bishops, Pocono Manor, Pennsylvania, October 24-29, 1971, in *Journal of the General Convention*, 1973, p. 1063.

2. Ibid., pp. 1072-3.

3. *PBS* 26, pp. 3-5.

4. Merriman, "Introduction," in *The Baptismal Mystery and the Catechumenate*, pp. 15, 17.

5. "Walk in Newness of Life," in Holeton (ed.), *Growing in Newness of Life*, p. 254.

6. Ibid., p. 229.

7. *Journal of the General Convention*, 1988, pp. 158-9.

Bibliography

LITURGICAL TEXTS

Prayer Books and other official liturgical texts

(in chronological order):

The Book of Common Prayer and Administration of the Sacraments and Other Rites and Ceremonies of the Church; According to the Use of the Protestant Episcopal Church in the United States of America; Together with The Psalter or Psalms of David. Philadelphia: Hall & Sellers, 1790.

The Book of Common Prayer and Administration of the Sacraments and Other Rites and Ceremonies of the Church; According to the Use of the Protestant Episcopal Church in the United States of America; Together with The Psalter or Psalms of David. New York: Thomas Nelson & Sons, 1892.

The Book of Common Prayer and Administration of the Sacraments and Other Rites and Ceremonies of the Church; According to the Use of the Protestant Episcopal Church in the United States of America; Together with The Psalter or Psalms of David. New York: Oxford University Press, 1928.

The Book of Offices: Services for Certain Occasions not provided for in the Book of Common Prayer; Compiled by the Liturgical Commission and commended for use by General Convention. New York: Church Pension Fund, 1940. 2nd ed., 1949. 3rd ed., 1960.

The Hymnal of the Protestant Episcopal Church in the United States of America 1940. New York: Church Pension Fund, 1940, 1943, 1961.

The Book of Common Prayer and Administration of the Sacraments and Other Rites and Ceremonies of the Church; Together with The Psalter or Psalms of David; According to the Use of The Episcopal Church. New York: Church Hymnal Corporation, 1979.

The Book of Occasional Services. New York: Church Hymnal Corporation, 1979. 2nd ed., 1988. 3rd ed., 1991. 4th ed., 1994.

The Hymnal 1982 according to the use of The Episcopal Church. New York: Church Hymnal Corporation, 1985.

Prayer Book Studies and other proposed liturgical texts

(in chronological order):

Prayer Book Studies: I. Baptism and Confirmation; II. The Liturgical Lectionary. New York: Church Pension Fund, 1950.

Holy Baptism with the Laying-on-of-Hands. Prayer Book Studies 18: On Baptism and Confirmation. New York: Church Pension Fund, 1970.

The Church Year: The Calendar and the Proper of the Sundays and Other Holy Days throughout the Church Year. Prayer Book Studies 19. New York: Church Hymnal Corporation, 1970.

Pastoral Offices. Prayer Book Studies 24. New York: Church Hymnal Corporation, 1970.

Services for Trial Use: Authorized Alternatives to Prayer Book Services. New York: Church Hymnal Corporation, 1971.

Holy Baptism, together with a Form for the Affirmation of Baptismal Vows with the Laying-on of Hands by the Bishop, also called Confirmation. Prayer Book Studies 26. New York: Church Hymnal Corporation, 1973.

Holy Baptism, together with a Form for Confirmation or the Laying-On of Hands by the Bishop with the Affirmation of Baptismal Vows, as Authorized by the General Convention of 1973. Prayer Book Studies 26. New York: Church Hymnal Corporation, 1973.

A Catechism. New York: Church Hymnal Corporation, 1973.

Authorized Services 1973. New York: Church Hymnal Corporation, 1973.

Holy Baptism. A Form for Confirmation, for Reception, and for the Reaffirmation of Baptismal Vows. New York: Church Hymnal Corporation, 1975.

The Draft Proposed Book of Common Prayer and Administration of the Sacraments and Other Rites and Ceremonies of the Church; According to the use of the Protestant Episcopal Church in the United States of America, otherwise known as The Episcopal Church; Together with The Psalter or Psalms of David. New York: Church Hymnal Corporation, 1976.

Proposed The Book of Common Prayer and Administration of the Sacraments and Other Rites and Ceremonies of the Church, Together with The Psalter or Psalms of David, According to the Use of The Episcopal Church. New York: Church Hymnal Corporation, 1976.

Unofficial liturgical texts

(in chronological order):

The American Missal. Being the Liturgy from the Book of Common Prayer According to the Use of the Church in the United States of America. With Introits, Graduals, and Other Devotions Proper to the Same, Together with Propers for Additional Holy Days and Saints' Days and for Requiem and Votive Masses. Milwaukee: Morehouse, 1931.

A Manual for Priests of the American Church, Complementary to the Occasional Offices of the Book of Common Prayer. Cambridge, MA: Society of St. John the Evangelist, 1944.

An American Holy Week Manual: The Liturgy from Palm Sunday through Easter Day together with Tenebrae. Cambridge, MA: Society of St. John the Evangelist, 1946.

Diekmann, Godfrey L. *The Easter Vigil: Arranged for Use in Parishes*. Collegeville, MN: Liturgical Press, 1953.

The Order for Holy Saturday When the Restored Vigil Is Observed. London: Church Literature Association, 1953.

Shepherd, Massey Hamilton, ed. *Holy Week Offices*. Greenwich, CT: Seabury, 1958.

Contemporary liturgical books of churches in the Anglican Communion

Anglican Church of Australia. *A Prayer Book for Australia*. Alexandria, New South Wales: Broughton Books, 1995.

Anglican Church of Canada. *The Book of Alternative Services*. Toronto: Anglican Book Centre, 1985.

Church in Wales. *The Book of Common Prayer for use in The Church in Wales*. Church in Wales Publications, 1984.

Church of England. *The Alternative Service Book*. Various publishers, 1980.

Church of Ireland. *Alternative Prayer Book*. London: Collins Liturgical Publications, 1984.

Church of the Province of Kenya. *Modern Services*. Nairobi: Uzima Press, 1991.

Church of the Province of New Zealand. *A New Zealand Prayer Book*. Auckland: William Collins Publishers, 1989.

Church of the Province of Southern Africa. *An Anglican Prayer Book*. London: Collins Liturgical Publications, 1989.

Liturgical books of other denominations

Book of Common Worship, prepared for the Presbyterian Church USA and the Cumberland Presbyterian Church. Louisville: Westminster/John Knox Press, 1993.

Book of Worship. New York: United Church of Christ Office for Church Life and Leadership, 1986.

Lutheran Book of Worship. Minneapolis: Augsburg; Philadelphia: Fortress, 1978.

Manual on the Liturgy—Lutheran Book of Worship. Minneapolis: Augsburg, 1979.

The Rites of the Catholic Church: as Revised by Decree of the Second Vatican Ecumenical Council and Published by Authority of Pope Paul VI. Translated by The International Commission on English in the Liturgy. Study ed., New York: Pueblo, 1975.

The United Methodist Book of Worship. Nashville, TN: United Methodist Publishing House, 1992.

OFFICIAL REPORTS AND PUBLICATIONS

Baptism and Confirmation: A Report submitted by the Church of England Liturgical Commission to the Archbishops of Canterbury and York in November 1958. London: SPCK, 1959.

Baptism, Eucharist, and Ministry. Faith and Order Paper No. 111. Geneva, Switzerland: World Council of Churches, 1982.

The Blue Book: Reports of the Committees, Commissions, Boards, and Agencies of The General Convention of the Episcopal Church. 1982-1988.

"Children and Communion. An International Anglican Consultation Held in Boston U.S.A. 29-31 July 1985." In *Nurturing Children in Communion: Essays from the Boston Consultation*, Grove Liturgical Study 44, pp. 42-49. Edited by Colin Buchanan. Bramcote, Nottingham: Grove Books, 1985. Reprinted in *Children at the Table: A Collection of Essays on Children and the Eucharist*, pp. 127-44. Edited by Ruth A. Meyers. New York: Church Hymnal Corporation, 1995.

Coleman, Roger, ed. *Resolutions of the twelve Lambeth Conferences 1867-1988*. Toronto: Anglican Book Centre, 1992.

Confirmation Crisis. Report of the Executive Council of the Episcopal Church. New York: Seabury, 1968.

Constitution & Canons for the Government of the Protestant Episcopal Church in the United States of America otherwise known as The Episcopal Church. Adopted in General Conventions 1789-1994.

Convocations of Canterbury and York. *Baptism and Confirmation Today: Being the Schedule attached to the Final Reports of the Joint Committees on Baptism, Confirmation, and Holy Communion, as presented to the Convocations of Canterbury and York in October, 1954*. London: SPCK, 1955.

_____. *Baptism Today: Being the Schedule attached to the Second Interim Reports of the Joint Committees on Baptism, Confirmation and Holy Communion, as presented to the Convocations of Canterbury and York in October, 1949*. London: Press and Publications Board of the Church Assembly, 1949.

_____. *Confirmation Today. Being the Schedule attached to the Interim Reports of the Joint Committees on Confirmation, setting forth certain major issues before the Church, as presented to the Convocations of Canterbury and York in October, 1944*. London: Press and Publications Board of the Church Assembly, 1944.

Hatchett, Marion J. "Architectural Implications of The Book of Common Prayer." Occasional Paper 7, March 1985. In *The Occasional Papers of the Standing Liturgical Commission*, Collection No. 1, pp. 57-66. New York: Church Hymnal Corporation, 1987.

Journal of the General Convention of the Protestant Episcopal Church in the United States of America. 1928-1988.

The Lambeth Conference 1948. *The Encyclical Letter from the Bishops, together with Resolutions and Reports*. London: SPCK, 1948.

The Lambeth Conference 1958. *The Encyclical Letter from the Bishops, together with Resolutions and Reports*. London: SPCK; Greenwich, CT: Seabury, 1958.

The Lambeth Conference 1968. *Resolutions and Reports*. London: SPCK; New York: Seabury, 1968.

Meyers, Ruth A., ed. *Baptism and Ministry*. Liturgical Studies 1. New York: Church Hymnal Corporation, 1994.

_____, ed. *A Prayer Book for the 21st Century*. Liturgical Studies 3. New York: Church Hymnal Corporation, 1996.

Office of Evangelism Ministries, The Episcopal Church Center. *The Catechumenal Process: Adult Initiation & Formation for Christian Life and Ministry: A Resource for Dioceses and Congregations*. New York: Church Hymnal Corporation, 1990.

Prayer Book Studies XV: The Problem and Method of Prayer Book Revision. New York: Church Pension Fund, 1961.

Price, Charles P. "Rites of Initiation." Occasional Paper 4, September 1984. In *The Occasional Papers of the Standing Liturgical Commission*, Collection No. 1, pp. 24-37. New York: Church Hymnal Corporation, 1987.

Price, Charles P., for the Standing Liturgical Commission. *Introducing the Draft Proposed Book: A Study of the Significance of the Draft Proposed Book of Common Prayer for the Doctrine, Discipline, and Worship of the Episcopal Church*. Prayer Book Studies 29. New York: Church Hymnal Corporation, 1976.

Ready and Desirous: Being the Report of the Commission on the Preparation for Confirmation of the Diocese of New York 1958-1962. New York: Morehouse-Barlow, 1962.

Stevick, Daniel B. *Holy Baptism, together with a Form for the Affirmation of Baptismal Vows with the Laying-on of Hands by the Bishop, also called Confirmation. Supplement to Prayer Book Studies 26*. New York: Church Hymnal Corporation, 1973.

The Theology of Christian Initiation: Being the Report of a Theological Commission appointed by the Archbishops of Canterbury and York to advise on the relations between Baptism, Confirmation and Holy Communion. London: SPCK, 1949.

"Walk in Newness of Life: The Findings of the International Anglican Liturgical Consultation, Toronto 1991." In *Christian Initiation in the Anglican Communion: The Toronto Statement "Walk in Newness of Life."* Edited by David R. Holeton. Grove Worship Series 118. Bram-56. Edited by David R. Holeton. Toronto: Anglican Book Centre, 1993.

White, Edwin Augustine, and Dykman, Jackson A. *Annotated Constitution and Canons for the Government of the Protestant Episcopal Church in the United States of America otherwise known as The Episcopal Church*. 2 vols. 1981 edition, revised and updated by the Standing Commission on Constitution and Canons of the General Convention, New York: Seabury, 1982. 1989 Supplement prepared by the Standing Commission on Constitution and Canons of the General Convention.

BOOKS AND MONOGRAPHS

Ahlstrom, Sydney E. *A Religious History of the American People*. New Haven, CT: Yale University Press, 1972.

Austin, Gerard. *Anointing with the Spirit: The Rite of Confirmation: The Use of Oil and Chrism*. New York: Pueblo, 1985.

Avis, Paul. *Anglicanism and the Christian Church: Theological Resources in Historical Perspective*. Minneapolis: Fortress, 1989.

Booty, John. *The Episcopal Church in Crisis*. Cambridge, MA: Cowley Publications, 1988.

Boston Clergy Group of the Episcopal Evangelical Fellowship. *A Prayer Book Manual*. Louisville: Cloister Press, 1943. 4th ed., 196-?

Bouyer, Louis. *Liturgical Piety*. Notre Dame, IN: University of Notre Dame Press, 1955.

Bradshaw, Paul F. *The Search for the Origins of Christian Worship: Sources and Methods for the Study of Early Liturgy*. New York: Oxford University Press, 1992.

Burnett, Charles P. A. *A Ritual and Ceremonial Commentary on the Occasional Offices of Holy Baptism, Matrimony, Penance, Communion of the Sick, and Extreme Unction*. New York: Longmans, Green, and Co., 1907.

Burson, Malcolm C., ed. *Worship Points the Way: A Celebration of the Life and Work of Massey Hamilton Shepherd, Jr*. New York: Seabury, 1981.

Cellier, Frank Stephen, ed. *Liturgy Is Mission*. New York: Seabury, 1964.

Confirmation or the Laying on of Hands. 2 vols. Vol. 1: *Historical and Doctrinal*. Vol. 2: *Practical*. London: SPCK, 1926.

Cully, Kendig Brubaker, ed. *Confirmation: History, Doctrine, and Practice*. Greenwich, CT: Seabury, 1962.

_____. *Confirmation Re-Examined*. Wilton, CT: Morehouse-Barlow, 1982.

Darling, Pamela W. *New Wine: The Story of Women Transforming Leadership and Power in the Episcopal Church*. Cambridge, MA: Cowley Publications, 1994.

DeWitt, William C. *Decently and in Order: Pastoral Suggestions in Matters Official and Personal*. Milwaukee: The Young Churchman Co., 1914.

Dix, Gregory. *The Shape of the Liturgy*. London: Dacre Press, 1945. New edition with additional notes by Paul V. Marshall, New York: Seabury, 1982.

_____. *The Theology of Confirmation in Relation to Baptism: A Public Lecture in the University of Oxford delivered on January 22nd 1946*. Westminster: Dacre Press, 1946.

Douglas, Winfred. *Church Music in History and Practice: Studies in the Praise of God*. New York: Charles Scribner's Sons, 1937.

Eastman, A. Theodore. *The Baptizing Community: Christian Initiation and the Local Congregation*. New York: Seabury, 1982. 2nd ed., Wilton, CT: Morehouse, 1991.

The First and Second Prayer Books of Edward VI. Introduction by E. C. S. Gibson. London: J. M. Dent and Sons, 1910.

Galley, Howard E. *The Ceremonies of the Eucharist: A Guide to Celebration.* Cambridge, MA: Cowley Publications, 1989.

Gallup, George, and Castelli, Jim. *The People's Religion: American Faith in the 90's.* New York: Macmillan, 1989.

Glover, Raymond F., ed. *The Hymnal 1982 Companion.* 4 vols. New York: Church Hymnal Corporation, 1990, 1994.

Graves, Anson Rogers. *The Farmer Boy Who Became a Bishop.* Akron, OH: The New Werner Company, 1911.

Gray, Donald. *Earth and Altar: The Evolution of the Parish Communion in the Church of England to 1945.* Alcuin Club Collections 68. Norwich: Canterbury Press, 1986.

Hall, Arthur C. A. *Notes on the Use of the Prayer Book.* New York: E. & J. B. Young, 1896.

Hart, Samuel. *The Book of Common Prayer.* Sewanee, TN: University Press, 1910.

Hatchett, Marion. *Commentary on the American Prayer Book.* New York: Seabury, 1980.

Hebert, Arthur Gabriel. *Liturgy and Society: The Function of the Church in the Modern World.* London: Faber and Faber, 1935.

————, ed. *The Parish Communion: A Book of Essays.* London: SPCK, 1937.

Holeton, David R. *Infant Communion—Then and Now.* Grove Liturgical Study 27. Bramcote, Nottingham: Grove Books, 1981.

————, ed. *Growing in Newness of Life: Christian Initiation in Anglicanism Today.* Toronto: Anglican Book Centre, 1993.

Holmes, Urban T. *Confirmation: The Celebration of Maturity in Christ.* New York: Seabury, 1975.

Howe, Reuel. *Man's Need and God's Action.* New York: Seabury, 1953.

Jagger, Peter J. *Clouded Witness: Initiation in the Church of England in the Mid-Victorian Period, 1850-1875.* Pittsburgh Theological Monographs, n.s., 1. Allison Park, PA: Pickwick Publications, 1982.

Johnstone, Verney. *The Story of the Prayer Book.* New York: Morehouse-Gorham, 1949.

Kavanagh, Aidan. *Confirmation: Origins and Reform.* New York: Pueblo, 1988.

————. *The Shape of Baptism: The Rite of Initiation.* New York: Pueblo, 1978.

Koenker, Ernest. *The Liturgical Renaissance in the Roman Catholic Church.* St. Louis: Concordia, 1966.

LaCugna, Catherine Mowry. *God for Us: The Trinity and Christian Life.* New York: HarperCollins, 1991.

Ladd, William Palmer. *Prayer Book Interleaves: Some Reflections on How the Book of Common Prayer Might Be Made More Influential in Our English-speaking World.* New York: Oxford University Press, 1942.

Lampe, Geoffrey W.H. *The Seal of the Spirit: A Study in the Doctrine of Baptism and Confirmation in the New Testament and the Fathers.* London: Longmans, Green, and Co., 1951. 2nd ed., London: SPCK, 1967.

Made, Not Born: New Perspectives on Christian Initiation and the Catechumenate. Notre Dame, IN: University of Notre Dame Press, 1976.

Marshall, Paul V. *Prayer Book Parallels: The Public Services of the Church Arranged for Comparative Study.* Anglican Liturgy in America, Vol. 1. New York: Church Hymnal Corporation, 1989.

Mason, Arthur James. *The Relation of Confirmation to Baptism as Taught in Holy Scripture and the Fathers.* New York: E. P. Dutton, 1891.

Merriman, Michael W., ed. *The Baptismal Mystery and the Catechumenate.* New York: Church Hymnal Corporation, 1990.

Meyers, Ruth A., ed. *Children at the Table: The Communion of All the Baptized in Anglicanism Today.* New York: Church Hymnal Corporation, 1995.

Michno, Dennis G. *A Priest's Handbook: The Ceremonies of the Church.* Wilton, CT: Morehouse-Barlow, 1983.

Micks, Marianne. *Deep Waters: An Introduction to Baptism.* Cambridge, MA: Cowley Publications, 1996.

Mitchell, Leonel L. *Baptismal Anointing.* Alcuin Club Collections 48. London: SPCK, 1966; reprint ed., Notre Dame, IN: University of Notre Dame Press, 1978.

_____. *Praying Shapes Believing: A Theological Commentary on the Book of Common Prayer.* Minneapolis: Winston, 1985.

_____. *Worship: Initiation and the Churches.* Washington, DC: Pastoral Press, 1991.

Moody, Dale. *Baptism: Foundation for Christian Unity.* Philadelphia: Westminster, 1967.

Moriarty, Michael. *The Liturgical Revolution: Prayer Book Revision and Associated Parishes: A Generation of Change in the Episcopal Church.* New York: Church Hymnal Corporation, 1996.

Myers, Chauncie Kilmer. *Baptized into the One Church.* New York: Seabury, 1963.

Paret, William. *The Pastoral Use of the Prayer Book: The Substance of Plain Talks Given to His Students and Younger Clergy.* Baltimore: Maryland Diocesan Library, 1904.

Parsons, Edward Lambe, and Jones, Bayard Hale. *The American Prayer Book: Its Origins and Principles.* New York: Charles Scribner's Sons, 1937.

Perry, Michael, ed. *Crisis for Confirmation.* London: SCM Press, 1967.

Pocknee, Cyril E. *Water and the Spirit.* London: Darton, Longman and Todd, 1967.

Price, Charles P., and Weil, Louis. *Liturgy for Living.* The Church's Teaching Series. New York: Seabury, 1979.

Puller, F. W. *What Is the Distinctive Grace of Confirmation?* A Paper Read before the Chapter of the South-Eastern Division of the Upper Llandaff Rural Deanery. London: 1880.

Robbins, Howard Chandler. *Charles Lewis Slattery.* New York and London: Harper & Brothers, 1931.

Schnitker, Thaddaeus A. *The Church's Worship: The 1979 American Book of Common Prayer in a Historical Perspective.* European University Studies, Series XXIII (Theology), Vol. 351. Frankfurt: Peter Lang, 1989.

Shepherd, Massey Hamilton. *The Liturgical Movement and the Prayer Book.* Evanston, IL: Seabury-Western Theological Seminary, 1946.

_____. *Liturgy and Education.* New York: Seabury, 1965.

_____. *The Living Liturgy.* New York: Oxford University Press, 1946.

_____. *The Oxford American Prayer Book Commentary.* New York: Oxford University Press, 1950.

_____. *The Reform of Liturgical Worship: Perspectives and Prospects.* New York: Oxford University Press, 1961.

_____. *The Worship of the Church.* Greenwich, CT: Seabury, 1952.

_____, ed. *The Eucharist and Liturgical Renewal.* New York: Oxford University Press, 1960.

_____, ed. *The Liturgical Renewal of the Church.* New York: Oxford University Press, 1960.

_____, Keene, John H.; Patterson, John O.; Bill, John R., eds. *Before the Holy Table: A Guide to the Celebration of the Holy Eucharist, Facing the People, According to The Book of Common Prayer.* Greenwich, CT: Seabury, 1956.

Slattery, Charles Lewis. *David Hammell Greer: Eighth Bishop of New York.* New York: Longmans, Green, and Co., 1921.

_____. *The New Prayer Book: An Introduction.* New York: Edwin S. Gorham, n.d. (1929?)

Stark, Rodney, and Glock, Charles Y. *American Piety: The Nature of Religious Commitment.* Berkeley and Los Angeles: University of California Press, 1968.

Stevenson, Kenneth. *Gregory Dix—Twenty-Five Years on.* Bramcote, Nottingham: Grove Books, 1977.

Stevick, Daniel B. *Baptismal Moments; Baptismal Meanings.* New York: Church Hymnal Corporation, 1987.

Stone, Darwell. *Holy Baptism.* London: Longmans, Green, and Co., 1899.

Stuhlman, Byron D. *Eucharistic Celebration 1789-1979.* New York: Church Hymnal Corporation, 1988.

_____. *Occasions of Grace: An historical and theological study of the Pastoral Offices and Episcopal Services in the Book of Common Prayer.* New York: Church Hymnal Corporation, 1995.

_____. *Prayer Book Rubrics Expanded*. New York: Church Hymnal Corporation, 1987.

Sumner, David E. *The Episcopal Church's History: 1945-1985*. Wilton, CT: Morehouse-Barlow, 1987.

Suter, John, and Cleaveland, George. *The American Book of Common Prayer: Its Origin and Development*. New York: Oxford University Press, 1949.

Thornton, Lionel S. *Confirmation: Its Place in the Baptismal Mystery*. London: Dacre Press, 1954.

_____. *Confirmation Today: An Address*. Westminster: Dacre Press, 1946.

Turner, Paul. *Confirmation: The Baby in Solomon's Court*. New York: Paulist Press, 1993.

Turner, Timothy J. *Welcoming the Baptized: Anglican Hospitality within the Ecumenical Enterprise*. Alcuin/GROW Joint Liturgical Studies 34. Cambridge: Grove Books, 1996.

Waterman, Lucius. *Prayer Book Papers*. Series II, No. 2. The Protestant Episcopal Church. *The Duty of Parties toward Proposals for Prayer Book Revision* and *Proposed Supplanting of Our Baptismal Offices*. New York: The Prayer Book Papers Joint Committee, n.d. (1925?)

White, James F. *The Cambridge Movement: The Ecclesiologists and the Gothic Revival*. Cambridge: Cambridge University Press, 1962.

Wilson-Kastner, Patricia. *Faith, Feminism, and the Christ*. Philadelphia: Fortress, 1983.

Wirgman, A. Theodore. *The Doctrine of Confirmation Considered in Relation to Holy Baptism as a Sacramental Ordinance of the Catholic Church; with a Preliminary Historical Survey of the Doctrine of the Holy Spirit*. London: Longmans, Green, and Co., 1897.

Wuthnow, Robert. *Rediscovering the Sacred: Perspectives on Religion in Contemporary Society*. Grand Rapids, MI: Eerdmans, 1992.

_____. *The Restructuring of American Religion: Society and Faith Since World War II*. Princeton, NJ: Princeton University Press, 1988.

ASSOCIATED PARISHES BROCHURES

(in chronological order)

The Parish Eucharist. 1950.

Christian Initiation: Part I—Holy Baptism. 1953.

Christian Initiation: Part II—Confirmation. 1954.

Ministry I: Holy Baptism. 1978.

Holy Baptism: A Liturgical and Pastoral Commentary. 1987, 1997.

The Catechumenate: Formation for Church Membership. 1991.

ARTICLES

Allen, Joseph L. "Continuity and Change: The Church and the Contemporary Social Revolution." *Interpretation* 22 (1968): 461-74.

Allison, C. FitzSimons. "Anglican Initiatory Rites: A Contribution to the Current Debate." *Anglican and Episcopal History* 56 (1987): 27-43.

Barton, Lane W. "Thoughts on Christian Baptism." *Anglican Theological Review* 30 (1948): 209-15.

Bradner, Lester. "The Educational Aspect of Confirmation." *Anglican Theological Review* 1 (1918): 133-47.

————. "Preparation for Confirmation." *Anglican Theological Review* 3 (1920): 125-36.

Breul, Henry. "Paul Dombey's Baptism." *The Anglican*, n.s. 6 (1976): 17-21.

Carroll, Jackson W. "Continuity and Change: The Shape of Religious Life in the United States, 1950 to the Present." In *Religion in America: 1950 to the Present*, pp. 1-45. By Jackson W. Carroll, Douglas W. Johnson, and Martin E. Marty. San Francisco: Harper & Row, 1979.

"Documentation and Reflection: Confirmation Today." *Anglican Theological Review* 54 (1972): 106-19.

Foster, Walter Roland. "Some Notes on Confirmation and Episcopacy." *The Anglican*, n.s. 5 (1974): 18-21.

Franklin, R. William. "The Nineteenth Century Liturgical Movement." *Worship* 53 (1979): 12-39.

Frederick, J. B. M. "The Initiation Crisis in the Church of England." *Studia Liturgica* 9 (1973): 137-57.

Hatchett, Marion J. "Initiation: Baptism or Ordination?" *St. Luke's Journal of Theology* 12 (1969): 17-22.

Holeton, David R. "Communion, Children, and Community." In *The Identity of Anglican Worship*, pp. 14-26. Edited by Kenneth Stevenson and Bryan Spinks. Harrisburg, PA: Morehouse, 1991.

_____. "Confirmation in the 1980s." In *Ecumenical Perspectives on Baptism, Eucharist and Ministry*, pp. 68-89. Edited by Max Thurian. Geneva, Switzerland: World Council of Churches, 1983.

Holmes, Urban T. "Confirmation as a Rite of Intensification: A Response to J. Robert Wright." *Anglican Theological Review* 57 (1975): 72-8.

Howe, Reuel L. "Personal and Social Implications of Baptism." *Anglican Theological Review* 27 (1945): 264-74.

Jordahl, Leigh. "Secularity: The Crisis of Belief and the Reality of Christian Worship." *Dialog* 9 (1970): 15-25.

Martinez, German. "Cult and Culture: The Structure of the Evolution of Worship." *Worship* 64 (1990): 406-33.

Marty, Martin E. "The Context of Liturgy: Here and Now, There and Then," *Worship* 43 (1969): 465-73.

Mitchell, Leonel L. "By Water and the Holy Spirit." *The Anglican*, n.s. 5 (1974): 1-7.

_____. "Communion of Infants and Little Children." *Anglican Theological Review* 71 (1989): 63-78.

_____. "The Eucharist and Christian Initiation." In *Worship in Spirit and Truth; Papers from a Conference Entitled Worship in Spirit and Truth*, pp. 37-41. Edited by Donald Garfield. New York: Jarrow Press, 1970.

_____. "The Place of Baptismal Anointing in Christian Initiation." *Anglican Theological Review* 68 (1986): 202-11.

_____. "Revision of the Rites of Christian Initiation in the American Episcopal Church." *Studia Liturgica* 10 (1974): 25-34.

_____. "The 'Shape' of the Baptismal Liturgy." *Anglican Theological Review* 47 (1965): 410-19.

_____. "The Theology of Christian Initiation and *The Proposed Book of Common Prayer*." *Anglican Theological Review* 60 (1978): 399-419.

_____. "What Does Confirmation Mean?" *The Anglican*, n.s. 4 (1973): 2-6.

_____. "What Is Confirmation?" *Anglican Theological Review* 55 (1973): 201-12.

_____. "What Shall We Do about Baptism and Confirmation?" *The Anglican* 25 (1969-70): 1-6.

Moriarty, Michael. "Associated Parishes and the 1979 Prayer Book." *Anglican and Episcopal History* 64 (1995): 195-227.

_____. "William Palmer Ladd and the Origins of the Episcopal Liturgical Movement." *Church History* 64 (1995): 438-51.

Porter, H. Boone. "Baptism: Its Paschal and Ecumenical Setting." *Worship* 42 (1968): 205-14.

"Primitive Teaching on Confirmation and Its Relation to Holy Baptism." *Church Quarterly Review* 34 (1892): 1-20.

Ramsey, A. Michael. "The Doctrine of Confirmation." *Theology* 48 (1945): 194-201.

Rasmussen, Niels. "The Chrism Mass: Tradition and Renewal." In *The Cathedral: A Reader*, pp. 29-33. Washington, DC: US Catholic Conference, 1979.

"The Relation of Confirmation to Baptism." *Church Quarterly Review* 45 (1898): 357-82.

Richardson, Cyril C. "The Proposed Revision of Our Liturgy: I. Baptism." *Anglican Theological Review* 35 (1953): 106-17.

_____. "The Proposed Revision of Our Liturgy: II. Confirmation." *Anglican Theological Review* 35 (1953): 174-80.

_____. "What Is Confirmation?" *Anglican Theological Review* 32 (1941): 223-30.

Senn, Frank C. "Lutheran and Anglican Liturgies: Reciprocal Influences." *Anglican Theological Review* 64 (1982): 47-60.

Slattery, Charles Lewis. "Essentials of Prayer Book Revision." In *The Church and Its American Opportunity: Papers by Various Writers Read at the Church Congress in 1919*, pp. 87-127. New York: Macmillan, 1919.

Spinks, Bryan D. "Mis-Shapen: Gregory Dix and the Four-Action Shape of the Liturgy." *Lutheran Quarterly* 4 (1990): 161-77.

Stookey, Laurence H. "Three New Initiation Rites." *Worship* 51 (1977): 33-49.

Vogel, Arthur A. "Are You My Type?" *Anglican Theological Review* 69 (1987): 376-84.

_____. "Note on the Gifts in Baptism and Confirmation." *Anglican Theological Review* 38 (1956): 276-85.

Weil, Louis. "Christian Initiation: A Theological and Pastoral Commentary on the Proposed Rites." *Nashotah Review* 14 (1974): 202-23. Reprint, Alexandria, VA: Associated Parishes, n.d.

_____. "Confirmation: Some Notes on Its Meaning." *Anglican Theological Review* 59 (1977): 220-24.

_____. "Disputed Aspects of Infant Communion," *Studia Liturgica* 17 (1987): 256-63.

_____. "Prayer Book Studies #26, Revised and Expanded," *Anglican Theological Review* 71 (1989): 88-94.

Westerhoff, John H. "Confirmation: An Episcopal Church Perspective." *Reformed Liturgy and Music* 24 (1990): 198-203.

Wright, J. Robert. "Prayer Book Studies 26: An Objection, Some Observations, and a Proposed Alternative." *The Anglican*, n.s. 5 (1974): 7-18.

_____. "Response: Prayer Book Studies 26: Considered Objections." *Anglican Theological Review* 57 (1975): 60-71.

UNPUBLISHED ARCHIVAL MATERIALS

The General Convention. Joint Commissions, Committees, and Boards. 1789-1973. Record Group 10. Archives of the Episcopal Church, Austin, Texas.

The General Convention. Standing Liturgical Commission. Office of the Coordinator for Prayer Book Revision. Prayer Book Revision Records for the *Book of Common Prayer*, 1979. Record Group 122. Archives of the Episcopal Church, Austin, Texas.

UNPUBLISHED SOURCES

Braun, Dorothy L. "A Historical Study of the Origin and Development of the Seabury Series of the Protestant Episcopal Church." Ph.D. Dissertation, New York University, 1960.

"Christian Initiation in the Diocese of Chicago: A Draft Proposal Submitted by the Task Force on the Catechumenate and the Commission on Liturgy." January 1990.

"The Committee on Liturgy of the Diocese of Northern Indiana: Guidelines for the Celebration of the Rites of Christian Initiation." 1989.

Evangelical Lutheran Church in America. "The Use of the Means of Grace." 1996.

Hatfield, M. Richard. "Baptism, Chrismation and Eucharist: Christian Initiation: A Recovery of the Primitive Pattern." S.T.M. Thesis, Nashotah House, 1988.

Jones, Edward W. "Present Practices of Bishops in the Episcopal Church, with Regard to the Rite of Confirmation." Report of survey conducted during sabbatical. Part I: "Introduction to a Questionnaire." Indianapolis, 1986.

Meyers, Ruth A. "Present Diocesan Practices in the Episcopal Church with Regard to Baptism and Confirmation, Reception, Reaffirmation of Baptismal Vows." Summary of responses to survey of members of the Association of Diocesan Liturgy and Music Commissions, November 1992.

Moriarty, Michael. "The Associated Parishes for Liturgy and Mission, 1946-1991; The Liturgical Movement in the Episcopal Church." Ph.D. Dissertation, University of Notre Dame, 1993.

Tracy, Paul John. "Christian Initiation Complete in Baptism? A Continuing Problem for Anglicans." M.A. Thesis, University of Notre Dame, 1985.

POPULAR LITERATURE

The Churchman. New York, 1934-1972.

The Episcopalian (continuation of *Forth*). Philadelphia, PA, April 1960–March 1990.

Episcopal Churchnews (continuation of *The Southern Churchman*). Richmond, VA, 1952-1957.

The Evangelical Outlook. Arlington, VA: Evangelical Education Society, 1964-1990.

Findings (*Christian Education Findings*). New York: Protestant Episcopal Church in the USA Department of Christian Education. 1953-1971.

Forth. New York: Protestant Episcopal Church in the USA National Council, January 1940–March 1960.

The Living Church. Milwaukee, WI, 1928-1990.

Open. Newsletter of Associated Parishes. Madison, WI, 1969-1990.
Sharers. Newsletter of Associated Parishes. Madison, WI, 1954-1962.
The Southern Churchman. Richmond, VA, 1935-1952.
The Witness. Ambler, PA, 1928-1990.

Index

Shepherd, Massey H.   33-35, 37, 42, 48, 54, 56, 58, 61-63, 76, 90, 106, 111, 113, 120-125, 132, 169, 171, 181, 184, 193, 204, 207

signing
    See consignation

Slattery, Charles   10, 15-16

Smith, Charles   115

Smith, Newland   x

Society of Saint John the Evangelist   56, 80, 105

Society of the Sacred Mission   27

Spencer, Bonnell   x, xii-xiii, 118, 132-140, 143, 145, 147, 149, 169, 171-173, 176-177, 180, 182, 201-202, 205-206, 210

Spilman, William   xiii, 133-134, 137, 144, 197, 201, 208

Spinks, Bryan D.   x

Spirit of the Liturgy, The   33

sponsors   8, 53-54, 76, 109, 167, 199-200, 204-205
    See also godparents

sprinkling, at renewal   194, 230

Stevenson, Taylor   164

Stevick, Daniel B.   x, 34, 94, 162, 176-178, 198-199, 233

Stone, Darwell   69

Stuhlman, Byron David   xi

T

Talley, Thomas   34, 201

Thanksgiving for the Birth or Adoption of a Child   218, 268

Thanksgiving over the Water   201, 207-208, 222, 229-230

The Secular City   23

Thornton, Lionel   xii, 72, 75, 133

trial use   125-127, 132, 152, 180

Trinitarian formula   114, 118, 209, 233-234, 242, 266, 270

Trinitarian theology   227-228

U

United Church of Christ   253

United Methodist Book of Worship   253, 255-257, 259-260

United Methodist Church   253, 257, 259-260

V

Vogel, Arthur   84, 233

W

Warnecke, Frederick   122-123

Watkins, Keith   198

Weil, Louis   34, 206, 235

Westerhoff, John   240

What Is the Distinctive Grace of Confirmation?   68

"White & Dykman"   46

Whitsunday   51, 60

Wilson, Frank   88

Wilson-Kastner, Patricia   227

Wirgman, A. Theodore   69

women, ministry of   28, 41, 47, 237-238
    See also ordination of women

World Conference on Christian Life and Work   88

World Conference on Faith and Order   88

World Council of Churches Commission on Faith and Order   166

Worship of the Church, The   111

Wright, J. Robert   179

Wuthnow, Robert   24-25

Y

Yerkes, R.K.   32

Z

"Zebra Book," The   127

Zimmerman, J. Robert   97